THE EVERYTHING Family Guides

New England, 2nd Edition

Dear Reader,

I have the best job in the world—sharing the region I love and call home with a global audience of travelers who read my books and visit my New England Travel Web site on About.com. Since 1998, I've had the opportunity not only to share my adventures but to inspire readers to escape to this historic and picturesque corner of the world. Even a brief New England getaway can be truly unforgettable.

My kindergartener frequently tells people, "My mommy touched a whale's tongue," and "I drove a lobster boat," and "We saw zucchinis flying through the air." And she's not making any of it up. Through her eyes, I've had the opportunity to appreciate New England's wonders in new ways and to understand the rewards—and, of course, the challenges—of taking little ones on vacation.

We've had more than our share of emergency bathroom stops, spilled juice boxes, and "Are we there yets?" not to mention hours upon hours of listening to the Wiggles, but we also have stories and memories to cherish forever.

Family time is precious. New England is the perfect place to watch children laugh, learn, and grow. I can't wait for you to get here!

Kim Knox Beckius

THE EVERYTHING® Series

Everything® Family Guides are designed to be the perfect traveling companions. Whether you're traveling within a tight family budget or feeling the urge to splurge, you will find all you need to create a memorable family vacation. Review this book to give you great ideas before you travel, and stick it in your backpack or diaper bag to use as a quick reference guide for activities, attractions, and excursions. You'll discover that vacationing with the whole family can be filled with fun and exciting adventures.

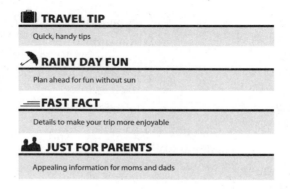

TRAVEL TIP

Quick, handy tips

RAINY DAY FUN

Plan ahead for fun without sun

FAST FACT

Details to make your trip more enjoyable

JUST FOR PARENTS

Appealing information for moms and dads

When you're done reading, you can finally say you know EVERYTHING®!

DIRECTOR OF INNOVATION Paula Munier

EDITORIAL DIRECTOR Laura M. Daly

EXECUTIVE EDITOR, SERIES BOOKS Brielle K. Matson

ASSOCIATE COPY CHIEF Sheila Zwiebel

ACQUISITIONS EDITOR Lisa Laing

DEVELOPMENT EDITOR Brett Palana-Shanahan

PRODUCTION EDITOR Casey Ebert

Visit the entire Everything® series at **www.everything.com**

THE

EVERYTHING®

FAMILY GUIDE TO

NEW ENGLAND

— 2nd Edition —

Where to eat, play, and stay in
America's scenic and historic Northeast

Kim Knox Beckius

Happy travels!,

Kim Knox Beckius

▲adamsmedia
Avon, Massachusetts

*In memory of my friend, Debby Fowles, who taught me
so much about Maine, moose, and life.*

• • •

An Everything® Series Book.
Everything® and everything.com® are registered trademarks of F+W Publications, Inc.

Published by Adams Media, an F+W Publications Company
57 Littlefield Street, Avon, MA 02322 U.S.A.
www.adamsmedia.com

ISBN 10: 1-59869-448-0
ISBN 13: 978-1-59869-448-2

Printed in Canada.

J I H G F E D C B A

Library of Congress Cataloging-in-Publication Data
is available from the publisher.

This publication is designed to provide accurate and authoritative information with
regard to the subject matter covered. It is sold with the understanding that the publisher is not engaged in rendering legal, accounting, or other professional advice.
If legal advice or other expert assistance is required, the services of a competent
professional person should be sought.
—From a *Declaration of Principles* jointly adopted by a Committee of the
American Bar Association and a Committee of Publishers and Associations

Many of the designations used by manufacturers and sellers to distinguish their
products are claimed as trademarks. Where those designations appear in this book
and Adams Media was aware of a trademark claim, the designations have been
printed with initial capital letters.

*This book is available at quantity discounts for bulk purchases.
For information, please call 1-800-289-0963.*

Contents

Top Ten Unforgettable Family Adventures in New England

1. Wade into the tank with a beluga whale at Connecticut's Mystic Aquarium & Institute for Exploration.

2. Photograph moose in the wild on a Maine moose safari.

3. Tour Boston in a World War II–era amphibious "Duck."

4. Shop at L.L. Bean's flagship store in Freeport, Maine, in the middle of the night.

5. Climb aboard Cinderella's pumpkin coach for a ride to her castle at Story Land in New Hampshire.

6. Stuff your own furry friend at Vermont Teddy Bear.

7. Hike with llamas in the Berkshires.

8. Experience the mesmerizing glow of ninety-seven bonfires during a WaterFire evening in Providence, Rhode Island.

9. Ride one of the world's best roller coasters, Superman: Ride of Steel, at Six Flags New England.

10. Build your own "zukapult" and compete for glory and prizes at the annual Vermont State Zucchini Festival.

Acknowledgments

I have my parents, George and Carol Snyder, to thank for instilling in me a love of books and writing. They also had a knack for turning even our short family vacations—often to New England destinations—into adventures that my brother, Michael, and I still remember vividly.

I am indebted to all of the visitors to my Web site (*www .gonewengland.about.com*) who have shared their travel experiences, provided insight into the questions New England travelers ask, and kept me on my toes. I also appreciate the assistance provided by tourism and public relations professionals who are always ready to answer my questions and who keep me abreast of what's new and exciting in the region. Special thanks to Adams Media Project Editor Lisa Laing for offering me the opportunity to write this updated guide for families and to my literary agent, Barb Doyen, for "finding me" and for helping to make my career dreams a reality.

My husband, Bruce, and daughter, Lara, are wonderful travel companions and my greatest fans, and I am fortunate to have their love and support for my creative endeavors.

Introduction

Have you been to New England? Even born and bred New Englanders may have difficulty answering that question with an authoritative
affirmative. Though New England is a relatively compact region by
size, its vacation possibilities are vast. You could literally spend a lifetime exploring New England's nooks and crannies, and then you'd
need at least another lifetime to revisit them all again at a different
time of year, when they are blanketed in fresh snow, bedazzled with
spring blossoms, baked in summer sun, or brush-stroked by autumn's
magical hues.

The good news is, the sheer variety of things to do, places to see,
and experiences to collect during all four unique seasons makes it
possible to tailor a New England vacation to your family's interests.
Do you love art? amusement parks? literature? lighthouses? history?
hiking? seafood? snow sports? museums? mansions? sandy beaches?
bargains? Then there is a New England travel itinerary just waiting
for you.

The bad news is, with all these options, once you decide to visit
New England, you may be overwhelmed by the number of choices
still to be made. Whether you're traveling with toddlers or teens,
grown children or grandparents, this *Everything® Guide* will help
you narrow the field of possibilities to the few that have the greatest appeal. Designed to spark your thinking with descriptions of a
little bit of everything that each state and region offers, this guide
will lay out ideas and travel basics and then point you to appropriate
resources for further planning and investigation. For each state, you'll
find information on what to see and do, where to stay and eat, and
more.

If you've never visited New England, there are a few things you
should know at the outset. The peak tourism season is definitely the
fall, when nature puts on its annual color bonanza. Many prospective
leaf peepers book their accommodations a year in advance for pre-
dicted peak foliage weeks, and you'd be hard-pressed to find a last-
minute opening anywhere in the region from late September through
mid-October.

Massachusetts is New England's most popular state with about 24 million visitors annually. Its central position within the region makes it a hub that many New England travelers arrive via or pass through, even if they are en route to other destinations. Its proximity to metropolitan New York also makes Massachusetts an ideal weekend getaway for a large population. With New England's largest city, Boston, and several of its most popular vacation hot spots including the Berkshires, Cape Cod, and the islands of Martha's Vineyard and Nantucket, within its boundaries, Massachusetts has drawing power that is unmatched in the region.

Some of the less obvious destination selections, however, may actually offer you a unique getaway that's more memorable and less crowded and harried.

If you are already familiar with New England, you'll also discover within these pages a wealth of information on lesser-known attractions that you may not have encountered. Even locals may find a few new haunts to frequent and some fun activities close to home.

Check the appendices for helpful New England Web sites and a comprehensive guide to state tourism organizations. These regional promotion organizations are happy to provide you with additional information and free brochures to help you design and enjoy a New England vacation all your own.

New England

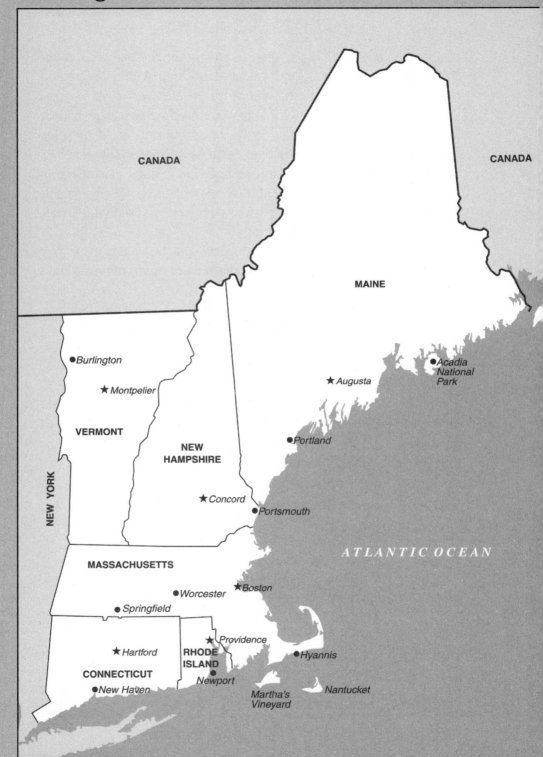

CANADA

CANADA

MAINE

●Burlington

★ Montpelier

★ Augusta

●Acadia
National
Park

VERMONT

NEW
HAMPSHIRE

●Portland

NEW YORK

★ Concord

●Portsmouth

ATLANTIC OCEAN

MASSACHUSETTS

●Worcester

★Boston

● Springfield

★ Providence

●Hyannis

★ Hartford

RHODE
ISLAND

CONNECTICUT

●Newport

Martha's
Vineyard

Nantucket

●New Haven

CHAPTER 1

Welcome to New England

NEW ENGLAND IS THE ultimate living classroom, a region where tales told in history books spring to life, where the diversity of nature is constantly on display, and where world-class museums and attractions transform learning into a hands-on, multisensory experience. But don't tell your kids. After all, New England is also the perfect backdrop for a family vacation that is relaxing, memorable, and fun. As you explore storied locales and embrace new adventures, the most important lesson is to cherish your time together.

Why Visit New England?

There's something about New England that has earned fans the world over, even among those who have visited it only through words and pictures. What is it that draws people to New England and makes the six-state region—Connecticut, Maine, Massachusetts, New Hampshire, Rhode Island, and Vermont—one that travelers return to again and again throughout their lives? While New England is a thoroughly modern region, there's a pervasive aura of timeless permanence that hearkens back to simpler times. Covered bridges and white-steepled churches, maple trees tapped for sap, horse-drawn sleighs, cider mills, and forests blazing with autumn hues are part of the reality families can experience when they choose New England as their vacation destination.

A Region Steeped in the American Tradition

No U.S. region is home to more historic sites, and none is more steeped in the American patriotic tradition. From the Pilgrims' first feast of Thanksgiving, re-created each year at Plimoth Plantation in Plymouth, Massachusetts; to the Revolutionary War battlefields at Lexington and Concord; to the seeds of political and intellectual influence embodied in the Adams and Kennedy families and writers such as Mark Twain, Harriet Beecher Stowe, Nathaniel Hawthorne, Herman Melville, Ralph Waldo Emerson, and Henry David Thoreau—many of the traditions and ideas that have shaped and continue to guide the destiny of America were born and nurtured in New England.

═FAST FACT

Mark Twain said, "There is a sumptuous variety about the New England weather that compels the stranger's admiration—and regret." The record high temperature recorded in New England was 107°F on August 2, 1975, in both New Bedford and Chester, Massachusetts. The record low was –50°F, recorded on December 30, 1933, in Bloomfield, Vermont.

Seasonal Variations

Adding to the region's appeal are the four distinct seasons that continually paint New England with a changing palette of colors, even as time seemingly stands still. Each change in weather and temperature opens the door to new recreational possibilities— skiing, snowmobiling, hiking, fishing, biking, boating, and raking up and jumping into piles of crunchy leaves. And, the region's compactness makes it feasible for families to plan a visit that incorporates an endless variety of activities. Travelers can spend a day walking the Freedom Trail in history-filled and bustling Boston and by evening find themselves either nestled inside a cozy cabin listening to the haunting cry of loons on a sleepy New Hampshire lake, breathing in salty ocean air and feasting on fresh seafood in a seaside Rhode Island town, or lazing on a blanket under the stars listening to the strains of a symphony at Tanglewood, the Boston Symphony Orchestra's summer home in Western Massachusetts's Berkshires.

Six Vacations in One

While history, climate, and identity unify the region, each of the six states that comprise New England also has its own distinct appeal. Connecticut is New England's gateway, and it provides interesting juxtapositions of old and new that blend in perfect harmony. Historic whaling towns are a stone's throw from the flashing lights and twenty-four-hour action of the world's largest casino. Maine visitors are equally entranced by outlet shopping bargains and frequent moose sightings.

Massachusetts can't be beat for historic attractions, miles of sandy beaches, delectable chowder, performing arts centers, quaint island escapes, scenic highways, and top-notch museums. New Hampshire satisfies vacationers' hunger for mountain vistas and lakeside retreats, while surprising them with the offbeat—from llama treks to sky rides to attractions such as America's Stonehenge and Clark's Trading Post with its dancing bears. Rhode Island may be America's most diminutive state, but it can boast 400 miles of coastline and one of the nation's densest concentrations of historic landmarks. Vermont's rural stretches and sparse population make it the cure for everyday hassles and a coveted destination for hikers and skiers.

Whether you are planning your first family trip to New England or your fiftieth, this guide will orient you to the region, provide destination inspiration, steer you toward helpful travel resources, and help you maximize your precious time. Hopefully, you will turn to it again and again as you join the legion of fans who have fallen in love with New England.

A Brief History of the Region

New England has long been the incubator for American ideas. Much of the region's mystique lies in its intricate and compelling history and its vital role in weaving the political, cultural, and intellectual fabric of American life. Visiting New England is truly akin to leaping inside the pages of a history textbook and meeting larger-than-life characters face-to-face on their own turf.

The "New" England

John Smith is credited with giving the region its Eurocentric nomenclature in 1614, but the land he called "New England" was home to native peoples long before European explorers and settlers arrived on the scene. Little is known, though, of New England's earliest inhabitants. Fossil evidence of human habitation found in Shawville, Vermont, places a date of 9000 B.C. on New England's earliest civilization, but no clear connection has been established between these early peoples and the thriving Algonkian civilization that arose during the fourteenth or fifteenth centuries and was firmly established by the time Europeans began to explore the area.

Though "related," the Algonkians were splintered into many small tribes—the Narragansett in Rhode Island, the Abenaki in Maine, the Massachuset in, of course, Massachusetts, and many others. They were frequently engaged in intertribal wars, and their lack of unity eventually contributed to European domination.

English interest in the land that would later be known as New England picked up in the early 1600s, but it would be several decades before the establishment of a permanent settlement. Although profit seekers found little in the way of gold or diamonds to entice them to stick around, a group of Puritans, known today as the Pilgrims, discovered something of immeasurable value on New England's shores—religious freedom.

In mid-December 1620, after more than two months aboard the *Mayflower*, the Pilgrims landed at Plymouth Rock; they first touched ground on what is now Provincetown on the outermost tip of Cape Cod. More than half died during the first miserable winter, but with spring came the help of Squanto and the Wampanoag tribe, and by fall, the Native Americans and Pilgrims joined in a feast to celebrate their first harvest—our country's first Thanksgiving.

≡FAST FACT

Included on the menu for the Pilgrims' first Thanksgiving were lobster and beer! President Abraham Lincoln proclaimed Thanksgiving a national holiday in 1863, three months after the Battle of Gettysburg in the American Civil War. Lincoln designated the last Thursday of November as Thanksgiving Day. President Franklin Delano Roosevelt changed it to the fourth Thursday in 1939.

In 1628, another group of Puritans formed the Massachusetts Bay Colony, settling in the Boston area, and from there, religious leaders dispersed with followers to establish settlements in neighboring states. Oddly enough in light of their own desire for freedom from religious persecution, the Puritans were an intolerant bunch, and in 1636, upstart preacher Roger Williams, who asserted, "forced worship stinks in God's nostrils," established the colony of Rhode Island after being banished from the Massachusetts Bay Colony.

Colonial Revolt

Mother England pretty much left her colonies to toddle along on their own until the 1760s, when King George III, Prime Minister Lord North, and Parliament began imposing new taxes on colonial subjects. Needless to say, the Americans were not amused, primarily because they lacked representation in Parliament and had little recourse as new taxes and laws—the Sugar Act of 1764, the Stamp Act of 1765, the Townshend Acts of 1767—were handed down. Tensions mounted, resistance reverberated, and in 1770, British troops opened fire on an angry crowd, killing five in the Boston Massacre.

Defiant patriots responded in 1773 by demanding that a ship loaded with tea leave Boston Harbor and return to England. When it did not, the rebels, including Sam Adams and John Hancock, disguised themselves as Native Americans, stormed the ship, and tossed its cargo of more than 300 crates of tea into the ocean.

You know what happened next. The American Revolution broke out in New England with Paul Revere warning of the coming of British troops on his famous midnight ride from Boston to Lexington and Minutemen standing in defense of freedom as the "shot heard round the world" was fired at Lexington. Massachusetts also saw the war's first major engagement, the Battle of Bunker Hill, where the Brits were victorious but suffered heavy losses. On July 4, 1776, fourteen New Englanders were among the signers of the Declaration of Independence.

═FAST FACT

The Old Farmer's Almanac is North America's oldest continuously published periodical and one of the best sources for New England lore. It's been around since 1792, during George Washington's second term! The secret formula for long-range weather forecasting devised by its first editor, Robert B. Thomas, is kept in a black tin box at its offices in Dublin, New Hampshire.

Post-Revolution New England

When the war was finally won in 1781, New Englanders returned to the business of building the economy of the Northeast. Some of the most prominent, including John Adams and his son John Quincy Adams, turned their attention to shaping the fledgling democracy. Much of New England's early prosperity was tied to its success in using the ocean, its key natural resource. The fishing, whaling, and shipbuilding industries and overseas trade bolstered the development of harbor towns.

The nineteenth century brought impediments to a maritime economy—wars and trade embargoes—but resilient New Englanders used their ingenuity to develop a new economic model: manufacturing. From the launch of Samuel Slater's cotton mill in Rhode Island in 1793 to the rise of mill towns in the Merrimack Valley of Massachusetts in the first half of the century, New England was at the forefront of the Industrial Revolution in America.

RAINY DAY FUN

The Lowell National Historical Park in Lowell, Massachusetts, portrays life during America's early industrial period. At the Boott Cotton Mills Museum, children can don aprons, punch their time cards, see how raw cotton was transformed into cloth, and even hear the cacophonous roar of a re-created 1920s weave room within the restored textile mill.

New England also took the lead in social reform during this era. Abolitionists spoke out against slavery and sheltered escaped slaves, helping them achieve freedom through the Underground Railroad. In 1800, Rhode Island was the site of the nation's first labor strike. In the mid-1800s, Dorothea Dix crusaded on behalf of the mentally ill in Massachusetts.

Artistic, literary, and intellectual accomplishments had their epicenter here, too. The 1800s saw the creation of the nation's oldest continuously operating art museum, the Wadsworth Atheneum (1842), in Hartford, Connecticut; the opening of the first free municipal public library, the Boston Public Library (1854); and the debut of the Boston Symphony (1881) and the Boston Pops (1885). Writers who shaped the thinking of the nation and the world called New England home—Henry David Thoreau, Emily Dickinson, Ralph Waldo Emerson, Henry Wadsworth Longfellow, Nathaniel Hawthorne, Herman Melville, Mark Twain, and Harriet Beecher Stowe.

The nineteenth century also saw an influx of "new" New Englanders. During the Great Potato Famine of 1845–1850, Irish immigrants arrived in Boston at the rate of more than 1,000 per month. Others arrived from Italy, Portugal, Eastern Europe, and Canada. Digestion of the new mass of opportunity seekers led to a few hiccups and bellyaches as these groups forged their own political and cultural identity in New England's cities and towns.

The Twentieth Century and Beyond

By the twentieth century's dawn, New England was losing its grasp on economic leadership as new methods of manufacturing made it possible for factories to move to locations where labor was less expensive. The stock market crash of 1929, World War II, and the postwar recession contributed to wild fluctuations in the region's fortunes. But the latter half of the century marked a resurgence of prominence.

The election of John Fitzgerald Kennedy from Massachusetts in 1960 showed that the region and the country were coming to terms with their anti-immigrant sentiments. (Kennedy was the first Irish Catholic and the youngest person ever elected to the nation's top office.) The growth, too, of an information economy in the late 1900s and early part of the twenty-first century boded well for the region's current and future economic strength as it became home to distinguished universities and leading technology companies.

New Englanders are proud of their rich history and traditions, but they do not opt for stagnancy and complacency. The next "revolution" in American history may well be nurtured inside the fertile minds of imaginative, ingenious New Englanders.

Getting to New England

One of the perks of New England is its accessibility. By air, sea, road, or rail, there is never a shortage of travel options for this first step in planning your northeastern getaway.

By Car

Most of New England is well connected by interstate highways, and traveling to and around the region by car allows the highest degree of flexibility. New England's compact geography makes it possible to explore multiple states even during a weekend getaway. If you are flying to New England or arriving by rail or bus, you may want to consider renting a car for the duration of your stay. Boston is really the only New England destination where you won't need a car—in fact, you're better off without one. Major interstate highways include:

- **I-95**, which runs north and east from New York City through Connecticut, Rhode Island, Massachusetts, New Hampshire, and Maine
- **I-84**, which enters Connecticut at Danbury and traverses the state, connecting to I-90, also known as the Massachusetts Turnpike, at Sturbridge
- **I-91**, which runs due north from New Haven, Connecticut, through Hartford, to Springfield, Massachusetts, bisecting the Massachusetts Turnpike, and then along the Vermont/New Hampshire border before taking a turn into northern Vermont
- **I-93**, which branches off I-95 near Boston and runs through New Hampshire, meeting I-91 at St. Johnsbury, Vermont

The speed limit on most interstate highways is 65 miles per hour, but it is often lower around major cities. Be alert for posted speed limits as you approach cities and towns. Also be sure to obey speed limits posted on local roadways. Highway routes may be your fastest option, but there may be more scenic alternatives if travel time is not a major issue.

Traffic can be a hassle, particularly if you are traveling a popular "escape route" on Friday afternoon. Traffic through Boston, into Maine, and especially entering Cape Cod can be nightmarish during peak travel weekends. If you can plan your drive for off-peak times, you may have a smoother journey.

By Plane

Boston's Logan International Airport is by far the region's busiest airport. Major carriers also serve Bradley International Airport in Windsor Locks, Connecticut; T.F. Green International Airport in Warwick (near Providence), Rhode Island; Manchester-Boston Regional Airport in Manchester, New Hampshire; and smaller airports in Portland and Bangor, Maine; Burlington, Vermont; and Hyannis, Massachusetts. New England is also accessible to New York airports in Albany, Westchester County, Newburgh, and New York City and to Montreal, Canada.

There are several other small airports for certain niches throughout New England. Some of the most popular serve Provincetown, Martha's Vineyard, and Nantucket in Massachusetts; Westerly and Block Island in Rhode Island; Nashua and Lebanon in New Hampshire; and New Haven in Connecticut.

By Train

Amtrak (800-872-7245, *www.amtrak.com*) is the region's major rail carrier. The Regional route connects Newport News, Virginia, with Boston, and stops in Washington, D.C., Baltimore, Philadelphia, New York's Penn Station, and New Haven, Connecticut. At New Haven, the line splits, and travelers may choose stops along the Hartford route including Springfield, Massachusetts, or along the shoreline route, including Mystic, Connecticut and Providence, Rhode Island.

TRAVEL TIP

The Acela Express, Amtrak's high-speed rail service, makes travel along the Washington, D.C.–New York–Boston corridor speedy and convenient. The train's top speed of 150 miles per hour is the fastest of any Amtrak service in the nation. The Acela schedule is designed specifically for business travelers going between New York and Boston, but it's also a good transportation choice for vacationers.

The Vermonter route is popular with skiers and fall foliage seekers. With daily service from Washington, D.C., and New York, this train stops in Vermont at Brattleboro, Bellows Falls, Windsor, White River Junction, Randolph, Montpelier, Waterbury, Essex Junction, and St. Albans. There are also stops at New Haven and Hartford, Connecticut, and Springfield and Amherst, Massachusetts, and you can continue on to Montreal by bus from St. Albans. The Ethan Allen Express route connects New York City to Rutland, Vermont, with several New York stops along the way.

Metro-North Railroad (212-340-3000 or 800-638-7646, *www .mta.info/mnr*) operates from New York's Grand Central Station and offers more affordable service to points in Connecticut. The New Haven line carries passengers between Grand Central and points along Connecticut's shoreline as far east as New Haven. There is connecting service from Stamford to New Canaan, from South Norwalk to Danbury, and from Bridgeport to Waterbury. Metro-North offers a wide variety of special excursion packages including round-trip rail transportation from New York City to Connecticut destinations such as The Maritime Aquarium at Norwalk and Mohegan Sun Casino.

By Cruise Ship

Though New England may not be the first destination that comes to mind when you're planning a cruise vacation, there are several cruise lines that stop at ports of call along New England's coast such as Boston, Portland, and the islands of Nantucket and Martha's Vineyard. The majority of departures coincide with fall foliage season, although some lines do offer late spring and summer sailings. Carnival Cruise Lines, Celebrity Cruises, and Holland America Line are particularly well known for their onboard programs for children and teens.

MAJOR CRUISE LINES SERVING NEW ENGLAND

Cruise Line	Phone Number	Web Site
Carnival Cruise Lines	☎888-CARNIVAL	✍www.carnival.com
Celebrity Cruises	☎800-647-2251	✍www.celebritycruises.com
CruiseWest	☎888-851-8133	✍www.cruisewest.com
Holland America Line	☎877-SAIL-HAL	✍www.hollandamerica.com
Norwegian Cruise Line	☎800-327-7030	✍www.ncl.com
Princess Cruises	☎800-PRINCESS	✍www.princess.com
Royal Caribbean	☎866-562-7625	✍www.royalcaribbean.com

By Bus

Interstate bus companies that provide service to many points in New England include Greyhound Lines (617-526-1800 or 800-231-2222, *www.greyhound.com*), Peter Pan Bus Lines (800-343-9999, *www .peterpanbus.com*), and Concord Coach Lines (617-426-8080 or 800-639-3317, *www.concordtrailways.com*).

Planning Your Trip

Peak and off-peak travel times are closely linked to the changing seasons. Overall, fall is New England's busiest tourism season as "leaf peepers" descend upon the region from near and far. Hotel reservations can be extraordinarily hard to come by if you have not made plans well in advance.

═FAST FACT

Why do leaves change colors? The one-word answer is photoperiodism. That's a fancy term that refers to the length of day and night. Trees need sunlight to produce chlorophyll, the pigment that gives leaves their green hue. As autumn nights get longer, less chlorophyll is produced, and leaves' "natural" tints come shining through. Rain, wind, and temperature influence the intensity and duration of fall colors.

You'll struggle with crowds, too, if you visit the area's seaside destinations during summer weekends and particularly the Fourth of July holiday week. Finding a ski chalet in Vermont can be tricky during school vacation weeks in December and February. Your best bet is to plan as far ahead as possible, to make sure you understand individual lodging properties' cancellation policies, and to be prepared for lines at attractions and restaurants if your trip coincides with peak season. Keep in mind that you can uncover special off-peak deals by visiting ski resort areas in the spring and summer, Cape Cod and other ocean-side spots in the fall through early spring, or just about any destination during the first few weeks of September before the annual foliage-viewing rush.

Time Zone

All six New England states are on U.S. Eastern Time (GMT minus five hours). Daylight-saving time is observed. Clocks are set forward one hour at 2 A.M. on the second Sunday morning in March, and Eastern Standard Time resumes at 2 A.M. on the first Sunday morning in November.

Public Holidays

These public holidays are observed in New England: New Year's Day (January 1), Martin Luther King Jr.'s Birthday (third Monday in January), Presidents' Day/Washington's Birthday (third Monday in February), Patriots' Day (third Monday in April—Massachusetts and Maine only), Memorial Day (last Monday in May), Independence Day (July 4), Labor Day (first Monday in September), Columbus Day (second Monday in October), Veterans Day (November 11), Thanksgiving (fourth Thursday in November), Christmas Day (December 25).

Business Hours

Typical public and private office hours are Monday through Friday, 8 or 9 A.M. to 5 P.M. Banking hours are typically Monday through Friday, 9 A.M. to 4 P.M., but many banks, particularly those with branch offices inside retail establishments such as grocery stores, offer extended hours on selected evenings and on Saturday mornings. Many gas stations and grocery/convenience stores are open day and night. Post offices are usually open from 8:00 or 8:30 A.M. until 5:00 P.M. Monday through Friday and until noon or later on Saturday. Most stores are open Monday through Saturday from 9 or 10 A.M. until 6 P.M. or later and on Sunday from 11 A.M. or noon until 5 or 6 P.M.

Finding Accommodations

Accommodations are abundant nearly everywhere you go in New England, except perhaps in the far northern wilderness reaches of Maine and New Hampshire. Your most difficult decision will be choosing a type of lodging from the array available—chain hotels, historic inns, spacious resorts, rental cottages, lakeside campsites, family-run motels, bed-and-breakfast inns (some even welcome children). This guide will point you to some family-friendly places to stay and to resources for researching lodging options. Contact regional and state tourism organizations for more leads on accommodations to suit your needs, and be sure to ask friends who have visited New England for their recommendations.

Advance reservations are always a good idea, and during fall foliage season, they are absolutely critical. After all, you don't want to spend valuable vacation minutes searching aimlessly for a place to catch some shuteye.

What to Pack

Two factors will influence the contents of your suitcase when you're packing for your trip to New England: the time of year and your planned activities. In general, you'll want to take lightweight clothing for visits between late June and early September, but be sure to pack jackets or sweaters, especially if you're visiting coastal areas, where breezes can have a decidedly cooling effect. Bathing suits, towels, and sunscreen are critical for ocean or lakefront getaways. Carry an insect repellent containing DEET for protection against Lyme disease, a tick-borne illness, if you're planning to spend time outdoors in wooded, brushy, or overgrown grassy areas.

In the spring and fall, temperatures can be quite cold at night even when daytime temperatures are comfortably moderate. Bring along warmer jackets or raincoats, and pack items that can be worn in layers.

Between November and March, be prepared with heavy winter coats, scarves, waterproof boots, and gloves or mittens. If you are planning a ski vacation, take your own gear or rent equipment at the slopes.

Many hotels provide hair dryers and toiletry items such as shampoo, soap, and body lotion, but it is always wise to inquire in advance. Smaller inns are less likely to offer these amenities. You may need to furnish your own linens at rental accommodations, so be sure to ask ahead.

An umbrella is always a good idea no matter what the season. Be sure to pack prescription medications, maps and brochures with information on the sights you plan to visit, airline and other tickets, passports, favorite stuffed animals, and games and activities to keep children amused while traveling. Don't forget your camera so that you'll have lasting images of your New England discoveries.

Health and Safety

Most sizable cities in New England have their own hospitals with emergency rooms. Highway signs with the hospital symbol—a white H on a blue background—can direct you to the nearest facility. Many cities and towns also have walk-in clinics for minor emergencies and ailments. Over-the-counter drugs are available at pharmacies, grocery and convenience stores, and even at many discount and department stores. If you require prescription medications, it is a good idea to bring along an adequate supply.

Safety Tips

As a general rule, New England is a safe place to travel. That said, visitors to the region should stay alert and use common sense to protect themselves and their belongings.

Here are a few things to keep in mind:

- **Don't carry large amounts of cash.** Traveler's checks and credit cards are much safer choices, or withdraw small amounts of cash at Automated Teller Machines (ATMs), which are commonplace throughout the region.
- **Carry valuables—passports, visas, money, jewelry—close to you at all times.** Do not leave valuables unattended in your hotel room. Check with your hotel for the availability of a safe.
- **Lock your hotel door and use the deadbolt where available.** Lock your car doors, whether you're parked or driving.
- **Do not leave luggage or purchases visible in your car.**
- **Whenever possible, stay in well-traveled, populated areas, particularly after dark.**
- **In most of New England, you can dial 911 from any telephone to access the emergency response system.** If 911 service is not available, dial 0, and an operator can connect you to the appropriate emergency services.
- **Fill your car with gas before heading to remote areas**, and don't underestimate the usefulness of a good map.
- **Deer, moose, and slick, wet fall leaves can all create driving hazards.** In the autumn, watch out, too, for drivers who are looking at leaves instead of watching the road.

Safety Belt and Child Restraint Laws

In New England, laws requiring the use of safety belts and child restraints vary by state. Here is a quick summary:

- **Connecticut**—Safety belts are required for all front-seat passengers ages seven and up. Children six years old and younger and less than sixty pounds must be secured in rear-seat child restraints.
- **Maine**—Passengers over age eight must wear seatbelts in all seats. Children ages eight and younger and less than 80 pounds must ride in the rear of the vehicle in a child-safety or booster seat. Children ages eleven and younger and less than 100 pounds must ride in the rear seat if available.

- **Massachusetts**—Safety belts are required for passengers ages five and up in all seats. Children four years old and younger or who weigh less than forty pounds must ride in a rear- seat child restraint.
- **New Hampshire**—Children five years old and younger who are less than 55 inches tall must be secured in a rear-seat child restraint. Children ages six through seventeen must wear a seatbelt in all seats. There is no safety belt law applying to adults in New Hampshire.
- **Rhode Island**—Passengers ages seven and up must wear safety belts in all seats. Children six years and younger and less than 54 inches and less than eighty pounds must ride in a car seat. Children six years and younger and greater than 54 inches and eighty pounds must be seated in the rear of the vehicle if space allows.
- **Vermont**—Everyone eight and up must wear a safety belt in any seat of a vehicle. Rear-seat child restraints are required for children ages seven and younger.

For more information about highway safety laws and potential fines, call the Insurance Institute for Highway Safety at 703-247-1500 or visit the nonprofit organization's Web site at *www.iihs.org*.

Helmet Laws

Laws pertaining to helmets for motorcycle drivers and passengers also vary by state. In Connecticut, helmets are required for riders seventeen and younger only. In Maine, they are required for riders fourteen and younger. In Rhode Island, riders twenty years old and younger are required to wear helmets. In Massachusetts and Vermont, all riders must wear helmets.

Connecticut, Maine, Massachusetts, New Hampshire, and Rhode Island also have laws requiring the use of helmets by young bicyclists. In Connecticut, Maine, New Hampshire, and Rhode Island, riders younger than sixteen must wear a helmet. In Massachusetts, bicycle riders ages one through sixteen must wear helmets; children under one are prohibited from riding on bicycles.

Connecticut

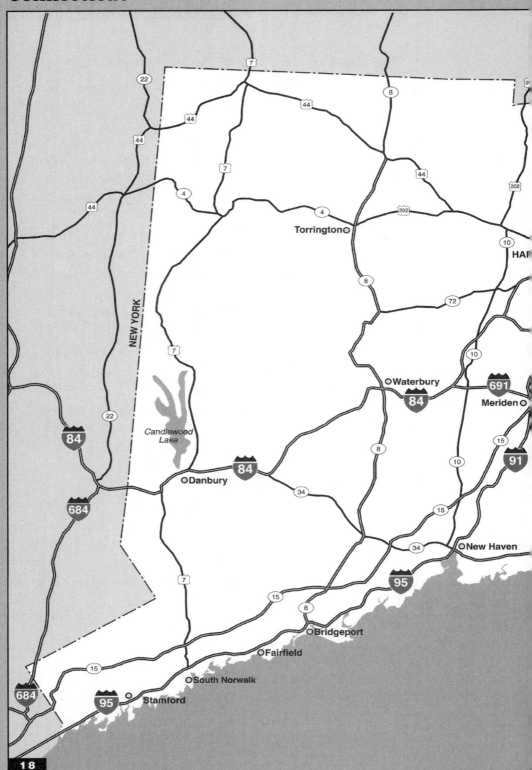

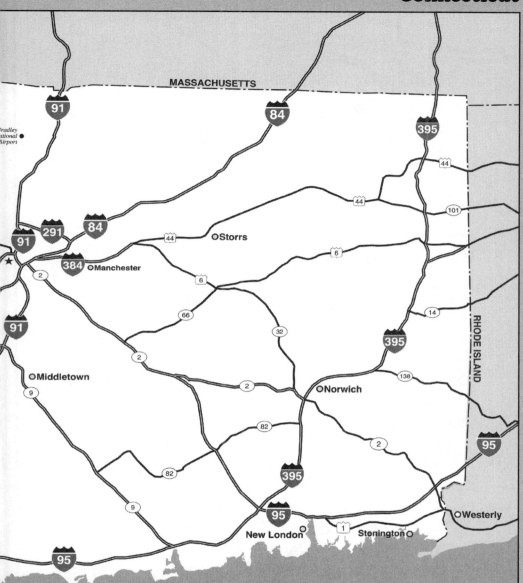

MASSACHUSETTS

Bradley
National
Airport

91

84

395

44

291

84

44

44

101

91

384 Manchester

Storrs

6

2

6

66

32

14

395

91

Middletown

2

2

Norwich

138

9

82

395

2

82

9

95

95

95 Westerly

395

New London

1 Stonington

95

LONG ISLAND SOUND

RHODE ISLAND

Hartford, Connecticut

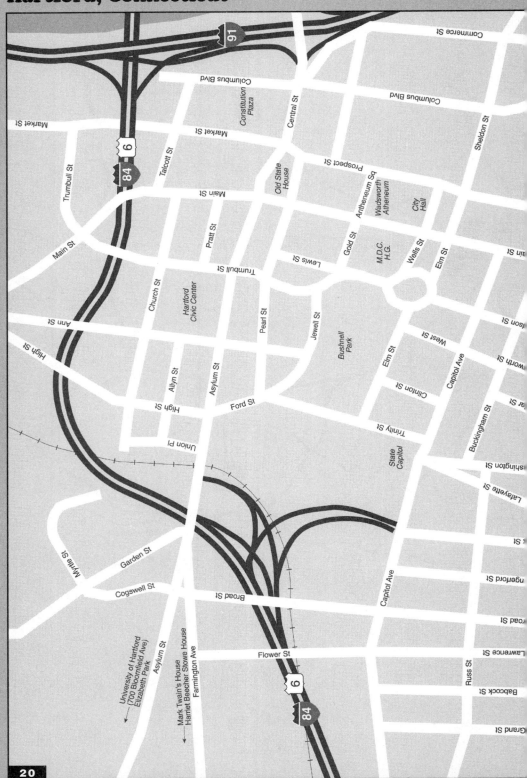

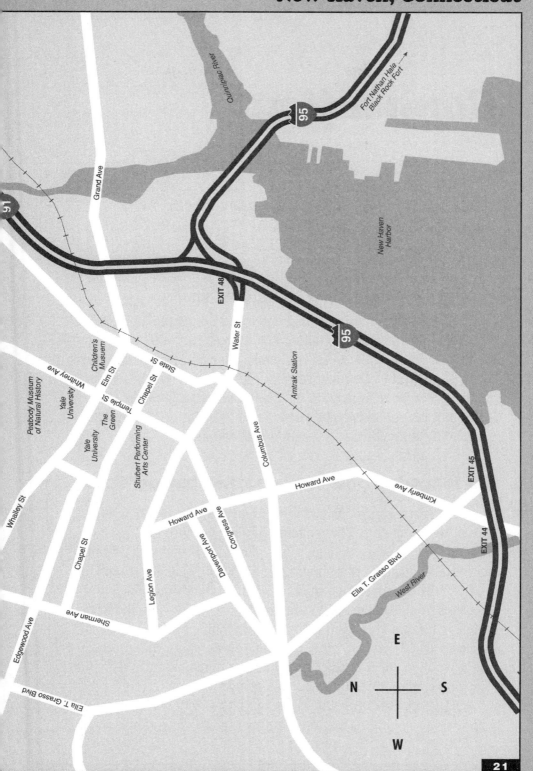

CHAPTER 2

Connecticut

CONNECTICUT PROVIDES MANY TRAVELERS with their very first glimpse of New England as they enter the region from New York City and other points south and west. Unfortunately, many see little more than the trees and green highway signs lining Interstates 84, 91, and 95 on their way to more distant New England destinations. Connecticut may be the third-smallest state in the United States, but it's no lightweight when it comes to historic sites, museums, family attractions, and vacation destinations.

An Introduction to the Constitution State

America's first turnpike, its first town library, and its first newspaper can all be credited to Connecticut. Connecticut inventors gave the world the first sewing machine, cotton gin, helicopter, nuclear submarine, and artificial heart. And we even have Connecticut to thank for the first Frisbee; bored Yale students got their hands on some empty pie plates from Mrs. Frisbie Pies in Bridgeport in 1920, and the rest is flying toy history. This "land of firsts" offers families much more than meets the eye. There's no other place in New England where you can ride a wooden roller coaster built into a mountainside, make your own dinosaur-track castings, or hug a beluga whale.

Along Connecticut's southern shore, you can explore lighthouses, a zoo, and a natural history museum that houses a world-class collection of dinosaur skeletons. The Mystic area, a whaling and ship-building center in the seventeenth through nineteenth centuries, is a popular family destination featuring historic and marine life attractions. Elsewhere along the Long Island Sound coastline and inland along the Connecticut River, you will discover spectacular scenery, steam train and riverboat rides, beaches, and even a castle. The central part of the state surrounding the capital, Hartford, is home to historic houses, apple orchards, kid-friendly museums, and one of the country's oldest amusement parks still in operation.

TRAVEL TIP

Request your free Connecticut Vacation Guide packed with information on attractions, accommodations, and recreational activities statewide by calling toll free, 888-CTVISIT, or by submitting your request online at *www.ctvisit.com.*

Connecticut can't be beat for a quick getaway—there's so much to experience in a close, accessible area. Couple compact geography with the state's amazing contrasts, and you'll be able to engage in a wide variety of vacation activities, even if your travel plans allow for little more than a weekend.

The Constitution State harmoniously blends old and new, large and small. Historic whaling towns are a stone's throw from the glamour and glitz of the world's largest casino, Foxwoods. Urban Fairfield County, an extension of the New York metropolitan region, is bisected by one of the nation's most scenic highways, the Merritt Parkway. Though only three states are more densely populated, nearly three-quarters of Connecticut is rural, and farm attractions beckon to families with petting zoos, pony rides, corn mazes, apple cider pressing, and harvest festivals. So don't speed through Connecticut; make savoring its sights your first New England travel priority.

When to Visit

Connecticut has New England's most temperate climate. Temperatures rarely top 90 degrees or fall below zero. Autumn is peak season, with dazzling foliage displays in the Litchfield Hills, the Connecticut River Valley, and along the Merritt Parkway. Winter offers lantern-light tours at Mystic Seaport, Christmas festivities in Bethlehem, and skiing. Spring brings opportunities to hike, bike, and explore the outdoors; summer offers swimming and boating along the shore and festivals celebrating seafood favorites from lobster to shad to oysters. Some attractions are closed in the winter, and beaches and amusement parks often do not open until the last weekend in May.

JUST FOR PARENTS

Looking for a quick escape without the wee ones? Consider Connecticut's "Quiet Corner" in the northeastern pocket or the Litchfield Hills in the western part. Both picturesque regions are known for vineyards, antiquing, outdoor recreation, scenic driving, and some of the state's most romantic and cozy bed-and-breakfast inns.

Getting There and Getting Around

Connecticut is an easy drive-to destination from the Northeast and Mid-Atlantic states. Alternative inbound transportation options include commercial bus lines, Amtrak and Metro-North rail service, and ferries that connect the southern shore with New York's Long Island. Connecticut's centrally located airport, Bradley International, offers travelers a convenient schedule of daily arrivals.

Bradley International Airport (BDL)

Bradley International Airport (860-292-2000 or 888-624-1533, *www .bradleyairport.com*), located just fifteen minutes north of Hartford in

Windsor Locks, is an easily accessible transportation hub that serves the Greater Hartford/Springfield area as well as western New England. It is the region's second-largest airport, serving nearly 7 million passengers annually. Bradley International Airport is located at exit 40 off I-91.

MAJOR AIRLINES SERVING BRADLEY INTERNATIONAL AIRPORT

Airline	Phone Number	Web Site
American	✆ 800-433-7300	✍ www.aa.com
Continental	✆ 800-525-0280	✍ www.continental.com
Delta	✆ 800-221-1212	✍ www.delta.com
Midwest	✆ 800-452-2022	✍ www.midwestairlines.com
Northwest	✆ 800-225-2525	✍ www.nwa.com
Southwest	✆ 800-435-9792	✍ www.southwest.com
United	✆ 800-864-8331	✍ www.ual.com
US Airways	✆ 800-428-4322	✍ www.usair.com

Airport Connections

In addition to limousine and taxi services, a number of shuttle operators and bus companies offer airport transfers. Connecticut Transit (860-522-8101, *www.cttransit.com*) operates buses that connect the airport and the Old State House in downtown Hartford. Valley Transporter (413-253-1350 or 800-872-8752, *www.valleytransporter .com*) shuttles students and others between Bradley and the towns and colleges of the Pioneer Valley in Massachusetts. Connecticut Limo (203-878-2222 or 800-472-5466, *www.ctlimo.com*) connects Bradley with these Connecticut destinations: Bridgeport, Danbury, Farmington, Hartford, Meriden, Milford, New Haven, Norwalk, Southbury, Stamford, Wallingford, and Waterbury.

Ferry Services

Two ferry companies link Long Island and Connecticut year-round. Cross Sound Ferry (860-443-5281, *www.longislandferry.com*) offers high-speed auto and passenger ferry service between Orient Point, New York, and New London, Connecticut. The Bridgeport & Port Jefferson Ferry (203-335-2040, *www.bpjferry.com*) provides car and passenger transport between Bridgeport, Connecticut, and Port Jefferson, New York. In addition, from late May until early September, Viking Fleet (631-668-5700, *www.vikingfleet.com*) offers passenger-only ferry service between Montauk, New York, and New London, Connecticut.

Getting Around

Once you arrive in Connecticut, you'll find that public transportation options are rather limited. Connecticut Transit (860-525-9181, *www .cttransit.com*) operates regularly scheduled bus services in Greater Hartford, New Haven, and Stamford. Metro-North Railroad (212-340-3000 or 800-638-7646, *www.mta.info/mnr*) has stations in Fairfield and New Haven counties along its 72-mile New Haven Line, which has offshoot branches extending north to New Canaan, Danbury, and Waterbury. Amtrak also has a presence in the state, with its Acela Express trains making stops in Stamford, New Haven, and New London, and the Regional line connecting Stamford, Bridgeport, New Haven, Wallingford, Meriden, Berlin, Hartford, Windsor, and Windsor Locks.

 TRAVEL TIP

> In 2005, transportation in downtown Hartford became a breeze for visiting families with the introduction of the Star Shuttle, a free bus service connecting the Connecticut Convention Center and Hartford's riverfront with downtown hotels, shops, restaurants, and museums. Simply climb aboard at any of the city's thirteen stops, which are designated with blue and gold Star Shuttle signs.

For maximum flexibility, and to reach many of Connecticut's finest family attractions, you will need a car. Most national car-rental chains have outlets in the state. Avis (800-331-1212, *www.avis.com*), Budget (800-527-0700, *www.budget.com*), Hertz (800-654-3131, *www.hertz .com*), and National (800-227-7368, *www.nationalcar.com*) all have cars available for pickup on-site at Bradley International Airport.

Must-See Activities and Attractions

The following are some of the must-see attractions in Connecticut. One of the beauties of touring this compact state is that you can most likely fit two or three appealing sites into one day's adventure.

Connecticut's Beardsley Zoo

⌸1875 Noble Avenue, Bridgeport

✆203-394-6565

✑*www.beardsleyzoo.org*

Connecticut's only zoo is home to nearly 300 animals including endangered Siberian tigers and red wolves that are being raised as part of the Species Survival Plan. While you're there, be sure to stroll through the indoor re-creation of a South American jungle in the Tropical Rainforest Building. Children will be delighted by the zoo's carousel museum, working carousel, and New England Farmyard.

Dino Sites

Peabody Museum of Natural History

⌸170 Whitney Avenue, New Haven

✆203-432-5050

✑*www.yale.edu/peabody*

Dinosaur State Park

⌸400 West Street, Rocky Hill

✆860-529-8423

✑*www.dinosaurstatepark.org*

Nature's Art & Dinosaur Crossing

⌸1650 Route 85, Oakdale

✆860-443-4367

✑*www.enaturesart.com*

Connecticut offers three fun destinations for young dinosaur enthusiasts and their families. Marvel at the size of the extinct beasts as you amble through the Great Hall of Dinosaurs at the Peabody Museum of Natural History at Yale University. Dig for dino bones and encounter twenty-five life-size dinosaur replicas along one-and-a-half miles of easy walking trails at Nature's Art & Dinosaur Crossing, one of the state's most eclectic attractions. Then, make tracks to Hartford County's Dinosaur State Park, where one of North America's largest collections of fossilized dino tracks, imprinted 200 million years ago, is housed under a dome.

Gillette Castle

⌨ 67 River Road, East Haddam

✆ 860-526-2336

✐ *www.ctrivervalley.com*

Yes, there is a castle in Connecticut. The fieldstone "castle" built by Connecticut actor William Gillette, known for his stage portrayals of Sherlock Holmes, is now a state park. Walk the picturesque grounds overlooking the Connecticut River, and then venture inside Gillette Castle, where you'll find creative décor including a table that moves on tracks, wooden light switches, and forty-seven distinctly different doors with intricately carved latches.

Lake Compounce

⌨ 271 Enterprise Drive, Bristol

✆ 860-583-3300

✐ *www.lakecompounce.com*

Connecticut is home to America's oldest amusement park, Lake Compounce. This 325-acre historic family attraction that dates to 1846 seamlessly blends the old and the new. You'll find a 1911 carousel, a vintage trolley, and a classic wooden roller coaster alongside modern bumper cars, thrill rides, and the Splash Harbor Water Park.

The Maritime Aquarium

⌨ 10 North Water Street, Norwalk

✆ 203-852-0700

✐ *www.maritimeaquarium.org*

More than 1,200 marine animals native to Long Island Sound and its watershed, including oysters, lobsters, sea stars, fish, sharks, sea turtles, and river otters, call the Maritime Aquarium home. You may have a difficult time getting the kids to leave when they discover the Ray Touch Pool, Jellyfish Encounter exhibit, Seal Pool, and larger-than-life IMAX movies. If you're looking for adventure, the aquarium offers a chance to see the animals in their natural habitat on summer-time study cruises, fall foliage cruises, and winter creature cruises on Long Island Sound.

RAINY DAY FUN

At The New England Carousel Museum (95 Riverside Avenue, Bristol, 860-585-5411, *www.thecarouselmuseum.org*), handcrafted carousel horses from bygone days are preserved and displayed. When the sun comes out, head to downtown Hartford's Bushnell Park, where you can clamber aboard a vintage 1914 carousel; it operates from May through mid-October.

Mystic's Aquarium and Seaport
Mystic Aquarium & Institute for Exploration
⌨55 Coogan Boulevard, Mystic
✆860-572-5955
✎*www.mysticaquarium.org*

Mystic Seaport
⌨75 Greenmanville Avenue, Mystic
✆860-572-5315 or ✆888-973-2767
✎*www.mysticseaport.org*

A shipbuilding and whaling center from the seventeenth to nineteenth centuries, Mystic is now home to several popular sights including Mystic Aquarium & Institute for Exploration, featuring thousands of water-loving creatures from around the world such as African penguins and the only captive whales in New England, and Mystic Seaport, a seventeen-acre living-history museum that recreates maritime life in the 1800s. A combination ticket will save you money when you visit both attractions.

Mashantucket Pequot Museum and Research Center

⌂110 Pequot Trail, Mashantucket

✆800-411-9671

✎*www.pequotmuseum.org*

In 1998, the Mashantucket Pequots opened the nation's largest museum dedicated to Native American culture. The 308,000-square-foot multimedia museum tells the tribe's story from prehistoric to present times in fascinating detail. Allow three to five hours to explore its life-size displays, interactive learning stations, and changing exhibits.

New England Air Museum

⌂36 Perimeter Road, Route 75, Windsor Locks

✆860-623-3305

✎*www.neam.org*

Located near Bradley International Airport, this museum has one of the world's largest collections of antique aircraft and aviation artifacts, including planes dating from 1909 to the present, helicopters and gliders, and exhibits on such fascinating themes as the Flying Tigers and Connecticut's role in aviation history. For a real treat, visit on one of the museum's regularly scheduled Open Cockpit Days.

TRAVEL TIP

Take your kids to a trashy place . . . The Children's Garbage Museum in Stratford (203-381-9571, *www.crra.org/pages/edu_museums.htm*). Home to the Trash-o-saurus, a dinosaur made from one ton of refuse (the amount an average person discards each year), the museum teaches kids the importance of recycling. Admission is free. Hours are limited.

Tubing and Skiing in the Farmington Valley
Farmington River Tubing

Satan's Kingdom State Recreation Area, Route 44, New Hartford

860-693-6465

www.farmingtonrivertubing.com

Ski Sundown

126 Ratlum Road, New Hartford

860-379-7669

www.skisundown.com

If your family is fond of outdoor recreation, you'll want to know about two cool activities in the Farmington River Valley. When hot and humid summer days arrive, try tubing on the river; it's exhilarating for ages ten and up. When winter sets in, Ski Sundown's gentle slopes are a great place for young ones to learn to ski or snowboard, and there are enough challenging runs to keep skilled parents and teens entertained, too.

USS Nautilus

One Crystal Lake Road, Groton

860-694-3174 or 800-343-0079

www.ussnautilus.org

The Submarine Force Museum is the permanent home of the world's first nuclear-powered submarine, the USS *Nautilus*. The historic ship was christened in 1954 by First Lady Mamie Eisenhower. It shattered all submerged speed and distance records and made a historic first journey under the North Pole. Climb aboard for a self-guided audio tour of this historic craft; then learn more about submarines by exploring the museum's exhibits of memorabilia, working periscopes, and even a re-created World War II submarine attack center.

Family Fun Plans

Whether you're planning a quick weekend getaway or a week-long family escape, there are many reasons to choose Connecticut as your destination. These Family Fun Plans offer suggestions to help you fill your days with enjoyable activities for kids, parents, and even grandparents. Use them as a starting point to design an itinerary that's right for you.

A Wet and Wild Summer Weekend

Who says a brief weekend getaway can't be fun-filled? Here's how to make the most of a two-night summer jaunt to Connecticut.

Friday Night: Check in to the Clarion Hotel in Bristol (42 Century Drive, 860-589-7766, *www.choicehotels.com*) early enough to allow time for a dip in the indoor heated pool. Then enjoy an all-you-can-eat seafood dinner at the hotel's Jillian's Restaurant.

Saturday: In the morning, wet your whistle by visiting Avery's Beverages (520 Corbin Avenue, New Britain, 860-224-0830, *www .averysoda.com)*, where soda is still made in small batches using generations-old recipes. Founded in 1904, Avery's is one of New England's oldest bottlers, and kids will love sipping soda flavors like strawberry, pink lemonade, and orange cream. Call ahead, and they'll give you a tour of the factory and even let you concoct your own unique beverage. Enjoy a light lunch at The Flatbread Company (110 Albany Turnpike/Route 44, Canton, 860-693-3314, *www.flatbreadcompany.com*), where chewy, wood-fired pizzas are topped with organic local ingredients. Then, get ready for a wild river ride at Farmington River Tubing (Satan's Kingdom State Recreation Area, Route 44, New Hartford, 860-693-6465, *www .farmingtonrivertubing.com*). Dry off back at the hotel, and head out to Frankies (1195 Farmington Avenue, Bristol, 860-584-9826, *www.frankies hotdogs.com*) for a famous "Frankie" topped with anything from chili to bacon; you'll find burgers, fried clams, chicken wings, Philly steaks, and plenty of kids' menu items, too.

Sunday: Spend the day at Lake Compounce (822 Lake Avenue, 860-583-3300, *www.lakecompounce.com*), home to Connecticut's largest water park, Splash Harbor, plus thrill rides, kiddie rides, shows, and more. There's plenty to do until it's time to bid Connecticut adieu.

Five Days in and Around Hartford

Connecticut's centrally located capital city makes a great home base for exploring the state. The Residence Inn Hartford Downtown (942 Main Street, 860-524-5550, *www.marriott.com/property/ propertypage/BDLRI*) is a good choice for extended family stays; all suites have full kitchens, and room rates include a hot buffet breakfast daily and a light supper weekdays. Hartford's free Star Shuttle picks up passengers at a stop across the street from the hotel.

Day One: Explore downtown Hartford: the State Capitol Building (210 Capitol Avenue, 860-240-0222), the Old State House (800 Main Street, 860-522-6766, *www.ctosh.org*), Bushnell Park (Trinity Street at Elm Street, 860-232-6710, www.bushnellpark.org), and the Wadsworth Atheneum art museum (600 Main Street, 860-278-2670, *www. wadsworthatheneum.org*).

Day Two: On the western outskirts of the city, visit the Mark Twain House (351 Farmington Avenue, 860-247-0998, *www.marktwainhouse .org*) and the Harriet Beecher Stowe Center (77 Forest Street, 860-522-9258, *www.harrietbeecherstowecenter.org*). If time allows, travel farther west on Farmington Avenue and explore the shops in West Hartford Center. Plan an early-evening picnic in the fragrant, historic rose gardens of Elizabeth Park (Prospect Avenue, 860-231-9443, *www .elizabethpark.org*), or dine at the park's Pond House Café (860-231-8823, *www.pondhousecafe.com*).

 RAINY DAY FUN

When it opens in Hartford in 2008, the Connecticut Science Center (*www.ctsciencecenter.org*) will be a must-see family attraction. The museum's dramatic riverfront building will house interactive exhibits that will inspire young imaginations and make scientific learning fun. In the Sports Lab, for example, kids can test their balance at the Skateboard Challenge and compare the aerodynamics of sports balls in a wind-stream tunnel.

Day Three: Take a day trip to Bristol, where you can explore The New England Carousel Museum (95 Riverside Avenue, 860-585-5411, *www.thecarouselmuseum.org*) and spend the rest of the day playing at Lake Compounce (822 Lake Avenue, 860-583-3300, *www.lakecompounce.com*).

Day Four: Spend a low-key day visiting some of the area's best free places for kids, including Jonathan's Dream (335 Bloomfield Avenue, West Hartford), the first playground designed for children of all abilities, and Westmoor Park (119 Flagg Road, West Hartford), a demonstration farm where you can walk nature trails and see barnyard animals up-close. If your kids are a bit older, head to Talcott Mountain State Park (57 Gun Mill Road, Bloomfield, 860-242-1158), and hike the mile-and-a-quarter Tower Trail to the summit, where you can climb Heublein Tower for panoramic views. After a day outdoors, treat yourselves to an entertaining dinner around the Japanese hibachi tables at Ginza (14 Wintonbury Mall, Bloomfield, 860-242-8289, *www.ginzacuisine.com*).

Day Five: Before you take off for home, visit the New England Air Museum (Route 75, Windsor Locks, 860-623-3305, *www.neam.org*), located about twenty minutes north of Hartford near Bradley International Airport. Here, kids can learn about aviation, participate in hands-on activities, and even take the controls of a computer flight simulator.

A Week along the Connecticut Coast

Connecticut's shoreline is rich in history, but kids will find this week-long escape anything but boring. Along the way, there's fun for Mom and Dad, too, and plenty of good food, including famous pizza and burgers, and of course, seafood.

Day One: Start out at the Maritime Aquarium in Norwalk (10 North Water Street, 203-852-0700, *www.maritimeaquarium.org*) to explore the marine life of Long Island Sound and take in a colossal IMAX movie. In the afternoon, take I-95 North to exit 27 and visit the Barnum Museum in Bridgeport (820 Main Street, 203-331-1104, *www.barnum-museum.org*), a monument to the Greatest Showman on Earth.

Day Two: Continue north on I-95 to exit 47 for New Haven, home of historic Yale University. Tour the campus in the morning, and spend the afternoon exploring one or two of the university's splendid museums of art, rare books, or natural history. When your gang gets hungry, be sure to stop by Louis' Lunch (261-263 Crown Street, 203-562-5507, *www.louislunch.com*) to eat flame-cooked burgers prepared just as Louis Lassen made them when he invented the hamburger in New Haven in 1900.

Day Three: Continue north on I-95 to exit 63, stopping in Clinton at the Clinton Crossing Premium Outlets (20-A Killingworth Turnpike, 860-664-0700, *www.premiumoutlets.com*), or to exit 65 for the Tanger Outlet Center in Westbrook (314 Flat Rock Place, 860-399-8656, *www.tangeroutlet.com*) to scout for bargains. If the temperatures are sweltering, spend some time relaxing and cooling off at nearby Hammonasset Beach State Park at exit 62 in Madison. Have dinner overlooking Long Island Sound at Bill's Seafood in Westbrook (548 Boston Post Road, 860-399-7224, *www.billsseafood.com*), located off I-95 at exit 65.

Day Four: Take Route 9 North from I-95 to explore the Connecticut River towns of Old Saybrook, Essex, and East Haddam. The quirky Gillette Castle in East Haddam (67 River Road, 860-526-2336, *www.dep. state.ct.us/stateparks/parks/gillettecastle.htm*) is a must-see. Essex is home to the Connecticut River Museum (67 Main Street, 860-767-8269, *www.ctrivermuseum.org*), whose changing exhibits focus on the region's history and eagle cruises depart during winter months. You'll find quaint shops, art galleries, and seafood restaurants tucked away in these river towns. Plan to dine aboard the 1920s-era Essex Clipper Dinner Train operated by The Valley Railroad Company in Essex (One Railroad Avenue, 860-767-0103 or 800-377-3987, *www. essexsteamtrain.com*).

Day Five: Well, I-95 should feel like an old friend by now. Heading north once again, stop at exit 90 for the town of Mystic, one of Connecticut's most popular destinations. Explore the town's whaling history at Mystic Seaport (75 Greenmanville Avenue, 860-572-5315 or 888-973-2767, *www.mysticseaport.org*). Grab a slice of heaven at

Mystic Pizza (56 West Main Street, 860-536-3700, *www.mysticpizza .com*), made famous by the movie. Then spend the afternoon with whales, sea lions, and penguins at Mystic Aquarium & Institute for Exploration (55 Coogan Boulevard, 860-572-5955, *www.mystic aquarium.org*). If it's a perfect summer evening, dine in nearby Noank at Abbott's Lobster in the Rough (117 Pearl Street, 860-536-7719, *www .abbotts-lobster.com*), where you can feast on the freshest seafood at a picnic table overlooking the Sound as the sun sets.

Day Six: Had enough family togetherness? Part ways for a bit at Mohegan Sun Casino (1 Mohegan Sun Boulevard, 888-226-7711, *www. mohegansun.com*), located just a short detour off I-95 in Uncasville. Grownups can gamble or shop while little ones ages six months to twelve years enjoy supervised play activities at Kids Quest. Reconnect for a memorable meal at an all-you-can-eat buffet, Geno Auriemma's Fast Break—the food court named for the Basketball Hall of Famer and University of Connecticut women's basketball coach, or one of the casino's fine restaurants.

Day Seven: If you're returning home on I-95 South, stop at exit 86 and submerge yourself in the nautical marvels of the Submarine Force Museum at Groton (One Crystal Lake Road, 860-694-3174 or 800-343-0079, *www.ussnautilus.org*), where you can tour the USS *Nautilus*, the world's first nuclear-powered submarine.

CHAPTER 3

The Connecticut Shore

NEW ENGLAND SNEAKS UP on you subtly as you travel north along Connecticut's shoreline. While Fairfield County is still part of the sprawling New York metropolitan region, it won't be long before you encounter coastal villages, classic town greens, and winding country lanes that seem a world away from the big city. For families craving diversity, Connecticut's coast can't be beat. Here, you'll find world-class restaurants and roadside seafood shacks, dazzling casinos and tranquil tidal marshes, and museums that house everything from British art to Tom Thumb's wardrobe.

An Introduction to Connecticut's Coastal Regions

Southwestern Connecticut's Fairfield County might remind you of the Buddhist parable of the blind men and the elephant. Just as each blind man experienced a very different creature depending on whether he touched the elephant's head or ears or tusk or trunk or tail, you'll find a variety of experiences awaiting you as you feel your way around Fairfield County.

Touch Greenwich, and you'll leave impressed with the affluence and sophistication of the region. Touch Stamford, and you'll swear you're in the heart of a major commercial center. Touch Westport, and you'll take home memories of seaside elegance and creative, cultured living. Touch Norwalk, and the sensation is of a former thriving seaport searching for a new life as a trendy shopping and sightseeing destination. Touch Bridgeport, and you'll get the notion that this is a blue-collar, post-industrial area struggling to find a new identity.

 TRAVEL TIP

Traffic on I-95 in Connecticut can be brutal on summer weekends. Be sure to pack snacks and some games and activities to keep children amused. You'll find service areas with fast-food and restroom facilities after exits 12, 21, 40, 53, and 61 as you travel northbound and after exits 93, 62, 54, 41, 22, and 10 as you travel southbound.

Fairfield County is above all a region of transition. The city of New Haven serves as an invisible line of demarcation between the Connecticut that could be construed to be part of New York City and the Connecticut that is truly New England. In fact, when you visit the southeastern coastal region, you will be treated to everything that New England is and has been.

You will find many reasons to return to Connecticut's coast, season after season. After all, where else can you go to the largest museum dedicated to Native American culture, to Captain Kidd's hideout, to one of the country's oldest universities, to the scene of the bloodiest battle of the American Revolution, to a re-created nineteenth-century seaport, to the birthplace of the world's first nuclear-powered submarine, and to the world's largest casino, all within an hour's driving distance?

What to See and Do

When the kids ask, "What are we going to do today?" you'll have no shortage of answers when you vacation along the Connecticut shore.

Whether you're an active or an inquisitive bunch, in search of simple pleasures or seeking unforgettable experiences, here are some of the best amusements and attractions southern Connecticut has to offer.

Aquariums and Zoos

With two aquariums and a zoo, the Connecticut shore is a great destination for animal lovers of all ages. These fine educational facilities offer interactive learning experiences and opportunities to appreciate the diversity of creatures that share our planet.

Connecticut's Beardsley Zoo

⌨1875 Noble Avenue, Bridgeport

✆203-394-6565

✐*www.beardsleyzoo.org*

Whether you spend an hour or an entire day at Connecticut's only zoo, you'll be charmed by the antics of playful prairie dogs and the majesty of birds that soar within the free-flight aviary and gain an appreciation for the challenges faced by endangered and threatened species. A carousel and farmyard appeal to the littlest visitors. Challenge older children by printing a scavenger hunt from the zoo's Web site before you go.

The Maritime Aquarium

⌨10 North Water Street, Norwalk

✆203-852-0700

✐*www.maritimeaquarium.org*

From IMAX movies shown on a giant screen to daily harbor seal feedings, there are plenty of activities to enthrall young visitors at Norwalk's aquarium. The focus here is on the unique ecosystem of Long Island Sound, and exhibits provide a peek under the surface at the variety of life sustained by this sheltered sea inlet.

Mystic Aquarium & Institute for Exploration

⌨55 Coogan Boulevard, Mystic

✆860-572-5955

✐*www.mysticaquarium.org*

Mystic Aquarium is not only a refuge for an amazing variety of marine creatures, it is home to the Institute for Exploration, an extraordinary oceanic research organization founded and led by Dr. Robert Ballard, discoverer of the *Titanic* and one of the world's preeminent marine scientists. Allow a full day to explore all of the aquarium's exhibits, dedicated to everything from the search for John F. Kennedy's World War II PT boat to the hidden inhabitants of the Amazon rainforest. There are also two close encounters available to visitors: the Penguin Contact Program, available for ages seven and up, and the Beluga Contact program, available to participants who are at least five feet tall. While the fees are somewhat steep, you're assured a truly unforgettable experience when you meet an African penguin face-to-face or hug a beluga whale.

Beaches

Because it is shallow and sheltered from the open sea by the largest island in the continental United States, Long Island Sound tends to be relatively warm and calm. As a result, these beaches are ideal for tots to build their first sandcastles and dip their toes in the waves. Here are the state's largest and most popular public beaches.

Hammonasset Beach State Park

⌨1288 Boston Post Road, Madison

✆203-245-2785

✐*www.ct.gov/dep/cwp/view.asp?a=2716&q=325210*

The two-mile stretch of sand within this 919-acre state park is Connecticut's largest beach. Admission is charged by the car, with higher rates assessed on weekends and for out-of-state vehicles. In the off-season, the park is free to all visitors, and it is still an inviting place for a stroll along the boardwalk. During the summer months, the Meigs Point Nature Center offers a variety of programs and hands-on activities for children.

Lighthouse Point Park

⌨2 Lighthouse Point Road, New Haven

✆203-946-8019

✑ *www.cityofnewhaven.com/Parks/ParksInformation/light housepoint.asp*

With its octagonal lighthouse, antique carousel, Splashpad fountains, and lifeguard-protected beach, New Haven's oceanfront park appeals to families. Nonresidents pay a parking fee.

Ocean Beach Park

⌨Ocean Avenue, New London

✆203-447-3031 or ✆800-510-SAND

✑*www.ocean-beach-park.com*

In addition to its sugar-sand beach and half-mile boardwalk, Ocean Beach Park boasts an Olympic-size pool with a waterslide, classic kiddie and adult rides, an arcade, a slot car raceway, an 18-hole miniature golf course, a café, and a roster of special events from concerts to beach-blanket movie nights. Pay one fee for parking and admission for everyone in your car. Some activities carry additional fees.

Rocky Neck State Park

⌨244 West Main Street / Route 156, East Lyme

✆860-739-5471

✑*www.ct.gov/dep*

You can do more than swim at this white sand beach. Picnic under the stone pavilion, follow a variety of easy walking trails, try crabbing or saltwater fishing, and camp overnight while the ocean sings you a lullaby. Admission is charged by the car; higher rates apply on weekends and for out-of-staters. Camping fees are additional. Admission is free in the off-season.

Sherwood Island State Park

⌨Sherwood Island Connector, Westport

✆203-226-6983

✑*www.ct.gov/dep*

Connecticut's oldest state park makes a fine destination for families in search of a place to play in the sand. Facilities include a picnic grove, bathrooms and showers, a food concession, and a platform from which to observe birds and other marsh life. Admission is charged by the car, with higher rates assessed on weekends and for out-of-state vehicles. There is no admission charge in the off-season.

Boat Tours

For scenery and history, book passage aboard a Long Island Sound cruise. These boat tours operate seasonally and provide family vacationers with a memorable way to experience Connecticut's coastal places.

DownEast Lighthouse Cruises

⌨Pine Island Marina, 916R Shennecossett Road, Groton

✆860-460-1802

✍*www.downeastlighthousecruises.com*

See lighthouses, tall sailing ships, and submarines on a cruise around New London Harbor and the mouth of the Thames River, or choose one of the other excursions including sunset cruises on Fisher's Island Sound and lobstering adventures.

═FAST FACT

Oyster cultivation has been an important Connecticut industry for more than a century. There are over 70,000 acres of oyster farms along Connecticut's Long Island Sound coast. Each September, this delectable mollusk's role in the economy of the Constitution State is celebrated at the Norwalk Seaport Association's annual Oyster Festival (203-838-9444, *www.seaport.org/oyster_festival.htm*).

Sabino Island Steamer

Mystic Seaport, 75 Greenmanville Avenue, Mystic

860-572-5315 or 888-973-2767

www.mysticseaport.org

At Mystic Seaport, visitors can book passage aboard *Sabino*, America's last wooden, coal-fired, steam-powered ferry. The 1908 steamboat makes leisurely trips along the Mystic River, and if you're lucky, you'll have an opportunity to see Mystic's bascule bridge, an engineering wonder, in operation. There is a fee for tickets in addition to regular Seaport admission.

Seamist Thimble Islands Cruise

Indian Point Road, Stony Creek

203-488-8905

www.seamistcruises.com

The Thimbles are a storied archipelago of tiny islands lying just off the coast of Connecticut near Stony Point. According to legend, seventeenth-century pirate Captain Kidd stashed treasure here that's never been found. On this narrated cruise, you'll hear tales of pirates and bootleggers, as well as the islands' current wealthy and celebrity inhabitants.

Casinos

It may come as a surprise that Connecticut is one of America's premier gambling destinations. It is the only New England state to permit gambling casinos on Indian reservation lands. While they cater to a primarily adult audience, many families visit the state's two casinos each year to attend concerts and sporting events, to dine at tantalizing buffets and fine-dining restaurants, to shop, and to marvel at these incredible facilities that contribute more than $400 million in slot revenues annually to the state's coffers.

Foxwoods Resort Casino

Route 2, Mashantucket

800-FOXWOODS

www.foxwoods.com

The world's largest casino isn't in Las Vegas, Monte Carlo, or Atlantic City. It's in Connecticut! The Mashantucket Pequot tribe's Foxwoods Resort Casino, which has grown exponentially since it opened in 1992, offers twenty-four-hour gaming action, more than 7,000 slot machines, and a Bingo Hall that goes on forever. You'll also find three on-site hotels, thirty-five dining options, headline entertainment in the 1,400-seat Fox Theatre, a spa, and more.

≡FAST FACT

Visitors to the casinos must be at least twenty-one years of age to gamble or even to set foot on the casino floor. The Bingo Hall at Foxwoods is open to players ages eighteen and up.

An MGM-branded casino, which will add 2 million square feet of additional gaming, dining, entertainment, and hotel space to the Foxwoods complex, is scheduled to open in the summer of 2008. While Foxwoods' sheer size will astound visitors of all ages, the casino offers few entertainment options for children. The Tree House Arcade has games that will appeal to everyone from preschoolers to teens, but children under age fourteen may not be left unattended.

Mohegan Sun
1 Mohegan Sun Boulevard, Uncasville
888-226-7711
www.mohegansun.com

The Mohegan tribe boosted Connecticut's draw as a gaming outpost in 1996 when it opened Mohegan Sun. A $1 billion expansion completed in 2002, which added a 1,200-room, thirty-four-story hotel; a spa, salon, and fitness center; more than 100,000 square feet of meeting space, including the largest ballroom in the Northeast; the Sky Casino, with 115,000 square feet of additional gaming space; an additional 175,000 square feet of premium retail and entertainment space; and a new 10,000-seat arena to the Mohegan Sun empire, has made it even more competitive with its neighbor to the south.

JUST FOR PARENTS

The Elemis Spa at Mohegan Sun blends Native American traditions and signature Elemis treatments to create unique rituals you won't find at any other spa. Celebrating an anniversary? The Ceremony of the Strawberry Moon begins with champagne and chocolate-covered strawberries served while you enjoy an exotic jasmine flower bath for two; it concludes with a couple's massage lesson.

It's also the more family-friendly of the two casinos. Older children can play video and arcade games in a supervised atmosphere at Cyber Quest. At Kids Quest, child care and even meal service are provided for ages six weeks to twelve years. Or, stick together, and enjoy the casino's incomparable sights, such as an indoor waterfall, and the many kid-friendly restaurants and shops.

Historic Attractions

In 1614, Dutch navigator Adriaen Block was the first European to sail into Long Island Sound. In the ensuing quarter-century, Dutch and English settlers purchased lands from Native inhabitants and established towns along Connecticut's shoreline. As you travel in this region, you'll discover historic attractions that tell the story of Connecticut's colonial period, as well its role in the conflict and commerce that contributed to the growth of a new nation.

Fort Griswold Battlefield State Park

57 Fort Street, Groton

860-449-6877

www.dep.state.ct.us/stateparks/parks/fort_griswold.htm

The Battle of Groton Heights lasted only forty minutes, but when it was over, 88 of the 165 defenders stationed at Fort Griswold and 51 British attackers were dead. Today, visitors to the site of this battle of the American Revolution can relive that September day in 1781 when Connecticut native Benedict Arnold, who had deserted the American cause a year earlier, led British troops into an area that he knew quite well.

Admission to tour the historic fort, a Revolutionary War museum, and the Ebenezer Avery House, which sheltered the wounded, is free. The park is open year-round, but its museum and monument are only open daily from Memorial Day weekend through Labor Day, and then on Saturdays and Sundays through Columbus Day weekend.

Fort Nathan Hale and Black Rock Fort

36 Woodward Avenue, New Haven

203-787-8790

www.fort-nathan-hale.org

Black Rock Fort and Fort Nathan Hale, a restored Revolutionary War fort and a restored Civil War fort, respectively, are open free to the public from Memorial Day weekend through Labor Day weekend.

TRAVEL TIP

It's much easier to get into Yale if you're not applying to be a student. Take a free, student-led tour of the historic Yale University campus, the alma mater for many U.S. presidents. Tours are available at 10:30 A.M. and 2:00 P.M. on weekdays and at 1:30 P.M. on weekends. They depart from the Visitor Information Center (149 Elm Street, New Haven, 203-432-2300).

Henry Whitfield State Museum

⌂248 Old Whitfield Street, Guilford

☎203-453-2457

The stone house built by Reverend Henry Whitfield, who led a group of English Puritans to Connecticut's shores in 1639, is the oldest house in Connecticut and New England's oldest stone house. Tours are offered April through mid-December.

Mystic Seaport

⌂75 Greenmanville Avenue, Mystic

☎860-572-5315 or ☎888-973-2767

✎*www.mysticseaport.org*

Climb aboard the *Charles W. Morgan*, the world's only surviving whaleship; chat with role players at work inside the nineteenth-century seaside village's thirty shops and businesses; and view exhibits that tell the story of Connecticut's ties to the sea. Mystic Seaport, one of America's premier maritime attractions, is open daily year-round.

≡FAST FACT

In 2006, after receiving several phone calls from visitors to Mystic Seaport who shared similar accounts, a team from the Rhode Island Paranormal Research Group investigated to see whether there might indeed by a ghost aboard the Charles W. Morgan. What did the ghost hunters conclude? "It is our opinion that the old ship is haunted . . . to what extent remains to be seen," they stated.

USS *Nautilus*

⌂One Crystal Lake Road, Groton

☎860-694-3174 or ☎800-343-0079

✎*www.ussnautilus.org*

Visit the U.S. Navy's only submarine museum, and step down into the world's first nuclear-powered submarine, the USS *Nautilus*, for a self-guided audio tour. The sub broke all submerged speed and distance records and achieved the first crossing of the North Pole by a ship. You'll see the torpedo room, the crew's quarters, officers' staterooms, the control room, and more. The USS *Nautilus* is open year-round.

Museums Kids Will Love

Museums don't have to be boring. You'll be able to prove it to your offspring when you include one of these stops on your Connecticut itinerary.

The Barnum Museum
820 Main Street, Bridgeport
203-331-1104
www.barnum-museum.org

P. T. Barnum, America's crown prince of oddities and the mastermind behind "The Greatest Show on Earth," was born in Connecticut. He and his cast of characters—General Tom Thumb, Chang and Eng the Siamese twins, Jumbo the Elephant, Jenny Lind, and others—come to life at the only museum dedicated to the famous showman.

Mashantucket Pequot Museum & Research Center
110 Pequot Trail, Mashantucket
800-411-9671

America's largest Native American museum will immerse you in the history and culture of Connecticut's first people. The five-story, 308,000-square-foot facility features lifelike dioramas, dramatic films, galleries of artifacts and crafts, hands-on activity stations, audio tours, and even an escalator that transports visitors back to the last Ice Age. You can drive to the museum directly, or take a free shuttle from nearby Foxwoods Resort Casino.

Peabody Museum of Natural History
170 Whitney Avenue, New Haven
203-432-5050
www.yale.edu/peabody

This Yale University Museum is filled with fascinating exhibits related to plant, animal, and human evolution, but it is the Great Hall of Dinosaurs that will really catch kids' attention. If you are traveling with older children, consider visiting one of the university's other museums. You can see a rare Gutenberg Bible and original Audubon bird prints at the Beinecke Rare Book and Manuscript Library; art from Europe, America, Africa, and the Near and Far East at the Yale Art Gallery; and the most extensive assemblage of British art outside of Britain at the Yale Center for British Art.

 ## RAINY DAY FUN

Youngsters will find interactive exhibits featuring science, art, music, culture, history, safety, and health to delve into at the Children's Museum of Southeastern Connecticut (409 Main Street, Niantic, 860-691-1111, *www.childrensmuseumsect .org*). There is even a Nursery Rhyme Land for toddlers.

Outdoor Recreation
Ready to stretch your legs or work your arms? From hiking trails to kayaking trips, Connecticut's coastal region is a great place for outdoor recreation.

Bluff Point State Park and Coastal Reserve
Depot Road, Groton
860-444-7591
www.dep.state.ct.us/stateparks/parks/bluffpoint.htm

This 800-acre park is the largest undeveloped tract of land along the Connecticut shore. It is a popular spot for kayaking, hiking, mountain biking, and wildlife watching. There is no admission fee.

Connecticut Coastal Kayaking

⌨18 Oak Tree Lane, Lyme

✆860-391-3837

✒*www.ctcoastalkayaking.com*

This outfitter offers half- and full-day kayaking tours that are suitable even for inexperienced paddlers.

≡FAST FACT

Lyme disease, a tick-borne illness, is named for Lyme, Connecticut, where it was first diagnosed. Connecticut remains one of the states with the highest number of cases of the disease each year. Lyme-carrying ticks are especially prevalent during spring and summer. Protect yourself while outdoors by wearing long pants and long-sleeved shirts, tucking pants into socks, using insect repellent, and checking yourself and your children for ticks daily. If you do discover a tick, remove it carefully with tweezers. Keep an eye on the bite area, and if any swelling or discoloration occurs, contact a physician.

Roy and Margot Larsen Wildlife Sanctuary

⌨2325 Burr Street, Fairfield

✆203-259-6305

✒*www.ctaudubon.org*

Stop by the Connecticut Audubon Society Center at Fairfield, and then explore this adjoining 152-acre habitat with its meadows, streams, woods, marshes, and ponds. Walkways and bridges offer access to bird and wildlife viewing areas.

Stamford Museum & Nature Center

39 Scofieldtown Road, Stamford

203-322-1646

www.stamfordmuseum.org

This multifaceted attraction boasts a working farm, planetarium, observatory, and nature exhibits. Miles of scenic walking trails wind through the 118-acre property, which is open year-round. Kids will adore Nature's Playground, where they can climb a spider's web, wiggle like worms across large maple leaves, crawl through an ant's nest, get a bird's eye view from a hawk's nest, and search for fossils in the sand pit.

Shopping

Whether you're hunting for souvenirs and bargains or seeking a singular shopping experience, you'll find plenty of opportunities for retail therapy along Connecticut's coast.

B.F. Clyde's Cider Mill

129 North Stonington Road, Old Mystic

860-536-3354

Sip sweet cider and munch on just-baked mini-doughnuts at the only remaining steam-powered cider mill in the United States and the country's longest continuous producer of hard cider. B.F. Clyde's Cider Mill is open daily from August through late December.

Clinton Crossing Premium Outlets

20-A Killingworth Turnpike, Clinton

860-664-0700

www.premiumoutlets.com/outlets/outlet.asp?id=12

This outlet village features seventy stores, from Off Saks Fifth Avenue and Polo Ralph Lauren to Nike and Little Me.

Shanti Bithi Bonsai Nursery

3047 High Ridge Road, Stamford

203-329-0768

www.shantibithi.com

This unique nursery is one of the largest American growers and importers of bonsai trees. It is a lovely place to stroll and to shop for a living remembrance of your time in Connecticut.

Stew Leonard's
⌨100 Westport Avenue, Norwalk
☎203-847-7214
🖥*www.stewleonards.com*
Designated the "World's Largest Dairy Store" by *Ripley's Believe It or Not*, this remarkable grocery store features animatronic animals dancing in the aisles, a petting zoo, and other surprises. It's a great place to pick up picnic foods.

Tanger Outlet Center
⌨314 Flat Rock Place, Westbrook
☎860-399-8656
✍*www.tangeroutlet.com*
Shop sixty-five designer outlet stores, including children's wear favorites like Old Navy, Carter's, OshKosh B'Gosh, and The Children's Place.

Sports
Enjoy a home game during your time away. Sporting events in southern Connecticut range from world-class tennis and professional women's basketball to minor league baseball.

Bridgeport Bluefish
⌨Ballpark at Harbor Yard, 500 Main Street, Bridgeport
☎203-345-4800
✍*www.bridgeportbluefish.com*
This Atlantic League baseball team entertains crowds at its Bridgeport Stadium. Check the team's Web site for fun-filled promotional events throughout the season.

Connecticut Sun

⌨Mohegan Sun, 1 Mohegan Sun Boulevard, Uncasville

✆877-SUN-TIXX

✎*www.wnba.com/sun*

The WNBA's Connecticut Sun plays its home games at Mohegan Sun Arena. See some of the top names in professional women's basketball by reserving tickets to a game.

JUST FOR PARENTS

At Sports Haven (600 Long Wharf Drive, New Haven, 203-946-3201, *www.jaialai.com/sportshaven.asp*), adults can watch and wager on horse and greyhound racing and jai alai in a 38,000-square-foot complex with four movie-size, high-resolution screens. But the wildest thing is the Shark Bar's 2,800-gallon tank teeming with exotic sharks.

Pilot Pen Tennis

⌨Connecticut Tennis Center at Yale, 45 Yale Avenue, New Haven

✆203-776-7331 or ✆888-99-PILOT

✎*www.pilotpentennis.com*

Each August, as the U.S. Open approaches, top men's and women's tennis players tune up their games at this exciting and intimate tournament.

Where to Stay

From vacation rentals to chain hotels, from historic inns to seaside resorts, southern Connecticut offers accommodations to suit the needs of all types of travelers. When you're traveling with little ones, it's always prudent to make reservations in advance. Here are some of the region's best choices for family vacationers. You'll find availability most limited and prices the highest on summer weekends.

Fairfield County

As a pseudosuburb of New York City, Fairfield County's lodging options are dominated by business-class and chain hotels. However, rates are often reduced on weekends at these establishments, making them worth consideration.

In Stamford, consider the Amsterdam Hotel (19 Clark's Hill Avenue, 203-327-4300, *www.stamfordamsterdam.com*), which offers a free continental breakfast, free wireless Internet, and a complimentary train station shuttle; Hampton Inn & Suites (26 Mill River Street, 203-353-9855) with its spacious rooms and complimentary breakfast; the Holiday Inn Select (700 Main Street, 203-358-8400), with an indoor pool and exercise facility; and the Stamford Marriott Hotel and Spa (2 Stamford Forum, 203-357-9555),with both indoor and outdoor pools.

In Old Greenwich, the B&B Harbor House Inn (165 Shore Road, 203-637-0145, *www.hhinn.com*) is located a short stroll from the beach; children are welcome.

In Norwalk, try the Homestead Studio Suites (400 Main Avenue, 203-847-6888), an extended-stay hotel with fully equipped kitchens; the Norwalk Courtyard by Marriott (474 Main Avenue, 203-849-9111), with an indoor pool and whirlpool and complimentary high-speed Internet access; or the Silvermine Tavern (194 Perry Avenue, 203-847-4558, *www.silverminetavern.com*), a traditional New England country inn with antique-furnished guest rooms.

Bridgeport's best family hotel is the Holiday Inn Bridgeport (1070 Main Street, 203-334-1234), which has a restaurant, exercise room, and heated indoor pool.

In Stratford, there's the Ramada Inn Stratford (225 Lordship Boulevard, 203-375-8866).

The Fairfield Inn (417 Post Road, Fairfield, 203-255-0491 or 800-347-0414) offers eighty rooms and a free continental breakfast.

New Haven

Stay in the heart of this shoreline city at the Omni New Haven Hotel at Yale (155 Temple Street, 203-772-6664, *www.omnihotels.com*). There is an indoor pool at New Haven's Econo Lodge (100 Pond Lily Avenue,

203-387-6651). For extended stays, consider the Residence Inn New Haven (3 Long Wharf Drive, 203-777-5337), an all-suite hotel with fully equipped kitchens and a complimentary breakfast buffet. The Three Chimneys Inn (1201 Chapel Street, 203-789-1201, *www.threechimneysinn.com*), dates to the 1870s and is just a block from Yale; this casually elegant Victorian inn welcomes children ages six and older.

The Mystic Region

You can find just about every type of accommodation imaginable in southeastern Connecticut. There are colonial homes filled with antiques, such as the Bee and Thistle Inn (100 Lyme Street, Old Lyme, 860-434-1667), which welcomes children twelve and over. Other notable choices are the Lighthouse Inn (6 Guthrie Place, New London, 888-443-8411, *www.lighthouseinn-ct.com*), a Mediterranean-style mansion built by steel magnate Charles S. Guthrie in 1902 and a former retreat for film stars such as Bette Davis and Joan Crawford; and Water's Edge Resort & Spa (1525 Boston Post Road, Westbrook, 860-399-5901 or 800-222-5901, *www.watersedgeresortandspa.com*), which offers large guest rooms and water-view dining and activities; a supervised children's program is available during the summer.

 TRAVEL TIP

You'll find three hotel choices at Foxwoods Resort Casino: Two Trees Inn, the Grand Pequot Tower, and the Great Cedar Hotel. Two Trees is the best option for families. Call 800-FOX-WOODS for reservations at any of the three hotels. Mohegan Sun has one on-site hotel, and reservations can be made by calling 888-777-7922.

Other Mystic-region hotels that cater to families include the Mystic Marriott Hotel & Spa (625 North Road, Groton, 860-446-2600), which has an indoor pool, whirlpool, and fitness center; The Inn at Mystic (Routes

1 & 27, Mystic, 860-536-9604 or 800-237-2415, *www.innatmystic.com*), a diverse property with a number of lodging options, a restaurant, and an outdoor pool; and the Best Western Mystic Hotel (9 Whitehall Avenue, Mystic, 860-536-4281), which boasts an indoor pool and sauna.

Family Dining

Coastal Connecticut restaurants dish up cuisine to please any palate. Here's a smattering of some of the region's notable places to nosh.

Seafood Delights

You haven't really been to the shore unless you've cracked open a lobster or slurped up some chowder. These seafood restaurants in southern Connecticut make great family dining destinations.

≡FAST FACT

In most of New England, a lobster roll is a lobster-salad sandwich made with mayonnaise. Connecticut, however, is deliciously different. Here, the same dish is a roll—sometimes toasted—stuffed with chunks of succulent lobster meat bathed in rich, sweet melted butter.

Abbott's Lobster in the Rough
117 Pearl Street, Noank
860-536-7719
www.abbotts-lobster.com
Sure, it's a bit touristy, but Abbott's is a perennial favorite where you can feast on lobster, steamers, and other seafood delights indoors or outdoors at picnic tables right at the ocean's edge from May through mid-October. Diners are allowed to bring their own alcoholic beverages.

Bill's Seafood

548 Boston Post Road (Route 1), Westbrook

860-399-7224

www.billsseafood.com

Watch the boats go by as you dine outdoors at a picnic table overlooking the Patchogue River, or head inside, where Bill's New England– and Rhode Island–style chowders will warm your soul all winter long. Kids fussy about seafood? Burgers, dogs, spaghetti, and grilled cheese are options, too.

Crab Shell

46 Southfield Avenue, Stamford

203-967-7229

www.crabshell.com

Snuggle up to a bowl of hot chowder by the fireplace in the winter or sit outside and watch the world sail by in the summer.

Jasper White's Summer Shack

Mohegan Sun, 1 Mohegan Sun Boulevard, Uncasville

860-862-9500

www.mohegansun.com/dining/summer_shack.jsp

Whatever the weather, it's always a summer day by the sea at the Mohegan Sun outpost of celebrity chef Jasper White's casual seafood eatery, where you may have a tough time deciding whether you want your lobster steamed, pan-roasted, wood-grilled, chilled, or stuffed and baked.

A Taste of History

Louis' Lunch (261–263 Crown Street, New Haven, 203-562-5507, *www.louislunch.com*) cooked the country's first hamburger sandwich in 1900, and you can still order one flame-seared on the original grill. New Haven also claims America's first pizza pie, and the same brick ovens at Frank Pepe's Pizzeria Napoletana (157 Wooster Street, 203-865-5762) still crank out what many call the state's most delectable pizza. Be sure to try the white clam pie.

And for something straight out of a movie scene, grab a bite at Mystic Pizza (56 West Main Street, Mystic, 860-536-3700, *www.mysticpizza .com*), the setting for the movie that launched Julia Roberts's career.

Memorable Meals

Want to gather the family for Sunday brunch? Three restaurants noted for their all-you-can-eat spreads are Norwalk's Silvermine Tavern (194 Perry Avenue, 203-847-4558, *www.silverminetavern.com*), Sono Brewhouse (13 Marshall Street, Norwalk, 203-853-9110, *www.sonobrewhouse .com*), and Water's Edge Resort (1525 Boston Post Road, Westbrook, 860-399-5901 or 800-222-5901, *www.watersedgeresortandspa.com*). Be sure to make reservations in advance, particularly for holiday Sundays.

 TRAVEL TIP

Hungry at midnight? You'll find round-the-clock dining at southeastern Connecticut's two casinos: Foxwoods and Mohegan Sun. Both offer expansive buffets and dozens of other enticing options from casual cafés and food courts to elegant steakhouses and New England seafood restaurants.

For an elegant dinner without the kids, consider Jean-Louis (61 Lewis Street, Greenwich, 203-622-8450, *www.restaurantjeanlouis.com*) for cosmopolitan French cuisine; Thomas Henkelmann (420 Field Point Road, Greenwich, 203-869-7500, *www.homesteadinn.com*) for French food in an atmosphere of Victorian high society; or Da Pietro's (36 Riverside Avenue, Westport, 203-454-1213) which offers Italian–southern French cooking in an atmosphere you'll find either cramped or cozy depending on whether your glass is half empty or half full.

For something truly extraordinary the whole family can enjoy, make reservations at Randall's Ordinary (Route 2, North Stonington, 860-599-4540, *www.randallsordinary.com*), where colonial recipes are prepared entirely in an open-hearth fireplace.

CHAPTER 4

Hartford and the Connecticut River Valley

FROM ITS HEADWATERS IN New Hampshire, New England's longest river flows 405 miles to its meeting with Long Island Sound. In its namesake state, the Connecticut River was a vital commercial waterway as early as the seventeenth century, and the first European settlements were founded along its banks. This scenic artery continues to be a focal point as Hartford strives to raise its profile as a tourism and convention destination.

An Introduction to Connecticut's Capital Region

Hartford is Connecticut's capital city and America's insurance capital, too. The American insurance industry was born in Hartford in 1810, largely to protect important Connecticut River shipping interests. Today, the Greater Hartford area remains home to many of the nation's largest insurance companies.

As cities go, Hartford suffers a bit of an identity crisis, situated as it is about halfway between the larger, more urbane cities of New York and Boston. Its petite skyline is punctuated by the glittering, gold-domed State Capitol Building and the "blue onion" dome atop the Colt Building. By day, downtown Hartford is a bustling commercial center. At night and on weekends, when the business crowd flees to suburbia, the city can seem somewhat ghostly unless a concert or sporting event at the Hartford Civic Center has drawn folks downtown or a group is booked at the Connecticut Convention Center. It remains to be seen whether a flurry of new residential real-estate development can invigorate Hartford and alter its 9 to 5 character.

Nevertheless, the 370-year-old city and its surrounding communities retain the cultural and intellectual flair and the air of prosperity and abundance that spurred American literary icon Mark Twain to make Hartford his home in 1871. You may just find, as Twain wrote in 1868 following his first visit to the city, "Of all the beautiful towns it has been my fortune to see this is the chief. … You do not know what beauty is if you have not been here."

What to See and Do

Whether your family's interests lean toward history, literature, and architecture, or riverboat rides, hikes, and amusement park thrills, you'll find attractions that will capture your imagination. There is so much to learn and do within an easy radius of Hartford.

Amusement Parks

Central Connecticut's amusement parks blend nostalgia and thrills, making them ideal destinations for families with toddlers or teens.

Lake Compounce
822 Lake Avenue, Bristol
860-583-3300
www.lakecompounce.com

Located in the southwest corner of Hartford County, Bristol is home to the region's top family attraction, Lake Compounce. It's America's oldest continuously operating amusement park, and its combination of antique and updated rides, games, and entertainment make it a full-day outing. Lake Compounce is open daily mid-June through Labor Day and operates on an abbreviated schedule in the spring and fall.

TRAVEL TIP

Each October, Lake Compounce hosts the Haunted Graveyard (*www.hauntedgraveyard.com*), southern New England's largest and scariest Halloween attraction. Founded in 1990 by a father who wanted to distract his diabetic daughter from thoughts of Halloween candy, the event—which is suitable for older children—moved to Lake Compounce in 2000 after outgrowing the family's backyard.

Quassy Amusement Park

⌨2132 Middlebury Road, Middlebury

✆203-758-2913 or ✆800-FOR-PARK

✐*www.quassy.com*

For affordable family fun, head for Quassy Amusement Park, located forty-five minutes west of Hartford at exit 17 off I-84. You'll find twenty acres of amusements on the shores of Lake Quassapaug including the Big Flush, a water coaster with a 400-foot vertical drop.

Boat and Train Tours

The Connecticut River is one of the country's fourteen American Heritage Rivers. Visitors to central Connecticut will find several intriguing ways to travel this historic and scenic waterway.

Bald Eagle Cruises

⌨Steamboat Dock, Connecticut River Museum, 67 Main Street, Essex

✆800-996-8747

✐www.*ecotravel.ctaudubon.org*

Each winter, bald eagles (and some golden eagles, too) leave their homes in Canada for the warmer waters of the lower Connecticut River. Families can view these majestic birds by booking passage aboard one of the Connecticut Audubon Society's two-hour Bald Eagle Cruises, which depart from Essex in February and March.

Essex Steam Train & Riverboat
One Railroad Avenue, Essex
☎860-767-0103 or ☎800-377-3987
www.essexsteamtrain.com

The Essex Steam Train & Riverboat is a great way to soak up the area's ambience in an economical time period. First, climb aboard a 1920s-era coach pulled by a steam-powered locomotive, then board a riverboat for a relaxing inland excursion.

Lady Katharine Cruises
☎866-86-RIVER
www.ladykatharinecruises.com

Whether you choose a sightseeing, dining, or live entertainment cruise, you'll have a memorable Connecticut River experience aboard the *Lady Katharine*, which departs from two Hartford locations—Charter Oak Landing and Riverfront Plaza—as well as from Harbor Park Landing in Middletown, depending on the event. Autumn is a particularly picturesque time to enjoy a lunch or brunch outing aboard this tour boat, named for Hartford native and legendary actress Katharine Hepburn.

Historic Attractions

From literary icons to eccentric actors, notable people have called central Connecticut home. Their former residences are not only architecturally significant, they provide a glimpse of life during an earlier era.

Gillette Castle
67 River Road, East Haddam
☎860-526-2336
www.ctrivervalley.com

In his will, eccentric Connecticut actor William Gillette, known for his stage portrayals of Sherlock Holmes, specified that he didn't want his castle home on the Connecticut River to fall to "some blithering saphead who has no conception of where he is or with what surrounded."

Luckily for the public, the incredible edifice is now a state park. Admission to the grounds is free year-round; there is a charge to tour the castle, which is open Memorial Day weekend through Columbus Day.

Mark Twain House & Museum

⌨351 Farmington Avenue, Hartford

✆860-247-0998

✎*www.marktwainhouse.org*

Just west of downtown Hartford, tour Mark Twain's whimsical Victorian house and sample the humor and achievements of this American literary giant. Young visitors will especially enjoy hearing stories about Twain's daughters and his cats. Museum exhibits include rare manuscripts and artifacts that provide insight into the triumphs and tragedies of Twain's life and career.

Harriet Beecher Stowe Center

⌨77 Forest Street, Hartford

✆860-522-9258

✎*www.harrietbeecherstowecenter.org*

Next door to the Mark Twain House, you'll find the Harriet Beecher Stowe Center, where you can tour the Victorian brick cottage that was home to the *Uncle Tom's Cabin* author from 1871–1896. Although she is best known for her moving antislavery novel, Stowe was a prolific and widely read writer who also penned everything from children's stories to poems to articles about household décor.

Museums Kids Will Love

You won't have to venture far from Hartford to find museums that are as entertaining as they are educational. Here are a few museums that will spark young imaginations.

The Children's Museum

⌨950 Trout Brook Drive, West Hartford

✆860-231-2824

✎*www.thechildrensmuseumct.org*

Igniting curiosity is the goal of this science and nature museum that is home not only to interactive and changing exhibits but a wildlife sanctuary and a planetarium. You'll know you've found the right place when you spy the life-size model of a sperm whale outside.

Connecticut Trolley Museum
⌨58 North Road, East Windsor
☎860-627-6540
✎www.ceraonline.org

You can relive the days of trolley transportation not only by viewing historic photos and artifacts at this museum, but by climbing aboard a vintage trolley for a three-mile electric rail ride.

Imagine Nation
⌨One Pleasant Street, Bristol
☎860-314-1400
✎www.imaginenation.org

Learning is a side benefit of all the creative ways to play at this museum for families. With two floors of interactive exhibits, you can easily spend a day making giant bubbles, sending secret messages through whisper dishes, and even portraying favorite sports heroes in front of the green screen at the Play Your Way area sponsored by ESPN.

New England Air Museum
⌨Route 75, Windsor Locks
☎860-623-3305
✎www.neam.org

The story of flight becomes larger than life at this repository of historic aircraft. Before you go, print out one of the themed scavenger hunts from the museum's Web site.

Old State House
⌨800 Main Street, Hartford
☎860-522-6766
✎www.ctosh.org

Visit the changing exhibits at one of the oldest state houses in the United States and the site of the signing of the country's first written constitution. Kids will like the second-floor Museum of Natural and Other Curiosities.

 TRAVEL TIP

> On weekdays year-round and also on Saturdays from April through October, take a free, one-hour tour of Hartford's gold-domed, Victorian Gothic State Capitol Building (210 Capitol Avenue, 860-240-0222, *www.cga.ct.gov/capitoltours*). Completed in 1878 and designed by cathedral architect Richard M. Upjohn, it is a National Historic Landmark.

Wadsworth Atheneum
600 Main Street, Hartford
860-278-2670
www.wadsworthatheneum.org

If you are traveling with older children, consider a stop at the Wadsworth Atheneum, one of the country's oldest art museums and home to more than 45,000 works of art. Check the museum's Web site to see if any family programs are being offered during your visit.

Outdoor Recreation

The Connecticut River corridor is heavily populated, but that doesn't mean you can't find places to enjoy the great outdoors. From pristine parks to public gardens, here are some of the region's best places for a breath of fresh air.

Bushnell Park
Between Elm and Jewell Streets, Hartford
860-232-6710
www.bushnellpark.org

America's oldest public park is home to the Soldiers and Sailors

Memorial Arch, a Civil War memorial; a Children's Play and Learning Environment; and many public events and festivals. Don't miss the Bushnell Park Carousel, which dates to circa 1914.

Devil's Hopyard State Park
⌨366 Hopyard Road, East Haddam
✆860-873-8566
✍*www.ct.gov/dep*
Go for a short walk to Chapman Falls, one of Connecticut's most photogenic cascades, and decide whether the "potholes" at its base are the work of the devil or of stones trapped and spun by the rushing water.

Elizabeth Park
⌨Prospect Avenue and Asylum Avenue, Hartford
✆860-231-9443
✍*www.elizabethpark.org*
Breathe in the sweet scents at Elizabeth Park, America's oldest municipal rose garden, which is at its blossoming peak in June. This is one of central Connecticut's most enchanting picnic spots and a great place to enjoy a free family concert on select summer evenings.

Farmington River Tubing
⌨Satan's Kingdom State Recreation Area, Route 44, New Hartford
✆860-693-6465
✍*www.farmingtonrivertubing.com*
This 2.5-mile ride offers plenty of thrills for parents and kids ten and up. Operating from Memorial Day weekend through mid-September, these tubing outings are a great way to cool off on a steamy summer day.

Ski Sundown
⌨126 Ratlum Road, New Hartford
✆860-379-7669
✍*www.skisundown.com*
Ski Sundown, located just west of Hartford County in the town of New Hartford, is a perfect place for children and adults to learn to ski

or snowboard. With 100-percent snowmaking on fifteen trails, you're sure to find winter fun here all season long.

White Memorial Conservation Center
🖃80 Whitehall Road, Litchfield
✆860-567-0857
✍*www.whitememorialcc.org*

The 4,000-acre White Memorial Conservation Center, located less than an hour's drive from Hartford, is Connecticut's largest nature center. The grounds are open free daily and boast thirty-five miles of trails for hiking, cross-country skiing, bird watching, picnicking, and boating. Two family campgrounds on the property make it affordable to turn your visit into a memorable overnight outing.

JUST FOR PARENTS

Each summer, the 152-acre Hill-Stead Museum (35 Mountain Road, Farmington, 860-677-4787, *www.hillstead.org*) hosts the largest free poetry reading event in the United States. The Sunken Garden Poetry Festival features distinguished poets reading from their works in the museum's garden on selected Wednesday evenings. Each evening of readings also features a special musical performance.

Shopping
When the shopping bug bites, these malls, shopping districts, and gift stores offer Connecticut visitors a chance to hunt for collectibles, souvenirs, attire, and more.

Connecticut Creative: A General Store
🖃25 Stonington Street, Hartford
✆860-297-0112

Souvenir seekers can't beat this shop filled with Connecticut-made goodies. Housed in the same building as the Connecticut Department of Agriculture and the Hartford Botanical Garden Project, it is open Tuesday through Saturday. Gift basket shipping is available.

Westfarms Mall
500 Westfarms Mall, Farmington
860-561-3024
www.shopwestfarms.com

Westfarms Mall on the Farmington/West Hartford town line is one of the state's most elegant shopping centers, offering more than 130 upscale stores and restaurants. Kids will especially like the Build-A-Bear Workshop and Rainforest Café.

West Hartford Center
Farmington Avenue, West Hartford
860-521-2300
www.whchamber.com/westhartfordcenter/index.htm

This old-fashioned, walkable shopping district centered around Farmington Avenue and LaSalle Street in West Hartford is home to more than 140 unique shops and eateries. If the kids have been good, treat them to a plaything from The Toy Chest, and if Fido is tagging along, be sure to stop by Three Dog Bakery for some gourmet treats.

 JUST FOR PARENTS

Antiquers would be hard-pressed to find a more ideal destination than Woodbury, located forty miles southwest of Hartford. The town is home to more than forty-five independent dealers. A directory of shops is available at *www .antiqueswoodbury.com*. On Saturdays from mid-March through December, the Woodbury Antiques & Flea Market (787 Main Street, 203-263-2841, *www.woodburyfleamarket.com*) offers browsers an ever-changing selection of antiques.

Sports

Spectator opportunities are plentiful in central Connecticut. Here's your guide to the region's home teams.

Hartford Wolf Pack

Hartford Civic Center, One Civic Center Plaza, Hartford

860-548-2000

www.hartfordwolfpack.com

The Wolf Pack is Hartford's American Hockey League (AHL) team and a minor league affiliate of the NHL's New York Rangers. Catch a home game at the Hartford Civic Center during the AHL season, which runs from October through mid-April.

 RAINY DAY FUN

It's been the training home of figure skating stars like Oksana Baiul and Sasha Cohen, and your future Olympians will love taking a twirl on the ice at the International Skating Center of Connecticut (1375 Hopmeadow Street, Simsbury, 860-651-5400, *www.isccskate.com*). Public skating sessions are available year-round at the indoor rink, and skate rentals are available.

New Britain Rock Cats

New Britain Stadium, 230 John Karbonic Way

860-224-8383

www.rockcats.com

You don't have to be a big baseball fan to enjoy a day or night game at New Britain Stadium. The Rock Cats are the Eastern League Double-A affiliate of the Minnesota Twins, and their home games frequently feature giveaways, entertainment, and even fireworks. After Sunday games, kids twelve and under get to run the bases.

UConn Basketball
Hartford Civic Center, One Civic Center Plaza
860-486-2724 or 877-AT-UCONN
www.uconnhuskies.com

From November through early March, UConn men's and women's basketball games at the Hartford Civic Center are the hottest tickets in town. Inspire young hoopsters by taking them to a Huskies game.

UConn Football
Rentschler Field, 615 Silver Lane, East Hartford
860-486-2724 or 877-AT-UCONN
www.uconnhuskies.com or *www.rentschlerfield.com*

Catch Big East football action at the Huskies' 40,000-seat stadium in East Hartford. Tailgating before the game is half the fun.

Where to Stay

Although central Connecticut has many extended-stay chain hotels that make fine choices for leisure travelers. Consider some of these options that offer family-friendly amenities and convenient access to the region's sights and attractions.

Downtown Hartford
Connecticut's capital is an easily navigable city. Once you've found your hotel, you'll be able to explore much of the downtown area on foot or by hopping aboard the free Star Shuttle. These hotels are all located near shuttle stops.

The Goodwin Hotel
One Haynes Street
860-246-7500 or 888-212-8380
www.goodwinhotel.com

The Goodwin Hotel combines classic styling with modern amenities. Located across the street from the Hartford Civic Center, it is a good choice for travelers who are coming to town for an event.

Hilton Hartford

315 Trumbull Street

860-728-5151

www.hilton.com

With its central location near the Hartford Civic Center and a self-park garage, the Hilton is a convenient choice. Remodeled in 2005, it has an indoor pool and fitness room. Cribs, playpens, high chairs, and children's video rentals are all available.

Residence Inn by Marriott Hartford Downtown

942 Main Street

860-524-5550

www.marriott.com

This 120-suite hotel features fully equipped kitchens and is ideal for extended family stays. Complimentary breakfast is included.

Hartford's Outskirts

If you are seeking more unique lodgings close to Hartford, there's The Simsbury Inn (397 Hopmeadow Street, 860-651-5700 or 800-634-2719, *www.simsburyinn.com*), a classic New England inn with full-service amenities, an indoor heated pool, a Jacuzzi, an art gallery, and complimentary airport or train station transportation. The Avon Old Farms Hotel (279 Avon Mountain Road 860-677-1651, *www.avonoldfarmshotel.com*) is a charming, 160-room hotel complex in the heart of the Farmington Valley.

For families flying in or out of Connecticut, there are many hotels located in Windsor Locks near Bradley International Airport. The Sheraton Bradley Hotel (1 Bradley International Airport, 877-422-5311, *www.sheratonbradley.com*) offers the greatest convenience; it is connected to both airport terminals and has a restaurant and indoor pool. Ask about family getaway packages that include admission to area attractions. Other hotels close to Bradley that offer free airport shuttle service include the Days Inn Windsor Locks at Bradley International Airport (185 Turnpike Road, 860-623-9417 or 800-894-1475, *www.daysinnbradley.com*), Doubletree Hotel Bradley International

Airport (16 Ella Grasso Turnpike, 860-627-5171), Homewood Suites by Hilton Hartford/Windsor Locks (65 Ella Grasso Turnpike, 860-627-8463) and Ramada Inn at Bradley International Airport (5 Ella Grasso Turnpike, 860-623-9494, *www.ramadainnbradley.com*).

The Connecticut River Valley

Lodging choices in the region are mostly limited to small bed-and-breakfast inns, many of which cater exclusively to couples. Families will, however, find a few suitable options.

 TRAVEL TIP

Planning a family reunion, church retreat, school trip, or other group getaway? Sunrise Resort (121 Leesville Road, Moodus, 800-225-9033, *www.sunriseresort.com*) offers an array of activities and excellent facilities for gatherings. Accommodations range from rustic cottages and spacious cabins to motel rooms and RV camping sites; all are affordably priced. Sunrise Resort also hosts public events including the Connecticut Jazz Festival.

The Wesley Inn & Suites (988 Washington Street, Middletown, 860-346-9251, *www.wesleyinnsuites.com*) offers simple but affordable rooms including some with kitchenettes. Bishopsgate Inn (Goodspeed Landing, East Haddam, 860-873-1677, *www.bishopsgate.com*), an 1818 shipbuilder's home accommodates well-behaved children in its six guest rooms. The historic Griswold Inn (36 Main Street, Essex, 860-767-1776, *www.griswoldinn.com*) has thirty individually decorated rooms and suites furnished with antiques and reproductions.

Family Dining

Even the most active families need to pause for sustenance. Here are a few eateries worth seeking out while you're vacationing in central Connecticut.

Quick Bites

McDonald's and Wendy's aren't the only choices when you're in the mood for fast food. Try something out-of-the-ordinary at one of these restaurants.

A. C. Petersen Farms

240 Park Road, West Hartford

860-233-8483

Step back in time at this old-fashioned family restaurant, where the homemade ice cream is impossible to resist.

Plan B Burger Bar Tavern

138 Park Road, West Hartford

860-231-1199

www.planbtavern.com

The kiddies will love the mini-cheeseburgers, and you won't be disappointed in the gourmet burgers—or the beer list. From buttery lobster sliders to the East Coast Burger topped with roasted tomato, fried onions, horseradish cream, and lobster, there are plenty of New England influences to make the menu distinctive.

City Steam Brewery Café

942 Main Street, Hartford

860-525-1600

www.citysteambrewerycafe.com

For Hartford's only original brews, hop on over to City Steam for a beer and a bite to eat. You'll have to make that a root beer for the kids, of course.

JUST FOR PARENTS

Hartford's City Steam Brewery Café is not only a brewpub and restaurant, it's home to the area's only comedy club. See up-and-coming stand-up comedians, including many who appear regularly on New York City stages, on Thursday, Friday, and Saturday nights at the Brew Ha Ha Comedy Club. Tickets are half-price on Thursdays.

Doogies
2525 Berlin Turnpike, Newington
860-666-6200
www.doogieshotdogs.com

Doogies is the home of the sixteen-inch monster hot dog—and more, including tasty Philly steaks and fried seafood. Parents of toddlers, be forewarned. Rule number one at Doogies is "If you're cranky, come back another time."

Frankies
1195 Farmington Avenue, Bristol
860-584-9826
www.frankieshotdogs.com

Fussy kids? Frankie Bites—mini–corn dogs—will put a smile on their faces while you indulge in a famous Frankie with hot cheddar cheese or a fried seafood plate.

A Bite of History

If you like your dinner with a dose of historic intrigue, then you'll want to make reservations at The Griswold Inn (36 Main Street, Essex, 860-767-1776, *www.griswoldinn.com*), which has catered to travelers since 1776. The inn's menu features New England game, fowl, and fresh-caught seafood, and the Hunt Breakfast served on Sundays is a feast not to be missed. Avon Old Farms Inn (One Nod Road, 860-677-2818, *www.avonoldfarmsinn.com*) claims an even earlier date of origin—1757—although it didn't become an inn and a popular stop on the Albany-Hartford-Boston stagecoach route until around 1678. Pettibone's Tavern (4 Hartford Road, Simsbury, 860-658-1118, *www .pettibonetavern.com*), established as a stagecoach stop in 1780, is a relative newcomer, but it is an even more alluring haunt, not only because it offers a choice of fine dining downstairs, a casual atmosphere in the second-floor pub, or outdoor beer-garden dining, but because it's rumored to have a resident ghost.

Memorable Meals

Sometimes, the cuisine is secondary to the scenery. In Greater Hartford, however, two family-friendly restaurants offer meals that are a match for their lovely settings. The Pond House Café (1555 Asylum Avenue, West Hartford, 860-231-8823, *www.pondhousecafe .com*) in Elizabeth Park is a great choice for lunch, dinner, or brunch overlooking a picture-perfect duck pond. The menu relies heavily on fresh, organic ingredients and is both familiar and adventurous with dishes like a mac and cheese just for adults. The Mill on the River (989 Ellington Road, South Windsor, 860-289-7929 or 888-344-4414, *www.themillontheriver.com*) offers river views and a multicultural menu.

For a special dinner sans offspring, consider Max Downtown (185 Asylum Street, Hartford, 860-522-2530, *www.maxrestaurant group.com*), which offers upscale dining in a classy atmosphere. It's a favorite among Hartford's preconcert/pretheater crowd, and reservations are a must on show nights. Black-eyed Sally's BBQ & Blues (350 Asylum Street, Hartford, 860-278-7427, *www.blackeyedsallys.com*) serves up great Cajun food and live blues music on Friday and Saturday evenings. For a relaxing and romantic evening meal, reserve a table at The Copper Beech Inn (46 Main Street, Ivoryton, 860-767-0330 or 888-809-2056, *www.copperbeechinn.com*), where French cuisine is served in three elegant and intimate dining rooms and the award-winning wine list features more than 5,000 bottles.

Rhode Island

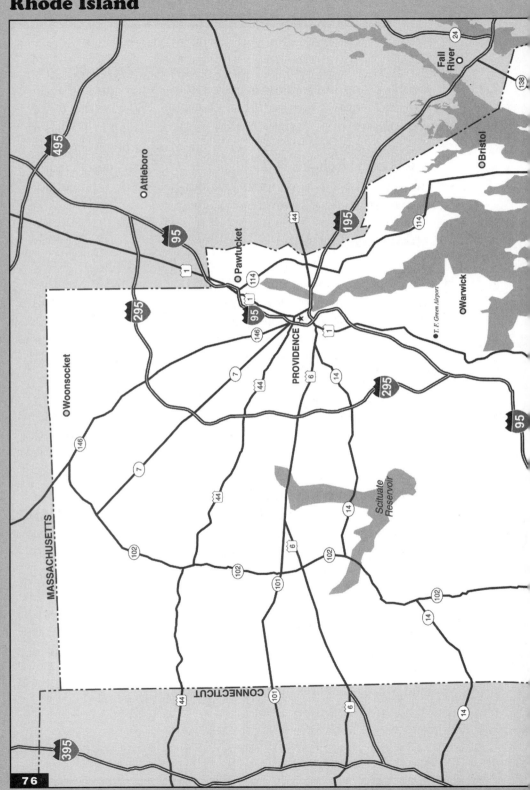

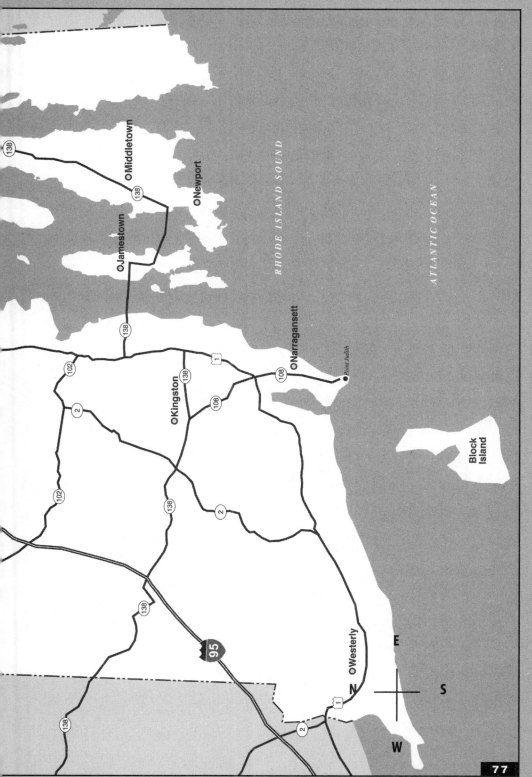

Newport, Rhode Island

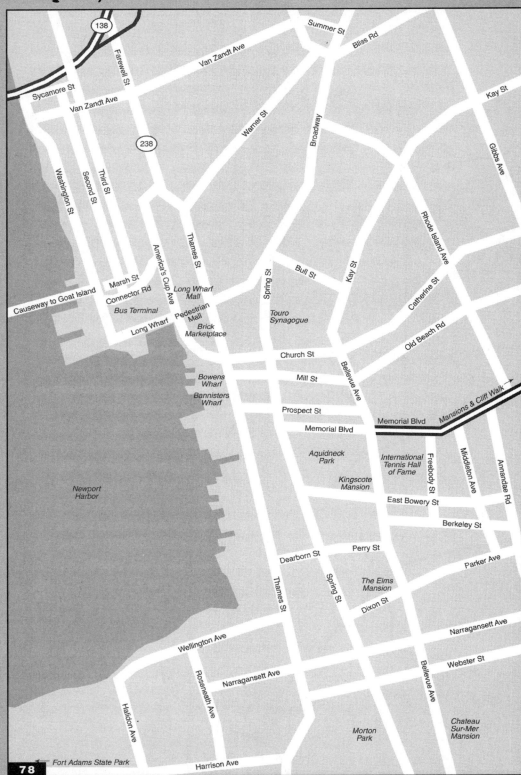

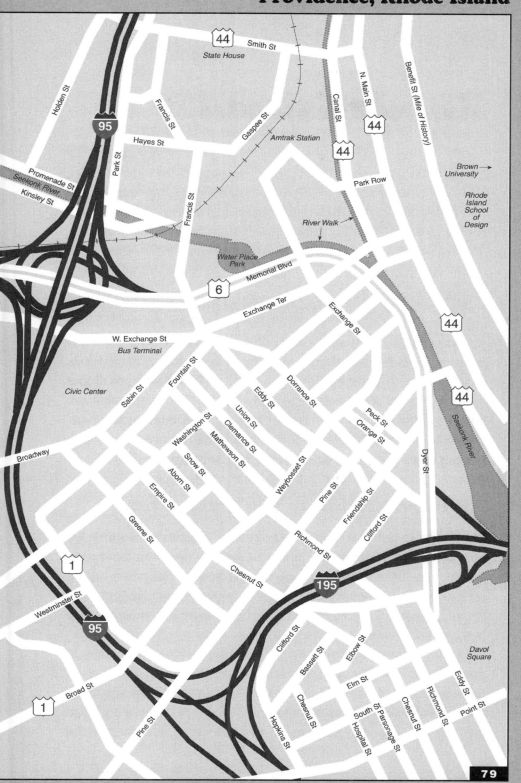

CHAPTER 5

Rhode Island

ONCE YOU'VE VISITED, YOU'LL think twice about calling Rhode Island "little." Facts are facts: Rhode Island is the smallest state not only in New England but in the entire United States. But this petite place is feisty. Did you know that Rhode Island declared its independence from Great Britain on May 4, 1776, two months before the Declaration of Independence was signed? And it is practically bursting at the seams with scenic, historic, and cultural wonders. Rhode Island may be compact, but it is home to an incredible 20 percent of the country's National Historic Landmarks.

An Introduction to the Ocean State

Rhode Island is blessed with 400 miles of coastline including 100 miles of sandy beaches. Combine that with its premium location— just 60 miles from Boston and 180 miles from New York City—and it is easy to see why some of the biggest names in America flocked to Rhode Island at the turn of the century, turning it into their summer playground.

Today, Rhode Island offers an astounding variety of vacation possibilities. Newport's marvelous mansions are a must-see, as is the natural beauty of Block Island, called "one of the twelve last great places in the Western Hemisphere" by the Nature Conservancy. Capital city Providence has undergone extensive urban renewal, and the

River Walk and Water Place Park are permanent monuments to the city's rejuvenation. Travelers and locals alike flock to see the spectacular WaterFire displays on the Providence riverfront; a musical score accompanies the crackling bonfires that float along the river, casting a warm, shimmering glow on the vibrant city center.

The Blackstone Valley in the northern part of the state was the birthplace of America's Industrial Revolution—Samuel Slater opened his famous cotton mill there in 1793. And, of course, you can't leave for home until you've played on the beaches of South County. Ocean lovers have been lured to these shores for more than a century.

≡FAST FACT

Rhode Islanders have stamped their state's name on their own variety of clam chowder. Unlike traditional, creamy, milk-based New England clam chowder or tomato-based Manhattan clam chowder, Rhode Island clam chowder features quahogs, celery, onions, and potatoes in a clear broth.

The good news is, these days, you don't need a name like Vanderbilt or Astor to immerse yourself in the pleasures of this seaside paradise. From mansions to boating excursions to beaches to outdoor concerts to seafood dinners, Rhode Island offers a little something for everyone.

When to Visit

While summer is still a spectacular time to enjoy beaches, boating, and famous outdoor music festivals, there are alternatives to fighting peak-season crowds.

Narragansett Bay breezes keep the summers relatively free from unbearable humidity, And those same breezes also keep the winters less frigid than elsewhere in New England. Off-season rates kick in after the summer tourist population swell subsides. Newport's mansions are especially spectacular when decked in Christmas finery, and if you bundle up, a wintertime stroll along the Cliff Walk can be invigorating. Keep in mind that some attractions close in the off season, and beaches and amusement parks are usually not open until the last weekend in May.

 TRAVEL TIP

Your complimentary copy of the official Rhode Island Travel Guide is just a phone call away. Contact the Rhode Island Tourism Division, 800-556-2484, to request a copy. You may also order a free guide by visiting the state's official tourism Web site, *www.visitrhodeisland.com*.

Getting There and Getting Around

Whether you fly, drive, or take mass transit, you will find that Rhode Island is an easily reachable destination. The state continues to invest in its transportation network, and while renting a car on arrival provides maximum flexibility, it isn't an absolute must. If you plan to rely on public transportation, be sure to consult the Rhode Island Public Transit Authority (RIPTA) Web site, *www.ripta.com*, for current routes and schedules.

T.F. Green International Airport (PVD)

T.F. Green International Airport (401-737-8222 or 888-268-7222, *www .pvdairport.com*) is located at exit 13 off I-95, just twelve minutes south of Providence in Warwick. It is an easily accessible, relatively hassle-free transportation gateway that serves the state as well as southern New England. It is even a reasonable alternative to busy Logan Airport in Boston. More than 5 million passengers utilize the airport each year.

MAJOR AIRLINES SERVING T.F. GREEN INTERNATIONAL AIRPORT

Airline	Phone Number	Web Site
Air Canada	☎888-247-2262	✍www.aircanada.com
American	☎800-433-7300	✍www.americanair.com
Cape Air	☎800-352-0714	✍www.flycapeair.com
Continental	☎800-525-0280	✍www.continental.com
Delta	☎800-221-1212	✍www.delta.com
Northwest	☎800-225-2525	✍www.nwa.com
Southwest	☎800-435-9792	✍www.southwest.com
Spirit	☎800-772-7117	✍www.spiritair.com
United	☎800-241-6522	✍www.ual.com
US Airways	☎800-428-4322	✍www.usair.com

Airport Connections

Aero-Airport Limousine Service (401-737-2868) offers regularly scheduled transportation service from T.F. Green International Airport to Providence hotels, the train station, Dunkin' Donuts Center, the Convention Center, Rhode Island School of Design (RISD), and Brown University. Cozy Cab, Inc. (401-846-1500 or 800-846-1502, *www.cozytrans.com*) operates a shuttle between the airport and Newport.

≡FAST FACT

In 2006, ground was broken for construction of the Warwick Intermodal Facility. That's the fancy name for a new train station that will provide the nation's closest rail link to a major airport terminal. The transportation hub, which will also incorporate a bus station, rental car facility, and commuter parking lot, will be connected to T.F. Green Airport by an enclosed skywalk with moving sidewalks. The facility is slated for completion in mid-2009.

Getting Around

For a small state, Rhode Island has a surprisingly well-developed system of ferry, train, bus, and trolley services. The Rhode Island Public Transit Authority (401-781-9400) serves thirty-eight of Rhode Island's thirty-nine communities with fifty-eight transportation routes statewide.

In Providence, RIPTA operates the downtown Providence LINK, vintage-style trackless trolleys. Two routes take visitors to stops at twenty city parking lots and at major city attractions. The cost is $1.50 per person, per ride. RIPTA also offers a Day Pass, which entitles the purchaser to unlimited rides on trolleys and buses statewide. Tokens and passes are available at the Kennedy Plaza Transportation Center in Providence.

TRAVEL TIP

RIPTA's Rack N' Ride program makes it easy for cyclists to take advantage of the state's miles of biking paths. The forty-foot buses are equipped with easy-to-use bike racks, which can be loaded and unloaded independently. There is no extra charge for transporting your bike on the bus.

In Newport, RIPTA offers year-round trolley service departing from the Gateway Visitors Center, with stops at the Bellevue Avenue mansions, the Cliff Walk, and more. All-day passes are priced at $6 per person or $18 for a family of four.

RIPTA also offers daily ferry service between Providence and Newport from mid-May through mid-October. The RIPTA ferry is operated by New England Fast Ferry Co. The trip from Conley's Wharf in Providence to Newport's Perrotti Park takes just over an hour. Reservations are recommended; call 401-453-6800.

Getting to Block Island

Block Island is located twelve miles off the coast of Rhode Island. It is not connected to the mainland and is accessible only by air or by boat.

The Block Island Ferry is operated by the Interstate Navigation Company (401-783-4613, *www.blockislandferry.com*). Year-round service is available between Point Judith, Rhode Island, and Block Island. In the summer, ferries also depart for Block Island from Newport. The trip takes about an hour from Point Judith and two hours from Newport. Call or visit the Web site for pricing information and scheduled departure times, which vary seasonally. Plan to arrive about an hour before your scheduled departure to allow ample time to park and board. Passenger tickets may be purchased on board the ferry.

FAST FACT

From early June through mid-October, Interstate Navigation Company also operates a high-speed, passenger-only ferry that will get you from Galilee to Block Island in just thirty minutes. Call ahead or visit their Web site for a schedule and rates. Reservations are recommended, and tickets are nonrefundable.

It is extraordinarily difficult to take a car to Block Island. All vehicle reservations need to be booked and paid for in advance by telephone. Vehicle reservations for summer weekends and holidays should be booked four to five months in advance. Your reservation will be forfeited if you do not check your car in at the ferry ticket window at least one hour prior to departure. Reservations are not necessary for passengers, bicycles, and motorcycles.

Without a vehicle reservation, you can inquire about traveling standby on your date of departure. However, even if you manage to secure a standby slot, you will not be guaranteed a return reservation.

New England Airlines (401-466-5881 or 800-243-2460) provides air service between Westerly State Airport and Block Island. The round-trip flight takes about twelve minutes, and adult airfare is about $85.

 TRAVEL TIP

> If you're looking for a very private retreat, consider renting a Block Island home for a week or longer. Ferreting out a suitable vacation rental can be a bit of a project, as most are rented independently by their owners, but you can research available rental properties online at Vacation Rentals by Owner (*www.vrbo.com*), CyberRentals (*www.cyberrentals.com*), or VacationRentals.com (*www.vacationrentals.com*).

Must-See Activities and Attractions

Rhode Island may be small, but it is no small task to list all the best places to visit while vacationing in the Ocean State. Seriously consider including these highlights on your itinerary.

Block Island
✆800-383-BIRI
✍*www.blockislandchamber.com*

Block Island is home to more than forty species of rare and endangered plants and animals. Highlights include beaches, boating, bicycling, fishing, lighthouses, and sweeping views of the sea from the 185-foot clay cliffs at Mohegan Bluffs.

Green Animals Topiary Garden
🖾Cory's Lane, Portsmouth
✆401-683-1267
✍*www.newportmansions.org*

This splendid Victorian estate boasts America's oldest topiary gardens, first planted in 1880. California privet, golden boxwood, and

American boxwood trees are artfully "carved" into geometric and ornamental designs and even whimsical animal shapes such as an elephant, a camel, and a teddy bear. Also visit the rose garden, the antique toy collection in the main house, and the plant shop.

Historic Carousels

Crescent Park Carousel
700 Bullocks Point Avenue, Riverside
401-433-2828
www.crescentparkcarousel.com

Looff Carousel
Slater Memorial Park, Route 1A, Pawtucket
401-728-0500, ext. 252

Flying Horse Carousel
Bay Street, Westerly
401-348-6007

Rhode Island is home to three historic carousels. In Riverside, you'll find the 1895 Crescent Park Carousel, designated a National Historic Site and a National Historic Landmark. Kids will have trouble choosing a mount from the sixty-six hand-carved figures designed by Charles I. D. Looff. Slater Memorial Park in Pawtucket is home to Looff's earliest carousel, built in 1894 and installed in the park in 1910. It features forty-two intricately carved horses, plus three dogs, a lion, a camel, and a giraffe. The oldest carousel in America, Westerly's Flying Horse Carousel, was constructed circa 1867 and has twenty horses that were each hand-carved from a single piece of wood.

International Tennis Hall of Fame
194 Bellevue Avenue, Newport
401-849-3990
www.tennisfame.com

The International Tennis Hall of Fame and the world's largest tennis museum are housed at the Newport Casino, where the first

American tennis National Championships were held in 1881. The complex also features thirteen grass tennis courts—the only competition grass courts in the country that are open to the public.

≡FAST FACT

The long-proposed Heritage Harbor Museum may finally become a reality in 2008, albeit on a smaller scale than was originally envisioned in 1999 when Narragansett Electric donated the decommissioned South Street Power Station in Providence to house a new museum dedicated to Rhode Island's legacy and traditions. The 55,000-square-foot museum will now be part of Dynamo House, a $140 million hotel and retail development. For updates on the museum's progress, visit *www.heritageharbor.org*.

Newport Mansions

A visit to Rhode Island isn't complete without a visit to at least one or two of Newport's magnificent seaside mansions. The Preservation Society of Newport (401-847-1000, *www.newportmansions .org*) operates eleven historic properties including Cornelius Vanderbilt II's seventy-room "cottage," The Breakers, and William K. Vanderbilt's Marble House, which features 500,000 cubic feet of marble. Don't miss the privately owned Astors' Beechwood Mansion (580 Bellevue Avenue, 401-846-3772, *www.astorsbeechwood.com*), where costumed guides portray family members, servants, and guests. Several other privately operated mansions are also open for tours. Make sure you leave time to stroll the three and one-half mile Cliff Walk along the Atlantic; it will take you past many of these famous, historic homes.

▐▌ TRAVEL TIP

Newport may have the mansion market cornered, but a lovely 33-acre turn-of-the-century mansion in Bristol is worth visiting. Blithewold Mansion and Gardens (101 Ferry Road / Route 114, 401-253-2707, *www.blithewold.org*), the former summer home of Pennsylvania coal magnate Augustus Van Winkle, has forty-five rooms. The landscaped grounds overlooking Narragansett Bay include an arboretum with 3,000 trees and one of the tallest giant sequoias on the East Coast.

Rhode Island Beaches

Rhode Island has 400 miles of coastline, so if the ocean calls to you, you'll be pleased to find dozens of places to play in the sand. South County boasts the state's most popular spots including South Kingstown Town Beach, Roger W. Wheeler State Beach, Blue Shutters Town Beach, Watch Hill Beach, and Misquamicut State Beach, which also offers family amusements. You'll also find public beaches in Bristol, Jamestown, Middletown, Narragansett, Newport, Portsmouth, Tiverton, Warwick, and on Block Island.

Roger Williams Park Zoo

⌂1000 Elmwood Avenue, Providence

✆401-785-3510

✐*www.rogerwilliamsparkzoo.org*

Providence is home to the country's third-oldest zoo, which has been a popular family attraction since 1872. The widely acclaimed zoo is home to more than 1,000 animals representing 139 species.

Slater Mill

🖿67 Roosevelt Avenue, Pawtucket

📞401-725-8638

✍*www.slatermill.org*

The mill that precipitated cataclysmic change in not only Rhode Island but also the nation is a must-see. Slater Mill, the birthplace of the American Industrial Revolution, is a museum complex that includes the original yellow-clapboard textile mill built by Samuel Slater in 1793, the 1810 Wilkinson Mill and machine shop, and the 1758 Sylvanus Brown House, home of a master craftsman who contributed to Slater's success by making machine patterns and wooden machine parts for the textile mill.

Water Place Park and River Walk

🖿Memorial Boulevard, Providence

Water Place is the four-acre urban park along the Woonasquatucket River that is the centerpiece of revitalization in Rhode Island's capital city. The charming cobbled walkways, footbridges, and amphitheater will remind you of Venice, and you'll do a double-take when you spot a gondola gliding along with a gondolier at the stern and a smiling, picnicking couple aboard. Believe it or not, a company called La Gondola (401-421-8877, *www.gondolari.com*) offers outings from a landing at Water Place; call ahead to make reservations.

Family Fun Plans

Active families will find plenty to do while vacationing in Rhode Island. These Family Fun Plans are just a starting point. Allow them to inspire your vacation dreaming; then make a plan that suits your family's style—or simply head to the beach, with no plan at all.

A Short and Sweet Summer Holiday

Transform a summer weekend into a memorable and educational escape with this two-night plan for fun in the sun.

Day One: Head straight to the state's summertime playground, Newport, and tour one or two of the city's historic mansions on your first morning. In the afternoon, view several other stately homes from the outside as you meander along the Cliff Walk. In the evening, picnic at Fort Adams State Park (Harrison Avenue, Newport, 401-847-2400, *www.riparks.com/fortadams.htm*), or feast on Rhode Island clam chowder and other seafood delights at one of the restaurants along the waterfront.

Day Two: Set the alarm for an early call and allow at least forty-five minutes for the drive to Galilee to catch the high-speed ferry operated by Interstate Navigation Company (401-783-4613, *www.block islandferry.com*), which will whisk you over to Block Island in just thirty minutes. Rent bicycles or mopeds and spend the day visiting the island's two historic lighthouses and enjoying its sandy beaches. Return to Newport in the evening for an adventurous dinner at The Red Parrot (348 Thames Street, 401-847-3800, *www.redparrotrestau rant.com*), where parents can tip back exotic drinks and chicken-nugget-weary kiddies can sample the batter-fried shark bites.

Day Three: Visit the International Tennis Hall of Fame (194 Bellevue Avenue, Newport, 401-849-3990, *www.tennisfame.com*). If time permits, take a short drive in the afternoon to Middletown, where you can hike the trails at the Norman Bird Sanctuary (583 Third Beach Road, 401-846-2577, *www.normanbirdsanctuary.org*) before heading for home.

JUST FOR PARENTS

One of New England's best places for busy parents to rekindle romance is The Chanler at Cliff Walk (117 Memorial Boulevard, Newport, 401-847-1300 or 866-793-5664, *www.thechanler .com)*, a historic, ocean-side Newport mansion that is now an intimate and luxurious inn with fourteen themed suites and six secluded villas.

A Five-Day Family Summer Sampler

Summer is truly family vacation season in Rhode Island. If you can get away for five days, you'll be able to see many of the state's highlights and enjoy some downtime by the sea.

Day One: Begin with a relaxing day at Misquamicut State Beach (257 Atlantic Avenue, Westerly, 401-596-9097, *www.riparks.com/misquamicut.htm*). You will enjoy the surf and the nearby games and amusements. If a quieter beach is more your speed, South County's seaside towns provide plenty of other options.

Day Two: Head for Galilee in the morning and take the half-hour trip to Block Island aboard the high-speed ferry operated by Interstate Navigation Company (401-783-4613, *www.blockislandferry.com*). One of the best ways to see the island's spectacular scenery is to rent bicycles—the whole island is ideal for cycling. Return to the mainland at the end of the day.

Day Three: Spend the morning in Newport viewing the magnificent mansions from the Cliff Walk. Choose one or two that intrigue you for an afternoon tour. Children might particularly like the Astors' Beechwood (580 Bellevue Avenue, 401-846-3772, *www.astorsbeechwood.com*), where costumed guides play period roles.

Day Four: Drive from Newport to Providence, stopping along the way to see the historic yachts at the Herreshoff Marine Museum (One Burnside Street, Bristol, 401-253-5000, *www.herreshoff.org*) and perhaps Bristol's Blithewold Mansion and Gardens (101 Ferry Road/Route 114, 401-253-2707, *www.blithewold.org*), as well. Take an evening gondola ride on the Woonasquatucket River in Providence from the urban park, Water Place, which is at the hub of the capital city. Call La Gondola (401-421-8877) for reservations.

Day Five: Spend the last day of your family road trip at Providence's Roger Williams Park Zoo (1000 Elmwood Avenue, 401-785-3510, *www.rogerwilliamsparkzoo.org*), before saying goodbye to Rhode Island.

CHAPTER 6

South County Seaside Escapes

OFFICIALLY, THERE IS NO Rhode Island county named South County, but this informal designation for the coastal area is pervasive. When you're tired of jumping waves and constructing sandcastles at the beach, you'll find plenty of other activities, from strolling classic New England Main Street shopping districts to exploring a Colonial-era working farm, to squealing along with the kids as you plummet down a fifty-foot waterslide.

An Introduction to Rhode Island's Coastal Region

Southern Rhode Island is definitely one of New England's top beach vacation destinations. It boasts 100 miles of dazzling coastline, more than a dozen public beaches, expansive ocean views, and some of New England's best surfing. Yes—die-hard surfers ride Rhode Island's waves year-round. Some of the best swells accompany storms in the spring and fall, when water temperatures are, oh, a bit on the chilly side.

Your kids will love riding summer's gentler waves; you'll find bodyboards for rent at the region's beaches if you haven't brought your own. But if you're traveling to one of the eleven South County towns—Charlestown, Coventry, East Greenwich, Exeter, Hopkinton, Narragansett, North Kingstown, Richmond, South Kingstown, West Greenwich, or Westerly—there are a bevy of non-beach attractions and enticements. After all, it may rain. Or you might all feel a bit waterlogged after a day or two of splashing in the salt water.

Though this seaside playland lies just ninety minutes from Boston and three and one-half hours from New York, you're bound to feel a world away if this is the place you choose to stay. There is just enough excitement in South County to keep kids entertained. While the little ones catch a wave or grasp for a brass ring on an antique carousel, grownups can catch a few rays and grasp those precious moments of relaxation they crave.

What to See and Do

For many families, a trip to the beach is adventure enough, and that makes the Rhode Island shore a popular place for a short getaway. While there's nothing wrong with heading home after a day of beach play, you'll miss some of the natural, historic, and artistic riches of this small but enticingly diverse state if you don't stick around South County long enough to explore. As you plan your vacation, consider complementing your time at the beach with a few activities destined to leave impressions that stick with you longer than sand between your toes.

The Beaches of South County

You certainly won't be disappointed with the vast selection of beaches that line the coast. However, individual usage and parking fees at each make it costly to "beach hop," at least within the course of a day. Call ahead for prices and parking information. The South County Tourism Council (401-789-4422 or 800-548-4662, *www .southcountyri.com*) is also a good central resource for help in selecting the best beach to suit your family's interests.

Charlestown
- **Blue Shutters Town Beach**, East Beach Road off Route 1, 401-364-1206. Amenities at this very popular family beach include restrooms, changing rooms, and a concession stand. Complimentary beach-accessible wheelchairs are available to visitors.

- **Charlestown Town Beach**, 557 Charlestown Beach Road, 401-364-1208, ext. 364. This clean, fine-sand beach has moderate to heavy surf.
- **Charlestown Breachway State Beach / Burlingame State Park**, off Route 1 at Charlestown Breachway exit, 401-364-7000 (summer), 401-322-8910 (winter), *www.riparks.com/charlesbreach.htm.* This state beach is popular for its campground; its 75 camper sites are available on a first-come, first-served basis.
- **East Beach**, off East Beach Road, 401-322-0450. This unspoiled and picturesque three-mile barrier beach has no concessions or facilities, but it can attract so many visitors on summer weekends that you'll need to arrive early to find a parking spot.

Narragansett

- **Narragansett Town Beach**, Ocean Road/Route 1A, 401-782-0658. With its nearby shops and restaurants and mile-long swath of sand, this beach—known for some of New England's best surfing—offers diverse appeal.
- **Roger W. Wheeler State Beach**, 100 Sand Hill Cove Road, 401-789-3563 (summer), 401-789-8374 (winter), *www.riparks .com/wheeler.htm.* This beach's sheltered area with no undertow makes it a good choice for families with small children.

TRAVEL TIP

If you are planning an extended vacation, consider purchasing a Season Pass, which entitles you and your vehicle's occupants to unlimited admission to the state's ten State Beaches. Passes, priced at $60 per car for nonresidents, may be purchased at any State Beach or at the Office of Parks and Recreation (2321 Hartford Avenue, Johnston, 401-222-2632).

- **Salty Brine State Beach**, 254 Great Road, 401-789-3563 (summer), 401-789-8374 (winter), *www.riparks.com/saltybrine.htm*. Small children will enjoy watching the fishing boats come and go and swimming in the gentle surf at this tiny, sheltered beach.
- **Scarborough State Beach**, 870 Ocean Road (Scarborough North), 401-789-2324, 970 Ocean Road (Scarborough South), 401-782-1319, 401-789-8374 (winter), *www.riparks.com/scarborough.htm*. This exceedingly popular family spot offers excellent bodysurfing and fine facilities including two pavilions, a boardwalk, an observation tower, food concessions, and restrooms.

South Kingstown

- **Carpenter's Beach Meadow**, 854 Matunuck Beach Road, 401-783-4412. There are snack bars and shops within walking distance of this privately owned beach, which is open to the public.
- **East Matunuck State Beach**, 950 Succotash Road, 401-789-8585 (summer), 401-789-8374 (winter), *www.riparks.com/eastmatunuck.htm*. This beach is popular for fishing and surfing and with teens and young adults.

 JUST FOR PARENTS

Picture this . . . professional musical theater, historical surroundings, fragrant gardens, the shore, all rolled into one enchanted evening. That's what you'll find at Theatre by the Sea (364 Card's Pond Road, Matunuck, South Kingstown, 401-782-8587, *www.theatrebythesea.com*), where professionally produced musicals and plays are performed in a 1933 theater that's on the National Register of Historic Places. Just steps from the theater, you'll find casual dining at the SeaHorse Grill, housed inside a 1929 inn and tavern.

- **Roy Carpenter's Beach**, 240 Card's Pond Road, 401-783-7418. You'll find moderate to heavy surf at this privately owned family beach with its own snack bar and restroom facilities.
- **South Kingstown Town Beach at Matunuck**, Matunuck Beach Road, 401-789-9301. This quaint family beach with moderate to heavy surf has a playground, pavilion, and restroom facilities.

Westerly

- **Atlantic Beach Park**, 321-338 Atlantic Avenue, Misquamicut, 401-322-0504, *www.atlanticbeachpark.com*. With its carousel, bumper cars, miniature golf course, and other family amusements, this beach spot is a great place to spend an entire day.
- **Dunes Park Beach**, 665 Atlantic Avenue. This small, family-oriented beach is privately owned.
- **Misquamicut State Beach**, 257 Atlantic Avenue, 401-596-9097 (summer), 401-322-8910 (winter), *www.riparks.com/misquamicut.htm*. This perennial favorite boasts seven miles of white sand beach, moderate surf, a playground, pavilion, picnic area, and restrooms.
- **Napatree Point**, Bay Street, Watch Hill. Napatree Point is primarily a walker's beach; limited access is provided by the conservation organization that manages this ecologically sensitive barrier beach that is home to nesting osprey.

≡FAST FACT

The Flying Horse Carousel in the village of Watch Hill in Westerly is both a National Historic Landmark and a lot of fun. This is the only surviving example of a flying horse carousel in America, where the horses are not attached to the floor but instead are suspended from a center frame and swing out as if flying. Only children ages two to twelve are permitted to ride.

- **Watch Hill Beach**, Bay Street, Watch Hill, 401-348-6007. This crowded family beach with a bathhouse and restrooms is located adjacent to the historic Flying Horse Carousel and offers views of the 1806 Watch Hill Lighthouse.
- **Westerly Town Beach**, 365 Atlantic Avenue, 401-322-0110. Picnicking and restroom facilities are available at this town beach, which hosts Wednesday night Blues on the Beach concerts in July and August.

Family Amusements

Break up your beach days with a visit to one of these family attractions.

Adventureland of Narragansett

⌨Point Judith Road, Narragansett

✆401-789-0030

✍*www.adventurelandri.com*

Challenge your kids to an eighteen-hole round of miniature golf, a Go-Kart race, or a duel against the batting cages, and then cool off by jostling and dousing each other on the bumper boat ride.

Water Wizz

⌨Atlantic Avenue, Misquamicut

✆401-322-0520

✍*www.waterwizzri.com*

This small waterslide park is a family favorite on blistering summer days. With more than 1,000 feet of slippery slides that twist, dip, and wind through tunnels, you'll find plenty of reasons to take the plunge. Opt for a forty-minute splash session or an all-day pass.

Museums and Historic Sites

Ready to trade your bodyboards for history books? Actually, the transition won't seem severe when you visit any of these museums and attractions, which bring the history of Rhode Island's coastal region to life.

Casey Farm

⌨2325 Boston Neck Road, Saunderstown

✆401-295-1030

✎*www.historicnewengland.org/visit/homes/casey.htm*

This plantation farm dates to about 1750. Tours of the working organic farm, now preserved and operated by Historic New England, are available Saturdays from June through mid-October.

Gilbert Stuart Museum

⌨815 Gilbert Stuart Road, Saunderstown

✆401-294-3001

✎*www.gilbertstuartmuseum.com*

Even if your kids aren't much into art, they probably know the work of Rhode Island–born portrait painter Gilbert Stuart. That's because his famous image of George Washington has graced the dollar bill for more than a century. Stuart's restored birthplace and the adjacent grist mill are open to visitors Thursday through Monday from May through October.

International Scholar-Athlete Hall of Fame

⌨Feinstein Building, 3045 Kingstown Road/Route 138, University of Rhode Island, Kingston

✆401-874-2375

✎*www.internationalsport.com*

Inspire your little superstars with a visit to this memorabilia-, art-, and photography-filled museum that celebrates inductees who have excelled in both academics and athletics. The museum features a variety of hands-on exhibits for all ages.

Mercy Brown's Grave

⌨Chestnut Hill Baptist Church Cemetery, Victory Highway, Exeter

There are several tales of Rhode Island vampires, but none more enduring than that of Mercy Brown. If you are traveling with older children and looking for an out-of-the-ordinary and slightly creepy experience, you can visit her gravesite in the cemetery behind Chestnut Hill

Baptist Church. According to stories, Brown died in 1892 at the age of nineteen, shortly following the deaths of her mother and sister. Her brother, Edwin, was also ill. In an effort to save him from what appeared to be a curse on the family, the women's bodies were exhumed. Mercy's body appeared to have shifted inside the coffin, and fresh blood was present in her heart, which was burned upon a nearby rock before she was reburied. Feeding poor Edwin the heart ashes, alas, did not save him—he died two months later. But Mercy's legend lives on.

Quonset Aviation Museum
⌨Eccleston Avenue, North Kingstown
✆401-294-9540
Located in a World War II hangar, this museum is a retirement home for a growing collection of historic aircraft, including several that can be viewed as restoration works-in-progress. It is open daily July through September and weekends the rest of the year.

Smith's Castle
⌨55 Richard Smith Drive, Wickford
✆401-294-3521
✐*www.smithscastle.org*
Built in 1678, Smith's Castle is one of the nation's oldest plantation houses. From May through October, house tours, led by docents in period costume, provide insight into four centuries of Rhode Island history. Hours vary seasonally, so call ahead.

South County Museum
⌨Boston Neck Road, Narragansett
✆401-783-5400
✐*www.southcountymuseum.org*
The South County Museum at Canonchet Farm exhibits more than 20,000 artifacts of life from the eighteenth to the early twentieth centuries at a 174-acre campus that also features a working print shop, carpentry shop, blacksmith shop, textile arts center, and farm.

Tomaquag Indian Memorial Museum
⊞ 390A Summit Road, Exeter
✆ 401-539-7213
✎ *www.tomaquagmuseum.com*

Introduce yourselves to the first Rhode Islanders, the Native American tribes that populated the area for hundreds of years before Europeans arrived. Open weekdays, this museum features local artifacts and a trading post where you can purchase hand-made items.

Outdoor Recreation

Outdoorsy families will find plenty of opportunities to bike, hike, boat, fish, bird-watch, and even ski in southern Rhode Island. Explore on your own, or enjoy a tour; either way, you'll gain a new appreciation for this coastal region's natural wonders.

Block Island
✆ 800-383-BIRI
✎ *www.blockislandchamber.com*

The seasonal, high-speed ferry from Galilee makes Block Island an easy day trip for South County vacationers. The tiny, pork chop–shaped island is just ten square miles in size, but its natural beauty and unique variety of flora, fauna, and feathered creatures are unparalleled.

Environmental preservation efforts began in earnest in 1971 with the formation of the Block Island Conservancy. Today, approximately a quarter of the island is protected as open space. Because it is home to more than forty species of rare and endangered plants and animals, visitors must protect this fragile environment as they enjoy Block Island's beaches, boating, bicycling, fishing, lighthouses, and sweeping views of the sea from the clay cliffs at Mohegan Bluffs.

Block Island is a favorite with walkers, cyclists, bird watchers, and other outdoor sports lovers. You'll find miles of walking trails at Rodman's Hollow (Black Rock Road, 401-466-2129), an Ice Age–carved glacial depression with rolling hills and scenic ocean vistas. Rodman's Hollow is situated along the twenty-five-mile Greenway network of interconnecting trails that starts at the heart of the island near Beacon Hill and traverses public and private lands.

For the island's most picturesque views, you'll want to climb Mohegan Bluffs (Mohegan Trail, 401-466-5009). These clay cliffs soar to more than 200 feet above the shimmering sea. A staircase is available to facilitate your climb and descent. While you're there, visit Southeast Light, one of two lighthouses on the island. Built in 1875, the Victorian brick structure was moved inland in 1993 because erosion jeopardized its position on the edge of the bluffs.

The Kayak Centre of Rhode Island
⌨9 Phillips Street, Wickford Village, North Kingstown
✆888-SEA-KAYAK
✐*www.kayakcentre.com*

This waterfront outfitter offers a variety of programs and tours, including outings specifically designed for families.

Ninigret Conservation Area
⌨Off East Beach Road, Charlestown

This protected area is home not only to pristine East Beach but to Ninigret Pond, a popular windsurfing, kayaking, and fishing destination. The adjacent Ninigret National Wildlife Refuge has four miles of well-marked trails for those who'd like to explore on foot. Or take a dune drive along the barrier beach; you must have your own four-wheel-drive vehicle and a permit, which can be obtained from the state's Coastal Resources Management Council (401-783-3370, *www .crmc.ri.gov*).

💼 TRAVEL TIP

Surprised that you can ski in Rhode Island? It is nicknamed the Ocean State, not the Mountain State, after all. But Yawgoo Valley Ski Area (160 Yawgoo Valley Road, Exeter, 401-294-3802, *www.yawgoo.com*) does offer day and night skiing. There's a snow-tubing park, too; kids must be at least 42 inches tall to snow-tube.

Southland Riverboat
🖃State Pier #3, Great Island Road, Port of Galilee, Narragansett
📞401-783-2954
✒*www.southlandcruises.com*

Hit the water without getting wet by taking a sightseeing cruise aboard the 149-passenger *Southland Riverboat*. You'll see dramatic coastal scenery and the historic Point Judith Lighthouse on a narrated eleven-mile tour.

Shopping

If you're looking for something more than tie-dyed T-shirts and trinkets, leave the souvenir shops near the beach behind for one of these eclectic shopping destinations.

The Christmas House
🖃1557 Ten Rod Road, Exeter
📞401-397-0097
✒*www.mychristmashouse.com*

It's Christmas year-round at this décor and gift store surrounded by twenty-three acres of scenic woodland.

The Fantastic Umbrella Factory
⌨4820 Old Post Road, Charlestown

☏401-364-6616

A one-of-a-kind shopping experience awaits year-round at the nineteenth-century farmyard that is now home to a collection of shops including an art gallery, a garden shop, and a natural foods restaurant. Children will enjoy feeding the small animals.

Sweenor's Chocolates
⌨21 Charles Street, Wakefield

☏401-783-4433

⌨Charlestown Village, Routes 1 & 2, Charlestown

☏401-364-3339

✎*www.sweenorschocolates.com*

Still owned by the third and fourth generations of the family, the confection company Walter Sweenor began in his basement kitchen during World War II is now Rhode Island's largest chocolate manufacturer. You'll find two Sweenor's stores in South County.

Wickford Village
⌨Brown Street, North Kingstown

☏401-295-5566 or 877-295-7200

✎*www.wickfordvillage.org*

Are you dreaming of the quintessential "Main Street New England" shopping experience: tree-lined streets, white picket fences, gardens, old homes, church spires, and a snug harbor forming the backdrop for antique shops brimming with unique treasures, boutiques with clever wares, art galleries, gourmet food shops, and outdoor cafés? Then close your eyes, and don't open them until you get to Wickford Village. Okay, that might not be feasible, but the picture-perfect image in your head is not far from the reality that you'll find at this historic North Kingstown village that is home to more than forty shops, galleries, and restaurants.

JUST FOR PARENTS

The first Wednesday of each month is "Westerly Arts Night." From 5 to 8 P.M., downtown nonprofit and commercial galleries and studios host opening receptions where you can meet artists, view their works, and enjoy refreshments and entertainment. For more information, call 401-348-0733.

Where to Stay

Families visiting South County's beach towns will find a variety of independently operated inns and motels with rates that vary widely, peaking on summer weekends. Here are a few of the available options that have particular appeal for families.

The fifteen-acre Willows Resort (Route 1, Charlestown, 401-364-7727 or 800-842-2181, *www.willowsresort.com*) is situated on a salt-water pond and located a five-minute drive from ocean beaches. Lodging options include efficiency units and one- and two-bedroom apartments, and rates include use of the outdoor pool, canoes, rowboats, kayaks, and sailboats.

Choose a room, efficiency, or cottage at Sand Dollar Inn (171 Post Road, Westerly, 401-322-2000, *www.visitri.com/sanddollarinn*), a quiet family property that is two miles from beaches.

You can hide away inside your own tiny "beach cottage" at Hathaway's Guest Cottages (4470 Old Post Road, Charlestown, 401-364-6665, *www.hathawaysguestcottages.com*), which has some efficiency cottages with cooking facilities that are ideal for longer stays.

Choose a deluxe room, suite, or private villa and have an eighteen-hole golf course at your doorstep at Winnapaug Inn (169 Shore Road, Westerly, 401-348-8350, *www.winnapauginn.com*), a fifty-six-room, year-round lodging facility where the kids will enjoy the heated outdoor pool. Guests can use complimentary passes to a private Misquamicut beach.

TRAVEL TIP

You can request your free South County Style vacation planner by calling the South County Tourism Council, 401-789-4422 or 800-548-4662 or visiting their Web site, *www.southcountyri.com*. This helpful guide includes an easy-to-scan chart that will help you select accommodations by price, distance to the beach, and availability of on-site amenities, such as a pool or restaurant.

While there are few accommodations right on the ocean, the Westerly area does have several beachfront options that are family-friendly but not fancy: the Andrea Hotel (89 Atlantic Avenue, Misquamicut, 401-348-8788, *www.andreahotel.com*), Pleasant View Inn (65 Atlantic Avenue, Watch Hill, 401-348-8200 or 800-782-3224, *www.pvinn.com*), Sandcastle Beachfront Inn (141 Atlantic Avenue, Misquamicut, 401-596-6900, *www.oceanviewinns.com/sandcastle.html*), and Sandy Shore Motel (149 Atlantic Avenue, Misquamicut, 401-596-5616, *www.sandyshore.com*).

If you're more comfortable with a chain hotel, stay eight miles from the beach and have access to an outdoor pool at the Holiday Inn (3009 Tower Hill Road, South Kingstown, 401-789-1051) or consider the Best Western West Greenwich Inn (99 Nooseneck Hill Road, West Greenwich, 401-397-5494), which has an indoor pool, whirlpool, fitness center, and complimentary continental breakfast. Coventry is home to two comfortable family hotels: Hampton Inn (Centre of New England Boulevard, 401-823-4041), which has a pool, hot tub, and fitness center; and Wingate Inn (4 Universal Boulevard, 401-821-3322), which offers a large indoor heated pool, oversize rooms, and a complimentary expanded continental breakfast.

Family Dining

From pizza places and casual pubs to delis and diners, there are plenty of budget-friendly dining options in South County. You'll also find one-of-a-kind restaurants when you're ready to treat your clan to a memorable meal.

Lobstermania

The only thing better than eating lobster on a vacation at the Rhode Island shore is eating an excessive amount of lobster! You can do just that at Nordic Lodge (178 East Pasquiset Trail, Charlestown, 401-783-4515, *www.nordiclodge.com*), home of the All You Can Eat Lobster Buffet featuring unlimited lobster and much more. The price is steep, although a sliding fee scale based on children's ages helps, but for the price, you're guaranteed access to a spread that is unlike anything you've ever seen. While you're there, be sure to sign the restaurant's guest book, as annual mailings include a free live-lobster-to-go offer. Nordic Lodge is open seasonally, as are many of the restaurants in this region.

 JUST FOR PARENTS

For a touch of romance, mosey over to the Watch Hill Inn Restaurant (38 Bay Street, Watch Hill, 401-348-6333, *www.watchhillinn .com*), where you can watch the sun sink from the outdoor Sunset Deck while sipping tropical beverages, and then retire to the dining room for a baked or steamed lobster feast.

If you know for certain that a fourth lobster won't tempt you, then you (and your wallet) may be better off heading to the self-proclaimed "Home of the Triple Lobster," Duffy's Tavern (235 Tower Hill Road, Wickford, 401-295-0073). If a single lobster is adequate for your appetite—and easier on your budget—you'll find tasty crustaceans and scenic views at Harbourside Lobstermania (38 Water Street, East Greenwich, 401-884-6363, *www.harboursideri.com*), or do as Rhode Island diners have done for more than eighty-five years—enjoy a traditional Rhode Island Shore Dinner in a casual environment at Aunt

Carrie's Seafood Restaurant (1240 Ocean Road, Narragansett, 401-783-7930, *www.auntcarriesri.com*).

Other Seafood Delights

Man (and woman and child) cannot live on lobster alone. Fortunately, there are many restaurants along Rhode Island's shoreline that prepare the bounty of the sea in all of its delicious variety.

In the village of Galilee, you can watch fishermen unloading the day's catch—which might just become your supper—and then dine on the outdoor deck at Champlin's Restaurant (Great Island Road, Narragansett, 401-783-3152) or overlooking Block Island Sound at George's of Galilee (250 Sand Hill Cove Road, Narragansett, 401-783-2306, *www.georgesofgalilee.com*), known far and wide for its chowder and fried clams.

≡FAST FACT

The word quahog evolved from the native Narragansett term, poquahock. Quahogs are found just below the surface of the sand between high and low tide and can be harvested by hand or rake. A quahog that is 1 to 2½ inches long is called a littleneck; a 2½- to 3-inch quahog is a cherrystone; and a 3-inch or larger quahog is a chowder. They're delicious raw, steamed in their shells, or in chowder and clam cakes.

For fish and chips made with the fresh local catch of the day, head to The Pump House (1464 Kingstown Road, Wakefield, 401-789-4944), where a diverse menu ensures the whole family will be happy.

Historic Settings

If you'd like a side of history with your meal, South County offers some unique places to dine.

The Coast Guard House, (40 Ocean Road, Narragansett, 401-789-0700, *www.thecoastguardhouse.com*) is known for its all-you-can-eat seaside Sunday brunches. Housed in a historic former Coast Guard lifesaving station that dates to 1888, the restaurant also serves lunch and dinner and has a small selection of children's menu choices.

Wilcox Tavern (5153 Old Post Road/Route 1, Charlestown, 401-322-1829, *www.wilcoxtavern.com*) serves traditional New England fare inside a 1730 house that was the birthplace of General Joseph Stanton, a member of the Colonial Congress who became Rhode Island's senator to the First Constitutional Congress. The children's menu has plenty of options for fussy eaters.

Children will also feel welcome at the Shelter Harbor Inn (10 Wagner Road, Westerly, 401-322-8883 or 800-468-8883, *www .shelterharborinn.com*), a lodging and dining property housed inside a farmhouse that dates to the early 1800s.

TRAVEL TIP

It's only a dozen years old, but the Middle of Nowhere Diner (Route 3, Exeter, 401-397-8855) is already legendary in Rhode Island not only for its quirky name but for its giant portions, excellent omelets, and affordable prices. The diner is open year-round for breakfast, lunch, and dinner.

CHAPTER 7

Providence and Newport

PROVIDENCE IS RHODE ISLAND'S capital and largest city, and it's home to New England's oldest zoo. Newport, with its historic mansions, beaches, boutiques, and seasonal activities, is the state's premier tourist destination. The good news for travelers torn between the two is that in a state as small as Rhode Island, the choice is easy—see both. From late spring until early fall, the Providence-Newport Ferry shuttles passengers between these two eclectic cities in just an hour.

Divine Providence

After Boston, if you can choose only one other New England city to visit, make it Providence. This urban enclave has emerged as one of the most dynamic centers of learning, culture, and architecture in the Northeast. Since the early 1980s, Rhode Island's capital has undergone a multimillion-dollar urban-renewal project focused on the city's waterfront, and yet, care has been taken to preserve the historical character of one of the oldest cities in America. Religious leader Roger Williams founded Providence in 1636, and today it is the only major U.S. city that has its entire downtown listed on the National Register of Historic Places.

Providence has a youthful exuberance that you'll sense as you meander its streets and the central River Walk. That's because it is home to several major colleges and universities including the Ivy League's Brown University, New England's third-oldest college; Rhode Island

School of Design, a forward-thinking college of the arts established in 1877; and Johnson & Wales University, which graduates some of the region's top chefs from its culinary school. Providence is quite compact and easily explored on foot. As you discover the Venice-inspired river-front walkways and bridges of Water Place Park, the bustling pubs and trendy shops of Thayer Street, and the cultural richness provided by the city's museums and performing arts centers, you'll understand why Providence has been nicknamed the "Renaissance City."

What to See and Do in Providence

Providence is an especially suitable vacation destination for families with tweens and teens. That's because Rhode Island's capital is best explored on foot, and many of its cultural and historic attractions won't hold the attention of younger children. That said, even the tiniest tots will love strolling through New England's oldest zoo.

Family Amusements

In Providence, history and fun go hand-in-hand.

Crescent Park Carousel

700 Bullocks Point Avenue, Riverside

401-433-2828

www.crescentparkcarousel.com

East of Providence, don't miss the 1895 Crescent Park Carousel, designated a National Historic Site and a National Historic Landmark. With sixty-two intricately carved wooden horses and four ornate chariots, this is the grandest of the carousels designed by Charles I. D. Looff. The carousel operates Thursday through Sunday from mid-June until Labor Day and weekends thereafter through Columbus Day.

Roger Williams Park Zoo

1000 Elmwood Avenue

401-785-3510

www.rogerwilliamsparkzoo.org

Just outside of downtown Providence, you can spy elephants, snow leopards, moon bears, and more in natural settings at the Roger Williams Park Zoo. The widely acclaimed zoo is home to more than 1,500 creatures. Don't miss the Marco Polo Silk Road, which traces explorer Marco Polo's three-year journey through Asia.

Splash Duck Tours
⊞ Corner of Fountain and Eddy Streets
✆ 401-421-3825
✎ *www.splashducktours.com*
See the best of Providence from the land and the water on a narrated tour aboard an amphibious vehicle, which travels the city's historic streets before splashing into the Providence River.

Museums and Historic Sites
Providence is an energetic and vibrant city that your kids will find hip—while they're learning a thing or two.

Benefit Street
History and architecture buffs won't want to miss the College Hill neighborhood, home to Benefit Street, Providence's "Mile of History." Wealthy businessmen began building houses along Back Street, now Benefit Street, in 1758; today this is the largest concentration of colonial homes in America. Early Federal period and interesting nineteenth- and twentieth-century architectural styles can be seen, too. The Providence Preservation Society (401-831-7440, *www.ppsri.org*) offers information on self-guided walking tours of Benefit Street.

While you're there, you can visit the Old State House (150 Benefit Street, 401-222-2678, *www.preservation.ri.gov/about/old_state_house.php*), where the Rhode Island General Assembly renounced allegiance to King George III of England a full two months before the rest of the American colonies officially did so with the signing of the Declaration of Independence.

Nearby, visit the John Brown House Museum (52 Power Street at Benefit Street, 401-273-7507, *www.rihs.org/Museums.html*). John

Brown was a prosperous Providence merchant, and this 1786 Georgian mansion is filled with examples of Rhode Island craftsmanship.

Providence Children's Museum
⌨100 South Street

☎401-273-5437

✎*www.childrenmuseum.org*

Providence is home to Rhode Island's only museum just for kids, and there are plenty of hands-on activities here to keep the under-twelve set entertained, whether they'd rather play vet at the mini–animal hospital or assemble a skeleton puzzle in the Bone Zone.

The RISD Museum
⌨224 Benefit Street

☎401-454-6500

✎*www.risd.edu/museum.cfm*

The RISD (Rhode Island School of Design) Museum is open to the public Tuesday through Sunday. It exhibits an impressive collection of more than 80,000 works ranging from ancient Greek and Roman sculpture to French impressionist paintings to contemporary art. Kids will be intrigued by the museum's Egyptian galleries, where a coffin and mummy are on display.

State House
⌨Smith Street

☎401-222-2357

✎*www.sec.state.ri.us/pubinfo/Tours/tours.html*

One of the most distinctive architectural gems of Providence's skyline is the State House, designed by McKim, Mead, and White and completed in 1901. It sports one of the largest self-supported domes in the world. Free, self-guided tours are available weekdays.

Roger Williams National Memorial
⌨282 North Main Street

☎401-521-7266

✎*www.nps.gov/rowi*

The National Park Service–operated Roger Williams National Memorial includes a landscaped park and a visitor's center, where the story of Rhode Island's founder is told.

Outdoor Recreation

Pack your walking shoes, your skates, and your bikes; Providence is a city best explored under your own power.

Bank of America City Center Skating Rink

⌨2 Kennedy Plaza

✆401-331-5544

✎*www.providenceskating.com*

Spend an exhilarating winter morning, afternoon, or evening, gliding on the outdoor ice at the city's centrally located skating rink. Skate rentals are available.

East Bay Bike Path

Looking for a safe, smooth place to cycle? The 14½-mile East Bay Bike Path is a paved trail that follows the course of an abandoned railroad line along the shore of Narragansett Bay, all the way from Providence to Bristol. The Bike Path is accessible from many points, including Haines Memorial State Park (Route 103, East Providence) and Colt State Park (Route 114, Bristol, 401-253-7482).

Water Place Park and River Walk

⌨Memorial Boulevard

The four-acre Water Place Park and River Walk in the heart of downtown Providence is the most visible manifestation of the city's renaissance. Creating the series of Venetian-like canals, bridges, and riverside walkways was no easy task. Railroad tracks were removed, and two rivers were rerouted through the city to create this scenic centerpiece where you can stroll, picnic, watch outdoor theater presentations, and even embark on a gondola ride. Contact La Gondola (401-421-8877, *www.gondolari.com*) May through October to reserve your forty-minute ride for up to six people.

 TRAVEL TIP

Try to time your visit to Providence to coincide with Water-Fire (401-272-3111, *www.waterfire.org*)! It is a fusion of fire, water, music, and art. Sculptor Barnaby Evans created the first WaterFire in 1994 and a second for the International Sculpture Conference in 1996. Today, WaterFire has ninety-seven flaming braziers that cast their gaze-monopolizing glow along the Woonasquatucket and Moshassuck Rivers on select evenings from May through October.

Shopping

Whether you're looking for an old-fashioned shopping experience, the latest fashion trends, or a Rhode Island souvenir, there are retail destinations to explore in Providence.

The Arcade
⌨ 65 Weybosset Street
✆ 401-598-1199

Even shopping can be a blast from the past. The Arcade is America's oldest indoor shopping mall, and it's a National Historic Landmark. The 1828 mall now houses three floors of shops, boutiques, and eateries. The Arcade is closed on Sundays.

Only in Rhode Island
⌨ 297 Thayer Street
✆ 401-276-0600
✍ *www.onlyinrhodeisland.com*

In the midst of Providence's eclectic, shop- and eatery-lined Thayer Street, you'll find this store devoted to products made in America's smallest state. From chowder to candles, from pine soap to pottery, this is the place to nab souvenirs.

Providence Place Mall
⌨1 Providence Place
✆401-270-1017
✍*www.providenceplace.com*

Providence also boasts a modern shopping center, which features popular restaurants and more than 170 department stores and specialty shops.

 RAINY DAY FUN

An IMAX movie—especially one in 3D—is a larger-than-life experience. Providence Place Mall is home to the Feinstein IMAX Theatre (9 Providence Place, 401-453-4629, *www.imax.com/providence*). You'll be amazed by the clarity of the sound and images of everything from documentaries to remastered Hollywood blockbusters on an immense screen.

Sports
Going to a game is fun for the whole family, and Providence won't disappoint sports fans.

Pawtucket Red Sox
⌨McCoy Stadium, Ben Monder Way, Pawtucket
✆401-724-7300
✍*www.pawsox.com*

From April through September, head north of Providence to see the PawSox play. McCoy Stadium has been the home of the Pawtucket Red Sox, the International League's AAA affiliate of the Boston Red Sox, since 1973. The historic stadium was a 1942 Works Progress Administration (WPA) project. General admission tickets are very affordable (just $6 for adults and $4 for children twelve and under) and can be ordered online or by calling 401-724-7300.

≡FAST FACT

McCoy Stadium was the setting for the longest professional baseball game ever played, an eight-hour and twenty-five minute duel between the Pawtucket Red Sox and the Rochester Red Wings. When the game was suspended after 4 A.M., the nineteen fans in the stands who had remained through thirty-two innings received lifetime passes to McCoy Stadium. Two months later, when the game was resumed, the PawSox won in the bottom of the thirty-third.

Providence Bruins
⊞Dunkin' Donuts Center, One LaSalle Square, Providence
✆401-273-5000
✐*www.providencebruins.com*

From October through April, catch Providence Bruins minor-league (AHL) hockey action at the Dunkin' Donuts Center.

Where to Stay in Providence

Like most urban destinations, Providence's lodging choices are primarily hotels. These options put you either in the heart of the city or close to the airport.

Downtown Providence Hotels

In the heart of downtown Providence, you'll find a grand old hotel that is an attraction in and of itself. Built in 1922, the Providence Biltmore (11 Dorrance Street, 401-421-0700, *www.providencebiltmore.com*) offers 291 rooms and suites and a rooftop Grand Ballroom with skyline and waterfront views.

The Westin Providence (One West Exchange Street, 401-598-8000, *www.starwoodhotels.com*) is the city's largest hotel. It's connected to the Rhode Island Convention Center and Providence Place Mall and has an indoor pool, restaurant, bar, and fitness center. If you're in the mood to splurge, consider the Hotel Providence (311 Westminster Street, 401-861-8000 or 800-861-8990, *www.thehotelprovidence.com*), an elegant small hotel with luxurious amenities.

You'll also find convenient, central accommodations at the Marriott Providence Downtown (1 Orms Street, 401-272-2400 or 866-807-2171) and at the Providence Plaza Hotel (21 Atwells Avenue, 401-831-3900).

Hotels Near T.F. Green Airport

For convenient accommodations right at T.F. Green Airport, located south of Providence, try the Comfort Inn Airport (1940 Post Road, Warwick, 401-732-0470, *www.choicehotels.com*); Hampton Inn & Suites Providence Warwick-Airport (2100 Post Road, Warwick, 401-739-8888, *www.hamptoninnprovidenceairport.com*); the Radisson Airport Hotel (2081 Post Road, Warwick, 401-739-3000, *www .radisson.com/warwickri*); or Sheraton Providence Airport Hotel (1850 Post Road, Warwick, 401-738-4000, *www.starwoodhotels.com*).

Family Dining in Providence

Foodies will discover much to savor in Providence. The city is home, after all, to Johnson & Wales University, a highly respected culinary school that provides an ongoing stream of new talent to shake up the local dining scene. Of course, when you're traveling with young mouths to feed, you may choose restaurants more for their monetary—and entertainment—value.

Mall Meals

For fun dining experiences that won't break the bank, look no farther than Providence Place. Among the mall's eateries, you'll find Fire + Ice (48 Providence Place, 401-270-4040, *www.fire-ice.com*), an all-you-can-eat "improvisational grill" where each family member can create a custom dish from an extensive array of meats, vegetables, seafood, and sauces that is then cooked before your eyes on an enormous round grill.

On the mall's entertainment level above the food court, you'll discover Dave & Busters (401-270-4555, *www.daveandbusters.com*), a game-filled emporium that also serves a diverse menu of food and beverages.

Johnny Rockets (59 Providence Place, 401-270-0902, *www .johnnyrockets.com*) on the mall's third floor has the look of an all-American diner and the food to match. Or if you're feeling indulgent, head to The Cheesecake Factory (94 Providence Place, 401-270-4010, *www.thecheesecakefactory.com*) and allow your brood to order dessert first.

A Taste of History

Federal Hill, the neighborhood west of downtown Providence, is home to the city's "Little Italy." Dine on classic Italian dishes at Camille's (71 Bradford Street, 401-751-4812, *www.camillesonthehill .com*), a dining landmark since 1914. Then pop into Roma Gourmet Foods (310 Atwells Avenue, 401-331-8620) for homemade pastries.

≡FAST FACT

If you find yourself addicted to coffee milk, Rhode Island's official beverage, after your visit to the Ocean State, despair not! The coffee syrup used to make this unique drink since the 1920s can be ordered from Lincoln-based Autocrat, Inc. by calling 800-AUTOCRAT or visiting *www.famousfoods.com*.

If you're craving something equally historic but much less fancy, try Haven Brothers Diner (77 Spruce Street, 401-861-7777). Providence is reputed to be the birthplace of the diner—a claim that stems from the ingenuity of Walter Scott, who launched his horse-drawn lunch cart in 1872. In 1893, the Haven family got into the lunch wagon business, and today, Haven Brothers Diner is still a restaurant on the move. Each evening, the silver diner truck with just three barstools parks next to City Hall, where it serves greasy diner grub until the wee hours.

Light Bites

Sometimes, all you really need to fuel your sightseeing adventures is a hot dog. At Spike's Junkyard Dogs (273 Thayer Street, 401-454-1459 and 485 Branch Avenue, 401-861-6888, *www.spikesjunk yarddogs.com*), you'll find affordable, all-beef tube steaks with an enticing lineup of toppings.

Even if hot dogs aren't your thing, head to Thayer Street, which runs through the Brown University campus. It's dotted with ethnic eateries and outdoor cafés, many of which cater to the college crowd by offering generous portions at reasonable prices.

 ## JUST FOR PARENTS

Beer enthusiasts should chug on over to the Union Station Brewery (36 Exchange Terrace, 401-274-2739, *www.johnharvards.com*) for a pint and some pub fare inside a historic brick building that was formerly the Providence train station. Or try the Trinity Brewhouse (186 Fountain Street, 401-453-2337, *www.trinitybrewhouse .com*), Rhode Island's largest brewery.

Get to Know Newport

Newport's population quadruples each year between May and September. That alone speaks to the enormous popularity of this New England destination that has been called America's first resort.

Newport was founded in 1639 at the southern tip of Aquidneck Island, and by the 1700s, it was already one of the American colonies' most important ports. Unfortunately, the British realized this as well; in 1776, they blockaded the port and occupied the town. By the time Newport was "freed" in 1780 by a fleet of French ships enlisted to support the colonies' cause in the American Revolution, the port city was in ruins. It would never recover its status as a thriving seaport.

No need to cry the blues for Newport, though. Surrounded by water on three sides and blessed with gentle summer breezes, it was discovered a century later by the nation's "aristocracy"—the Astors and Vanderbilts and other wealthy capitalists who transformed Newport into their own summer playground. During Newport's Gilded Age, its socially elite seasonal residents strove to outdo each other by building larger, more ornate "cottages" and by hosting more and more lavish parties.

Today, Newport still knows how to celebrate summer, and the incomparable mansions that once were the setting for the grandest events open their doors to tourists for a gander at the lifestyle of a bygone era. The summer season is packed with music festivals, yachting events, and opportunities to see and be seen at the town's delightful shops and eateries and to stroll along the Cliff Walk, the only obstacle between the mansions and the churning sea. But the tourism industry has made a conscious effort to expand its "peak" season beyond that May to September time frame. December is another particularly busy month, as Santa arrives by Coast Guard cutter and the Newport mansions dress up in fabulous holiday fashion. A month-long schedule of "Haunted Newport" events has also made October an appealing month for a trip to the "City by the Sea"—if you dare.

💼 TRAVEL TIP

Newport is home to America's oldest synagogue. Touro Synagogue (85 Touro Street, 401-847-4794, *www.tourosynagogue.org*), established by Spanish and Portuguese Jews fleeing religious persecution, was dedicated in 1763 and is now a National Historic Site. Designed by Peter Harrison, it is renowned for its architecture. Tours are available, and services are open to the public.

What to See and Do in Newport

Though the mansions, of course, are a must-see, there's so much more to do in historic Newport. Whether strolling wharves lined with shops and restaurants, unfurling a picnic blanket at an outdoor music festival, lazing on a beach, setting out on a sailing adventure, or ice skating with an ocean view, you'll easily fill your days.

Newport's Magnificent Mansions

Their wealthy owners called them "summer cottages," but visitors may find that even the word *mansion* seems hopelessly inadequate to describe the magnificently monstrous residences built in Newport by nineteenth-century industrialists and entrepreneurs seeking a seasonal escape. It's hard to imagine living in these splendid palaces, much less spending just a few short months each year.

There are so many mansions to see that plotting a plan of action can be daunting. Here's a quick description of each mansion that is open to the public, listed in order from those that families must see to those might be saved for another visit. Those marked with an asterisk (*) are under the umbrella of the Newport Preservation Society (401-847-1000, *www.newportmansions.org*), which offers discounted, multiproperty admission passes that are available at each mansion it operates.

The Astors' Beechwood Mansion
580 Bellevue Avenue
401-846-3772
www.astors-beechwood.com
Built in 1851 and bought in 1881 by William Backhouse Astor and his wife, Caroline, the undisputed queen of American society, this Victorian mansion was the setting for the 1911 wedding of their son, John Jacob Astor IV, who later embarked on an ill-fated honeymoon aboard the *Titanic*. Today's visitors return to the year 1891 and are welcomed as guests of Mrs. Astor by actors and actresses in period character and costume.

The Breakers*
⌨44 Ochre Point Avenue
✆401-847-1000
✍*www.newportmansions.org*

This seventy-room villa was completed in 1895 for Cornelius Vanderbilt II, heir to the family shipping and railroad fortune. It was designed by Richard Morris Hunt to resemble a sixteenth-century Italian palace. This is the grandest of all of the Newport mansions.

Green Animals*
⌨380 Cory's Lane, Portsmouth
✆401-683-1267
✍*www.newportmansions.org*

Located just outside of Newport, Green Animals is worth the trip to see its amazing topiary gardens. Eighty topiary figures represent geometric shapes, ornamental designs, and over twenty birds and animals. The Victorian country house that was home to the Brayton family features a collection of antique toys and dollhouses.

Belcourt Castle
⌨657 Bellevue Avenue
✆401-846-0669
✍*www.belcourtcastle.com*

This sixty-room mansion was built for Oliver Hazard Perry Belmont, who inherited his fortune from his father, and served as the Rothschild banking representative in America. It was designed by Richard Morris Hunt to resemble a Louis XII–style castle. Although privately owned, it is open daily for guided tours.

Rough Point
⌨680 Bellevue Avenue
✆401-849-7300
✍*www.newportrestoration.com*

Rough Point is the "newest" old mansion in Newport. Opened to the public in 2000, the dramatic, Gothic-style home was originally built in 1889 for Frederick W. Vanderbilt and was the home of tobacco heiress Doris Duke until her death in 1993. Rough Point houses one of the area's most significant private art collections.

Marble House*
⌨596 Bellevue Avenue
✆401-847-1000
✐*www.newportmansions.org*

This "summer cottage" was built between 1888 and 1892 for William K. Vanderbilt and his wife, who envisioned it as her "temple to the arts" in America. Of the $11 million spent on construction, $7 million went toward the purchase of the 500,000 cubic feet of marble that inspire the mansion's name.

Rosecliff*
⌨548 Bellevue Avenue
✆401-847-1000
✐*www.newportmansions.org*

This structure was completed in 1902 for Theresa Fair Oelrichs, daughter of one of the discoverers of the Comstock Silver Lode. Designed by Stanford White of the famed architectural firm McKim, Mead, and White to resemble the neoclassical Grand Trianon at Versailles, it houses Newport's largest ballroom.

≡FAST FACT

If you would just as soon avoid the crowds of summer, there's another "most wonderful time of the year" to visit Newport. These ostentatious mansions are even more stunning when adorned with lush greenery, baubles, and bows. The Preservation Society of Newport County selects a few of its prized properties each year to decorate and open for holiday season tours, and other privately owned mansions get into the spirit, as well.

Chateau-sur-Mer*

⌨474 Bellevue Avenue

✆401-847-1000

✎*www.newportmansions.org*

This Victorian mansion was built in 1852 and enlarged in 1872 for retired banker William S. Wetmore. Until the Vanderbilts arrived on the social scene in the 1890s, this Victorian villa was Newport's most palatial residence.

The Elms*

⌨367 Bellevue Avenue

✆401-847-1000

✎*www.newportmansions.org*

Built in 1901 as a summer vacation home for Pennsylvania coal magnate Edward J. Berwind, The Elms is a nearly perfect replica of a circa-1750 Parisian chateau.

Chepstow*

⌨120 Narragansett Avenue

✆401-847-1000, ext. 165

✎*www.newportmansions.org*

Chepstow was designed by local Newport architect George Champlin Mason and built in 1860. It houses the possessions of the Morris family, which acquired the property in 1911. Tours are by appointment only from May through October.

Kingscote*

⌨253 Bellevue Avenue

✆401-847-1000

✎*www.newportmansions.org*

This Gothic Revival–style mansion was the first Newport "cottage" built exclusively for summer use. Completed in 1841 for George Noble Jones, a Georgia planter, it was sold in the 1860s to Newport China trade merchant William Henry King and christened Kingscote. His collection of Oriental furnishings remains on view inside the house.

Outdoor Recreation

Newport is so breathtakingly scenic, you'll find it difficult to stay indoors. This seaside city offers unparalleled opportunities for outdoor fun in every season.

The Cliff Walk

On all but the bitterest days, you'll want to meander along the Cliff Walk (*www.cliffwalk.com*), the National Recreation Trail that provides breathtaking views of Newport's shoreline and of the historic Bellevue Avenue mansions. Development of the Cliff Walk began in the 1880s, and while at times there have been disputes waged by homeowners along the trail, its public access has been preserved. The walk starts at the western end of Easton's Beach at Memorial Boulevard and continues south with major entrance points at Narragansett Avenue, Webster Street, Sheppard Avenue, Ruggles Avenue, Marine Avenue, Ledge Road, and Bellevue Avenue at the east end of Bailey's Beach. While the trail makes for a quite leisurely walk, you'll still want to wear comfortable shoes and to watch where you're going.

Easton's Beach

175 Memorial Boulevard

401-845-5810

www.cityofnewport.com/4538.aspx

Newport's largest public beach is a ¾-mile crescent of fine sand with a boardwalk, snack bar, showers, a beach store, playground, carousel, and skateboard park. Although the beach is free, fees are charged for parking and some amenities.

Fort Adams State Park

Harrison Avenue

401-847-2400

www.riparks.com/fortadams.htm

Fort Adams was the second-largest U.S. bastioned fort from 1799 to 1845. Volunteers and staff of the Fort Adams Trust (401-841-0707, *www.fortadams.org*) conduct guided tours of the twenty-one-acre stone fort daily from 10 A.M. until 4 P.M. on the hour from mid-May through October. There is no admission fee. You'll find famous events such as the Newport Jazz and Folk Festivals, plus a beach, picnic areas, fishing piers, a boat ramp, a Museum of Yachting, and a sailing center. Tickets for festival events are generally available through TicketWeb (866-468-7619, *www.ticketweb.com*).

 JUST FOR PARENTS

There are three wineries near Newport. Greenvale Vineyards (582 Wapping Road, Portsmouth, 401-847-3777, *www.greenvale .com*), Newport Vineyards (909 East Main Road, Middletown, 401-848-5161, *www.newportvineyards.com*), and Sakonnet Vineyards (162 West Main Road, Little Compton, 800-919-4637, *www.sakonnetwine.com*). Contact each winery for tour information and hours of operation.

Gooseberry Beach
⌨Ocean Avenue
✆401-847-3958
✍*www.gooseberrybeach.com*
The parking fees are a bit steep at this privately owned beach club, but it is open to the public and the gentle waves are ideal for young swimmers and snorkelers. Have lunch at the Gooseberry Café, and make a day of it.

Norman Bird Sanctuary
⌨583 Third Beach Road, Middletown
✆401-846-2577
✍*www.normanbirdsanctuary.org*
Love birds? Flock to this 300-acre preserve in nearby Middletown that offers seven miles of walking trails through diverse habitats.

Sovereign Bank Family Skating Center

⌨Newport Yachting Center, America's Cup Avenue

✆401-846-3018

✎*www.skatenewport.com*

Day and night, Newport's ocean-view ice-skating rink is the place to be when chilly weather arrives. Skate rentals, food, and beverages are available.

Shopping

Whether you're in search of a souvenir, something to wear to dinner, an antique treasure, or a perfect gift made in Rhode Island, Newport's three centrally located waterfront shopping areas—Bannister's Wharf and Bowen's Wharf, both located off America's Cup Avenue, and the Brick Market Place between Thames Street and America's Cup Avenue—won't disappoint.

Bannister's Wharf

✎*www.bannisterswharf.net*

When Bannister's Wharf was established in 1742, its shops provided townspeople and sailors with basic necessities. Today, you're not likely to find anything you absolutely need in the wharf's twenty shops and galleries, but you will find plenty of enticing items to purchase, from leather goods at the Brahmin Handbags Factory Outlet to waffle cones piled high with Ben & Jerry's distinctive ice cream.

Bowen's Wharf

✎*www.bowenswharf.com*

Bowen's Wharf has a special charm with its cobblestone and brick walkways, boat docks, raw bars, and blend of eighteenth-, nineteenth-, and twentieth-century architecture. You'll find Newport's oldest fine-arts gallery here; the Roger King Gallery of Fine Art (21 Bowen's Wharf, 401-847-4359, *www.rkingfinearts.com*) exhibits an ever-changing selection of New England regional and marine art. Scrimshaw artist Brian Kiracofe's Newport Scrimshanders (14 Bowen's Wharf, 401-849-5680, *www.scrimshanders.com*) features jewelry and other ivory items engraved using traditional techniques.

Brick Market Place

✍*www.brickmarketnewport.com*

The sprawling Brick Market Place is home to both one-of-a-kind boutiques and high-end national retailers. It's a perfect place to window-shop.

Sports

Not surprisingly, the sports that Newport is known for are those traditionally associated with the social upper crust. Nowadays, the city's attractions and tour operators make it possible for anyone to experience these rarefied sporting pursuits.

International Tennis Hall of Fame

🖃194 Bellevue Avenue

✆401-849-3990

✍*www.tennisfame.com*

The legends of tennis are immortalized in the world's largest tennis museum. It's also the spot where the first American tennis National Championships were held in 1881. The complex features thirteen grass tennis courts, and they're open to all ages and abilities for play in season. Reservations can be made by calling 401-846-0642.

Newport Sailing School and Tours

🖃Goat Island Marina, Dock A5

✆401-848-2266

✍*www.newportsailing.com*

What better place to learn to sail than the "Sailing Capital of the World"? Newport Sailing School and Tours offers short-term instruction for beginning, intermediate, and advanced students, including children. Or simply relax aboard a one- or two-hour sailing tour of Newport Harbor and Narragansett Bay.

JUST FOR PARENTS

Although live jai alai action is history at Newport Grand (Admiral Kalbfus Road, 401-849-5000, *www.newportgrand .com*), this gaming and entertainment facility offers a state-of-the-art simulcast theater where you can bet on thorough-bred, harness, and greyhound racing and jai alai year-round. There are also more than 1,000 video poker, blackjack, and slot machines inside. Admission is free; you must be at least eighteen to get in.

Sightsailing of Newport
⌨32 Bowen's Wharf
✆401-849-3333 or ✆800-709-SAIL
✍*www.sightsailing.com*

Enjoy an intimate sailing excursion aboard one of three sailing yachts; you may even be offered a chance to take the wheel. Day and sunset departures are offered daily from early May through early November.

Where to Stay in Newport

Though you're not likely to find accommodations to rival those the Vanderbilts and Astors had when they visited Rhode Island, there are many lodging options that will spoil your family. The Hyatt Regency Newport (1 Goat Island, 401-851-1234, *www.newport.hyatt.com*) has 264 water-view rooms, an indoor pool, an outdoor saltwater pool, a spa, three restaurants, and a complimentary shuttle to downtown Newport. The 237-room Hotel Viking (One Bellevue Avenue, 401-847-3300 or 800-556-7126, *www.hotelviking.com*), listed on the National Register of Historic Places, was built by 100 of Newport's wealthiest residents in the 1920s to accommodate their numerous guests.

 TRAVEL TIP

Have you ever dreamed of being a lighthouse keeper? Newport's Rose Island Lighthouse (401-847-4242, *www .roseislandlighthouse.org*), built in 1870 and refurbished in 1993, is now a museum open to the public by day and a fantasy getaway for lighthouse lovers at night. The two keepers' bedrooms are available for overnight stays year-round. Or, your family could be "Keepers for a Week." Your "rent" would include daily work projects.

For more down-to-earth room rates, consider the Newport Marriott (25 America's Cup Avenue, 401-849-1000, *www.marriott.com*), which provides a convenient location for exploring Newport's sights, or Best Western The Mainstay Inn (151 Admiral Kalbfus Road, 401-849-9880, *www.bestwestern.com*), which is a mile out of town. You can also save money, particularly in the off-season, by staying at hotels in neighboring Middletown, such as the cozy Courtyard by Marriott (9 Commerce Drive, Middletown, 401-849-8000, *www .marriott.com*). Just remember, parking in Newport for the day can be expensive.

Newport claims the largest number of individual inns and B&Bs in the United States, but most are romantic hideaways where children are unwelcome. Newport Reservations (800-842-0102, *www .newportreservations.com*), a free reservation service, can assist you in locating available rooms at properties that do accommodate young visitors. The Newport County Inns and Bed & Breakfasts Association (*www.newportinns.com*) provides an online showcase for its member inns if you prefer to do your own research.

Keep in mind that, especially during peak season, it will likely be impossible to book a stay in Newport for just one weekend night. Don't let that thwart your quick getaway plans, though. Remember that Rhode Island is tiny—just thirty-seven miles east to west and forty-eight miles north to south—so staying in another part of the state or even in neighboring Connecticut or Massachusetts may help you to get around this restriction.

Family Dining in Newport

Just when it's time for lunch or dinner and you think you'll get a brief respite from the rigors of having to decide what to do next, you'll find that the local restaurant selection once again leaves you with decisions, decisions, decisions.

Seafood Delights

If you eat chowder in only one place, make it The Black Pearl (Bannister's Wharf, 401-846-5264, *www.blackpearlnewport.com*). This crowded, noisy, casual tavern is an especially good choice for lunch. For a traditional New England lobster dinner, the Atlantic Beach Club (55 Purgatory Road, Middletown, 401-847-2740, *www.atlantic beachclub.com*) is always a solid choice, or take the kids to Aquidneck Lobster Company (31 Bowen's Wharf, 401-846-0106), Newport's closest thing to a lobster zoo, and select some tasty crustaceans to take home for a souvenir dinner. Scales & Shells Restaurant and Raw Bar, (527 Thames Street, 401-846-3474, *www.scalesandshells.com*) is another favorite with seafood lovers. If you're spending time at Easton's Beach, be sure to sample the fried clams at the ultracasual Flo's Clam Shack (4 Wave Avenue, Middletown, 401-847-8141).

Memorable Meals

Pizza, chicken nuggets, and burgers may be the mainstay of most kids' vacation diets, but in Newport, you really should challenge them to try something new. There's spicy food on the menu at the Newport Blues Café (286 Thames Street, 401-841-5510, *www.newport blues.com*), where kids eat free before 7 P.M. with the purchase of an adult entrée. Unfortunately, live music doesn't start most nights until after young ones' bedtime.

The Red Parrot (348 Thames Street, 401-847-3800, *www .redparrotrestaurant.com*), housed in a former meat-packing house built in 1898, serves dishes with Caribbean flair, and your kids might just try the shark bites on a dare.

Meals on the Move

For a completely out-of-the-ordinary dining experience, book passage aboard the Newport Dinner Train (19 America's Cup Avenue, 401-841-8700, *www.newportdinnertrain.com*). You'll enjoy a lovely meal served in a luxury dining car while you ride the rails for twenty-two miles along the scenic shore of Narragansett Bay.

Luncheon and dinner outings aboard the Newport Cruise Company's *Majestic* (2 Bowen's Ferry Landing, 401-849-3575, *www* *.newportcruiseco.com*), a yacht that plies the waters of Newport Harbor and Narragansett Bay from May through October, are fine way to combine eating and sightseeing.

 JUST FOR PARENTS

The White Horse Tavern (26 Marlborough Street, 401-849-3600, *www.whitehorsetavern.com*) is America's oldest continuously operating tavern—it's been hosting guests since 1687. But don't let the tavern moniker and the restaurant's rustic New England appearance fool you. This is one of Newport's most sophisticated dining enclaves featuring cuisine that highlights fresh local ingredients. Reservations are a must.

Massachusetts

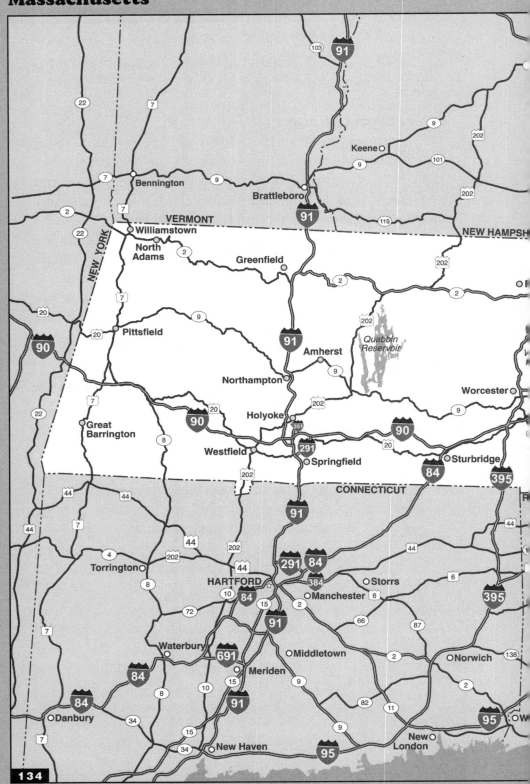

Massachusetts

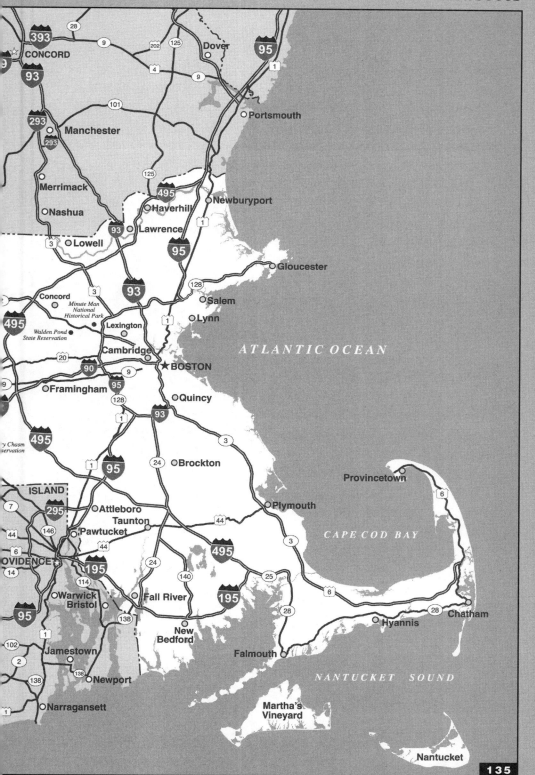

Boston and Cambridge, Massachusetts

LEGEND

-T- Subway line & station

HIH Commuter rail line

···· Freedom Trail

ⓘ Visitor information center

Msgr O'Brien Highw

Windsor St
Plymouth
Portsmouth
Bristol St
Clark St
Webster Ave
St
Moore St
Davis St
Portland St

Fifth St
Lopez St
First St
Third St
Second St
Bent St

Land Blvd
Cambridge Pkwy

Binney St

Tech Square
Broadway
Galileo Way
Mid-Block Connector

Potter St

Athenaeum St

Cha
Pla

Main St

T Kendall
Main St
Wadsworth
Red Line
③ Longfellow Bridge
Ch

Dock St
Carleton St
Ames St
Amherst St

Memorial Dr

Re

Community Boating
Embankment Rd
Pin
Brittne

③

Massachusetts Ave
Amherst St

Charles River

Chestnut St
Beaver Pl

②⑧

Harvard Bridge

Beacon St
Berkeley St
Arlington St
Marlborough St

②⑧

②

2A

James J. Storrow Dr

Fairfield St
Exeter St
Dartmouth St
Clarendon St

Commonwealth Ave

Newbury

②⑧

Beacon St
Herford St
Gloucester St
Marlborough St
Commonwealth Ave

②

Copley T

Stuart St
Stanhope s

State Rd
Beacon St
Charlesgate W
Charlesgate E
Massachusetts Ave

②

Newbury St
Boylston St

Green Line

Blagden St
Dartmouth St
Trinity Pl

②⑧

ore
are

Westbound 90 only
Ipswich St
Cambria St
Scotia St
Dalton St

T

Green Line
Garrison St
Harcourt St
Orange Line

T
Back Bay
South End

St Cha
Columbus Ave
Cazenove

Boylston St
Haviland St
Belvidere St

Chandler St
Lawrence St

Boston and Cambridge, Massachusetts

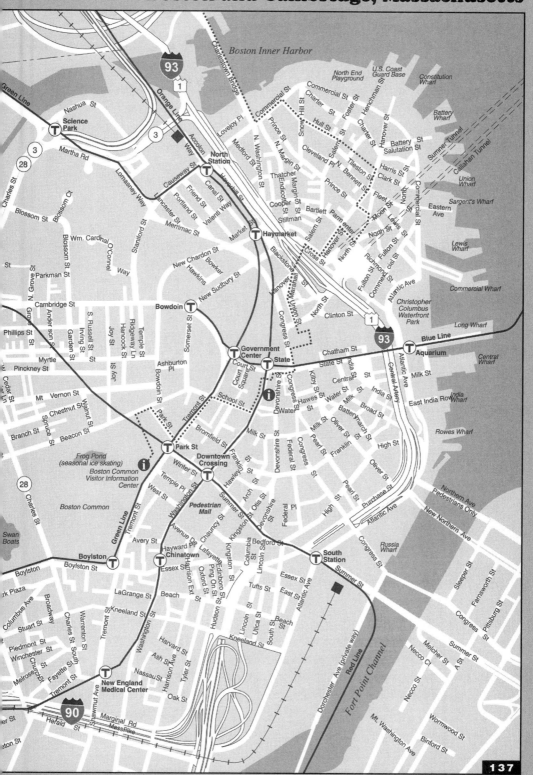

Boston Inner Harbor

Springfield, Massachusetts

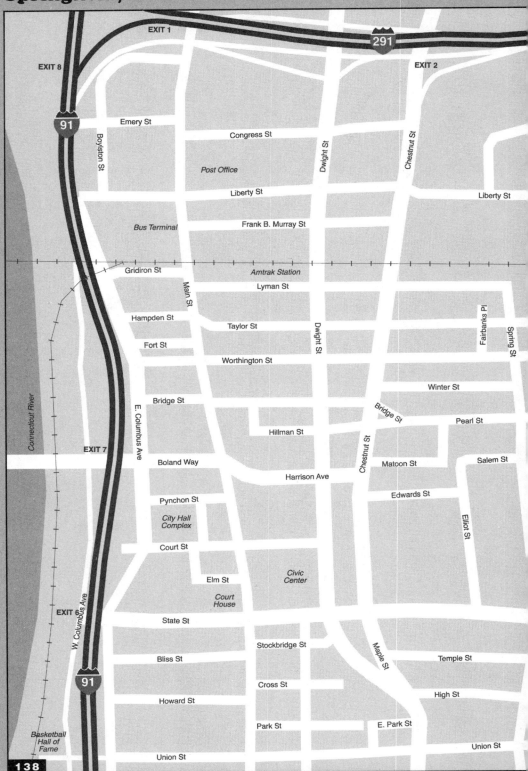

EXIT 1

EXIT 8

EXIT 2

91

291

Emery St

Boylston St

Congress St

Dwight St

Chestnut St

Post Office

Liberty St

Liberty St

Bus Terminal

Frank B. Murray St

Gridiron St

Amtrak Station

Lyman St

Main St

Hampden St

Taylor St

Dwight St

Fairbanks Pl

Spring St

Fort St

Worthington St

Winter St

Connecticut River

Bridge St

Bridge St

Pearl St

E. Columbus Ave

Hillman St

Chestnut St

EXIT 7

Boland Way

Harrison Ave

Matoon St

Salem St

Pynchon St

Edwards St

City Hall
Complex

Elliot St

Court St

Civic
Center

Elm St

EXIT 6

W. Columbus Ave

Court
House

State St

Stockbridge St

Maple St

Temple St

Bliss St

91

Cross St

High St

Howard St

Park St

E. Park St

Basketball
Hall of
Fame

Union St

Union St

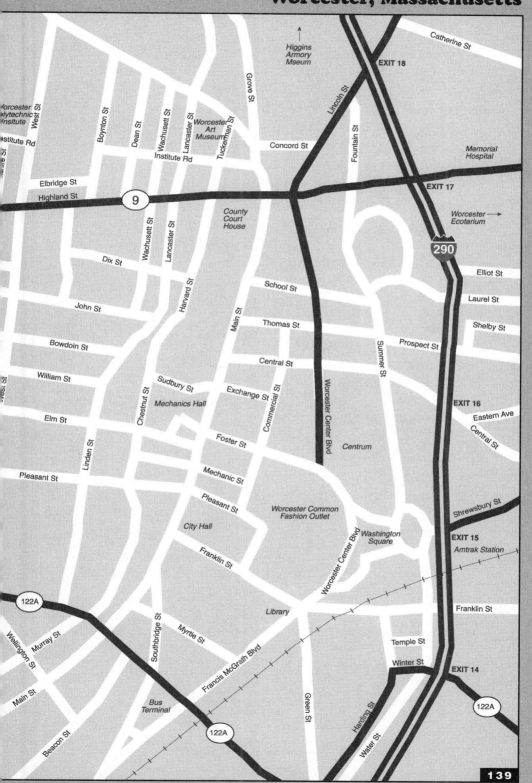

Springfield, Massachusetts

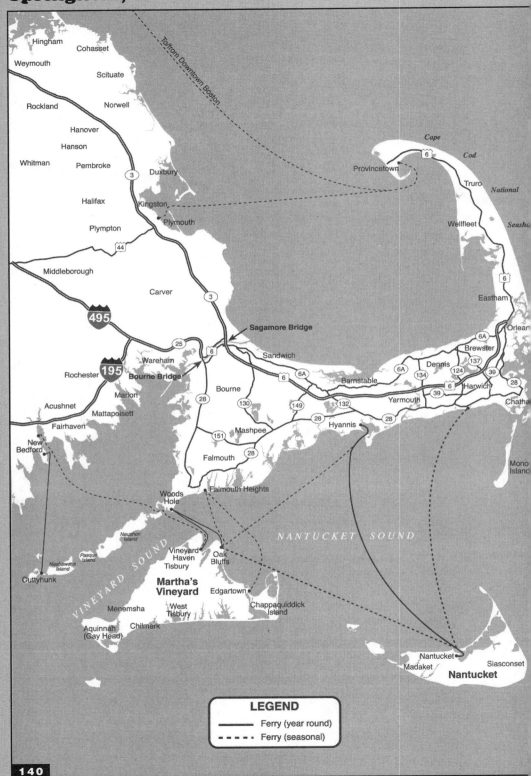

Hingham
Cohasset
Weymouth
Scituate
Rockland
Norwell
Hanover
Hanson
Whitman
Pembroke
Halifax
Plympton
Middleborough
Carver
Duxbury
Kingston
Plymouth
Toll from Downtown Boston
Provincetown
Cape
Cod
Truro
National
Wellfleet
Seasho
44
3
495
25
6
Sagamore Bridge
Sandwich
Eastham
6
Rochester
195
Bourne Bridge
Wareham
Bourne
6A
6
Barnstable
Orlean
6A
Brewster
137
Acushnet
Marion
28
130
149
6A
134
Dennis
124
39
Mattapoisett
Fairhaven
151
Mashpee
132
Yarmouth
39
6
Harwich
28
New
Bedford
Falmouth
28
28
Hyannis
Chatha
Woods
Hole
Falmouth Heights
Naushon
Island
Pasque
Island
Vineyard
Haven
Tisbury
Oak
Bluffs
NANTUCKET SOUND
Mono
Island
Cuttyhunk
Nashawena
Island
VINEYARD SOUND
Martha's
Vineyard
Edgartown
Chappaquiddick
Island
Menemsha
West
Tisbury
Aquinnah
(Gay Head)
Chilmark
Nantucket
Madaket
Siasconset
Nantucket

LEGEND
—— Ferry (year round)
- - - - Ferry (seasonal)

CHAPTER 8

Massachusetts

MASSACHUSETTS PRACTICALLY PULSATES WITH possibilities as it provides a matchless mix of past and present. A Massachusetts vacation allows families to mix learning with pure fun, and at many historic attractions, the line between the two is blurred. Choose this land of patriots, Pilgrims, painters, and presidents—not to mention the Wiggles—as your launching pad for a grand tour of all of New England or as your primary destination.

An Introduction to the Bay State

Massachusetts is truly the heart of New England. It borders every other New England state except for Maine, and even the Maine state line is just a handful of miles away. But geography alone is insufficient to explain the state's vital position. Historically, politically, intellectually, and culturally, Massachusetts has long been at the center of developments not only in the region, but the nation.

Massachusetts, after all, took the lead in forging a separate national identity for the American colonies. From the fiery speeches of the Sons of Liberty at Boston's Faneuil Hall to the Boston Massacre to the Boston Tea Party to the midnight ride of Paul Revere to the Battle of Lexington and Concord that marked the start of war between the colonies and the motherland, Massachusetts ignited the rebellion and bore more than its share of the burden in America's fight for independence.

Some of the nation's greatest thinkers have called the Bay State home: authors Ralph Waldo Emerson and Henry David Thoreau, social reformers Dorothea Dix who crusaded on behalf of the mentally ill and Horace Mann who lobbied for universal education, beat generation spokesman Jack Kerouac, and popular illustrator Norman Rockwell, who captured enduring images of American life, plus several members of the Adams and Kennedy families who rose to positions of political prominence.

≡FAST FACT

April 19 is the anniversary of the outbreak of the American Revolution at Lexington and Concord. Maine and Massachusetts honor that event with a holiday on the third Monday in April. Patriots' Day is also the day of the annual Boston Marathon (*www.bostonmarathon.org*).

Travelers will find their own heartbeats quickening as they discover a multitude of historic sites, museums, performing arts centers, scenic byways, beaches, and theme parks. Boston is not only the state capital but also New England's major metropolitan area. It boasts some of the country's finest cultural institutions, museums, and professional sports arenas and more than 100 colleges and universities that keep Massachusetts at the forefront of intellectual debate and scientific discovery. North of Boston, Cape Ann's beaches and eclectic towns and the witchcraft lore of Salem are popular with visitors. The Merrimack Valley is home to the battlefields of Lexington and Concord and the former residences of Massachusetts literary legends. South of Boston, you can explore the state's whaling past and the lives of its first European settlers, the Pilgrims. Cape Cod, Nantucket, and Martha's Vineyard have a flavor all their own; they're the perfect ocean-side antidote to Boston's urban bustle. In the western part of the state, you'll find Springfield, the birthplace of basketball and Dr. Seuss, and college towns such as Amherst and Northampton. The Berkshire Hills are a summer haven for arts lovers, a photo-perfect paradise in autumn, and a winter wonderland for skiers.

When to Visit

The moderate climate makes Massachusetts a draw to tourists in each of its four distinct seasons. Although Chicago is known as the "Windy City," Boston is actually America's windiest major city. The wind chill factor can make temperatures feel substantially colder. In contrast, Cape Cod and the Islands get little snow and remain warmer even during the winter months. Summer is the high season on the Cape and along the North Shore; accommodations are harder to come by and pricier. The Berkshires are at their best during summer's arts season or in winter if you're a skier. Because Boston is primarily a walking city, late spring and fall are the most comfortable times to visit and to see the sights. Autumn can be breathtaking statewide—there are plenty of opportunities for scenic driving.

Getting There and Getting Around

Massachusetts has the region's most extensive transportation infrastructure, including a busy international airport, a cruise port that welcomes ships from eleven major cruise lines, and New England's only subway system—the "T" in Boston. If your primary destination is the capital city, it's actually a good idea to leave your car at home. If you plan to visit other parts of the state, such as the Berkshires or Cape Cod, renting a car or driving your own vehicle is often the best and sometimes the only option.

Logan International Airport (BOS)

Logan International Airport (617-561-1800 or 800-23-LOGAN, *www.massport.com/logan*) is located in East Boston. The nation's twentieth busiest airport, it serves more than 27 million passengers each year. This 2,400-acre transportation center is New England's largest. More than 25 domestic and international airlines fly into and out of Logan.

To reach Logan from points west and south, follow the Massachusetts Turnpike (I-90 East) through the Ted Williams Tunnel to exit 26. From the north, follow Route I-93 South to exit 24B for the Callahan Tunnel and Route 1A North toward Logan.

TRAVEL TIP

Looking for something fun to do while you wait for your flight? Logan has two Kidport (*www.massport.com/logan/insid_kidpo.html*) play areas featuring airplane and control-tower climbing structures, baggage-claim slides, hands-on activities, and more. One is located near Gate A18 in terminal A; the other is on the departure level of terminal C.

Airport Connections

The Logan Shuttle offers complimentary transportation between airport terminals, to the airport's subway station on the MBTA Blue Line, and to the Water Transportation Terminal. Boat service to downtown Boston is provided by the MBTA Harbor Express (617-222-6999, *www.harborexpress.com*), Boston Harbor Water Taxi (617-593-9168), City Water Taxi (617-422-0392, *www.citywatertaxi.com*), and the Rowes Wharf Water Transporter (617-406-8584, *www.roweswharfwatertransport.com*). The MBTA Harbor Express also provides boat service to Quincy and Hull on the South Shore.

The MBTA's Silver Line Rapid Transit Bus Service connects Logan Airport with Boston's South Station in the Financial District, where other bus and train connections can be made. Logan Express (800-23-LOGAN) has bus stations with secure parking in Braintree to the south, Framingham to the west, and Peabody and Woburn to the north, from which buses depart regularly for the airline terminals. Logan Direct (508-746-0378, *www.p-b.com*) offers bus connections between the airport and the southern Massachusetts towns of Rockland, Plymouth, Sagamore, Barnstable, and Hyannis.

Shared van transportation between Logan Airport and destinations within the Greater Boston area and beyond is provided by a number of companies including Ace American (800-517-2281), City Transportation (617-561-9000), Easy Transportation (617-869-7760, *www.easytransportationinc.com*), Flight Line (800-245-2525, *www .flightlineinc.com*), JC Transportation (800-517-2281, *www.jctranspor tationshuttle.com*), Knights Airport Limousine Service (800-822-5456, *www.knightsairportlimo.com*), Logan/Boston Hotel Shuttle (617-331-8388), Star Shuttle (617-230-6005 or 877-970-7827, *www.starshut tleboston.com*), Thomas Transportation Services (603-352-5550 or 800-526-8143, *www.thomastransportation.com*), Worcester Airport Limousine (800-660-0992, *www.wlimo.com*), and Zebra Airport Shuttle (508-481-7300 or 800-242-0064, *www.zebrashuttle.com*). Call ahead for pricing and schedule information. Some services require twenty-four-hour advance reservations.

Taxi service is also readily available day and night to transport you from Logan to your destination. All drop-off points within a twelve-mile radius of downtown Boston are charged at a metered rate. Beyond the twelve-mile radius, a flat fee is assessed. Passengers are responsible for tunnel tolls and a $2 airport fee. Credit-card taxis are available on request. For sample fares, see Massport's Logan Airport Web site, *www.massport.com/logan/getti_typeo_taxis.html*.

Eight rental car companies operate at or near Logan International Airport: Alamo (800-327-9633, *www.goalamo.com*), Avis (800-831-2847, *www.avis.com*), Budget (800-527-7000, *www.budget.com*), Dollar (800-800-4000, *www.dollar.com*), Enterprise (800-325-8007, *www.enterprise.com*), Hertz (800-654-3131, *www.hertz.com*), National (800-227-7368, *www.nationalcar.com*), and Thrifty (800-367-2277, *www.thrifty.com*).

Trains and Buses

Amtrak (800-872-7245, *www.amtrak.com*) operates regional and high-speed Acela trains connecting Washington, D.C., Philadelphia,

New York's Penn Station, and New Haven, Connecticut, with Boston's Back Bay, Westwood, North, and South Stations. Amtrak also has routes that serve Massachusetts stations in Amherst, Framingham, Haverhill, Pittsfield, Springfield, Worcester, and Woburn.

≡ FAST FACT

If you're willing to sacrifice comfort for cost savings, you can travel between New York City and Boston for just $15. Two Chinese bus companies—Fung Wah Bus (617-345-8000 or 212-925-8889, *www.fungwahbus.com*) and Lucky Star Bus (617-426-8801, *www.luckystarbus.com*)—offer daily connections between New York's Chinatown and Boston's South Station.

Boston has bus terminals at South Station (Summer Street and Atlantic Avenue) and Back Bay Station (145 Dartmouth Street). Interstate bus companies that carry passengers to Boston include Greyhound Lines (617-526-1800 or 800-231-2222, *www.greyhound.com*), Peter Pan Bus Lines (800-343-9999, *www.peterpanbus.com*), and Concord Trailways (617-426-8080 or 800-639-3317, *www.concordtrail ways.com*).

The T—The Mass Transit System of Eastern Massachusetts

Driving in Boston is notoriously tricky. Even though the Central Artery/Tunnel Project, more commonly known as the "Big Dig," which caused additional detours and confusion for more than a decade, is now essentially complete, out-of-towners often still find it difficult to navigate the one-way streets and crowded highways. If you must drive in Boston, verify directions with someone at your destination shortly before your departure. You may also want to check the Massachusetts Turnpike Authority's Web site (*www.masspike .com*) for updates on road construction in the Boston area that may affect traffic patterns. Parking is expensive in Boston, too—you'll pay $25 to $30 or more per day.

The good news is that even before Boston gave birth to the notion that the American colonies should be a free and independent nation, it had already originated another modern concept we take very much for granted today—mass transit. In 1631, Thomas Williams began operating ferry service from Chelsea to Charlestown and on to Boston. In 1897, the nation's first subway line connected Boston's Park and Boylston Streets. Today, more than one million one-way passenger trips are taken each weekday on the subway, bus, water ferry, and commuter rail systems operated by the Massachusetts Bay Transportation Authority (MBTA). Their service connects seventy-eight communities in the Greater Boston area, and commuter rail and interdistrict bus routes branch out to an additional sixty-four communities. The system encompasses a total of 181 routes and 252 stations. Stations and stops are marked with a black T on a white circle, thus, the transportation system's nickname—the T.

TRAVEL TIP

Up to two children ages eleven and under can ride Boston's subway free when accompanied by a paying adult. Substantially discounted T-fares are also available for senior riders, who must first obtain a Senior ID by visiting the Senior & Access Pass Office at Back Bay Station or the Senior/T.A.P. ID Center at Downtown Crossing Station weekdays between 8:30 A.M. and 5:00 P.M.

Boston's mass transit system is known for being efficient, safe, and clean, and it provides visitors with an easy means of getting around the city. Travelers can purchase one-way fares or day or week passes valid for unlimited travel on the subway, local buses, and the inner harbor ferry.

MBTA maps are posted at all stations and may be viewed online at *www.mbta.com*. Route and schedule information is also available by calling the MBTA Traveler's Information Center (617-222-3200 or 800-392-6100) or by visiting the MBTA Information Booth located at Park Street station. There's also a handy online Trip Planner to help you navigate between city landmarks or addresses using public transit at *www.mbta.com/rider_tools/trip_planner*.

≡FAST FACT

Plan ahead and save time and money by ordering a plastic CharlieCard at *http://commerce.mbta.com*. Available precharged with $5, $10, or $20, the CharlieCard is the most affordable option for subway and bus riders. CharlieCards may be reloaded at more than 500 in-station fare-vending machines and at retail sales locations in Boston. You will need to purchase a card for each member of your family over the age of eleven.

There is no subway service between about 1 A.M. and 5 A.M. Ferries stop running even earlier. If you plan to stay out late, have an alternate means of transportation in mind.

Getting Around by Car

The 138-mile Massachusetts Turnpike (617-248-2800, *www .masspike.com*), I-90, runs the east-west length of the state, connecting West Stockbridge near the New York State line with Logan Airport in East Boston. You'll speed your trip along this toll road substantially by using the Turnpike Authority's FAST LANE system. You can apply to receive a FAST LANE electronic transponder online at *www.masspike .com/travel/fastlane/fastlane_signup.html*. If you return your transponder in good condition within ninety days, you will receive a full refund of the transponder fee and any money that remains in your account.

FAST LANE can also be used to pay tolls electronically on the Maine Turnpike and at the Hampton (I-95), Hooksett (I-93), and Bedford (F.E. Everett Turnpike) toll plazas in New Hampshire. FAST LANE is compatible with E-ZPass, so it is also accepted on E-ZPass–enabled toll roads in other states. Likewise, your E-ZPass transponder can be used in Massachusetts, New Hampshire, and Maine.

The Massachusetts Turnpike intersects with major north-south highways, including I-91 in Springfield, I-290 in Worcester, I-495 (encircles Boston and leads to points north and south including Cape Cod), I-95 (the East Coast's major highway linking Maine's Canadian border with Miami, Florida), and I-93 (leads north into New Hampshire).

Getting to Cape Cod and the Islands

A bit of advance planning will ensure your travels go smoothly if your destination is Cape Cod or the islands of Martha's Vineyard or Nantucket.

Getting to Cape Cod

To reach Cape Cod, you must cross the Cape Cod Canal via the Bourne or Sagamore bridges. From the bridges, Provincetown at the Cape's tip is about seventy miles. Traffic crossing the bridges can back up significantly in the summer, particularly on Fridays if you're trying to get to the Cape, and on Sundays if you are departing. The $59 million "rotary flyover" project, completed in 2007, is expected to relieve some of this congestion by eliminating the Sagamore Rotary and connecting Route 3 directly to the Sagamore Bridge.

 TRAVEL TIP

Want to find ways to get around Cape Cod and the Islands without a car? Call toll free, 888-33-CAPECOD, to request your free Smart Guide to car-free travel choices, or visit *www .smartguide.org* to learn about options for reaching Cape destinations by plane, ferry, bus, or bicycle.

During the summer, Boston Harbor Cruises (617-227-4321, *www .bostonharborcruises.com*) operates a high-speed ferry that connects Boston with Provincetown.

You can fly to the Barnstable Municipal Airport in Hyannis from Nantucket, Boston, Providence, and LaGuardia in New York. Hyannis is a destination for Cape Air (508-771-6944 or 800-352-0714, *www .flycapeair.com*), Colgan Air/US Airways Express (703-368-8880, *www.colganair.com*), and Nantucket Airlines (508-228-6234 or 800-635-8787, *www.nantucketairlines.com*).

Getting to Martha's Vineyard

Martha's Vineyard is situated seven miles off the coast of Cape Cod. The Steamship Authority (508-477-8600 or 508-693-9130, *www.steamshipauthority.com*) provides regularly scheduled, year-round ferry service to the island from Woods Hole. The Steamship Authority's ferry is the only means of transporting a car to Martha's Vineyard. Vehicle reservations are absolutely required in the summer and highly recommended at other times of the year. If your stay on Martha's Vineyard will be three days or fewer, leaving your car behind may be your best bet. Take advantage of other transportation options including public shuttle buses, taxis, rental cars, mopeds, and bicycles.

New England Fast Ferry Co. (49 State Pier, New Bedford, 866-683-3779, *www.mvexpressferry.com*) offers year-round passenger service between New Bedford and Martha's Vineyard on a high-speed catamaran that makes the trip in just under one hour. Other passenger ferry service is provided seasonally: Falmouth Ferry Service (508-548-9400, *www.falmouthferry.com*) transports passengers from Falmouth to Edgartown; the *Island Queen* (508-548-4800, *www.islandqueen .com*) will whisk you from Falmouth Harbor to Oak Bluffs in thirty-five minutes; Hy-Line Cruises (508-778-2600 or 800-492-8082, *www .hy-linecruises.com*) connects Hyannis and Oak Bluffs; Viking Fleet Interstate Fast Ferry (631-668-5700, *www.vikingfleet.com*) departs from Montauk, New York, for Oak Bluffs; Vineyard Fast Ferry (401-295-4040, *www.vineyardfastferry.com*) operates a ferry from Quonset

Point, Rhode Island, to Oak Bluffs that makes the crossing in ninety minutes.

Martha's Vineyard can also be reached by air. Cape Air (508-771-6944 or 800-352-0714, *www.flycapeair.com*) offers flights to the island from Boston, New Bedford, Hyannis, Nantucket, and Providence, Rhode Island.

If you wish to reach the island via your own boat, contact the harbormaster in Edgartown (508-627-4746), Menemsha (508-645-2846), Oak Bluffs (508-693-9644), or Vineyard Haven (508-696-4249).

Getting to Nantucket

The Steamship Authority (508-477-8600 or 508-693-9130, *www.steamshipauthority.com*) provides regular, year-round ferry service to Nantucket from South Street Dock in Hyannis, and, as with Martha's Vineyard, this is your only option if you're planning to take a car to the island. Reserve your vehicle's spot early if you're traveling during the summer months. The car ferry makes the crossing to Nantucket in two hours and fifteen minutes. From mid-May through mid-October, the Steamship Authority also offers a high-speed, passengers-only ferry that makes the trip from Hyannis to Nantucket in just one hour.

Passenger ferry service to Nantucket is also provided year-round by Hy-Line Cruises (508-778-2600 or 800-492-8082, *www.hy-linecruises.com*), departing from the Ocean Street dock in Hyannis. Freedom Cruise Line (508-432-8999, *www.nantucketislandferry.com*) offers seasonal passenger crossings between Harwich Port and Nantucket; their high-speed ferries make the trip in one hour and fifteen minutes, and free parking is available for day-trippers.

If you would like to visit both islands, Hy-Line Cruises (508-778-2600 or 800-492-8082, *www.hy-linecruises.com*) offers "Around the Sound" one-day trips from Hyannis in the summer months with stops at Nantucket and Martha's Vineyard.

Nantucket Memorial Airport (*www.nantucketairport.com*) is served by Cape Air (508-771-6944 or 800-352-0714, *www.flycapeair.com*), Colgan Air / US Airways Express (703-368-8880, *www.colganair.com*), Continental (800-525-0280, *www.continental.com*),

Island Airlines (508-228-7575 or 800-248-7779, *www.islandair.net*), Jet-Blue (800-538-2583, *www.jetblue.com*), and Nantucket Airlines (508-228-6234 or 800-635-8787, *www.nantucketairlines.com*).

Must-See Activities and Attractions

From Boston to the Berkshires, from Cape Ann to Cape Cod, there are many must-see attractions in the state. Although Massachusetts may appear small on a map, it is actually larger in land area than New Hampshire or Vermont, so you'll need to book accommodations in several Massachusetts destinations if you hope to experience all of the state's highlights.

Boston's Museums

The Boston metropolitan area is home to more than fifty museums for people of all ages, including the Boston Children's Museum (300 Congress Street, 617-426-8855, *www.bostonchildrensmuseum .org*), which underwent a major expansion and renovation in 2007. Whether you're traveling with avid artists or budding scientists, curious naturalists or history buffs, Boston is teeming with learning experiences waiting to be discovered.

Cape Cod and the Islands

Cape Cod juts out from Massachusetts, extending seventy miles into the Atlantic Ocean. The Cape and islands of Nantucket and Martha's Vineyard offer miles of glorious beaches; quaint villages; art galleries; outdoor recreation including biking, hiking, and golf; and attractions that are a mix of past and present.

The Freedom Trail

⌨Information booth on Boston Common at Tremont Street
☎617-357-8300
✑*www.thefreedomtrail.org*

One of the best ways to see Boston's major historic landmarks is to follow the two and one-half mile Freedom Trail. It's easy to follow the red line that has been painted or bricked to permanently mark the route, and you'll find each of the sixteen stops along the trail marked with a sign. Boston Common, your best starting point, is the oldest public park in the United States.

Minute Man National Historical Park
⌨174 Liberty Street, Concord
✆978-369-6993
✎*www.nps.gov/mima*

Relive the "shot heard 'round the world" that marked the beginning of the American Revolution when fighting broke out between the British and the American colonists at the Battle of Lexington and Concord. This 900-acre National Historic Site encompasses significant structures and landscapes associated with the Revolution's opening battles, plus original segments of the Battle Road traveled by the minutemen on April 19, 1775. Also within the park, you'll find the Hartwell Tavern, a restored eighteenth-century home and tavern where costumed park rangers demonstrate musket firing and talk about America's first soldiers, and the Wayside, home at different times to noted American authors Louisa May Alcott, Nathaniel Hawthorne, and Margaret Sidney.

The Mohawk Trail
⌨Route 2
✆413-743-8127
✎*www.mohawktrail.com*

There are more than 100 attractions along this 63-mile stretch of highway that begins at the Massachusetts–New York border. A particularly scenic drive in autumn, Route 2, better known as the Mohawk Trail, is also lined with country inns, public and private camping areas, and quaint shops. This is also a spectacular region for winter skiing and summer whitewater rafting adventures.

Naismith Memorial Basketball Hall of Fame

1150 West Columbus Avenue, Springfield

413-781-6500

www.hoophall.com

Did you know that Springfield, Massachusetts, is the birthplace of basketball? It's also home to the Naismith Memorial Basketball Hall of Fame, where you can pay tribute to the game's great players, teams, and coaches and even get into the game with interactive exhibits.

New Bedford Whaling Museum and Battleship Cove

New Bedford Whaling Museum

18 Johnny Cake Hill, New Bedford

508-997-0046

www.whalingmuseum.org

Climb aboard a full-size replica of a whaling ship's forecastle, marvel at a 66-foot blue whale skeleton, and view the largest collection of artifacts and art devoted to America's whaling history at the New Bedford Whaling Museum.

Battleship Cove

Five Water Street, Fall River

508-678-1100

www.battleshipcove.org

In nearby Fall River, board a very different kind of ship—the battleship *Massachusetts* at Battleship Cove, which is also home to the destroyer *Joseph P. Kennedy, Jr.* and the submarine *Lionfish*.

Old Sturbridge Village

1 Old Sturbridge Village Road, Sturbridge

508-347-3362 or 800-SEE-1830

www.osv.org

One of the area's leading attractions, this village recreates life in New England in the early 1800s. There are more than forty period buildings to explore at this 200-acre site, and costumed interpreters demonstrate spinning, weaving, blacksmithing, period cooking, and more as they interact with visitors and tell of their lives. There is also a working historical farm. Old Sturbridge Village hosts special events throughout the year; attend a gardening workshop, a re-creation of a traditional muster day, or special Christmas holiday celebrations.

Plimoth Plantation

137 Warren Avenue, Plymouth

508-746-1622

www.plimoth.org

A visit to the land of Pilgrims and Promise should include a stop at Plimoth Plantation, the living history museum that re-creates the lives of New England's first English settlers and their Native American friends and neighbors. While you're in Plymouth, you'll also want to tour the *Mayflower II*, a replica of the famous ship that carried the Pilgrims to New England's shores, and see Plymouth Rock—unimpressive in size but nostalgia-inspiring nonetheless. Both are located on the waterfront in Plymouth.

≡FAST FACT

Nearly one million people visit Plymouth Rock at Pilgrim Memorial State Park (Water Street, Plymouth, 508-866-2580, *www.mass.gov/dcr/parks/southeast/plgm.htm*) each year. Since the earliest efforts to preserve the symbolic rock began in 1774, it has been dropped a few times and vandalized by tourists. The rock you'll see today has been sheltered since 1921 within a canopy designed by famed architects McKim, Mead, and White.

Salem

Forever branded by the hysteria in 1692 that led to the infamous witchcraft trials, Salem takes advantage of its wicked past, offering up its own trail of attractions that not only tell the story for which the town is best known but also celebrate the city's seafaring heritage and its most notable former resident, author Nathaniel Hawthorne. Must-see stops include the Salem Witch Museum (Washington Square North, 978-744-1692, *www.salemwitchmuseum.com*), where you'll hear and see a compelling retelling of the accusations, hysteria, trials, and executions of 1692 through life-size dioramas; the Witch Dungeon Museum (16 Lynde Street, 978-741-7770, *www.witchdungeon.com*), where actors re-create the trials based on transcripts; the Salem Wax Museum of Witches and Seafarers (288 Derby Street, 800-298-2929, *www .salemwaxmuseum.com*), where characters from Salem's past are re-created in wax; and the House of the Seven Gables (115 Derby Street, 978-744-0991, *www.7gables.org*), the inspiration for Hawthorne's novel of the same name. While appropriate for older children, keep in mind that younger children may find the witch attractions frightening.

Six Flags New England

⌨ 1623 Main Street / Route 159, Agawam

✆ 413-786-9300

✐ *www.sixflags.com/parks/newengland*

You can bet your kids will be pleased if you include a stop at the region's premier amusement park. With ten phenomenal roller coasters, the Hurricane Harbor water park, and a full slate of shows and entertainment, the park caters to visitors of all ages. In 2007, Six Flags even debuted a Wiggles World–themed section of the park with rides and a restaurant that appeal to the youngest tots.

Family Fun Plans

Some families want to spend a lazy week by the shore. Others want to pound the pavement and pack as much sightseeing as they can into a weekend in Boston. You'll need to evaluate your priorities and make some tough decisions as you design a Massachusetts itinerary that's right for your family. These Family Fun Plans are just a sample of some of the myriad ways you can make the most of a Massachusetts vacation.

A Long Fall Weekend in Western Massachusetts

If you have preschool-age children, or if your kids have school holidays in the fall that allow you to plan a long weekend away, you can experience the most colorful season and enjoy autumn events while avoiding the summer crowds at Six Flags. Look for hotels in the Springfield area if you're planning to follow this itinerary, and make reservations in advance, as you'll be competing with leaf peepers for lodging.

Day One: Spend the morning exploring the eclectic shops in Northampton. You'll find plenty of great choices for lunchtime dining in this famously liberal college town. In the afternoon, squeeze in a visit to the Naismith Memorial Basketball Hall of Fame (1150 West Columbus Avenue, Springfield, 413-781-6500, *www.hoophall.com*), where kids can burn off energy playing a virtual game of one-on-one against NBA stars or practicing their shooting and passing at Center Court. Not sports fans? Spend the afternoon at the scent-sational Yankee Candle Village (Route 5 and 10 North, South Deerfield, 413-665-2929 or 877-636-7707, *www.yankeecandle.com*), the largest candle store in the world, where you can pick up autumn-scented souvenirs. Cinnamon stick, spiced pumpkin, harvest, fireside, and cranberry chutney are just some of the scents that will remind you of your stay in Massachusetts.

Day Two: Six Flags New England (1623 Main Street/Route 159, Agawam, 413-786-9300, *www.sixflags.com/parks/newengland*) not only stays open on fall weekends, it adds to the fun each October with Fright Fest happenings that are tame enough for small kids by day and decidedly scary after dark. You could easily spend an entire day at the park. Alternatively, if you plan your visit for mid- to late-September, you may want to check out the Eastern States Exposition (1305 Memorial Avenue/Route 147, West Springfield, 413-737-2443, *www.thebige.com*) for all or part of the day. Better known as "The Big E," this is New England's largest fair featuring midway rides, farm animals, headline entertainers, and buildings showcasing the products of all six New England states.

Day Three: End your long weekend with a leisurely drive along the scenic, 63-mile Mohawk Trail. Stop often to visit such engaging sights as the Bridge of Flowers in Shelburne Falls and the Natural Bridge in North Adams—they're even more spectacular against a backdrop of fall colors.

A Five-Day Summer Escape to the Cape

Cape Cod seems custom-made for family summer vacations. Here's a five-day plan for you to follow; feel free to tack on days or even weeks if you can, and spend the extra time savoring salty breezes, reading good books at the beach, munching on fried clams, and exploring the Cape's charming communities. Keep in mind that by starting your vacation on a weekday, you can avoid some of the Cape's worst traffic headaches.

Day One: Travel to Cape Cod, find your accommodations, and then find a beach. With more than 550 miles of coastline and literally dozens of beaches, you won't have to venture far from your home base to dip your toes in the water and walk along the sand. Get to bed early and rest up for an active second day.

Day Two: Journey to Provincetown at the far tip of the Outer Cape. Here, your choice of two adventures awaits. Book passage with Dolphin Fleet of Provincetown (MacMillan Pier, Provincetown, 508-240-3636 or 800-826-9300, *www.whalewatch.com*) for an unforgettable whale-watching excursion, or make reservations for an exhilarating drive along the Cape's legendary dunes with Art's Dune Tours (4 Standish Street, 508-487-1950, *www.artsdunetours.com*). While you're in Provincetown, try to squeeze in a climb to the top of the Pilgrim Monument (One High Pole Hill Road, 508-487-1310, *www .pilgrim-monument.org*).

Day Three: America has only ten national seashores, and Cape Cod claims the first and one of the finest. Start your morning at the Cape Cod National Seashore's Salt Pond Visitor Center (Route 6, Eastham, 508-255-3421, *www.nps.gov/caco*), where you can watch a short orientation film and learn about all your options for spending the day within this 44,600-acre coastal habitat, from swimming, hiking, and biking to photographing lighthouses or participating in ranger-led programs.

Day Four: Chatham is one of the Cape's cutest towns. It's also the departure point for the seal tours offered by Chatham Water Tours (508-432-5895, *www.chathamwatertours.net*); even little kids will enjoy these boat trips, which afford up-close views of the Cape's playful gray and harbor seals on Monomoy Island. Make reservations for a morning excursion, and then return to Chatham for lunch and a bit of shopping in the afternoon.

Day Five: Leaving Cape Cod is never easy. If you have time to make one last stop, visit the Heritage Museums & Gardens (67 Grove Street, Sandwich, 508-888-3300, *www.heritagemuseumsandgardens .org*), home to everything from a round barn filled with antique automobiles to lush gardens to a hand-carved antique carousel.

A Whirlwind Week in Massachusetts

If you like to cram as much as possible into a week's vacation, Massachusetts is a great destination.

Day One: Start your trip with a day at Old Sturbridge Village (1 Old Sturbridge Village Road, Sturbridge, 508-347-3362 or 800-SEE-1830, *www.osv.org*), where you can immerse yourself in the happenings of an early New England community. In the evening, dine on traditional Yankee fare at the Publick House (277 Main Street/Route 131, Sturbridge, 508-347-3313 or 800-PUBLICK, *www.publickhouse.com*).

Day Two: Head east to Boston, "the Hub of the Universe." Get acquainted with the city by taking in the view from the Skywalk Observatory on the fiftieth floor of the Prudential Center (800 Boylston Street, 617-859-0648, *www.prudentialcenter.com/play/skywalk.html*). In the afternoon, explore the shops at Faneuil Hall Marketplace (off State Street, 617-523-1300, *www.faneuilhallmarketplace.com*), also known as Quincy Market, or tour the New England Aquarium (Central Wharf, 617-973-5200, *www.neaq.org*). Dine at the Union Oyster House (41 Union Street, 617-227-2750, *www.unionoysterhouse.com*), America's oldest continuously operating restaurant; it dates to 1826.

Day Three: Wake up a bit early and walk Boston's Freedom Trail. Take a full, leisurely day exploring Boston's landmarks along the trail, or maintain a brisker pace and leave time in the afternoon to visit the Museum of Science (Science Park, 617-723-2500, *www .mos.org*) or one of Boston's other fine museums. If your legs are tired, you'll appreciate the opportunity to sit back and watch an IMAX film at the Museum of Science.

Day Four: Your week is nearly half over. Head north from Boston for a day trip to Salem. Visit the Salem Witch Museum (Washington Square, 978-744-1692, *www.salemwitchmuseum.com*), the Witch Dungeon Museum (16 Lynde Street, 508-741-3570, *www.witchdungeon .com*), the House of the Seven Gables (115 Derby Street, 978-744-0991, *www.7gables.org*), and other sights along the Heritage Trail. The witch attractions may frighten younger children. Dine overlooking Salem Harbor on slow-roasted prime rib at Victoria Station (Pickering Wharf, 978-745-3400, *www.victoriastationinc.com*).

Day Five: Drive south from Boston to New Bedford and Fall River, where you can board a whaling ship at the New Bedford Whaling Museum (18 Johnny Cake Hill, New Bedford, 508-997-0046, *www .whalingmuseum.org*) and stroll the decks of a destroyer at Battleship Cove (Five Water Street, Fall River, 508-678-1100, *www.battleshipcove. org*).

Day Six: Head for Cape Cod and a relaxing day of biking or basking on the beach. Hyannis is a good central base to enjoy a taste of the Cape.

Day Seven: If you don't need to rush home, drive to the Outer Cape for a visit to the Cape Cod National Seashore, which extends for 40 miles from Chatham to Provincetown, or book a morning boat trip with Chatham Water Tours (508-432-5895, *www.chathamwatertours.net*) for a memorable chance to mingle with the seals that live off the coast.

Find a unique piece for your home or a one-of-a-kind gift at Holsten Galleries (Elm Street, Stockbridge, 413-298-3044), which represents dozens of contemporary glass sculptors. While you're in Stockbridge and thinking about sprucing up your décor, stop into the headquarters of mail-order success story Country Curtains on Main Street (413-298-5565), founded in 1956.

CHAPTER 9

New England's Hub: Boston and Cambridge

BOSTON BECKONS TO FAMILIES who want to immerse themselves in history while enjoying the conveniences and excitement of a vibrant metropolitan area. The capital city blends all the benefits of a modern urban center with a pervasive sense of the past. Boston is architecturally intriguing, culturally rich, and historically unequaled. It's also, quite simply, a lot of fun.

An Introduction to Boston

March 5, 1770—The Boston Massacre leaves five residents dead at the hands of British troops. December 16, 1773—Colonists disguised as Mohawks clamber aboard British ships and dump 342 chests of tea into Boston Harbor. June 16, 1775—Before the Battle of Bunker Hill, Colonel Prescott gives American militiamen the command, "Don't fire until you see the whites of their eyes."

Legendary Boston lives in the pages of history books, but the string of dates and events familiar to practically every American is transformed from tedious text to vivid reality when you set foot in the nation's most historic and fascinating city. You can practically hear Paul Revere's horse galloping and his pulse pounding as you gaze up at the tower of the Old North Church, where the silversmith's eyes searched to see . . . one if by land, and two if by sea. The high drama of the Boston Tea Party will be forever etched in your mind when you participate in the annual December re-enactment.

Each year Boston and nearby Cambridge (home to America's first institution of higher learning, Harvard University) welcome hundreds of thousands of students to the area's more than 100 colleges and universities, giving the city and its surrounding neighborhoods a youthful energy. While not as frenetic as New York, Boston has a lively tempo that will propel you as you walk the Freedom Trail, slurp chowder from a bread bowl, root for the Red Sox, shop for antiques on Beacon Hill, ice-skate in the winter, or laze aboard a swan boat in the summer in Boston Public Garden. The possibilities are endless, so be prepared to make tough choices once you've made the first easy choice to visit Boston.

What to See and Do

It is impossible to describe the many things to do and see in Boston and Cambridge. Among these highlights, you'll discover some of the city's most family-friendly attractions and activities. The Greater Boston Convention & Visitors Bureau Web site (*www.bostonusa.com*), is a good source for information on seasonal events that coincide with your visit.

City Tours

For first-time visitors to Boston, a tour that provides an overview of the city's sights is a must. If you are traveling with older children, a walk along the Freedom Trail is the best way to experience Boston. If you are traveling with younger kids or have only a short time, several tour operators that will help you see the city's landmarks efficiently. Already familiar with Boston? Consider one of the specialty tours that will allow you to experience a unique aspect of the city.

The Black Heritage Trail
14 Beacon Street
617-725-0022 or 617-742-5415
www.afroammuseum.org/trail.htm or *www.nps.gov/boaf*
For a look at the history and life of Boston's nineteenth-century African-American community, walk the Black Heritage Trail, which features fourteen sites primarily in the Beacon Hill area. You can

venture inside two of the sites, the African Meeting House and the Abiel Smith School. For a self-guided walking tour map and guide, contact the Museum of African American History. The National Park Service offers free guided trail walks daily from Memorial Day weekend through Labor Day weekend.

Boston By Foot

⌨77 North Washington Street
📞617-367-2345
✐*www.bostonbyfoot.com*

The city's oldest walking-tour company offers a variety of tours May through October including Boston By Little Feet, designed to accommodate young walkers, and Boston Underfoot, a look at Boston's subways, Big Dig, sewers, and other subterranean engineering feats. Reservations are not required.

TRAVEL TIP

Want to sightsee outside Boston without a car? Brush Hill Tours (781-986-6100 or 800-343-1328, *www.beantowntrolley* *.com*) offers fall foliage, Newport, Plymouth, Salem, Cape Cod, and other bus tours with pickups from Boston and suburban hotels. They also operate the Beantown Trolley, which offers unlimited hop-on, hop-off service at twenty stops in the city. Trolley tickets include a harbor cruise in season.

Boston Duck Tours

📞617-267-DUCK
✐*www.bostonducktours.com*

If you want to see Boston's sights but aren't sure you have the time or the stamina to do a lot of walking, waddle over to the Prudential Center or the Museum of Science and book yourself on a Duck Tour. You'll tour Boston's roads and waters in a World War II–era amphibious vehicle—a "duck." Your captain will point out famous landmarks as you motor through the streets of Boston and, once you've plunged into the Charles River, he might even let you take the wheel. Duck Tours are available from late March through late November.

The Freedom Trail

⊞Information booth on Boston Common at Tremont Street

☏617-357-8300

✍*www.thefreedomtrail.org*

Each year, about 3 million people follow the red line that links the sixteen most significant sites related to Boston's role in the American Revolution. If this is your first visit to Boston, walking the Freedom Trail is likely one of the first things you'll want to do. The trail can be blitzed through in about an hour if you're in a real hurry and don't plan to actually stop and look at anything. Your best bet, though, is to allow three hours or more to walk the trail at a leisurely pace and see all of its Revolutionary War landmarks.

≡FAST FACT

Seven of the sites along the Freedom Trail are part of the Boston National Historical Park (*www.nps.gov/bost*), and National Park Service rangers conduct free ninety-minute walking tours of the heart of the trail seasonally. Call 617-242-5642 for a schedule, and arrive early at the Boston National Historical Park Visitor Center (15 State Street), as tours are limited to thirty people and offered on a first-come, first-served basis.

While technically you can pick up the trail at any point, the best starting spot is the information booth at Boston Common. Here, you can pick up a map and brochure describing the trail sites. The two and one-half-mile trail is not a loop—it begins at Boston Common and ends in

Charlestown at the Bunker Hill Monument. Admission to the sites along the trail is free with three exceptions: Paul Revere House, Old South Meeting House, and the Old State House. If you'd like to tour the Freedom Trail with a costumed guide, the Freedom Trail Foundation offers ninety-minute "Walk into History" tours daily from April through October; tickets may be purchased at the Boston Common information booth or online.

Old Town Trolley Tours
Ticket booth at Central Wharf and Milk Street
℡800-213-2474
✎*www.trolleytours.com*
Old Town offers hop-on, hop-off service that allows you to see major Freedom Trail sites, the New England Aquarium, Cheers Boston, Chinatown, and other attractions at your own pace. You can board at any stop. Old Town Trolley Tours is also famous for its Boston Chocolate Tours (*www.trolleytours.com/ChocolateTour*) from late January through late April.

Family Amusements
Don't think for a minute that Boston is boring. It's not just a city teeming with museums and historic landmarks, it's a place to see lions, whales, and Swan Boats, too. When you're ready for a taste of adventure, these family attractions await.

Boston Bike Tours
℡617-308-5902
✎*www.bostonbiketours.com*
This tour company offers a number of casually paced, family-friendly guided outings. Bikes, helmets, and water are included in the cost of the tour.

Boston Harbor Cruises Whale Watch
Long Wharf
℡617-227-4321 or ℡877-SEE-WHALE
✎*www.bostonharborcruises.com*
Grab your binoculars and sunscreen and head out to sea from April through October on a memorable three-hour voyage, narrated by

researchers from the Whale Center of New England. Whale sightings are guaranteed; if you don't see whales, you'll receive tickets for a future trip.

Boston Harbor Islands

&617-223-8666

✍*www.nps.gov/boha* or ✍*www.bostonislands.com*

Hadn't thought of Boston as an island getaway? The Boston Harbor Islands, thirty-four islands off the coast of the capital city, were designated a National Park in 1996. Several of the islands are open to the public during the summer months and accessible by ferry from Boston's Long Wharf or South Boston's EDIC Pier. Ferry service is also available from South Shore departure points. Ferries are operated by Harbor Express (617-222-6999, *www.harborexpress.com*). Private boats can also land on some islands. Georges Island, the park system's central point of arrival, is home to Fort Warren, a Civil War landmark. Other islands feature beaches that call to sunbathers, walking trails, birding opportunities, camping facilities, and historic lighthouses. Paved walkways on Georges and Peddocks Islands make these the best choices for families with young children in strollers.

Boston Public Garden

⌖Along Charles Street adjacent to Boston Common

&617-723-8144

✍*www.friendsofthepublicgarden.org*

The Boston Public Garden is America's oldest botanical garden. Images of the pedal-powered Swan Boats (617-522-1966, *www.swanboats.com*) that have occupied the garden's pond since 1877 are some of the city's most enduring. You don't even have to pedal, so sitting back and enjoying a summer day from your swan perch is a fabulously relaxing thing to do after all of the walking and sightseeing that Boston demands. In the winter, the pond is open to ice skaters.

Franklin Park Zoo

⌖One Franklin Park Road, Dorchester

&617-541-LION

✍*www.zoonewengland.com*

Lions, giraffes, and zebras call a seventy-two-acre park in Boston's Emerald Necklace park system "home." Founded in 1913, Franklin Park Zoo is open year-round, although some animals are off view in the winter.

New England Aquarium
⊞Central Wharf
✆617-973-5200
✎*www.neaq.org*

Watch three species of penguins at play in the 150,000-gallon Penguin Pool, see a whale skeleton, participate in hands-on activities at the Curious George Discovery Corner, visit a coral reef without donning scuba gear, see a colossal IMAX movie, and more at this popular family attraction. If you don't want to pay the aquarium's admission price, you can still see the free, outdoor harbor seal exhibit.

Tomb Boston
⊞186 Brookline Avenue
✆617-375-9487
✎*www.5-wits.com*

Located near Fenway Park, Tomb is an interactive adventure that's great for families with teens or tweens. Join a forty-five-minute expedition inside the Pharaoh's lair, where you'll need to work together to solve puzzles . . . or face the consequences.

Museums
Boston is home to museums that rival those found anywhere else in the world. Whatever your interests, you're likely to find a museum you'll want to visit.

Boston Children's Museum
⊞300 Congress Street
✆617-426-8855
✎*www.bostonchildrensmuseum.org*

Founded in 1913 and renovated and expanded in 2007, this museum inspires the imaginations of young visitors through hands-on activities, live performances, and changing exhibits that focus on science, culture, health and fitness, and the arts.

Harvard University Museums
✎*www.harvard.edu/museums*

Harvard University in Cambridge is home to a bevy of museums. Start with the historic university's three art museums (32 Quincy Street, Cambridge, 617-495-9400). The Arthur M. Sackler Museum houses collections of ancient, Asian, Islamic, and later Indian art. Treasures include Chinese jades, bronzes, sculptures, and cave paintings; Korean ceramics; Japanese woodblock prints; Greek and Roman sculpture and vases; and ancient coins. The Busch-Reisinger Museum is the nation's only museum devoted to the arts of Central and Northern Europe, particularly the German-speaking countries. The Fogg Art Museum is Harvard's oldest art museum, focusing on Western art from the Middle Ages to the present. Among the highlights are impressionist and post-impressionist works and the Boston area's most important collection of works by Picasso.

≡FAST FACT

Free campus tours of history-laden Harvard University leave from the Events & Information Center (Holyoke Center Arcade, 1350 Massachusetts Avenue, Cambridge, 617-495-1573, *www.harvard.edu*). From mid-August through late June, tours depart at 10:00 A.M. and 2:00 P.M. Monday through Friday and at 2:00 P.M. on Saturday. From late June through mid-August, tours are available at 10:00 A.M., 11:15 A.M., 2:00 P.M. and 3:15 P.M. Monday through Saturday.

While art museums may not be appropriate for young children, Harvard also has a Museum of Natural History (26 Oxford Street, Cambridge, 617-495-3045), comprised of a Botanical Museum, the

Museum of Comparative Zoology, and the Mineralogical and Geological Museum, where kids will be impressed by everything from the world's only mounted Kronosaurus—a forty-two-foot prehistoric marine reptile—to meteorites that they can touch.

John F. Kennedy Presidential Library & Museum

⌨ Columbia Point

☏ 617-514-1600 or ☏ 866-JFK-1960

✍ *www.jfklibrary.org*

This museum celebrates the legacy and leadership of one of America's most celebrated twentieth-century presidents, Boston native John F. Kennedy. It is an ideal place for teenagers to learn about the 1960s through the words and deeds of America's youngest elected president.

MIT Museum

⌨ 265 Massachusetts Avenue, Cambridge

☏ 617-253-4444

✍ *http://web.mit.edu/museum*

This museum at the Massachusetts Institute of Technology is home to the world's largest collection of holograms and other fascinating exhibits of science, technology, and the potential of the human mind.

 TRAVEL TIP

Save money and see six of Boston's most popular attractions. Boston CityPass is available for purchase at any of the six participating locations: Harvard Museum of Natural History, John F. Kennedy Presidential Library and Museum, Museum of Fine Arts, Museum of Science, the New England Aquarium, and the Skywalk Observatory. The CityPass price comes to about 50 percent of what the combined admission prices would be. For more information, call 888-330-5008 or visit *www.citypass.com*.

Museum of Fine Arts, Boston
465 Huntington Avenue
617-267-9300
www.mfa.org

The Museum of Fine Arts is the largest art repository in New England. Its holdings include the largest collection of works by French impressionist Claude Monet outside France. Intriguing special exhibitions add to the museum's draw. Weekends are the best time for families to visit; look for the Family Place cart, where you can pick up art activities for kids ages four and up to take along on your museum tour.

Museum of Science
Science Park
617-723-2500
www.mos.org

The city's most visited cultural institution has more than 550 interactive exhibits, an IMAX theater, and a planetarium. Each year, the museum also hosts phenomenal traveling and special exhibits that engage visitors of all ages. Allow at least a half-day—a full day if possible—to allow your children to explore everything from the human body to the solar system.

Shopping

Faneuil Hall Marketplace, aka Quincy Market, is probably Boston's best-known shopping area, and its location right on the Freedom Trail makes it a natural stop for visitors. Upscale fashion purveyors dominate the more than seventy-five shops, and you'll also find dozens of carts where you can buy eclectic souvenirs.

When you're ready to get off the trail and do some serious browsing and buying, head for one of the city's other hot shopping spots.

CambridgeSide Galleria
100 Cambridgeside Place
617-621-8666

✑*www.cambridgesidegalleria.com*

This urban waterfront shopping mall is home to more than 120 stores: everything from the Apple Store to Yankee Candle Company. A free shuttle runs every twenty minutes from the MBTA Kendall Square T Stop to the CambridgeSide Galleria.

 JUST FOR PARENTS

Charles Street on Beacon Hill is the city's premier hunting ground for antiques. Among the more than forty antique shops here is the Boston Antique Co-op (119 Charles Street, 617-227-9811, *www.bostonantiqueco-op.com*), which sells estate antiques of all sorts.

Copley Place
🖳2 Copley Place
📞617-369-5000
✑*www.shopcopleyplace.com*

This shopping mall in the Back Bay has more than 100 stores including glamour leaders such as Neiman Marcus, Gucci, and Tiffany & Co.

Filene's Basement
🖳426 Washington Street
📞617-348-7848
✑*www.filenesbasement.com*

If you're a bargain stalker, you won't want to miss the original Filene's Basement at the Downtown Crossing. Nearly a century ago, Edward A. Filene devised a clever scheme to deal with unsold merchandise from his father's department store: He moved it to the basement and automatically discounted it every few weeks until it sold. Today, the Basement is often mobbed with shoppers, and yes, the store admits that especially good deals have ignited tugs of war.

Newbury Street

✐*www.newbury-st.com*

Along the Back Bay neighborhood's Newbury Street, which stretches from the Public Garden to Massachusetts Avenue, and, to a lesser extent, Boylston Street, a block away, you can drift in and out of fancy boutiques, clever gift shops, high-end jewelers, and galleries. Don't miss Kitty World (279 Newbury Street, 617-262-5489), a shop dedicated to all things Hello Kitty.

The Prudential Center

⌨800 Boylston Street

✆617-236-3100 or ✆800-SHOP-PRU

✐*www.prudentialcenter.com*

From 1965 until 1976, Boston's tallest building was the Prudential Center, or the Pru. Still one of the most recognizable landmarks in the Boston skyline, the building offers extensive shopping options on its bottom floors and, fifty floors up, a Skywalk Observatory (617-859-0648, *www.prudentialcenter.com/play/skywalk.html*). Top of the Hub (617-536-1775, *www.topofthehub.net*), on the fifty-second floor, is considered one of the most romantic restaurants in the city.

Quincy Market

⌨Off State Street

✆617-523-1300

✐*www.faneuilhallmarketplace.com*

When you reach Faneuil Hall on your Freedom Trail tour, visit neighboring Quincy Market, also known as the Faneuil Hall Marketplace. This always lively indoor/outdoor market is home to more than seventy-five shops, souvenir and flower carts, seventeen full-service restaurants and pubs, forty food stalls offering the flavors of Boston and the world, street performers, and even a Build-A-Bear Workshop (617-227-2478, *www.buildabear.com*), where kids can stuff their own Boston souvenirs.

Sports

In Boston, sports are not a pastime; they are an obsession. While you're visiting the city where Bobby Orr skated, Larry Bird dominated, and the Curse of the Bambino was finally eradicated, try to tour a legendary sports venue or catch a game.

Fenway Park

⌨4 Yawkey Way

☎617-226-6666 or ☎877-REDSOX9

✎*www.bostonredsox.com*

Completed in 1912, Fenway Park, home of the Boston Red Sox, is the oldest active baseball park in Major League Baseball. Guided tours are available daily on an hourly basis; tickets are sold on a walk-up basis at the Souvenir Store across Yawkey Way.

═FAST FACT

You can use a credit card to purchase up to eight tickets for any home game by calling the Red Sox twenty-four-hour Touchtone Ticket System, 617-482-4SOX. Tickets can also be purchased online and printed at home or bought in person at the Red Sox Ticket Office, 4 Yawkey Way, weekdays from 10 A.M. until one hour after game time, or until 5 P.M. on non-game days. Many games are sellouts; purchase tickets well in advance.

Gillette Stadium

⌨One Patriot Place, Foxborough

☎508-543-1776

✎*www.gillettestadium.com*

Located south of Boston in Foxborough, Gillette Stadium seats 68,756 fans when the NFL's New England Patriots and Major League Soccer's New England Revolution are at home. The stadium also hosts other concert and sporting events. The ticket office is located in the northwest corner of the stadium; tickets for stadium events may also be reserved through Ticketmaster (617-931-2000, *www.ticketmaster.com*). Keep in mind, however, that Patriots tickets are very hard to come by, and ticket brokers sell seats at a substantial markup. What are the parents of young Pats fans to do? Plan to visit Gillette Stadium in late July or early August, when the Patriots welcome spectators to watch training camp practices free, and the Patriots Experience gives kids a chance to try their hand a football-themed interactive challenges. Call the training camp hotline (508-549-0001) for practice dates and times.

The Sports Museum
TD Banknorth Garden, 100 Legends Way
617-624-1234
www.sportsmuseum.org
Remember great moments in New England sports as you view memorabilia at this museum, located inside the TD Banknorth Garden. There is an admission fee, and hours may vary based on events at the arena, so call ahead.

TD Banknorth Garden
100 Legends Way
617-624-1000
www.tdbanknorthgarden.com
This 19,600-seat arena built in 1995 is home to the NHL's Boston Bruins and the NBA's Boston Celtics and hosts a variety of other sporting, music, and family events year-round. Purchase tickets via Ticketmaster (617-931-2000, *www.ticketmaster.com*).

Where to Stay

Boston gives Manhattan chase when it comes to room rates, which is an unfortunate reality for families and other leisure travelers. Fortunately, prices are frequently lower on weekends when the business travel crowd ebbs. In addition to the rate quoted for your overnight stay, you may also be charged to park your vehicle, even if you are a guest parking in the hotel's garage. You may also be assessed a fee each time you move your car in or out of the garage throughout the duration of your stay.

Lodgings Near Logan

If you will be flying in and out of Logan, staying at a nearby hotel may be a smart choice. Logan is well connected to downtown Boston via public transportation. Rates at airport hotels tend to be a bit less expensive than at downtown lodging properties, so consider an airport hotel as your home base for exploring the city, even if you do not need convenient access to the airport.

The Hilton Boston Logan Airport (One Hotel Drive, Boston, 617-568-6700, *www.hilton.com*), which has a complimentary airport shuttle, as well as a skybridge that connects the hotel to the terminals, is your best bet if you have a late arrival or early departure. The hotel also offers a free shuttle to the subway and water taxis, a health club and spa with an indoor pool, a coffee bar, restaurant, pub, and twenty-four-hour room service.

Within about three miles of Boston's airport, you'll find a number of family-friendly hotels including the Comfort Inn & Suites Logan Airport (85 American Legion Highway, Revere, 781-485-3600 or 888-283-9300, *www.comfortinnboston.com*), which offers free parking, a free twenty-four-hour airport shuttle, an indoor pool, and complimentary deluxe continental breakfast; and the Holiday Inn Boston–Logan Airport (225 McClellan Highway, Boston, 617-569-5250 or 888-465-4329, *www.holiday-inn.com/bos-loganapt*), where kids eat free and the complimentary airport shuttle operates around the clock.

Although it is eight miles away from Logan, the Days Inn Saugus Logan Airport (999 Broadway, Saugus, 781-233-1800, *www.daysinnsaugus.com*) has a courtesy airport shuttle, free high-speed wireless Internet access, a complimentary deluxe breakfast, and room rates under $100 per night, which are not easy to find in the Boston area.

Family-Friendly Boston Hotels

While an entire chapter could be devoted to the horde of hotels and inns located in and around Boston and Cambridge, here's a selection of some of the most convenient and popular options for families.

Be sure to consider location, along with price and amenities, especially if you are intimidated by the prospect of using the subway system.

If you're looking for a hotel situated right on the Freedom Trail, consider the Omni Parker House (60 School Street, 617-227-8600 or 888-444-OMNI, *www.omniparkerhouse.com*), the oldest continuously operating luxury hotel in America, famous for inventing Parker House rolls and Boston cream pie. Ask about the Omni Kids Program and special sightseeing packages designed for families.

The Boston Marriott Long Wharf (296 State Street, 617-227-0800, *www.marriott.com*) also boasts a location near the New England Aquarium and a block from Faneuil Hall and Quincy Market, it's one of the best choices for parents combining business with a family getaway.

The Sheraton Boston Hotel (39 Dalton Street, 617-236-2000, *www .starwoodhotels.com*) and the Colonnade (120 Huntington Avenue, 617-424-7000 or 800-962-3030, *www.colonnadehotel.com*) are both located near the Prudential Center and Copley Place in the Back Bay, and both have great swimming pools. The Sheraton's pool is one of the largest in New England, and its retractable roof allows year-round enjoyment. The Colonnade, a Back Bay landmark that has hosted three U.S. presidents, has a seasonal rooftop pool.

If you're looking for unique, moderately priced accommodations, Newbury Guest House (261 Newbury Street, 800-437-7668, *www .newburyguesthouse.com*) has a few rooms that can accommodate families. This thirty-two-room B&B on swanky Newbury Street was formerly three single-family Victorian residences.

In search of budget-priced lodging downtown, consider the Midtown Hotel (220 Huntington Avenue, 617-262-1000 or 800-343-1177, *www.midtownhotel.com*), where the rooms are basic but spacious, and the rates are considerably lower than elsewhere.

To pamper your brood, try the Four Seasons Boston (200 Boylston Street, 617-338-4400, *www.fourseasons.com/boston*), which overlooks the Public Garden, provides welcome goodies for kids, child-size bathrobes, toiletries for babies and children, and complimentary bedtime milk and cookies. The chic Langham Hotel Boston (250 Franklin Street, 617-451-1900, *www.langhamhotels.com*) has a V.I.B. Concierge to cater to your Very Important Baby and very important big brothers and sisters, too. Packages include everything from unlimited Huggies during your stay and use of a double stroller to pre-ordered food based on your little ones' preferences and a red velvet staircase that allows wee ones to check in at the front desk.

 JUST FOR PARENTS

XV Beacon (15 Beacon Street, 617-670-1500 or 877-XVBEACON, *www.xvbeacon.com*) is one of the city's boldest and most romantic hideaways featuring individually styled, luxurious rooms and suites with unique features such as four-poster beds, heated towel racks, and fireplaces. Complimentary chauffeured Lexus sedan transportation to wherever you're going in Boston is provided.

Although its location across from Boston's World Trade Center is not quite as central, the pet-friendly Seaport Hotel (One Seaport Lane, 617-385-4000 or 877-SEAPORT, *www.seaportboston.com*) is located close to the Boston Children's Museum, and families will like its service-inclusive (no tipping) policy and its indoor pool with underwater music. The Seaport Hotel is also easily accessed from the Massachusetts Turnpike.

In Cambridge, hotels that will place you within walking distance of Harvard, shopping, and more include the Charles Hotel (1 Bennett Street, 617-864-1200, *www.charleshotel.com*), which blends charming décor with state-of-the-art amenities; and the Harvard Square Hotel

(110 Mount Auburn Street, 617-864-5200, *www.harvardsquarehotel .com*), where all rooms have refrigerators and flat-panel TVs. The Residence Inn by Marriott Boston Cambridge (6 Cambridge Center, 617-349-0700, *www.marriott.com*) is a good choice for long-term stays in the Boston area.

Affordable Options on the Outskirts

Boston is a walking city, so there is a definite benefit to staying downtown. However, you will find some less-expensive accommodations options on the outskirts of the city. An outlying hotel that is close to public transportation may be one way to keep your Boston vacation affordable.

The Doubletree Guest Suites Boston (400 Soldiers Field Road, 617-783-0090, *www.doubletree.com*), located just off the Massachusetts Turnpike, is one of the city's better values when you consider that all rooms are spacious, two-room suites. The hotel has an indoor pool and a complimentary shuttle to downtown Boston; they'll even throw in a warm chocolate-chip cookie at check-in.

The no-frills Cambridge Gateway Inn (211 Concord Turnpike, 617-661-7800 or 866-427-6660, *www.cambridgegatewayinn.com*) will save you some money, and their free shuttle will take you to the Alewife T station.

In Brookline, the Courtyard by Marriott (40 Webster Street, 617-734-1393, *www.brooklinecourtyard.com*) is located just one block from the Coolidge Corner T station.

In Quincy, the Best Western Adams Inn (29 Hancock Street, 617-328-1500 or 800-368-4012, *www.bwadamsinn.com*) is an affordable choice, and it's just a quarter-mile from an MBTA station. The hotel offers an outdoor pool, free parking, and continental breakfast, plus a complimentary shuttle to Logan Airport and Boston's South Station.

In Braintree, the Holiday Inn Express Boston/Braintree (190 Wood Road, 781-848-1260, *www.ichotelsgroup.com*) offers free deluxe continental breakfast and complimentary shuttle transportation to the subway station.

West of Boston in Watertown and easily accessible from the Massachusetts Turnpike, the Super 8 (100 North Beacon Street, 617-926-2200 or 800-800-8000, *www.super8.com*) is adjacent to an MBTA station and offers free parking and continental breakfast.

Family Dining

Boston is without a doubt New England's dining capital, so pack an appetite. After all, this is the city that has given its name to such widely loved dishes as Boston baked beans, Boston brown bread, and Boston cream pie. Boston restaurants can be busy, so make reservations when possible.

A Taste of History

Daniel Webster liked to toss back oysters at the Union Oyster House (41 Union Street, 617-227-2750, *www.unionoysterhouse.com*). John F. Kennedy's favorite booth in the upstairs dining room is marked with a plaque. This historic restaurant, located on the Freedom Trail near Faneuil Hall, lays claim to the title of America's oldest continuously operating restaurant—it's been serving seafood since 1826. The building actually dates to the 1600s, and its hand-hewn wood beams and floor boards and warm atmosphere will transport you back to old New England. And yes, they serve Boston cream pie.

For well over a century, Durgin-Park (340 Faneuil Hall Marketplace, 617-227-2038, *www.durgin-park.com*) has delighted tourists with its notoriously surly waitresses, casual vibe, noisy atmosphere, and hearty portions of classic Yankee favorites. Save room for strawberry shortcake or Indian pudding.

 TRAVEL TIP

Although it is not yet twenty years old, the Langham Hotel's all-you-can-eat Chocolate Bar is already legendary in Boston. Available seasonally on Saturday afternoons, it features an amazing array of treats to delight any sweet tooth. For reservations, call 617-956-8751.

Your kids don't remember Sam and Diane, but if you do, you may want to grab a bite at Cheers Beacon Hill (84 Beacon Street, 617-227-9605, *www.cheersboston.com*), formerly the Bull & Finch Pub, where you can dine on casual fare and see plenty of memorabilia from the hit television show, *Cheers*, which aired from 1982 until 1993 and was inspired by this Boston setting.

Seafood Delights

Seafood is the main event when you're dining in the Bay State's capital. A reliable choice for reasonably priced seafood is the regional chain of Legal Sea Foods restaurants (*www.legalseafoods.com*): in Boston at Park Square (617-426-4444), Copley Place (617-266-7775), Long Wharf (617-742-5300), the Prudential Center (617-266-6800), Logan Airport Terminal B (617-568-2811), and Logan Airport Terminal C (617-568-2800); and in Cambridge at Kendall Square (617-864-3400) and Charles Square (617-491-9400). There are also LTK—Legal Test Kitchen (*www.ltkbarandkitchen.com*)—locations in Boston (225 Northern Avenue, 617-330-7430) and in Terminal A at Logan Airport (617-568-1888). Here, the menu is multicultural, and the theme is high-tech. Not only does the restaurant have WiFi and digital menus, you can dock your iPod at your table.

For something very casual, try the Barking Crab (88 Sleeper Street, 617-426-2722, *www.barkingcrab.com*), where you can sit on the deck peeling your own shrimp and cracking your own crabs to your heart's and tummy's content. Kids will also feel at home at Jasper White's Summer Shack (*www.summershackrestaurant.com*), with locations in the Back Bay (50 Dalton Street, 617-867-9955) and in Cambridge (149 Alewife Brook Parkway, 617-520-9500).

Where's the best clam chowder? It's a tough choice between these Chowderfest Hall of Fame members that have won the annual Boston Chowderfest three times and been retired from competition: Turner Fisheries at the Westin Copley Place (10 Huntington Avenue, 617-424-7425) and the Chart House (60 Long Wharf, 617-227-1576, *www.chart-house.com*). Other recent Chowderfest title holders include Ned Devine's Irish Pub (Faneuil Hall Marketplace, 617-248-

9900, *www.neddevinesboston.com*) and Houston's (60 State Street, 617-573-9777, *www.hillstone.com*).

Cuisines from Many Cultures

You can take a culinary trip around the world without ever leaving the Boston area. In Chinatown, the three-story Chau Chow City (83 Essex Street, 617-338-8158) may be the largest Chinese restaurant you have ever seen. The restaurant, which has a children's menu, serves Cantonese cuisine and specializes in seafood and fish dishes; Chau Chow City's third floor is devoted to dim sum.

Cajun food is on the menu and jazz is on stage at Bob's Southern Bistro (604 Columbus Avenue, 617-536-6204, *www.bobthechefs.com*); treat your family to Bob's Sunday jazz brunch. Fajitas & 'Ritas (25 West Street, 617-426-1222, *www.fajitasandritas.com*) is a fun, affordable Mexican restaurant near Boston Common; here you can build your own nachos by buying only the ingredients you crave: lettuce for forty-eight cents, sour cream for seventy-one cents, and so on.

Just outside the city in Brookline is a Japanese restaurant that claims to be New England's largest. With or without the kids, Fugakyu (1280 Beacon Street, 617-734-1268, *www.fugakyu.net*) will dazzle you with its artful sushi preparations.

For hearty, traditional German fare and a beer-hall atmosphere, Bostonians and visitors alike have been heading to the Jacob Wirth Restaurant (31 Stuart Street, 617-338-8586, *www.jacobwirth.com*) since 1868. The kids' menu features everything from foot-long franks to butternut-squash ravioli.

The North End is the place to head for Italian delights. Maurizio's (364 Hanover Street, 617-367-1123, *www.mauriziosboston.com*) is named for its talented chef, Maurizio Loddo, who will surprise you with generous portions of sumptuous Italian and Mediterranean specialties. At Bricco (241 Hanover Street, 617-248-6800, *www.bricco .com*), you can savor some of the city's finest Italian cuisine, or indulge your late-night cravings with a wood-fired pizza, served from 11 P.M. until 2 A.M. Tuesday through Saturday. You'll also find one of Boston's best family-owned, old-school pizzerias in the North End. Pizzeria

Regina (11½ Thacher Street, 617-227-0765, *www.pizzeriaregina.com*) is known for its fresh ingredients and brick oven–fired pies; be prepared to wait for a table.

Make the trip to Cambridge for Indian food at Tanjore in Harvard Square (18 Eliot Street, 617-868-1900, *www.tanjoreharvardsq.com*), featuring fresh preparations from a variety of regions.

For a taste of medieval Europe, reserve a spot at the banquet tables at Medieval Manor Theatre-Restaurant (246 East Berkeley Street, 617-423-4900, *www.medievalmanor.com*), where you'll be entertained by jesters and minstrels while eating with your hands.

≡FAST FACT

Boston has a long and proud Irish tradition. More than 600,000 visitors celebrate St. Patrick's Day in Boston each year. In 1999, the Boston Irish Tourism Association (617-696-9880, *www .irishmassachusetts.com*) was founded to promote and preserve Irish history and culture and to promote Irish events in the city. One of its first major accomplishments was to create the Irish Heritage Trail (*www.irishheritagetrail.com*).

Irish pubs are, of course, another Boston tradition—there are about 100 of them in Boston and Cambridge, and most are perfectly fine places to take children for lunch or an early dinner. The Black Rose at Faneuil Hall Marketplace (160 State Street, 617-742-2286, *www .irishconnection.com*) features Guinness on tap and live Irish music nightly. Kitty O'Shea's first restaurant was in Dublin, and the Boston incarnation of this Irish-themed pub (131 State Street, 617-725-0100, *www.kittyosheas.com/boston.asp*) is located in a Victorian building in the heart of the Financial District. The Purple Shamrock (1 Union Street, 617-227-2060, *www.irishconnection.com*), located on the Freedom Trail across from Boston City Hall, serves Irish and New England dishes and has nightly entertainment that ranges from live bands to karaoke.

CHAPTER 10

Plymouth and Cape Cod

IN THE 1950S, PATTI Page sang, "You're sure to fall in love with Old Cape Cod," and in the 1970s, Rupert Holmes sang about "piña coladas" and the "dunes of the Cape." You'll be singing the Cape's praises, too, once you've discovered its sea-scented breezes, sandy beaches, family resorts, enticing shops, and uncanny ability to recharge your life force. The land of Pilgrims also makes for an appealing family vacation pick, not only for its selection of historic attractions, but also for its proximity to Boston—without the city's family-unfriendly prices.

An Introduction to Cape Cod and the South Shore

Cape Cod and the nearby islands of Martha's Vineyard and Nantucket are surrounded not only by glittering water but also by a mystique and nostalgia that is unmatched in New England. There is a pervasive sense of a simpler time preserved in the rituals and rhythms of day-to-day living. And at night, the stars shine brighter than you remembered they could, the crickets croon, and the churning surf lulls you to sleep. Whatever the length of your stay, you'll long for just another day in this much-loved corner of New England.

Many families combine a trip to the Cape with a visit to the South Shore's historic attractions. Your youngsters will never dismiss history as dull again once they've chatted with Myles Standish in person at the re-created Pilgrim village at Plimoth Plantation.

The region south of Boston is comprised of three counties: Norfolk, Plymouth, and Bristol. It's a compact area with sights that can be savored in the space of a short getaway. Or, you may decide to stay longer, just as the *Mayflower*'s occupants did in 1620. Regardless of the duration of your visit, you're bound to depart with a new appreciation for the enduring American traditions that originated on this stretch of New England shore.

What to See and Do

Summer is the busiest tourism season along the South Shore and on Cape Cod, and it is easy to understand why this scenic and historic coastal region appeals to so many vacationers. You'll find all of the ingredients here for a memorable getaway filled with time to play and unwind and opportunities to understand one of the earliest chapters in America's history. Want to avoid summer's tourist swell? Plan a November pilgrimage, and give thanks along with Pilgrim re-enactors, or head to the Cape and islands during the quiet off-season. Warm ocean breezes help keep the climate more moderate than other New England spots.

Beaches

Cape Cod has more than 550 miles of coastline, and you're never far from a public beach where you can swim, sunbathe, and breathe deeply of the salty air. Most beaches have a parking or admission fee; some require season permits. In general, waters are warmer on the southern Nantucket Sound coast than on the northern Cape Cod Bay side. The most vigorous surf can be found along the Outer Cape at the beaches that are within the National Seashore.

Here are a few major beach destinations, but be sure to ask the staff at your hotel or inn for their recommendations.

Cape Cod National Seashore

⌨ Salt Pond Visitor Center, Route 6, Eastham

☎ 508-255-3421

⌨ Province Lands Visitor Center, Race Point Road, Provincetown

☎ 508-487-1256

✎ *www.nps.gov/caco*

Cape Cod National Seashore is New England's most visited national park, drawing about 4 million visitors annually. The park features lighthouses and historic structures, numerous Cape Cod–style houses, six beaches for swimming, self-guided nature trails for walking and hiking, and a variety of picnic and scenic overlook areas. The Salt Pond Visitor Center off Route 6 in Eastham is a good place to get oriented. Vehicle entrance fees are charged at beaches from late June through early September, and a vehicle season pass may be your best buy if you plan to visit for several days.

Craigville Beach

⌨ Craigville Beach Road, Centerville

☎ 508-790-6345

✎ *www.town.barnstable.ma.us/Recreation/beaches.asp*

Known for its warm waters, this popular Cape beach is one of thirteen ocean and freshwater beaches under the jurisdiction of the Town of Barnstable's Recreation Division. Visitors may purchase a daily vehicle permit at Craigville Beach. A bathhouse is available, and lifeguards are on duty during the season.

Nantasket Beach Reservation

⌨ Route 3A, Hull

☎ 617-727-5290

✎ *www.mass.gov/dcr/parks/metroboston/nantask.htm*

Bostonites have fled the city for the fine sands of Nantasket since the mid-1800s. Lifeguards look over this mile-plus-long South Shore beach in the summer months, and the twenty-six-acre reservation is open for public enjoyment year-round. A per-vehicle parking fee is charged during the summer season.

Veterans Beach

⌨Ocean Street, Hyannis

☏508-790-6345

✎*www.town.barnstable.ma.us/Recreation/beaches.asp*

With its playground and picnic area, this lifeguard-protected beach, under the jurisdiction of the Town of Barnstable, is a good choice for families. A daily vehicle permit may be purchased at the beach.

Boat and Train Tours

Many of the best excursions are on the water. If you'd rather stay on land, consider a leisurely train ride along the coast.

Cape Cod Central Railroad

⌨252 Main Street, Hyannis

☏508-771-3800 or ☏888-797-RAIL

✎*www.capetrain.com*

Embrace the nostalgia of the rail era during a two-hour journey past cranberry bogs and tidal marshes as you chug along from Hyannis to the Cape Cod Canal and Sandwich. There is a regular schedule of scenic train excursions from Memorial Day weekend through October.

Catboat Rides

⌨Ocean Street Dock, Hyannis

☏508-775-0222 or ☏800-308-1837

✎*www.catboat.com*

See Kennedy family homes and other landmarks from the Catboat, a thirty-four-foot sailing vessel that will whisk you out to sea on an exhilarating ninety-minute trip. Six daily departures are offered in July and August, and a more limited schedule is available in late spring and early fall.

Chatham Water Tours

☏508-432-5895

✎*www.chathamwatertours.net*

Make reservations for these boat tours departing from Chatham for an unforgettable opportunity to see harbor and gray seals cavorting in their natural environment. You'll also enjoy splendid views of the Cape from the water and spy a variety of shorebirds.

Dolphin Fleet of Provincetown
MacMillan Pier, Provincetown
508-240-3636 or 800-826-9300
www.whalewatch.com

Provincetown is a popular departure point for whale watches. In the unlikely event that you don't see a whale, Dolphin Fleet will give you a free pass for another excursion. Onboard naturalists will help you spy these fascinating marine mammals, and hands-on displays give kids something to do as you cruise toward the whales' habitat.

Hy-Line Cruises
Ocean Street Dock, Hyannis
508-778-2600 or 800-492-8082
www.hy-linecruises.com

Hy-Line operates both fishing trips and leisurely harbor sightseeing outings from Hyannis. Hy-Line's ferry to Nantucket and Martha's Vineyard also departs from the Ocean Street Dock.

Family Amusements

If you long for old-fashioned fun and a chance to introduce your children to the simple pleasures of a seaside getaway, you'll be hard-pressed to find a better vacation destination than Cape Cod and the nearby South Shore. While there are many attractions with family appeal, don't slot too many activities into your itinerary. Collecting seashells, playing card games, reading good books, and taking long walks can all be enjoyable diversions.

Art's Dune Tours
4 Standish Street, Provincetown
508-487-1950
www.artsdunetours.com

Rob Costa carries on the family business founded by his father,

Art Costa, in 1946, taking visitors on memorable drives over the Cape's sand dunes in an air-conditioned Suburban. The views are remarkable, and the stories are equally entertaining. In addition to daily dune tours in season, you can also book a two-hour sunset tour and even add a beach clambake or barbecue.

Cape Cod Baseball League
✍*www.capecodbaseball.org*

The ten-team Cape Cod Baseball League is a nonprofit organization that aims to make family entertainment affordable each summer, while also fostering the talents of up-and-coming amateur ball players. There are no tickets for games; some teams pass the hat or request a donation at the gate. From mid-June through early August, games are played at fields Cape-wide, so check the online schedule and plan to take your family out to the ballgame.

Cape Cod Melody Tent
⌨21 West Main Street, Hyannis
✆508-775-5630

On a summer's eve, nothing quite beats a concert at the Cape Cod Melody Tent, which hosts popular performers and features a round, revolving stage. If your children are too young for a concert, check the Melody Tent's schedule of morning children's shows. The South Shore Music Circus (130 Sohier Street, Cohasset, 781-383-9850, *www.southshoremusiccircus.org*) hosts many of the same performers and children's programs, so you may want to check their schedule, as well.

Edaville USA
⌨Pine Street, South Carver
✆877-EDAVILLE
✍*www.edaville.com*

Admission to this small family amusement park located southwest of Plymouth includes unlimited train rides and kiddie rides. Edaville USA, which also exhibits antique cars, locomotives, and cranberry harvesting equipment, opens for the season in mid-June and hosts a variety of seasonal events, including the National Cranberry Festival each Columbus Day weekend and a Christmas Festival of Lights in November and December.

 ## JUST FOR PARENTS

Tucked away between New Bedford and Fall River in Westport, you'll find one of the country's leading producers of sparkling wines and New England's largest vineyard. Westport Rivers Vineyard and Winery (417 Hixbridge Road, 800-993-9695, *www.westportrivers.com*) offers free tours on weekends year-round. There is a fee for tastings, which are also offered weekdays from May through December.

Flying Horses Carousel
⌨ Oak Bluffs Avenue, Oak Bluffs
☎ 508-693-9481
✐ *www.mvpreservation.org/carousel.html*

If you make it out to Martha's Vineyard, you'll definitely want to treat your tots to a ride on the oldest operating platform carousel in the United States. The Flying Horses Carousel is a National Historic Landmark.

Wellfleet Drive-In Theater
⌨ Route 6 at the Eastham/Wellfleet town line
☎ 508-349-7176
✐ *www.wellfleetdrivein.com*

The whole family will enjoy the retro vibe at the drive-in movie theater, which screens first-run double features every night from late April through early October. Movies are shown rain or shine, and there's a snack bar, plus a playground for kids to enjoy before the show and during intermission.

☂ RAINY DAY FUN

Children will enjoy seeing where potato chips are born on a free tour of Cape Cod Potato Chip Company (100 Breed's Hill Road, Hyannis, 508-775-3358, *www.capecodchips.com*). There are free chips at the end of the self-guided tour, which is available Mondays through Fridays from 9 A.M. until 5 P.M.

Museums and Historic Sites

You may be reluctant to interrupt your relaxation for a visit to a historic site or museum, but consider taking in some of these attractions.

Battleship Cove

⌨ Five Water Street, Fall River
☎ 508-678-1100
✎ *www.battleshipcove.org*

At this waterfront attraction, you'll see the world's largest collection of historic World War II ships including the battleship *Massachusetts*, the submarine *Lionfish*, and the destroyer *Joseph P. Kennedy Jr.* Inside a Victorian-style pavilion, you'll also find an antique 1920 carousel, rescued after Lincoln Park shut down. Battleship Cove is open year-round.

Heritage Museums & Gardens

⌨ 67 Grove Street, Sandwich
☎ 508-888-3300
✎ *www.heritagemuseumsandgardens.org*

This sprawling and beautifully landscaped attraction is home to diverse collections of Americana, an automobile museum, a military museum, plus gardens and an antique carousel. The facility is open April through October.

John F. Kennedy Hyannis Museum

⌨ 397 Main Street, Hyannis

☎508-790-3077

✐*www.jfkhyannismuseum.org*

This museum's collection of photographs and video tells the story of our thirty-fifth president's love for Cape Cod.

New Bedford Whaling Museum

⌨18 Johnny Cake Hill, New Bedford

☎508-997-0046

✐*www.whalingmuseum.org*

At the largest American museum devoted to the history of the whaling industry, you'll be awed by a complete skeleton of a rare blue whale, the world's largest ship model, and the world's most extensive collection of whaling artifacts. The museum is open daily.

Pilgrim Hall Museum

⌨75 Court Street, Plymouth

☎508-746-1620

✐*www.pilgrimhall.org*

Located in the center of Plymouth, this museum, which was built in 1824, exhibits Pilgrim possessions and Native American artifacts.

 **TRAVEL TIP**

Colonial Lantern Tours (508-747-4161, *www.lanterntours.com*) provides you with tin lanterns and leads you on an evening exploration of Plymouth's past or of local ghosts and legends. These 90-minute walking tours are offered nightly April through Thanksgiving. Tickets may be purchased online or by calling 800-979-3370.

Pilgrim Monument

⌨High Pole Hill Road, Provincetown

☎508-487-1310

✐*www.pilgrim-monument.org*

You might expect the Pilgrim Monument to be located in Plymouth . . . but it's not. The 252-foot tower that commemorates the site of the Pilgrims' first landing in America is located in Provincetown at the tip of Cape Cod. The Pilgrims spent five weeks exploring the Cape before they decided to sail across Cape Cod Bay to Plymouth, which they found more suitable for settlement. The monument is open to visitors from April through November. You'll get a workout climbing the 116 steps to the top; the view is worth the climb.

Plimoth Plantation
⌨137 Warren Avenue, Plymouth
✆508-746-1622
✍*www.plimoth.org*

Time is frozen in 1627 at this re-created Pilgrim village. Nearly half a million people descend upon this living history attraction each year to interact with costumed interpreters and to glimpse the life of New England's first settlers and their Native American neighbors. The attraction operates daily from late March through late November. Purchase a combination ticket, and you'll also be able to visit the nearby *Mayflower II* (Water Street at the State Pier), a replica of the Pilgrims' ship.

Shopping

It would be easier to list the places where you can't find cool shops on the South Shore, Cape, and islands than it is to point to all the retail riches of this region. Shopaholics should definitely plan to spend some concentrated time in Plymouth, Hyannis, Chatham, Wellfleet, Provincetown, Vineyard Haven, Oak Bluffs, Edgartown, in the heart of Nantucket Town, and cruising along the Cape's Route 6A. Keep in mind that Provincetown is a very open-minded community and a popular gay and lesbian resort, and some shop window displays may evoke questions from younger children.

If you want to take home a souvenir made in this region, popular choices include scrimshaw, cranberry food products, chichi and very expensive Nantucket lightship baskets, pottery, nautical wood carvings, braided rugs, shell gifts, and designer clothing. Antique shops and flea markets are very popular in this region, too.

Cape Cod Factory Outlet Mall
1 Factory Outlet Road, Sagamore
508-888-8417
www.capecodoutletmall.com
For bargains, take exit 1 off Route 6, and visit the twenty name-brand factory stores at this indoor outlet mall.

Christmas Tree Shops
888-287-3232
www.christmastreeshops.com
You'll find these wildly popular discount centers located in Falmouth, Hyannis, North Attleboro, North Dartmouth, Orleans, Pembroke, Sagamore, West Dennis, and West Yarmouth. The name of the chain is a bit misleading, as the merchandise offered is diverse and always in season.

Davoll's General Store
1228 Russell's Mills Road, Dartmouth
508-636-4530
www.davolls.com
You can visit one of the oldest general stores in America in Dartmouth. Davoll's has been in business since 1793 and today sells an assortment of clothing, antiques, and collectibles.

Northeast Knitting Mills Factory Outlet Store
Tower Outlet Mill, 657 Quarry Street, Fall River
508-678-1383
www.neknitting.com
You'll save 50 percent or more off retail prices at this factory outlet store, which sells closeouts and overstocked merchandise manufactured at Northeast Knitting Mills in Fall River. The fourth-generation, family-owned company has been making sweaters and other knitwear for children and adults for more than eighty-five years.

The Red Balloon Toy Shop
⌨114 Route 6A, Orleans
☏508-255-4208 or ☏800-901-TOYS
✍*www.redballoontoyshop.com*

In business since 1970, the Cape's best-loved toy store has puzzles, games, and other playthings to stimulate young imaginations.

Where to Stay

Lodging in Plymouth and the South Shore runs the full gamut from motor lodges and historic hideaways to elegant luxury hotels. Ocean view or not you won't miss with this these choices.

South Shore Sleepovers

Plymouth is a popular family destination, and reasonably priced accommodations abound. The kids will adore the Pilgrim Cove Indoor Theme Pool at the John Carver Inn (25 Summer Street, 508-746-7100 or 800-274-1620, *www.johncarverinn.com*), which is on the site of the original Pilgrim settlement; the John Carver's Beach Plum Spa is kid-friendly, too, and a perfect place for moms and daughters to enjoy manicures or pedicures. The Best Western Cold Spring (188 Court Street, 508-746-2222 or 800-678-8667, *www.bestwestern.com*) offers comfortable accommodations within walking distance of waterfront attractions, plus free breakfast and a heated outdoor pool. The Governor Bradford on the Harbour (98 Water Street, 508-746-6200 or 800-332-1620, *www.governorbradford.com*) features ninety-four guest rooms and an enviable location overlooking Plymouth Harbor. At the Radisson Hotel Plymouth Harbor (180 Water Street, 508-747-4900, *www.radissonplymouth.com*), enjoy the indoor pool and proximity to Plymouth Rock and other attractions.

For Nantasket Beach vacations, Clarion's Nantasket Beach Hotel & Conference Center (45 Hull Shore Drive, 781-925-4500, *www.nantasketbeachhotel.com*) offers an ideal waterfront location, plus an indoor/outdoor pool with a retractable roof and an on-site restaurant with an outdoor deck.

In the Fall River/New Bedford area, try the eighty-four-room Comfort Inn New Bedford/Dartmouth (171 Faunce Corner Road, North Dartmouth, 508-996-0800 or 800-228-5150, *www.comfortinn dartmouth.com*) or the Best Western Fall River (360 Airport Road, Fall River, 508-672-0011 or 800-780-7234, *www.bestwestern.com*), which has free breakfast and an indoor pool.

Family Resorts on Cape Cod and the Islands

Cape Cod has lodging establishments of every conceivable size and type, from family motor inns to chain hotels to rental homes to distinctive B&Bs to elegant inns to exclusive resorts. For a first-class stay, there are a number of fine resorts with amenities galore, from private beaches and golf courses to supervised children's programs and even an indoor water park.

The 400-acre Ocean Edge Resort & Club (Route 6A, Brewster, 508-896-9000 or 800-343-6074, *www.oceanedge.com*), has a private beach, four outdoor pools, two indoor pools, an 18-hole golf course, four restaurants, two tennis complexes, a fitness center, bike trails, and five hot tubs. In the summer, the optional half-day or full-day Ocean EdgeVenture program keeps kids ages four to twelve active and entertained. Kid's Night Out–themed dinner programs are also offered on select summer evenings. The whole family can enjoy a variety of offerings, from beach bonfires to bingo nights to barbecues on the front lawn of the historic mansion. The focal point of the resort, the mansion was a private estate. Accommodations range from hotel-style mansion rooms to one-, two- and three-bedroom villas. They are situated on both sides of Route 6A, and shuttles provide transportation around the resort.

The Red Jacket Beach Resort (1 South Shore Drive, South Yarmouth, 508-398-6941 or 800-672-0500, *www.redjacketresorts.com*) is a smaller-scale property, but it has three amenities that can really enhance your family's vacation: a private beach and indoor and outdoor swimming pools. Choose from a full range of accommodations, from hotel-style rooms to multibedroom cottages. A supervised children's program is available in the summer, and guests have access to an on-site spa, tennis courts, water sports, and a restaurant, as well as facilities at other Red

Jacket properties on the Cape, including the Blue Rock Golf Course.

At the Cape Codder Resort & Spa (1225 Iyanough Road, Hyannis, 508-771-3000 or 888-297-2200, *www.capecodderresort.com*), year-round water fun is on tap. That's because the property is home to an indoor water park featuring a wave pool, whirlpool, waterfalls, and two water slides. The resort also features a spa, an on-site Hearth 'n Kettle restaurant, a wine bar, a tennis court, and a playground. A full schedule of activities and entertainment for kids and families is also offered in the summer months.

The centrally located Bayside Resort Hotel (225 Main Street, West Yarmouth, 508-775-5669 or 800-243-1114, *www.baysideresort.com*) has 128 rooms and suites, a private beach, indoor and outdoor pools, fitness and fun centers, free wireless Internet access, and a customer rewards program that can earn you a free stay.

Sea Crest Resort (350 Quaker Road, North Falmouth, 508-540-9400, *www.seacrest-resort.com*) offers a private beach, indoor and outdoor pools, an arcade, a fitness center, and a summer day camp program for children ages three to twelve.

For family getaways on Nantucket, Harbor House Village (South Beach Street, 508-228-1500 or 866-325-9300, *www.harborhousevillage .com*) makes a good home base; you can even take your dog and board him at the Woof Hotel. If you're taking the kids to Martha's Vineyard, the Winnetu Oceanside Resort (South Beach, Edgartown, 508-310-1733 or 866-335-1133, *www.winnetu.com*) was just built in 2000 and caters to families with well-furnished suite accommodations and organized programs for children in the summer.

Budget-Friendly Cape Cod Lodgings

If your family vacation budget is limited, don't rule Cape Cod out. There are many independently owned hotels and motels with reasonable rates. Rates are always highest during the peak summer season, but the Cape is lovely year-round. So take advantage of off-season discounts and a quieter Cape if you're looking for value.

The centrally located Seacoast Inn (33 Ocean Street, Hyannis, 800-466-4100, *www.seacoastcapecod.com*) offers basic motel-style accommodations with a few perks, including complimentary continental breakfast and wireless Internet access. Best Value Inn & Suites (206 Main Street, Hyannis, 508-775-5225 or 866-327-9416, *www .bestvalueinncapecod.com*) is another affordable and central choice with indoor and outdoor pools and a free continental breakfast.

For an extended family stay, Cape Cod Harbor House Inn (119 Ocean Street, Hyannis, 800-211-5551, *www.harborhouseinn.net*) offers eighteen mini-suites with kitchenettes.

≡FAST FACT

Want to find a rental property on the Cape? The All Seasons Vacation Rental Network (online at *www.weneedavacation .com*) connects you to hundreds of houses, cottages, and condos that can be rented directly from homeowners. Getting away at the last minute? The Cape Cod and Islands Current Vacancies Web site, updated daily, lists available accommodations at *www.capecodchambers.com.*

A stay at Centerville Corners Inn (1338 Craigville Beach Road, Centerville, 508-775-7223 or 800-242-1137, *www.centervillecorners.com*) may save you some money on beach parking fees if you're up for the half-mile walk to Craigville Beach. The budget-priced, pet-friendly, WiFi-equipped motel also has an indoor pool and free continental breakfast.

In South Yarmouth, All Seasons Motor Inn (1199 Main Street, 508-394-7600 or 800-527-0359, *www.allseasons.com*) has heated indoor and outdoor pools and a game room for the kids, plus prices that will please parents.

If you're headed to the Outer Cape, Cove Bluffs Motel and Efficiencies (25 Seaview Road, Eastham, 508-240-1616, *www.capecod -orleans.com/covebluffs*) is a rare Cape property with motel rooms priced under $100 in-season; kids will like the swings, sandbox, and outdoor pool. Or, insure yourselves against rainy days by booking an affordable room or efficiency unit at Mainstay Motor Inn (2068 Route

6, South Wellfleet, 508-349-2350 or 800-346-2350, *www.mainstay motorinn.com*), which has an indoor heated pool.

Cape Cod is home to a number of campgrounds, which offer families another affordable alternative in the summer months. Two of the largest facilities are Bourne Scenic Park (370 Scenic Highway, Bourne, 508-759-7873, *www.bournescenicpark.com*), located on the banks of the Cape Cod Canal, and Peters Pond RV Resort (185 Cotuit Road, Sandwich, 508-477-1775, *www.peterspond.com*), which has two sandy lake beaches for swimming and other recreational facilities. Visit the Massachusetts Association of Campground Owners Web site (*www.campmass.com*) for more options.

Be sure to call the Cape Cod Chamber of Commerce (888-33-CAPECOD) to request your free guide to the area, including extensive accommodations listings. You can also download the guide from the Chamber's Web site (*www.capecodchamber.org*).

Family Dining

Traveling with little ones tends to involve a spur-of-the-moment approach to dining decisions. On the Cape, especially, there are so many restaurants that you'll be overwhelmed. Here, however, are a few eating experiences that are worth planning for. Be sure to ask hotel staff and folks you meet for additional restaurant recommendations.

A Taste of History

Each November, the public can break bread with the Pilgrims as Plimoth Plantation (137 Warren Avenue, Plymouth, 508-746-1622, *www.plimoth.org*) hosts Thanksgiving dinner. Advance reservations are required for the Victorian Thanksgiving Dinner and the Thanksgiving Day Buffet, and they book up fast. Call 800-262-9356, ext. 8366, for a schedule, prices, and reservations. If you've procrastinated and all seats are reserved, walk-in Thanksgiving Day dining is also available at Plimoth Plantation on a first-come, first-served basis.

JUST FOR PARENTS

Dine inside the stately mansion Captain Ebeneezer Linnell built for his bride in 1840. The chef-owned Captain Linnell House (137 Skaket Beach Road, Orleans, 508-255-3400, *www .linnell.com*) has several intimate dining rooms, including one overlooking a lily pond, and romantic dinners are served nightly year-round. Stroll the restaurant's lush grounds before or after your meal.

If you're celebrating an event with older children, have dinner inside a 200-year-old barn at the Red Pheasant (905 Route 6A, Dennis, 508-385-2133 or 800-480-2133, *www.redpheasantinn.com*), which specializes in local ingredients and traditional New England cooking.

Seafood Delights

Seafood, seafood, seafood! That should be your dining mantra when you're vacationing in this region. Something about the salty air and the laid-back surroundings makes lobster, clams, scallops, fish, and other fruits of the sea taste even more succulent.

For outdoor dining overlooking Plymouth Harbor, head to Wood's Seafood (15 Town Pier, Plymouth, 508-746-0261 or 800-626-1011, *www.woodsseafoods.com*), which has been serving seafood for more than seventy-five years.

In New Bedford, grab a bite at Freestone's City Grill (41 William Street, 508-993-7477, *www.freestones.com*), a two-time first-place winner in the Newport Chowder Cook-Off that is also known for its fish chowder. The kid-friendly restaurant is housed in a historic 1877 bank building and is also a showcase for funky art.

Slurp seafood chowder and enjoy fried scallops, Cape oysters, and other seafood specialties with a view of Hyannis Harbor at the upscale Black Cat (165 Ocean Street, Hyannis, 508-778-1233, *www .blackcattavern.com*). At the Dolphin Restaurant (3250 Main Street/

Route 6A, Barnstable Village, 508-362-6610, *www.thedolphinrestaurant .com*), sit beside the fireplace and enjoy sophisticated dishes, including some of the freshest and tastiest seafood offerings you'll find anywhere. The Impudent Oyster (15 Chatham Bars Avenue, Chatham, 508-945-3545) serves fresh-caught seafood and some of the Cape's most clever culinary combinations.

For fried clams you'll be talking about long after you leave the Cape, head to Baxter's (177 Pleasant Street, Hyannis, 508-775-4490, *www.baxterscapecod.com*), a casual waterfront restaurant. Cobies Clam Shack (3260 Main Street, Brewster, 508-896-7021, *www.cobies .com*) is another good choice for fried clams and other casual fare; save room for the cranberry soft-serve ice cream.

Memorable Meals

In Fall River, you can watch tomorrow's chefs prepare your meal in the kitchen laboratory of the Abbey Grill (100 Rock Street, 508-679-9108, *www.iicaculinary.com/abbey.htm*), the dining room at the International Institute of Culinary Arts, where lunch is served daily and dinner is served on weekends.

Kids love picnics, so stop at one of the Box Lunch restaurants (*www.boxlunch.com*), located in Brewster, Falmouth, Hyannis, North Eastham, Provincetown, South Dennis, or Wellfleet, to pick up their signature Rollwich sandwiches to take with you on your Cape Cod meanderings.

Combine eating and sightseeing on an elegant dinner train or family supper train excursion with Cape Cod Central Railroad (252 Main Street, Hyannis, 508-771-3800 or 888-797-RAIL, *www.capetrain .com*). Reservations and entrée selections are required in advance.

CHAPTER 11

Central and Western Massachusetts

BOSTON AND CAPE COD are the Bay State's best-known destinations, but you'll find that there is so much more. From Worcester—the state's second largest city—to the Pioneer Valley and continuing westward to the verdant hills of the Berkshires, inland Massachusetts offers inspiring landscapes, charming and dynamic towns, cultural and historic attractions, natural wonders, and family play places, including New England's largest theme park.

An Introduction to Worcester and Central Massachusetts

Worcester is New England's second largest city, out-populated only by Boston. A destination for quite a few business travelers, the city and its surrounding central Massachusetts environs are often overlooked by tourists. What are vacationers missing? A host of cultural and historic attractions, prime recreational facilities, one of New England's finest living history museums, and more.

Central Massachusetts also offers that hard-to-quantify but nevertheless all-important benefit—location. If you're looking for a central spot from which to explore New England, Worcester puts you within a few hours' drive of most of Massachusetts and parts of Connecticut, Rhode Island, and New Hampshire, too.

What to See and Do in Central Massachusetts

Have you always passed through central Massachusetts on your way to somewhere else? Here are some reasons to spend a day or two in this part of the state.

Family Amusements

Agritourism is alive and well in central Massachusetts. So is the nineteenth century. It all adds up to unique opportunities for family fun.

Davis' Farmland

⌨145 Redstone Hill, Sterling
☎978-422-MOOO
✍*www.davisfarmland.com*

This playful place with interactive farm-themed activities for children ages one to eight also has a serious mission: to protect rare barnyard breeds. The seventh-generation, family-run farm is North America's largest private sanctuary for endangered livestock. Meet baby animals in the spring, cool off at the Adventure Play & Spray (a zero-depth water sprayground) in the summer, and pick your own apples in the fall.

 TRAVEL TIP

Each autumn, Davis' Farmland is home to Davis' Mega Maze, the oldest and largest corn maze in New England. With the help of renowned English maze designer Adrian Fisher, an eight-acre cornfield is transformed into a three-dimensional puzzle; there's a new design and theme every year. Your family will enjoy the challenge of navigating the elaborate maze, which features bridges, dead ends, and plenty of surprises.

Old Sturbridge Village
⌨1 Old Sturbridge Village Road, Sturbridge
☎508-347-3362 or ☎800-SEE-1830
✐*www.osv.org*

This living history site, which re-creates New England life in the 1830s, attracts thousands of tourists each year. Visitors can get in on the act by talking with costumed "Village People," watching artisans at work, tasting foods prepared hearthside, learning nineteenth-century crafts, and attending special annual events such as an old-fashioned Independence Day celebration in July and Christmas by Candlelight evenings in December.

Museums and Historic Sites

Worcester is home to several museums, including two with terrific kid-appeal.

EcoTarium
⌨222 Harrington Way
☎508-929-2700
✐*www.ecotarium.org*

This science museum and environmental center, open Tuesday through Saturday, has indoor and outdoor wildlife habitats, a planetarium, nature trails, a railroad, and interactive exhibits.

☂ RAINY DAY FUN

Tatnuck Bookseller & Café (18 Lyman Street, Westborough, 508-366-4959, *www.tatnuck.com*) is one of America's largest independent book stores with more than five miles of books. Enjoy a light lunch at the café; then spend a rainy afternoon browsing the children's department.

Higgins Armory Museum
⌨100 Barber Avenue
📞508-853-6015
✎*www.higgins.org*

Catch a glimpse of a past that predates New England's at the only museum in the Americas dedicated to arms and armor. The amazing collections of John Woodman Higgins are grandly displayed in a Great Hall that resembles those found in European castles. Children will enjoy making their own brass rubbings and modeling medieval garb. The museum is open Tuesday through Sunday.

Outdoor Recreation

Love to explore the outdoors? Whether you prefer to ski, walk, bike, or drive, recreational opportunities await.

≡FAST FACT

Johnny Appleseed was real. John Chapman was born in Leominster, Massachusetts. What possessed him to travel an area of about 100,000 square miles sowing the seeds of apple trees? No one is completely certain, but legend has it that Chapman had a dream in which he saw a vision of a land filled with blossoming apple trees where no one went hungry.

Johnny Appleseed Trail
⌨Along Route 2
📞978-534-2302
✎*www.appleseed.org*

If a scenic country drive past farm stands, orchards, vineyards, and other points of interest appeals to you, explore the Johnny Appleseed Trail, the nickname given to the stretch of Route 2 that runs from I-495 west until it connects with the Mohawk Trail around

Westminster. This stretch of Route 2 traverses more than twenty-five classic New England towns and offers dozens of reasons to park and stretch your legs. Stop first at the Johnny Appleseed Visitor Center, located on the westbound side of Route 2 in Lancaster, for information on trail attractions.

Purgatory Chasm State Reservation
⌂ Purgatory Road, Sutton
☎ 508-234-3733
✎ *www.mass.gov/dcr/parks/central/purg.htm*

Hike, climb, or simply picnic beside the seventy-foot granite walls left behind by the last Ice Age at this natural landmark.

Quabbin Reservoir
⌂ 485 Ware Road / Route 9, Belchertown
☎ 413-323-7221
✎ *www.mass.gov/dcr/parks/central/quabbin.htm*
or ✎ *www.friendsofquabbin.org*

Built in the 1930s, Quabbin Reservoir—a popular free spot for hiking, fishing, and bicycling—is one of the largest human-made reservoirs in America. Beneath its tranquil surface lie the "lost towns" of Dana, North Dana, Greenwich, Enfield, and Prescott, all flooded and destroyed so that metropolitan Boston could have an additional water supply. Though the towns no longer exist, their history and fate are preserved by the Swift River Valley Historical Society at the Whitaker-Clary House (Elm Street, New Salem, 978-544-6882), which is open on Wednesday and Sunday afternoons from June through mid-October.

Wachusett Mountain
⌂ 499 Mountain Road, Princeton
☎ 978-464-2300
✎ *www.wachusett.com*

This ski area located on the tallest peak in Massachusetts east of the Connecticut River offers twenty-two trails and eight lifts. The

Polar Kids program provides ski and snowboard instruction for ages four to twelve. After the ski season, the mountain hosts a variety of festivals and events each summer and fall.

An Introduction to Western Massachusetts

Mom wants to shop and tour old houses. Dad's a sports nut. And the kids won't be satisfied until they get on a roller coaster. No need for anyone to pout—if they've selected Pioneer Valley for their holiday. The valley offers a monumental mix of sightseeing and amusement opportunities along the Connecticut River, including two historic villages, the Basketball Hall of Fame, New England's premier amusement park, and Yankee Candle's headquarters. Familial harmony is practically guaranteed.

≡FAST FACT

The Eastern States Exposition (1305 Memorial Avenue / Route 147, West Springfield, 413-737-2443, *www.thebige.com*), or "The Big E," is a New England extravaganza! This seventeen-day celebration of the history and agriculture of the six New England states is one of North America's largest fairs. It's held each September and features carnival rides, top entertainment, regional foods, and much more.

Speaking of harmony, what would you get if you took the sophisticated cultural enticements of Boston or Manhattan and transplanted them to a place of wide-open spaces, lush vegetation, statuesque mountains, sleepy towns, vigorous rivers, and tranquil country roads? You'd get the Berkshire Hills, of course. And you can drive there in just over two hours from Boston or New York City. You'll be joined by the Boston Symphony Orchestra, which takes up residence at Tanglewood each summer; by the nation's leading actors, who escape Manhattan and Los Angeles for summer stock stages; by world-renowned ballet troupes; and by dozens of other artists, writers, and performers. Don't be intimidated—tourists are welcome, too!

This accessible mountain destination offers four-season recreational possibilities, from whitewater rafting during the spring runoff to scenic autumn explorations along one of New England's oldest and most picturesque routes to downhill schussing. You just may find, as generations of vacationers have, that transplanting yourself regularly to a hotel, inn, or even a weekend or summer home here allows you to leave the hassles of city life behind without sacrificing the richness.

What to See and Do in Western Massachusetts

Tie on your running shoes—there are so many unique things to see and do that you may have to scurry to fit them all in. Of course, you don't have to do them all on your first visit.

Family Amusements

Western Massachusetts offers all-season fun for all ages. Catch March Madness at the Basketball Hall of Fame. Spend a summer day at New England's top amusement park. Leaf-peep from an antique train. And marvel at hundreds of thousands of twinkling lights as you drive through an illuminated holiday wonderland.

Berkshire Scenic Railway Museum
Housatonic Street and Willow Creek Road, Lenox
413-637-2210
www.berkshirescenicrailroad.org

On summer weekends and holidays, board a historic train for a one-and-a-half-hour scenic ride from Lenox to Stockbridge, or opt for the shorter, forty-five-minute trip from Lenox to Lee if your little ones are likely to get fidgety.

Magic Wings

⌨281 Greenfield Road, South Deerfield

✆413-665-2805

✍www.magicwings.com

Winter, spring, summer, or fall, it's tropically warm and enchanting inside this 8,000-square-foot glass butterfly conservatory that is home to thousands of fluttering specimens. If you're lucky, one may land right on your shoulder. Open daily year-round, Magic Wings is also home to a one-acre outdoor butterfly garden and Monarchs Restaurant, which serves family fare for lunch and dinner Wednesday through Saturday and brunch on Sunday.

Naismith Memorial Basketball Hall of Fame

⌨1150 West Columbus Avenue, Springfield

✆413-781-6500

✍www.hoophall.com

Basketball was invented in Springfield by Dr. James Naismith, and the Basketball Hall of Fame celebrates this truly American sport and the great players, coaches, and teams that have captured fans' imaginations. Open daily year-round, the hall even offers a chance to get in the game, although without the typical NBA player's salary.

Six Flags New England

⌨1623 Main Street/Route 159, Agawam

✆413-786-9300

✍www.sixflags.com/parks/newengland

The Six Flags theme park company made its mark on New England in 2000 when it took over the former Riverside amusement park. Six Flags New England features thrill rides such as the Superman Ride of Steel (one of the fastest and tallest roller coasters in the world), children's rides and amusements, shows, Looney Tunes Movietown, Wiggles World, and the Hurricane Harbor Water Park. The park is open daily from late May through Labor Day and on weekends and select holidays in the spring and fall. Admission includes all rides and shows; save money by purchasing your tickets online. If you arrive early, you may be able to purchase one of the limited number of Flash Passes available for the day. This ride reservation device will cut your time spent waiting in lines.

The Zoo in Forest Park

⌨302 Sumner Avenue, Springfield

☎413-733-2251

✍*www.forestparkzoo.org*

This small zoo is home to a variety of domestic and exotic animals, and children will enjoy meeting and feeding some of the furry residents. The zoo operates daily from April through mid-October and weekends only the rest of the year.

 TRAVEL TIP

Historic, 750-acre Forest Park (Sumner Avenue, Springfield) is transformed each holiday season into Bright Nights (413-733-3800, *www.brightnights.org*), a two and one-half-mile, drive-through display featuring more than 350,000 lights. One of New England's largest holiday light displays, it features Jurassic World, Seuss Land, North Pole Village, Winter Woods, and a Victorian Village.

Museums and Historic Sites

This culturally rich region is home to many museums and historic attractions; here are just a few with distinct family appeal. You can even rub elbows with the Cat in the Hat and the Grinch.

Berkshire Museum

⌨39 South Street / Route 7, Pittsfield

☎413-443-7171

✍*www.berkshiremuseum.org*

See a diverse collection of art, history, and science exhibits year-round and a breathtaking display of Christmas trees during the annual Festival of Trees from mid-November through December. Kids will especially like the hands-on Dinosaur Dig; there are more activities in the Dino Den.

FAST FACT

For a study in contrasts, visit Hancock Shaker Village (Route 20, Pittsfield, 413-443-0188 or 800-817-1137, *www .hancockshakervillage.org*) for a firsthand look at the simplicity advocated by the Shaker religious sect. Then, head to the Museum of the Gilded Age (104 Walker Street, Lenox, 413-637-3206, *www.gildedage.org*) for a look at living at the opposite, extravagant extreme.

Chesterwood
4 Williamsville Road, Stockbridge
413-298-3579
www.chesterwood.org
Chesterwood was the home of sculptor Daniel Chester French, best known for the statue of the sitting president at the Lincoln Memorial. Visit his studio and gardens late May through mid-October.

Emily Dickinson Museum
280 Main Street, Amherst
413-542-8161
Tours of two historic houses, The Homestead and The Evergreens, are available from March through early December and provide fascinating insight into the life of the reclusive poet, who lived in Amherst for most of her life.

Historic Deerfield

⊡Old Main Street, Deerfield

✆413-775-7214

✐*www.historic-deerfield.org*

This 330-year-old, mile-long street is one of the Pioneer Valley's most popular day-trip destinations. Admission includes guided tours of the village's eighteenth- and nineteenth-century houses, a self-guided tour of the Flynt Center of Early New England Life, and all special programs on the day of your visit, including hands-on activities at the Children's History Workshop. Historic Deerfield is open weekends from January through March and daily the remainder of the year.

Norman Rockwell Museum

⊡9 Glendale Road/Route 183, Stockbridge

✆413-298-4100

✐*www.nrm.org*

Norman Rockwell was one of America's best-loved artists, and his gift for capturing a slice of American life is even more evident when you see his original works up-close. This museum, which has the world's largest collection of original Rockwell art, is open daily year-round.

Springfield Museums at the Quadrangle

⊡21 Edwards Street, Springfield

✆413-263-6800 or ✆800-625-7738

✐*www.springfieldmuseums.org*

Where can you see art masterpieces, ancient treasures, dinosaurs, an aquarium, a planetarium, and arms and armor all in one place? At this unique collection of four museums, clustered around a central green. They include the Museum of Fine Arts, the George Walter Vincent Smith Art Museum, the Springfield Science Museum, and the Connecticut Valley Historical Museum. One admission fee admits you to all four, which are open daily except Monday year-round.

TRAVEL TIP

A national memorial dedicated to beloved children's book author and Springfield native Theodor Geisel, better known as Dr. Seuss, was unveiled at the Quadrangle in Springfield in 2002. The Dr. Seuss National Memorial Sculpture Garden (*www.catinthehat.org/memorial.htm*) is open free to the public year-round. It's a great place to photograph your kids with their favorite Seuss characters, sculpted by Geisel's step-daughter, Lark Grey Dimond-Cates.

Music, Theater, and Dance

The Berkshires have been called "America's Premiere Cultural Resort," and it's no wonder; the bucolic region is home to dozens of renowned cultural institutions. Summer is the most vibrant season for arts here, and many esteemed organizations offer opportunities to introduce young people to the enchantment of theater, music, and dance.

Barrington Stage Company

30 Union Street, Pittsfield

413-236-8888

www.barringtonstageco.org

Kids five to thirteen are admitted free with an adult to MainStage productions, except for preview and Saturday shows, at this critically acclaimed theater, which presents dramas and musicals from mid-May through mid-October.

Berkshire Theatre Festival (BTF)

Main Street, Stockbridge

413-298-5536

www.berkshiretheatre.org

One of the country's oldest theaters, BTF presents several family plays each summer, in addition to its schedule of professional productions on two stages.

Jacob's Pillow

⌨358 George Carter Road, Becket

✆413-243-9919

✎*www.jacobspillow.org*

If you're a dance fan, catch a summertime ballet, modern, or ethnic dance performance at America's oldest dance festival. Many free talks and demonstrations are open to the public, too. For families, the free Inside/Out performances, held Wednesday through Saturday evenings in a casual outdoor setting, are the best bet.

Shakespeare & Company

⌨70 Kemble Street, Lenox

✆413-637-1199

✎*www.shakespeare.org*

Introduce your teens to the Bard's best at this Shakespearean playhouse, which offers free outdoor prelude performances before each evening's show at the Founders' Theatre.

Tanglewood

⌨297 West Street, Lenox

✆413-637-1600

✎*www.tanglewood.org*

Imagine lazing on your picnic blanket, feasting on gourmet goodies, sipping something bubbly, and listening to the rich strains of a symphony or the cool sounds of jazz. A musical evening at Tanglewood, the Boston Symphony Orchestra's summer home in the Berkshires since 1936, may be the most memorable event of your stay in the region. Located in Lenox, Tanglewood is open from late June through early September each year and hosts a variety of performances. Call SymphonyCharge at 617-266-1200 or 888-266-1200 for tickets, or purchase them online. Even if you haven't planned ahead, you may still be able to get Shed or lawn tickets at the gate.

Children younger than five are not permitted in the Koussevitzky Music Shed and other indoor concert venues, and families with young children may only sit on the rear half of the lawn.

Outdoor Recreation

Whether your idea of outdoor enjoyment is schussing down slopes or stopping to smell the roses at a historic garden, western Massachusetts will delight your senses. Even if you're only able to get away for a weekend, you'll feel totally away from it all at these outdoor attractions.

Bash Bish Falls State Park

⌨Falls Road, Mt. Washington

☎413-528-0330

✐*www.mass.gov/dcr/parks/western/bash.htm*

The striking twin cascades of Bash Bish Falls—the state's highest waterfall—await at the end of a short, easy hike. Hidden in the southwest corner of the state, the scenic falls make a worthy day-trip destination; you can even take Baby along in a backpack-style carrier.

Berkshire Botanical Garden

⌨Junction Routes 102 and 183, Stockbridge

☎413-298-3926

✐*www.berkshirebotanical.org*

Stroll through fifteen acres of pretty plantings at one of America's oldest public display gardens, open daily May through mid-October.

Hawkmeadow Farm

⌨322 Lander Road, Lee

☎413-243-2224

✐*www.hawkmeadowllamas.com*

Introduce youngsters to the joy and adventure of hiking with llamas. Pack a picnic to enjoy by the pond after your outing.

Natural Bridge State Park

⌨McCauley Road, North Adams

☎413-663-6392

✐*www.mass.gov/dcr/parks/western/nbdg.htm*

Stand atop North America's only marble bridge, a geologic wonder located on the site of a former quarry. There is a parking fee at this seasonal park, open Memorial Day weekend through Columbus Day.

Skiing in the Berkshires

With a half-dozen ski areas, the Berkshires are the state's top winter destination. While the peaks here can't rival those farther north in Vermont, the region's ski mountains are a good choice for families with children who are just learning to snowboard or ski.

SKI AREAS IN THE BERKSHIRES

Ski Area	Town	Phone Number	Web Site
Berkshire East	Charlemont	413-339-6617	www.berkshireeast.com
Bousquet Ski Area	Pittsfield	413-442-8316	www.bousquets.com
Butternut Basin	Great Barrington	413-528-2000	www.skibutternut.com
Catamount	South Egremont	413-528-1262	www.catamountski.com
Jiminy Peak	Hancock	413-738-5500	www.jiminypeak.com
Otis Ridge	Otis	413-269-4444	www.otisridge.com

Shopping

As you ramble this region, you'll find shopping surprises around every bend—antique shops, flea markets, church tag sales, galleries, boutiques. Here are some of prime places to splurge.

Downtown Northampton
Main Street
413-584-1900
www.explorenorthampton.com

You may just believe you've reached nirvana when you discover Main Street in Northampton. This funky little college town is the perfect destination for an afternoon drifting in and out of clever shops, discovering the works and wares of New England artists and entrepreneurs. Don't miss the endless greeting card department at Faces (175 Main Street, 413-584-4081, *www.facesmainst.com*), one of the quirkiest gift shops on the planet.

Kenver LTD.
⌨39 Main Street, South Egremont Village
✆413-528-2330 or ✆800-342-7547
✑*www.kenver.com*
Even if you're not in the market for ski gear and warm outerwear, it's worth the trip to Kenver, where winter sports equipment and fashions are displayed in a former eighteenth-century stagecoach stop, and free apples, cider, and coffee are served by a roaring fire.

TRAVEL TIP

Want to stretch your vacation dollars in the Berkshires? Trade your U.S. currency for BerkShares (413-528-1737, *www.berkshares .org*). At participating regional banks, the exchange rate is ninety cents per BerkShare—that is, you'll receive 100 BerkShares for every $90—and this local currency is accepted at a variety of local shops, eateries, and other businesses.

Prime Outlets at Lee
⌨50 Water Street, Lee
✆413-243-8186
✑*www.primeoutlets.com*
Save some serious shopping time to search for deals at Prime Outlets, home to more than sixty name-brand outlet stores including Little Me, Gap, J. Crew, Jones New York, Liz Claiborne, and Polo Ralph Lauren.

Tom's Toys
⌨307 Main Street, Great Barrington
✆413-528-3330
✑*www.tomstoys.com*
With an inventory of 16,000 different toys, you're sure to find a plaything to enchant every little one on your list at this colorful store, where young patrons can climb up into the treehouse . . . if they're brave enough to walk through the jungle of stuffed animals.

Yankee Candle Village
⌨Routes 5 and 10 North, South Deerfield
✆877-636-7707
✐*www.yankeecandle.com*

The Yankee Candle flagship store draws millions of visitors each year and is one of New England's most popular tourist attractions. You can spend hours lost inside its cavernous showrooms. The world's largest candle store features a Candlemaking Museum, a dip-your-own-candle area, a Bavarian Christmas Village, the Black Forest where it snows indoors year-round, Santa's Enchanted Toy Works, animatronic musical entertainers, a restaurant with an award-winning kids' menu, and more.

Where to Stay

In central and western Massachusetts, you'll find business-class hotels and classic inns beset with nostalgic allure. The Berkshires, in particular, are known for romantic, historic, and extraordinary inns. Although many are not appropriate for travelers with children, there are plenty of alternatives for family vacationers.

Central Massachusetts Home Bases

The list of lodging possibilities in Worcester reads like a laundry list of who's who in hotels: Courtyard by Marriott, Crowne Plaza, Hampton Inn, Hilton, Quality Inn, Residence Inn by Marriott. That said, there are some more distinctive choices, too. The boutique-style Beechwood Hotel (363 Plantation Street, 508-754-5789 or 800-344-2589, *www .beechwoodhotel.com*) has elegant touches and business amenities and is a popular choice for parents visiting their children at local colleges. About ten away in Spencer, you'll find the Red Maple Inn (217 Main Street, 508-885-9205, *www.theredmapleinn.com*), a circa-1780 Federal-style colonial home turned B&B that is on the National Register of Historic Places; the owners welcome well-behaved children over the age of ten.

Staying in Sturbridge? You'll find charming, family-friendly choices such as the Publick House Historic Inn (277 Main Street/

Route 131, 508-347-3313 or 800-PUBLICK, *www.publickhouse.com*). Built in 1881, it features seventeen rooms and suites, many with canopied beds and other period touches. Just a short walk from the main inn, the Country Motor Lodge has an additional ninety-two rooms, an outdoor pool, and budget rates.

For extensive amenities, try the Sturbridge Host Hotel & Conference Center (366 Main Street, 508-347-7393, *www.sturbridgehosthotel .com*), which offers four restaurants, an indoor pool, a fitness center, miniature golf, and a private lake with a beach and paddleboats. The Sturbridge Comfort Inn & Suites (215 Charlton Road/Route 20, 508-347-3306, *www.sturbridgecomfortinn.com*) also has family appeal with its indoor pool and whirlpool, outdoor pool, complimentary deluxe continental breakfast, and on-site Cracker Barrel Restaurant.

The Central Massachusetts Convention & Visitors Bureau (508-755-7400 or 800-231-7557, *www.worcester.org*) lists many other lodging properties at its Web site and in its downloadable guide for visitors.

Springfield Sleepovers

After a day at Six Flags or one of the Pioneer Valley's other attractions, you'll definitely need a place to rest your weary heads. Not only do hotels in the Greater Springfield area welcome families, they often provide enticements, such as admission tickets for area sights, so be sure to inquire about special deals when you book your room.

≡FAST FACT

Want free tickets for Six Flags New England? At *www .sixflagshoteldeals.com*, you'll find information about hotels in Massachusetts and Connecticut that have partnered with the theme park to offer accommodations packages that include Six Flags admission. Contact participating hotels directly to check availability and confirm details.

If you're planning to visit the Basketball Hall of Fame, you won't find more convenient accommodations than those at the Hilton Garden Inn (800 West Columbus Avenue, Springfield, 413-886-8000, *www .hiltongardeninn.com*), just a short walk from the Hoop Hall. The Sheraton Springfield Monarch Place Hotel (One Monarch Place, Springfield, 413-781-1010, *www.starwoodhotels.com*) is the city's largest hotel. It overlooks the Connecticut River from its convenient location off I-91 and offers guests an indoor heated pool, room service, fitness classes, spa treatments, racquetball courts, and a game room.

In Northampton, the grandeur of an old New England hotel awaits at the Hotel Northampton (36 King Street, 413-584-3100 or 800-547-3529, *www.hotelnorthampton.com*), a 1927 Colonial Revival gem that is a member of Historic Hotels of America.

In Amherst, the Lord Jeffery Inn (30 Boltwood Avenue, 413-253-2576 or 800-742-0358, *www.lordjefferyinn.com*) dates to 1926 and offers both authentic New England fare in the Windowed Hearth Restaurant and a lighter menu at Elijah Boltwood's Tavern, in addition to forty-eight guest rooms and suites. Children under twelve stay at no additional charge, although there is a fee for use of a crib or cot. For reasonable rates, book a room at the Campus Center Hotel at the University of Massachusetts (1 Campus Center Way, 413-549-6000, *www.aux.umass.edu/hotel*). This 116-room "teaching hotel" is a training ground for students majoring in Hospitality and Tourism Management.

If you're looking for the quintessential New England inn, look no further than the Deerfield Inn (81 Old Main Street, Deerfield, 413-774-5587 or 800-926-3865, *www.deerfieldinn.com*). Located in the heart of Historic Deerfield, this 1884 National Historic Landmark has twenty-three individually furnished guest rooms with four-poster beds and other pleasing touches.

Bedtime in the Berkshires

Whether you choose to save a few dollars by booking a standard hotel room or to treat yourselves to a true New England experience by reserving a room at an historic inn, you'll sleep soundly at the end of each active vacation day in the Berkshires.

The Red Lion Inn (30 Main Street, Stockbridge, 413-298-5545, *www.redlioninn.com*) was originally a 1773 stagecoach stop rebuilt in 1897 after a devastating fire. The inn was immortalized in Norman Rockwell's painting, *Main Street, Stockbridge*. The historic property accommodates families in both the main inn and the spacious guest-house suites located in adjacent homes.

Children under twelve stay free in a room with their parents at Cranwell Resort, Spa, and Golf Club (55 Lee Road, Lenox, 413-637-1364 or 800-272-6935, *www.cranwell.com*), a 380-acre estate with an 1894 Tudor mansion as its focal point. Resort guests can enjoy a host of recreational activities including golf, tennis, cross-country skiing, and swimming indoors or out.

For a rustic retreat, consider Race Brook Lodge Bed & Breakfast (864 South Undermountain Road/Route 41, Sheffield, 413-229-2916 or 888-RB-LODGE, *www.rblodge.com*), a 200-year-old New England timber-peg barn with exposed-wood beams, wide plank floors, and warm, inviting nooks that has been transformed into an inn with thirty-two cozy rooms and suites.

JUST FOR PARENTS

Lenox is home to one of the world's most highly regarded health spas, the Canyon Ranch Health Resort (165 Kemble Street, 413-637-4100 or 800-742-9000, *www.canyonranch.com*), where you can relax, be pampered, and learn healthy-living secrets that will extend your spa vacation long past your stay in the Berkshires.

If you're seeking something a bit more standard, you'll find hotels and motor inns as well. Among the larger options are the 179-room Crowne Plaza in Pittsfield (One West Street, 413-499-2000, *www .berkshirecrowne.com*); the modern and convenient Comfort Inn & Suites (249 Stockbridge Road/Route 7, Great Barrington, 413-644-3200 or 800-437-3260, *www.berkshirecomfortinn.com*); the Econo Lodge (130 Pittsfield Road, Lenox, 413-637-4244 or 877-424-6423, *www .choicehotels.com*); Yankee Inn (461 Pittsfield Road, Lenox, 413-499-3700 or 800-835-2364, *www.yankeeinn.com*); the Best Western Black Swan Inn (435 Laurel Street, Lee, 413-243-2700 or 800-876-7926, *www .bestwestern.com*) overlooking Laurel Lake; and the Orchards Hotel (222 Adams Road, Williamstown, 413-458-9611 or 800-225-1517, *www .orchardshotel.com*), an upscale, forty-nine-room retreat.

For additional help in locating accommodations, contact the Berkshire Visitors Bureau's Lodging Reservation Service, 800-237-5747, ext. 140.

Family Dining

So many places to dine, so little time. That may be your lament in this region, where you'll find an eclectic dining scene and plenty of opportunities to sample Yankee cooking at its finest.

A Taste of History

From hearty chowder to baked New England scrod to lobster pie to Indian pudding, if it's traditional Yankee cooking you're seeking, the dining room at the Publick House (277 Main Street/Route 131, 508-347-3313 or 800-PUBLICK, *www.publickhouse.com*) delivers. Every day is Thanksgiving—even the pint-sized will find roast turkey dinner on their menu. Also in central Massachusetts, the historic Salem Cross Inn (260 West Main Street/Route 9, West Brookfield, 508-867-2345, *www.salemcrossinn.com*) serves lunch and dinner, but call ahead to try to time your visit with one of their special Fireplace Feasts, when you can sample early American fare including prime rib roasted on the only known roasting jack still operating in America and apple pie baked in a 1699 beehive oven.

Another historic dining choice is the Cocke 'n Kettle Restaurant (240 South Main Street/Route 122, Uxbridge, 508-278-5518, *www .cockenkettle.com*), housed in a Georgian-style mansion that was built in the early 1800s by Revolutionary War veteran the Honorable

Bazaleel Taft. The dinner menu features hearty steak and seafood preparations; children's portions are available.

For one blowout eating experience, make reservations for the main dining room at the Deerfield Inn (81 Old Main Street, Deerfield, 413-774-5587 or 800-926-3865, *www.deerfieldinn.com*) in the heart of Historic Deerfield. Children's selections are pricey; kids can opt to order small portions of entrées on the dinner menu.

A culinary blast from the past also awaits at the Old Mill (Route 23, South Egremont, 413-528-1421), a 1797 grist mill and blacksmith shop turned restaurant. Or chug on over to Sullivan Station (Railroad Street, Lee, 413-243-2082, *www.sullivanstationrestaurant.com*), and dine inside an old train depot. If you're celebrating a special occasion, you can even book a private dinner party inside a caboose.

Light Bites

Bluebonnet Diner (324 King Street, Northampton, 413-584-3333, *www.bluebonnetdiner.net*), a landmark since 1950, caters to late risers and the enormous local college student population by serving breakfast all day.

For a taste of New England at lunchtime, grab a sandwich at Hayfields (48 Main Street, Northampton, 413-586-7114), a Vermont-style deli.

The Northampton Brewery (11 Brewster Court, Northampton, 413-584-9903, *www.northamptonbrewery.com*), the oldest operating brewpub in the Northeast, is a good choice for lighter fare and locally crafted seasonal beers, including Pumpkin Ale in the fall. You'll also find pub food and beers microbrewed in the Pioneer Valley at Amherst Brewing Company (24-36 North Pleasant Street, Amherst, 413-253-4400, *www.amherstbrewing.com*). Both brewpubs offer children's menus.

For beer brewed in the Berkshires and hearty burgers and sandwiches, head for Barrington Brewery & Restaurant (420 Stockbridge Road/Route 7, Great Barrington, 413-528-8282, *www.barringtonbrewery.net*).

If you're in the mood for soup for supper, the sixteen-ounce Super Bowls of clam chowder, lobster bisque, and other hearty seasonal soups at the '6 House Pub at The 1896 House Country Inn and Motels (Cold Spring Road/Route 7, Williamstown, 413-458-1896 or 888-999-1896, *www.1896house.com*) will fill you up on a budget.

Memorable Meals

Bountiful, all-you-can-eat buffet breakfasts featuring pancakes, French toast, scrambled eggs, home fries, bacon, sausage, ham, milk, juice, coffee, tea, and pure maple syrup (hungry yet?) are served on weekends during sugaring season (late February through early April) and in the fall at High Hopes Farm Sugar House (Route 112, South Worthington, 413-238-5919 or 800-627-5374, *www.highhopesmaple.com*). Get there early, or plan on a wait.

Didn't think you could enjoy a luau in New England? Then you haven't heard of the Hu Ke Lau Restaurant & Dinner Theater (705 Memorial Drive, Chicopee, 413-593-5222, *www.hukelau.com*), which serves an Asian- and Polynesian-inspired menu and hosts family-friendly Hawaiian-themed shows most Friday and Saturday evenings.

If your accommodations have a kitchen and you'll be cooking breakfast in, stop by the Otis Poultry Farm (1570 North Main Road/Route 8, Otis, 413-269-4438 or 800-286-2690, *www.otispoultryfarm.com*) and pick up custom-laid eggs. Owned by the same family since 1904, the farm is also known for its home-baked breads, chicken and turkey pies in five sizes, and homemade fudge.

Dining at the Red Lion Inn (30 Main Street, Stockbridge, 413-298-5545, *www.redlioninn.com*) is not just an experience—it's three! That's because you can select from the formal main dining room, the more casual Widow Bingham's Tavern, or the dark and intimate pub atmosphere of the Lion's Den. The inn's menus feature fresh Berkshire-grown ingredients, and all three restaurants offer children's menus. Whichever you choose, make a reservation.

Maine

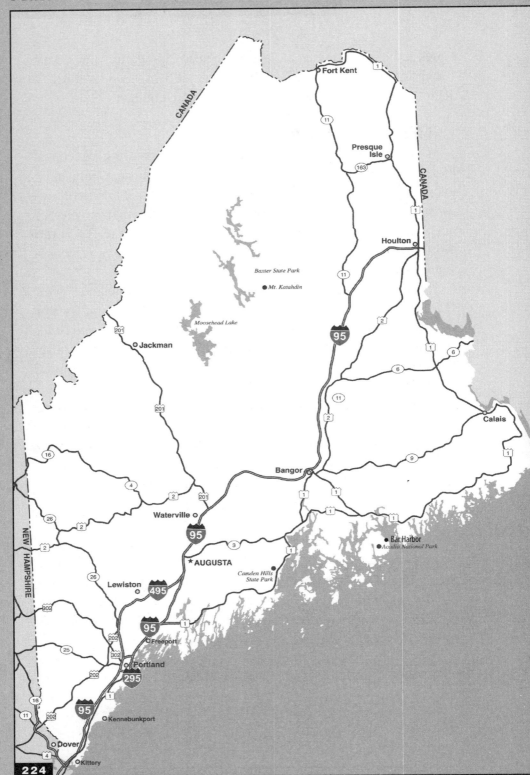

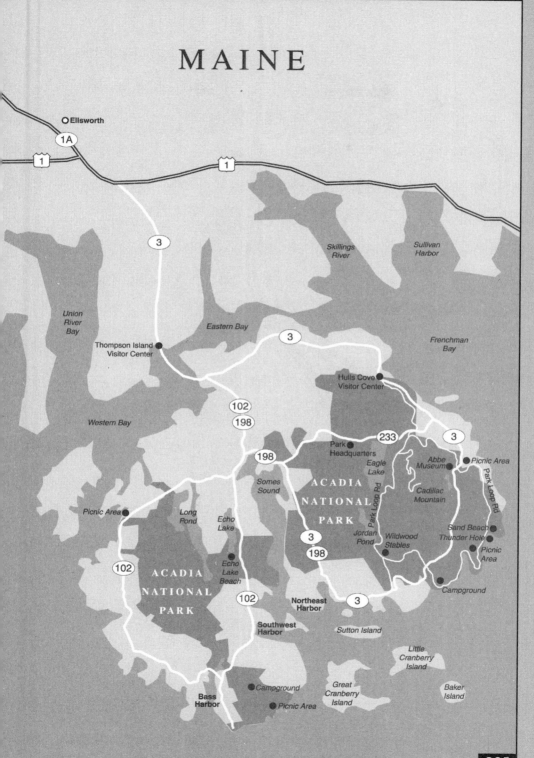

MAINE

○ Ellsworth

1A

1

3

Skillings River

Sullivan Harbor

Union River Bay

Eastern Bay

3

Thompson Island Visitor Center ●

Frenchman Bay

Western Bay

Hulls Cove Visitor Center ●

102

198

3

Park Headquarters ●

233

3

198

Eagle Lake

Abbe Museum ●

Picnic Area ●

Somes Sound

Cadillac Mountain

Picnic Area ●

Long Pond

Echo Lake

ACADIA NATIONAL PARK

Park Loop Rd

Park Loop Rd

ACADIA NATIONAL PARK

3

198

Jordan Pond

Wildwood Stables

Sand Beach ●
Thunder Hole ●
Picnic Area ●

102

Echo Lake Beach ●

102

Northeast Harbor

Campground ●

Southwest Harbor

3

Sutton Island

Little Cranberry Island

Baker Island

Bass Harbor

Campground ●
Picnic Area ●

Great Cranberry Island

Portland, Maine

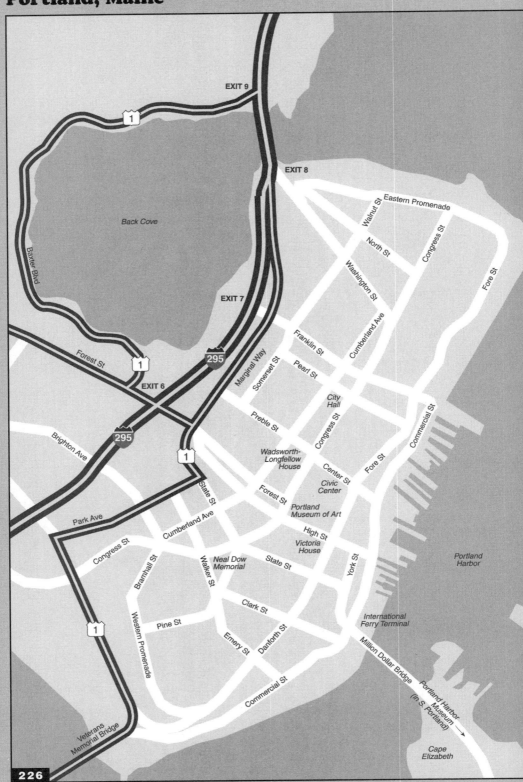

CHAPTER 12

Maine

IF YOU LIKE TO strap kayaks or mountain bikes to the roof of your SUV and head for remote places, then Maine is for you. If you enjoy oceanside amusement rides, playing in the surf, and feasting on fresh lobster, then Maine is also for you. If you're always up for adventure, whether on a snowmobile, a dogsled, a raft, or a windjammer, then Maine is for you, too. If you like to shop for casual clothing and outdoor gear at 3 A.M., then Maine is definitely for you.

An Introduction to the Pine Tree State

Warning: Travelers who spend time in New England's northernmost state are in grave danger of becoming Maine-iacs! Once you've got Maine on your mind, you'll find that the addiction runs deep—to the cellular level, even. But it still won't compare to the true blue affection harbored by Mainers whose families have called the state home for generations. In fact, even if you fall in love with Maine, move there, and have children, your young'uns will still be considered to be "from away." As the locals just might tell you, "Hatchin' chickens in the stove doesn't make 'em muffins, does it?"

The rule of thumb is that if at least three generations of your ancestors aren't from Maine—or even if your ancestors are from Maine, but you've moved away and then returned—you're "from away." But don't for a moment think that you won't feel welcome among the natives.

Mainers are renowned for their hospitality, and tourism is one of the state's most important industries.

The vast territory that is Maine was actually governed by Massachusetts until 1820, when it was admitted to the Union as the twenty-third state. Early European settlement attempts at St. Croix Island in 1604 and at Popham Beach in 1607 were unsuccessful, but in 1641, York became the first city in America with a charter from the English Crown. Today, while much of Maine's jagged, 3,478-mile Atlantic coastline is quite well developed, the northern inland regions are largely uninhabited. Keep in mind that Maine's large size means distances between cities and towns can be much more significant than in other New England states.

Choose Maine for a family beach vacation or a sailing adventure aboard a tall-masted windjammer, for a frenetic weekend of outlet shopping, or for quiet time in a woodsy lakefront cabin, for a wet and woolly whitewater adventure, or for a more leisurely but nevertheless stimulating moose safari. Whatever type of escape you choose, don't let being "from away" cause you to stay away.

When to Visit

Overall, temperatures are a bit cooler than in the rest of the region. While this can be an impediment to winter travelers, summers are more comfortable, particularly for outdoor activities such as biking and hiking. Maine's four seasons also begin and end on a slightly different timetable. Summers get off to a slower start, and peak fall colors can arrive two weeks or more ahead of the rest of New England. Summer and fall are definitely the tourism "high season," so look for bargain accommodations at other times.

Getting There and Getting Around

Mainers have been known to tell travelers, "You can't get there from here," and while their tongues are usually firmly planted in their cheeks, there's some truth to this old refrain. While it's not terribly difficult to get to Maine, getting around inside the state can indeed present a challenge. If you plan to travel far off the beaten path (i.e., the Maine Turnpike), it's a good idea to invest in a Maine road atlas. You'll also want to pack snacks and drinks, as Maine's winding and scenic byways aren't lined with golden arches.

Portland International Jetport (PWM)

Portland International Jetport (207-874-8877, *www.portlandjetport .org*), serves northern New England from its convenient location off the Maine Turnpike at exit 46. Passenger traffic through the jetport has grown to more than 1.4 million travelers annually.

MAJOR AIRLINES SERVING PORTLAND INTERNATIONAL JETPORT

Airline	Phone Number	Web Site
Continental	800-525-0280	*www.continental.com*
Delta	800-221-1212	*www.delta.com*
JetBlue Airways	800-538-2583	*www.jetblue.com*
Northwest	800-225-2525	*www.nwa.com*
United	800-241-6522	*www.ual.com*
US Airways	800-428-4322	*www.usair.com*

Companies offering airport shuttle service include Mermaid Transportation (207-772-2509, *www.gomermaid.com*) and VIP Tour and Charter/Portland Explorer (207-772-4457, *www.transportme.org*), which operates seasonally. Many Portland-area hotels also provide courtesy vans for their guests. Taxis and limousine service are also readily available.

Bangor International Airport (BGR)

Bangor International Airport (207-992-4600 or 866-359-2264, *www .flybangor.com*), serves northern Maine and Canada from its convenient location off I-95. To reach the airport, take exit 184 for Union Street off I-95 and follow signs. There are more than fifty domestic flights to and from Bangor daily.

MAJOR AIRLINES SERVING BANGOR INTERNATIONAL AIRPORT

Airline	Phone Number	Web Site
American	☎800-433-7300	🖰 www.aa.com
Continental	☎800-525-0280	🖰 www.continental.com
Delta	☎800-221-1212	🖰 www.delta.com
Northwest	☎800-225-2525	🖰 www.nwa.com
US Airways	☎800-428-4322	🖰 www.usair.com

Companies offering scheduled airport shuttle service include Bar Harbor–Bangor Shuttle (207-479-5911, *www.barharborshuttle.com*), Concord Trailways (207-945-4000 or 800-639-3317, *www.concordtrailways .com*), The Bus (207-992-4670), and West's Coastal Connection (207-546-2823 or 800-596-2823, *www.westbusservice.com*). Several local hotels offer free airport shuttle service. Taxis and limousine service are also readily available.

Trains, Buses, and Ferries

Flying and driving aren't the only ways to arrive in Maine. Amtrak (800-872-7245, *www.amtrak.com*) provides regularly scheduled rail service to Portland. The Downeaster travels from Boston's North Station to Portland in under three hours and makes stops in three other coastal Maine towns: Wells, Saco, and Old Orchard Beach.

Vermont Transit Lines (207-772-6587 or 800-552-8737, *www .vermonttransit.com*), an affiliate of Greyhound Lines (800-231-2222, *www.greyhound.com*), provides inbound bus service from Boston to several Maine destinations. Concord Trailways also provides bus transportation to a dozen communities in Maine.

Visiting from Canada, or want to take a side trip while you're traveling in Maine? The Cat High Speed Car Ferry (877-359-3760, *www .catferry.com*) connects Portland and Bar Harbor with Yarmouth, Nova Scotia, from June through early October. Be sure to make advance reservations. Travel time is approximately three hours from Bar Harbor, five and a half hours from Portland.

Getting Around

While seasonal shuttle services in Portland and Bar Harbor make it relatively easy for vacationers to get around town without a car, you'll need your own wheels in the off-season or if you plan to visit other prime vacation destinations in the state.

≡FAST FACT

If it's been a few years since you visited Maine, or if you're looking at older maps or travel brochures, the exit numbers along the Maine Turnpike (I-95) and Interstate 295 were changed in 2004. Speed your trip along the Maine Turnpike by using an E-ZPass–compatible transponder (*www.ezpassmaineturnpike.com*); turnpike toll booths were equipped to accept electronic payment in 2005.

There's an excellent chance that you'll find yourselves on Interstate 95, the Maine Turnpike, during your travels. This major north-south highway runs from Kittery north to Houlton near the Canadian border. The Maine Turnpike Authority (877-682-9433, *www.maineturnpike.com*) has a helpful Web site featuring maps and news about road conditions. You'll enjoy a more scenic, albeit slower, trip if you opt to follow Route 1, an alternative north-south route that hugs the Maine coast from Kittery to Fort Kent.

There is no major east-west highway, so you may need to follow a circuitous route without the usual rest stops and travel amenities if you plan to explore the interior of the state. Ask someone at your lodging property to recommend a driving route. Keep in mind that you won't be able to travel at top speed on many of Maine's interior roads, so ask locals as well how much time it will take to reach your destination. In the northernmost reaches of the state, it's not uncommon to encounter unpaved roads— and moose—so you'll need to exercise extreme caution.

If you're determined to see Maine without a car, be sure to visit the special Web site created by the Maine Department of Transportation, *www.exploremaine.org*, to discover alternative ways to navigate the state via bike, bus, ferry, train, or charter plane.

Must-See Activities and Attractions

Maine is not only visually stunning, it is a place that will stimulate all of your senses. From the sweet smell of pine to the exhilarating saltiness of sea air, from the tartness of wild blueberries to the decadent richness of lobster morsels dunked in butter, you'll have multisensory memories of your Maine vacation. While these highlights for family vacationers are mostly clustered along the coast, don't overlook the opportunities for outdoor recreation and quiet escape offered by other regions. Some of the best attractions have no signs and no admission price.

Acadia National Park

⊞Hulls Cove Visitor Center, Route 3, Bar Harbor

✆207-288-3338

✑*www.nps.gov/acad*

Acadia was the first National Park established east of the Mississippi River. Each year, millions flock to this 47,633-acre preserved paradise. Popular activities include driving the 27-mile Park Loop Road to view spectacular mountain and coastal scenery; walking, hiking, and biking on 45 miles of carriage roads; hiking 115 miles of trails rated from easy to strenuous; fishing; boating; horse-drawn carriage rides; cross-country skiing; snowshoeing; and ranger-led bird walks and other nature programs.

Funtown Splashtown U.S.A.

⊞774 Portland Road / Route 1, Saco

✆207-284-5139

✑*www.funtownsplashtownusa.com*

Maine's largest theme park is actually two parks in one. Enjoy the wooden roller coaster and other thrill rides, classic amusements, and kiddie attractions at Funtown. Cool off at Splashtown, home to the Fun Lagoon and more than a dozen water slides including two that are seven stories tall.

Kittery Outlets

⊞Route 1, Kittery

✆888-KITTERY

✑*www.thekitteryoutlets.com*

The densely packed factory outlet stores of Kittery can get even reluctant shoppers' blood pumping. You'll find savings on men's, women's, and children's wear, footwear, housewares, giftware—even underwear—at the more than 100 outlet stores that line a mile stretch of Route 1.

L.L. Bean Flagship Store
⌨95 Main Street, Freeport
✆800-559-0747, ext. 37222
✐*www.llbean.com*

What's open 365 days a year, twenty-four hours a day, and draws more than 3 million visitors each year? It's the flagship store of legendary Maine retailer L.L. Bean, a Main Street fixture in Freeport since 1917. The locks on the doors were removed in 1951 when the twenty-four-hour schedule was initiated.

Maine Lobster
Lobstering is one of Maine's oldest industries, and it remains a major contributor to the economy today. Believe it or not, the ultimate "other white meat" has less cholesterol than an equivalent serving of skinless chicken. Of course, you don't usually dunk skinless chicken in drawn butter before you devour it! Feasting on lobster is a must in Maine. Lobster boat excursions are offered along the shore if you'd like to see firsthand the life of a Maine lobsterman.

☂ RAINY DAY FUN

The Wyeth Center at the Farnsworth Art Museum (16 Museum Street, Rockland, 207-596-6457, *www.farnsworthmuseum.org*) is home to the world's most extensive collection of works by the Wyeth family's three generations of celebrated Maine painters. N. C. Wyeth relocated his family to the small fishing harbor of Port Clyde in 1920. His son, Andrew, and his grandson, Jamie, continued the family legacy of capturing some of the most striking and enduring images of the state.

Old Orchard Beach

West Grand Avenue and East Grand Avenue, Old Orchard Beach

207-934-2500

www.oldorchardbeachmaine.com

When summer shines, so does this seaside family playground that hearkens back to an earlier era with its arcades, rides, amusement pier, and boardwalk lined with pizza and fried dough vendors. Best of all, the main attraction—the seven-mile sandy beach—is open free to the public.

Portland Head Light

Fort Williams Park, 1000 Shore Road, Cape Elizabeth

207-799-2661

www.portlandheadlight.com

You've probably seen photographs of Portland Head Light in lighthouse books and calendars. Join the 350,000 to 400,000 people who visit the first lighthouse erected on Maine's seacoast each year. Portland Head Light was first lit in 1791, and George Washington appointed its first keeper.

Whitewater Rafting

www.raftmaine.com

There are more than a dozen whitewater adventure outfitters in Maine, where river rafting is serious business. From late April until mid-October, controlled daily releases from hydropower dams on the Penobscot and Kennebec Rivers guarantee excellent rafting conditions. Ask about minimum age requirements when booking your trip.

Maine Windjammer Cruises

800-807-WIND

www.sailmainecoast.com

Maine is home to America's most historic fleet of sailing vessels, and the Maine Windjammer Association represents twelve of these privately owned and operated tall ships, which take passengers of all ages on memorable voyages. While the accommodations are simple—a bit like camping on the water—the experiences are unforgettable as you ply the island-dotted waters of Maine's Midcoast region.

York's Wild Kingdom
⌨Route 1, York Beach
☎207-363-4911
✐*www.yorkzoo.com*

This wild place is part zoo, part amusement park. The attractions range from a walk-through aviary to a Ferris wheel, from a petting zoo to paddleboats, from a monkey exhibit to a merry-go-round.

Family Fun Plans

Because Maine is large, and you may have to spend hours in the car just to get there, it's perfectly acceptable to choose a home base. You can easily spend a week or more in vacation spots like Bar Harbor or Kennebunkport or even at a lakeside camping resort. If you're determined, however, to explore as much of Maine as possible, these suggested itineraries will provide some ideas for navigating around the state.

A Four-Day Shore and Shopping Escape
Whether you want to book yourself into a few different hotels or choose one central spot on the shore, this itinerary will keep you on the go.

Day One: Start in Kittery—Maine's outlet shopping capital—and spend a half-day searching for bargains. You won't be able to see it all, so plan your outlet strategy ahead of time. If you just can't wait for your first taste of lobster, follow Route 1 South to Warren's Lobster House (11 Water Street/Route 1, Kittery, 207-439-1630, *www.lobster house.com*), and order a lobster roll or lobster croissant for lunch.

In the afternoon, enjoy a leisurely drive north along coastal Route 1 to Kennebunkport. The forty-five-minute, narrated tour offered by Intown Trolley (Ocean Avenue, 207-967-3686, *www.intowntrolley .com*) is a good way to get acquainted with the town. Have a casual dinner overlooking the water at Federal Jack's Restaurant and Brewpub (8 Western Avenue, 207-967-4322, *www.federaljacks.com*).

Day Two: Start with a hearty breakfast at the Maine Diner (2265 Post Road/Route 1, Wells, 207-646-4441, *www.mainediner.com*); yes, they have lobster quiche, lobster omelets, and Lobster Benedict on the menu. Then, travel north on Route 1 to Old Orchard Beach, and spend the bulk of the day relaxing beside the ocean, browsing boardwalk stores, and riding the rides at the Pier. For dinner, try to score a table on the outdoor deck at Surf 6 Oceanfront Grille & Bar (6 Cortland Street, Old Orchard Beach, 207-934-2058, *www.oldorchardbeachlodging.com/Surf6/Surf6home.htm*).

Day Three: Spend the day exploring Portland, including the shops and restaurants of the Old Port District. On your way north, stop at Len Libby Chocolates (419 U.S. Route 1, Scarborough, 207-883-4897, *www.lenlibby.com*) to visit Lenny, the 1,700-pound, life-size chocolate moose. You may also want to detour out to Cape Elizabeth to see Maine's oldest lighthouse, Portland Head Light (Fort Williams Park, 1000 Shore Road, Cape Elizabeth, 207-799-2661, *www.portlandheadlight.com*). In the evening, catch a baseball game at Hadlock Field (271 Park Avenue, Portland, 800-936-3647, *www.portlandseadogs.com*) if the Portland Sea Dogs are in town.

Day Four: On your last day, continue north to Freeport. Get there as early as you like—the L.L. Bean flagship store (95 Main Street, 800-559-0747, ext. 37222, *www.llbean.com*) is open twenty-four hours a day. The assortment of other outlets and retail stores in town will keep you busy until it's time to head for home.

A Midcoast Maine Lighthouse Tour

Lighthouses are beautiful and functional structures that beckon to many vacationers. Maine has 65 historic beacons. This two-day tour will allow you to view several distinctive lights, as well as coastal sights. Don't forget your camera!

Day One: Start at Camden Hills State Park (Route 1, Camden, 207-236-3109 or 207-236-0849), where you can hike or drive to the summit of Mt. Battie. There's no lighthouse on Mt. Battie, but with a pair of binoculars, you can spot as many as sixteen lighthouses on a clear day.

Before leaving Camden, drive along Beacon Avenue for a view of Curtis Island Light, which dates to 1896. Its island home was named for *Saturday Evening Post* publisher Cyrus Curtis.

From Camden, take Route 1 North to Lincolnville, where you can board the Maine State Ferry Service (207-734-6935, *www.state .me.us/mdot/opt/ferry/maine-ferry-service.php*) ferry to Isleboro. Grindle Point Light is located near the ferry landing; the keeper's house is now the Sailor's Memorial Museum. This active beacon was first built in 1851, and the present lighthouse dates to 1874. The ferry trip is about twenty minutes. You'll want to call ahead for a schedule.

Day Two: Travel to Rockport, where Indian Island Light is visible from Rockport Marine Park (Andre Street, 207-236-4404). The present light was built in 1875 and taken out of service in 1934.

Continue south on Route 1 to Rockland, where you can visit the 1902 Rockland Breakwater Light (*www.rocklandlighthouse.com*), visible from the end of Samoset Road. Tread carefully if you decide to walk out on the mile-long breakwater for a closer look.

Also see Owls Head Light in nearby Owls Head; it's located on the grounds of Owls Head Light State Park (Lighthouse Road, 207-941-4014). This 1825 lighthouse, which is not open to the public, is still an active navigational aid. To get to the lighthouse, you'll have to walk up a steep ramp and climb dozens of steps, but the views are worth the exertion.

A fitting end to your expedition is a stop at the Maine Lighthouse Museum (One Park Drive, Rockland, 207-594-3301, *www.mainelight housemuseum.com*), open year-round. The museum contains a variety of exhibits and lighthouse artifacts, including the nation's largest collection of historic Fresnel lighthouse lenses. Lighthouse lovers will find terrific souvenirs in the gift shop.

═══FAST FACT

If you have time, you may want to drive out to the fishing village of Port Clyde for a visit to Marshall Point Light (Marshall Point Road, *www.marshallpoint.org*). If you feel a sense of déjà vu as you jog along the white ramp leading out to this picturesque beacon, you've probably seen the movie *Forrest Gump*.

A Long Weekend of Leaf Peeping

Maine is a popular choice for travelers who want to experience New England's autumn splendor. While it is impossible to predict exactly when foliage colors will be at their peak, you'll have a good chance of seeing vibrant leaves sometime between mid-September and early October.

Day One: Travel to Bethel in the western Lakes and Mountains region. This will be your home base for a long weekend of leaf peeping. If you arrive early enough in the day, pick your own apples at Lyon Orchard (684 Grover Hill Road, Bethel, 207-824-2842).

Day Two: Drive along Route 26 through Grafton Notch State Park (207-824-2912 or 207-624-6080, *www.state.me.us/cgi-bin/doc/parks/ find_one_name.pl?park_id=1*). On your way, stop in Newry to view The Artist's Bridge, one of Maine's most painted and photographed covered bridges. Stop often along this scenic drive; there are plenty opportunities for hiking, picnicking, and waterfall viewing.

Day Three: From Bethel, travel east on Route 2, then head north on Route 17 to Rangeley. There are many scenic places to pull over along this trip, including Coos Canyon in Byron, where you can actually pan for gold, although the water may be a bit cold in the fall. As you approach Rangeley, a spot known as Height of Land, which overlooks Mooselookmeguntic Lake, affords remarkable views; you'll even be able to see New Hampshire's White Mountains in the distance. While you're in the Rangeley area, rent a canoe at River's Edge Sports (Route 4, Oquossoc, 207-864-5582, *www.etravelmaine .com/riversedge*), located next to the public boat launch, and go for a paddle on Rangeley Lake. Call ahead to check availability.

Day Four: Before you depart for home, travel south from Bethel to New Gloucester and visit the Sabbathday Lake Shaker Village (Shaker Road, 207-926-4597, *www.shaker.lib.me.us*) and its museum and store. This is the home of the last few remaining followers of the Shaker faith. Whether you take a tour or simply stroll around for views of fields and farm animals, you'll find this to be a scenic and lovely place to appreciate nature's gifts.

CHAPTER 13

Portland and Southern Maine

PORTLAND IS MAINE'S BOSTON—a city that is old and new all at once, but unlike Boston, Maine's largest city is compact and easily navigable. The forty-two-mile stretch of the Maine Turnpike between Kittery and Portland holds many temptations, however, and families needn't venture far north to discover why the state has earned the nickname, "Vacationland." The southern coast is home to Maine's best beaches, oldest towns, choicest outlet shopping . . . and largest crowds.

An Introduction to Portland and Maine's Southern Shore

Portland was first settled in 1632, and in spite of two devastating fires that destroyed early landmarks, it retains the character etched upon it over its centuries of existence as a thriving commercial port. Today, history is well preserved in Portland, but this is also a thoroughly hip city—home to sophisticated hotels, coffee nooks, brewpubs, swank shops, ethnic eateries, a minor league baseball team, and world-class entertainment. Portland remains New England's largest tonnage seaport, and it is also emerging as a cruise ship destination, with more than 40,000 passengers exploring the port city each year.

Freeport, a town synonymous with shopping, is located a short drive north of Portland. Since venerable Maine retailer L. L. Bean set up shop here in 1917, the town has mushroomed into a retail bonanza of designer outlets and specialty stores selling everything from home furnishings and apparel to Maine-made products and mooselania. It was also in Freeport that Maine citizens contemplated a revolution in the early 1800s. Mainers were seeking their independence not from Britain but from governance by Massachusetts. In 1819, Massachusetts gave Maine the go-ahead to petition for statehood, and in 1820, Maine became the last New England state to join the Union.

Southern Maine is home to the state's two oldest towns—Kittery and York—but it isn't history that lures hordes of travelers to the region. This part of Maine, unlike the far northern reaches, is close to the rest of New England, and it's also an area that most Maine visitors must traverse on their way to more remote destinations. Of course, many vacationers never get much farther than the south shore once they discover the allure of outlet stores, cozy harbors, coastal towns, and beaches.

FAST FACT

Southern Maine is just over an hour's drive from Boston, and it is a popular day-trip destination and weekend escape for city dwellers. On a Friday evening in season, you can definitely spend a bit longer than you'd hoped snarled in traffic heading into Maine on I-95.

Of course, southern Maine isn't exactly the most tropical place. Ocean temperatures may make you say, "Brr!" even in July and August, so the peak season in this waterside destination is a bit abbreviated. On the flip side, if you plan your vacation for the off-season, you're likely to find lodging deals and to feel as if you have the place largely to yourself. That is, until you make your obligatory stop at the legendary outlets in Kittery, where bargain hunting is always in season.

What to See and Do

Some families are fond of tradition; they spend the same summer week at the same beach house enjoying the same simple pleasures year after year. Other folks like to mix things up, hopping from beach to beach, taking in historic sites, hitting the water, and testing the limits . . . of their physical endurance or their credit cards. Southern Maine appeals to families at both ends of the vacation spectrum, and everywhere in between.

Beaches

There are more than thirty public beaches between Kittery and Portland. They range from small, quiet patches of sand known mostly to locals to rollicking, hotel-lined resorts where the beach is just one of many attractions. Here are some of the largest Maine beaches with the greatest appeal for families.

Kennebunk Beach

⌨Beach Avenue, Kennebunk

Gooch's Beach at the northern end is the largest of the three beaches that constitute the mile-and-a-half-long Kennebunk Beach. It's popular with swimmers, sunbathers, bodysurfers, and sandcastle makers. Sidewalks connect Gooch's Beach with both rocky Middle Beach and the petite, sheltered Mother's Beach, where families with small children will enjoy the gentler waves. Lifeguards are on duty at Gooch's Beach and Mother's Beach in season. Parking stickers for all three beaches can be purchased at the chamber of commerce, town hall, or police station.

Ogunquit Main Beach

⌨Beach Street, Ogunquit

✆207-646-5139

Ogunquit's lovely beach is separated from the mainland by the Ogunquit River. Parking at the main beach is scarce, but visitors can park elsewhere in town and board one of the trolleys operated by the Ogunquit Trolley Company (207-646-1411, *www.ogunquittrolley.com*) to reach the beach.

TRAVEL TIP

The Marginal Way is one of Maine's most scenic—and most popular—walks. This mile-and-a-quarter-long paved foot-path runs from Ogunquit Beach to Perkins Cove, providing dramatic views of rocky cliffs along the shore. There are thirty memorial benches where you can rest when little family members' legs tire.

Old Orchard Beach
⌖Along West Grand Avenue and East Grand Avenue, Old Orchard
  Beach
☏207-934-2500
✍www.oldorchardbeachmaine.com
The perennial favorite among southern Maine's beaches is Old Orchard Beach, which is not just a seven-mile sandy strip but a family amusement center with rides, games, arcades, restaurants, and fireworks popping near the pier every Thursday night from late June through Labor Day.

Wells Beach
⌖Mile Road and Atlantic Avenue, Wells
☏207-646-7912
Wells Beach is the largest and best known of the three public beaches in Wells. This broad stretch of sand is lifeguard-protected in the summer months, and restrooms and a playground are available to visitors. Parking fees are charged at town-operated lots near the beach.

Willard Beach
⌖Preble Street, South Portland
☏207-767-3201

This crescent-shaped beach between two lighthouses appeals to families because of its soft sand and calm Casco Bay surf. It is located just three miles from downtown Portland.

Boat and Trolley Tours

A boat tour will give you an entirely different perspective of coastal Maine and a chance to see everything from lighthouses to whales. For landlubbers, trolley tours offer an old-fashioned way to see the sights.

Atlantic Seal Cruises

⌨Freeport Town Wharf, South Freeport

✆207-865-6112 or ✆877-ATLSEAL

From Memorial Day weekend through late October, head out to sea to spy on seals with this boat tour operator, which stops at Eagle Island for visits to the former home of North Pole explorer Admiral Peary on its daytime excursions.

Casco Bay Lines

⌨56 Commercial Street, Portland

✆207-774-7871

✎*www.cascobaylines.com*

Casco Bay Lines is the nation's oldest continuously operating ferry company. Check their summer sailing schedule for scenic cruises. You can even ride along on the mail boat that delivers letters and parcels to the residents of the islands in Casco Bay.

First Chance Whale Watch

⌨4 Western Avenue / Route 9, Kennebunk

✆207-967-5507 or ✆800-767-2628

✎*www.firstchancewhalewatch.com*

Don't miss the chance from Memorial Day through Columbus Day to head out to sea with First Chance Whale Watch Cruises. They offer not only whale-watch expeditions but also scenic lobster-harvesting and evening-storybook cruises. Reservations are a good idea.

Intown Trolley

⌨Ocean Avenue, Kennebunkport

✆207-967-3686

✍*www.intowntrolley.com*

Traffic in Kennebunkport can be brutal in the summer, so sit back and enjoy a narrated tour of the seaside town. Intown Trolley's forty-five-minute sightseeing outings take you past photogenic places and points of interest, including former president George Bush's coastal home.

 RAINY DAY FUN

For another dose of transportation nostalgia, visit the Seashore Trolley Museum (195 Log Cabin Road, Kennebunkport, 207-967-2712, *www.trolleymuseum.org*), where you can ride the rails in an early 1900s streetcar and learn about the bygone trolley era. The world's largest electric railway museum is open daily rain or shine from Memorial Day weekend through Columbus Day weekend, and weekends only in early May and late October.

Family Amusements

While the simple joys of playing in the sand, hopping over waves, and collecting shells will keep kids entertained for days, southern Maine delivers additional diversions.

Funtown Splashtown U.S.A.

⌨774 Portland Road / Route 1, Saco

✆207-284-5139

✍*www.funtownsplashtownusa.com*

Northern New England's largest amusement park celebrated its fortieth anniversary in 2007 by doubling the size of its Splashtown water park. You'll like the flexible ticket options, which allows you to choose either the wet side or the dry side of the park or both and to save money after 4 P.M. Funtown Splashtown U.S.A. is open from mid-May through mid-September.

Maine Wildlife Park
Route 26, Gray

207-657-4977

www.state.me.us/ifw/education/wildlifepark/index.htm

Ready for something wild? Head inland to the Maine Wildlife Park, home to animals that need protection or rehabilitation including moose, lynx, bobcats, mountain lions, coyotes, bald eagles, turkey vultures, and more.

 TRAVEL TIP

New England is not exactly known for its deserts, but thanks to a glacier that left behind a large sand deposit some 11,000 years ago, Freeport is home to a genuine desert. Tour the Desert of Maine (95 Desert Road, Freeport, 207-865-6962, *www.desertofmaine.com*) from early May to mid-October.

Portland Sea Dogs
Hadlock Field, 271 Park Avenue, Portland

207-879-9500 or 800-936-3647

www.portlandseadogs.com

When the dog days of summer arrive, it's time to cheer on the Portland Sea Dogs, the Eastern League Double-A Affiliate of Major League Baseball's Boston Red Sox. Kids will love the antics of the team's mascot, Slugger the Sea Dog, and a day at the ballpark makes for an affordable outing for the whole family. Tickets may be purchased by phone, in person, or online at the team's Web site.

York's Wild Kingdom
Route 1, York Beach
207-363-4911
www.yorkzoo.com

Visit and learn about exotic animals, plus enjoy a variety of rides and classic amusements at this family park, which operates from Memorial Day weekend through late September. Don't miss the ocean views from the Ferris wheel.

Museums, Lights, and Historic Sites

Whether it's too cold for the beach or you simply want to interrupt your days of frivolity for a learning opportunity, you'll find kid-friendly museums and historic landmarks to explore along Maine's southern shore.

Cape Neddick Light
Sohier Park, Nubble Road, York

Don't miss the Cape Neddick "Nubble" Light, a picturesque 1879 lighthouse that can be viewed from the free parking area at Sohier Park in York. The lighthouse is particularly spectacular when it is illuminated each year during the Christmas holiday season.

Children's Museum of Maine
142 Free Street, Portland
207-828-1234
www.childrensmuseumofme.org

With an ever-changing lineup of activities designed to inspire learning and wonder in addition to its permanent exhibits, this downtown museum strives to give kids something new to discover during each visit. Even older children will appreciate the optical magic of the museum's Camera Obscura, which allows visitors to see panoramic views of Portland from a room with no windows; call ahead for demonstration times.

The Museums of Old York
⌨York Street and Lindsay Road, York

✆207-363-4974

✎*www.oldyork.org*

In 1632, York became America's first chartered city. Walk through three centuries in Old York, the collection of historic buildings along York Street and Lindsay Road operated by the Old York Historical Society. Costumed guides lead tours of eight museum buildings Monday through Saturday from June through Columbus Day weekend.

Portland Harbor Museum
⌨Fort Road, South Portland

✆207-799-6337

✎*www.portlandharbormuseum.org*

See a working lighthouse, a nineteenth-century fort, and historic exhibits at this ocean-side museum. Located on the campus of Southern Maine Technical College, it is open to visitors daily Memorial Day through mid-October, Friday through Sunday from mid-April until Memorial Day and from mid-October through Thanksgiving weekend.

Portland Head Light
⌨Fort Williams Park, 1000 Shore Road, Cape Elizabeth

✆207-799-2661

✎*www.portlandheadlight.com*

The grounds of Fort Williams Park are open free year-round to see and photograph Maine's oldest lighthouse, built in 1791. The keeper's quarters now house a museum, which is open daily from Memorial Day through mid-October and on weekends from mid-April through May and from Columbus Day through late December. Fort Williams Park also offers a beach, tennis courts, and areas for cross-country skiing and ice skating in the winter and kite flying on breezy days. The ruins of the large, old fort entice to children and adults alike.

Portland Museum of Art
7 Congress Square, Portland
207-775-6148
www.portlandmuseum.org

Maine's largest art repository is a must for art lovers visiting the state. The museum focuses on the artistic heritage of the United States, particularly Maine, and features works by Winslow Homer, Andrew Wyeth, John Singer Sargent, and other acclaimed American painters. The museum is open daily Memorial Day through Columbus Day and every day except Monday the rest of the year. Check their Web site for a schedule of Family Festivals and other programs for children.

Two Lights State Park
Off Route 77, Cape Elizabeth
207-799-5871
www.state.me.us/cgi-bin/doc/parks/find_one_name.pl?park_id=28

This forty-acre state park is home to remnants of a World War II coastal defense installation. Enjoy picnicking, hiking, and scenic views of Maine's rocky coast.

Wadsworth-Longfellow House
489 Congress Street, Portland
207-774-1822
www.mainehistory.org/house_overview.shtml

Portland's first brick home dates to 1785. It was the childhood residence of one of Maine's most famous native sons, the poet Henry Wadsworth Longfellow. The house is open for tours daily May through October and during special holiday hours in December. It is also open weekends in November.

Wells Auto Museum
Route 1, Wells
207-646-9064

Have you ever dreamed of riding in a Model T? At the Wells Auto Museum, you can literally travel through automotive history. More than seventy cars of forty-five makes are on display daily from mid-June through September. The museum operates weekends only in late May and early June, as well as in early October.

Shopping

Few travelers can resist the allure of Kittery and Freeport's factory outlet stores. But the outlets aren't the only places to drop some cash in southern Maine. When you're finished scouring the outlets for deals, there are a few other interesting spots to shop.

Dock Square
Dock Square, Kennebunkport

You can easily lose hours wandering in and out of boutiques, gift shops, and art galleries in this charming shopping district.

Haven's Candies
87 County Road, Westbrook
207-772-1557 or 800-639-6309
www.havenscandies.com

Haven's Candies has been making saltwater taffy, fudge, chocolate lobsters, and other sweets since 1915. Their retail store is open daily. Make an appointment and treat yourselves to a behind-the-scenes tour of the candy factory on weekdays.

Freeport Outlet and Specialty Shopping
Main Street / Route 1 area, Freeport

There's more to Freeport than L.L. Bean. There are more than 170 outlet stores and specialty shops concentrated in this vibrant town. Other name-brand retailers with factory stores here include Banana Republic, Brooks Brothers, Cuddledown, Nine West, Polo Ralph Lauren, and Reebok. And, unlike Kittery, Freeport goes beyond outlets to offer shoppers a nifty array of specialty stores selling made-in-Maine gifts and unique souvenirs. Wander into The Mangy Moose (112 Main Street, 207-865-6414 or 800-606-6517, *www.themangymoose.com*), and just try to get out of there without purchasing one moose-shaped or emblazoned item. Plan your Freeport shopping trip by calling the Freeport Merchants Association at 207-865-1212 or 800-865-1994 to request a free visitor guide.

JUST FOR PARENTS

While you're in Freeport, stop by Cold River Vodka (437 Route 1, 207-865-4828, *www.coldrivervodka.com*) for a tour of the distillery and an opportunity to purchase a memorable souvenir or gift—vodka made with Maine potatoes and pure river water.

Kittery Outlets
⌨ Route 1, Kittery
☎ 888-KITTERY
✎ *www.thekitteryoutlets.com*

Finding Route 1 in Kittery is akin to discovering the pot at the end of the rainbow for retail addicts and casual shoppers alike. More than 100 brand-name outlets are packed into this stretch of highway. Plan your outlet-shopping strategy before you get to Maine by viewing the online map at the Kittery Outlets' Web site.

Len Libby Candies
⌨ 419 Route 1, Scarborough
☎ 207-883-4897
✎ *www.lenlibby.com*

Len Libby is not just a candy store. It's home to the world's only life-size chocolate moose—Lenny is made of 1,700 pounds of chocolate! The kids will love Len Libby's homemade ice cream, too.

Lighthouse Depot
⌨ 2178 Post Road /Route 1, Wells
☎ 207-646-0608
✎ *www.lighthousedepot.com*

Lighthouse Depot lays claim to the title of "world's largest lighthouse gift store." Next door, you'll find the American Lighthouse Foundation Museum of Lighthouse History (*www.lighthousefoundation.org/museum/mlh_landingpage.htm*), which displays artifacts from the U.S. Lighthouse Service. The museum is free and open daily from Memorial Day through Columbus Day and weekends thereafter until Christmas.

L.L. Bean Flagship Store
⌨ 95 Main Street, Freeport
✆ 800-559-0747, ext. 37222
✎ *www.llbean.com*

Leon Leonwood Bean invented the Maine Hunting Shoe in 1911. In 1912, he initiated mail-order sales with a four-page flyer sent to out-of-state sportsmen. In 1917, L.L. Bean set up shop on Main Street in Freeport, and the rest, as they say, is history. Today, visitors can shop 24 hours a day, 365 days each year. Part of L.L. Bean's mystique comes from the company's 100 percent satisfaction guarantee—a promise that was born in 1912 and remains to this day. Any purchase, whether made at the flagship store, at outlet shops, or via mail order, can be returned at any time for a replacement or refund.

≡ FAST FACT

You'll find L.L. Bean Factory Stores in these New England locations:
Maine: Bangor, Ellsworth, Freeport, Portland
New Hampshire: Concord, Manchester, Nashua, North Conway

Portland's Old Port
⌨ Commercial Street, Portland
✎ *www.portlandmaine.com/op.html*

Portland's Old Port District, with cobblestone walkways and Victorian red-brick buildings housing dozens of specialty boutiques, galleries, restaurants, antique emporiums, and craft shops selling Maine-made items, is well worth a visit. This easily walkable area extends from the bustling, working waterfront to Congress Street between Exchange and Pearl streets. If uniquely Maine jewelry is your desired souvenir, there are several distinctive jewelers you should visit in this area. Cross Jewelers (570 Congress Street, 207-773-3107 or 800-433-2988, *www.crossjewelers.com*) creates unique, nature-inspired pieces. Lovell Designs (26 Exchange Street, 207-828-5303 or 800-533-9685, *www.lovelldesigns.com*) specializes in Maine-inspired pins, pendants, and earrings in pewter, silver, and gold plate.

RAINY DAY FUN

Free tours of the Tom's of Maine manufacturing facility (27 Community Drive, Sanford, 800-985-3874, *www.tomsofmaine .com*) are available by reservation Monday through Friday in the summertime. Call 800-775-2388 to reserve your spot. The forty-five minute tour is recommended for children ages five and up.

Tom's of Maine Natural Living Store
302 Lafayette Center, Kennebunk
207-985-6331
www.tomsofmaine.com

Kennebunk is the birthplace of natural health and beauty products maker Tom's of Maine, and visitors to the Natural Living Store will find sizable discounts on factory seconds, plus an opportunity to learn about and shop for first-quality products.

Where to Stay

There are so many lodging properties in Portland and southern Maine that you may find it difficult to choose. Thankfully, the Internet makes it easy to investigate options, check availability, and compare prices. Read a variety of professional and traveler-generated online reviews, too. Whether you prefer a motel or a campground, a resort or a rental cottage, it's a good idea to decide on a location first and then begin your search.

Portland Overnights

Portland is Maine's largest city, and places to stay in the Greater Portland area are plentiful. Most of the major hotel chains are represented: Best Western, Comfort Inn, Days Inn, DoubleTree, Econo Lodge, Embassy Suites, Holiday Inn, Howard Johnson, Marriott, Motel 6, Sheraton. Among the city's largest hotels are the 239-room Holiday Inn by the Bay (88 Spring Street, Portland, 207-775-2311 or 800-345-5050, *www.innbythebay.com*), which boasts Greater Portland's largest indoor hotel pool, free parking and airport transportation, and proximity to the Old Port's shops and restaurants; and the 227-room Portland Marriott at Sable Oaks (200 Sable Oaks Drive, South Portland, 207-871-8000, *www.marriott.com/property/propertypage/PWMAP*), which allows pets and has an indoor pool and business amenities.

You'll also find quieter, seaside accommodations close to the city. Families will be quite comfortable at Inn by the Sea (40 Bowery Beach Road, Cape Elizabeth, 207-799-3134 or 800-888-4287, *www.innbythesea.com*), where each of the forty-three one- and two-bedroom suites and cottages has a porch or deck with ocean views, a kitchen, living room, dining area, two televisions, and a VCR. The more affordable Lighthouse Inn at Pine Point (366 Pine Point Road, Scarborough, 800-780-3213, *www.lighthouseinnatpinepoint.com*) is just fifteen minutes from Portland, and it's steps from the beach.

The Freeport area offers value-priced family motels and historic inns. Best Western Freeport Inn (32 Route 1, 207-865-3106 or 800-99-VALUE, *www.freeportinn.com*) has eighty rooms, an outdoor pool and play area for children, and two restaurants on-site. White

Cedar Inn (178 Main Street, 207-865-9099 or 800-853-1269, *www.whitecedarinn.com*) is a seven-room, historic Victorian B&B that is just two blocks from L.L. Bean; well-behaved children are welcome. Ask about the "Serious Shopper" package at the Harraseeket Inn (162 Main Street, 207-865-9377 or 800-342-6423, *www.harraseeketinn.com*), a classic, eighty-four-room, antique-filled New England inn with twenty-three fireplaces and an indoor pool.

Accommodations along the Shore

Family motels, beachside cottages, antique inns, spacious resorts, sea captains' homes turned B&Bs . . . the only option conspicuously absent for the most part from the list of available accommodations in southern Maine is large, name-brand hotel chains. But that's okay. After all, staying in a place with local character is all a part of getting to know Maine. Take extra care in asking questions before you book your reservations, and keep in mind that competition for rooms along the shore can be fierce during the peak summer season.

In Kittery, York Harbor, and Ogunquit

If you want to be right in the thick of the outlet shopping opportunities, the forty-three-room Coachman Inn (380 Route 1, 207-439-4434, *www.coachmaninn.net*) is located across the street from the Kittery Outlet Mall in the heart of the Route 1 shopping strip. It has an outdoor pool and complimentary supreme continental breakfast.

The York Harbor Inn (Route 1A, York Harbor, 207-363-5119 or 800-343-3869, *www.yorkharborinn.com*) offers fifty-four rooms with all of the warmth and individuality of a small B&B, yet the oceanside inn with a beach across the street also boasts a restaurant and pub and other amenities you'd associate with a larger hotel. Some of the inn's five buildings are better suited to families than others; ask about options when you call for reservations.

At the Anchorage Inn (Route 1A/Long Beach Avenue, York Beach, 207-363-5112, *www.anchorageinn.com*), you'll find family accommodations right on Long Sands Beach, plus indoor and outdoor pools, an exercise room, and a restaurant with a deck overlooking the beach. Cutty Sark Motel (58 Long Beach Avenue, York Beach, 207-363-5131 or 800-363-5131, *www.cuttysarkmotel.com*) is also located right on the water.

Ogunquit Resort Motel (719 Main Street, 207-646-8336 or 877-646-8336, *www.ogunquitresortmotel.com*) is a solid choice for extended family stays. Features include a pool, hot tub, exercise room, and free WiFi and continental breakfast, plus kids twelve and under stay free, and it's right on the trolley route for convenient beach access. If you're able to splurge, consider the historic Cliff House Resort & Spa (Shore Road, Ogunquit, 207-361-1000, *www.cliffhousemaine.com*), dramatically situated on Bald Head Cliff. Every room has a balcony with an ocean view, and the roar of the sea will lull you to sleep. Children twelve and under stay free with their parents in the resort's Ledges building.

In Wells and Kennebunkport

Village by the Sea (Route 1, Wells, 207-646-1100 or 800-444-8862, *www.vbts.com*) is an all-suite resort situated on eleven acres abutting the Rachel Carson Wildlife Preserve and tidal salt marsh, where you'll be surrounded by Maine's natural riches without sacrificing easy access to the region's attractions, including nearby Wells Beach. If you want to stay right on Wells Beach, book a room at Lafayette's Oceanfront Resort (Mile Road, Wells Beach, 207-646-2831, *www.wells beachmaine.com*); five of the property's nine buildings are directly on the beach. A playground, arcade, and indoor pool add to the fun.

 **TRAVEL TIP**

After summertime, the next best season to visit Kennebunk-port is the holiday season, when the town goes all out for its annual, old-fashioned Christmas Prelude (*www.christmas prelude.com*) the first two weekends in December. Events include candlelight caroling, walking tours, tree lightings, bonfires, and Santa's arrival by lobster boat.

For a full menu of amenities and the historic charm of an inn that has welcomed guests since 1884, the Nonantum Resort (Ocean Avenue, Kennebunkport, 207-967-4050 or 800-552-5651, *www .nonantumresort.com*) provides 115 rooms including some with kitchenettes, a restaurant, a heated outdoor pool, and more.

Families in search of a quiet, affordable retreat within a half-mile walk of Kennebunkport's beaches and shops should consider spending the night at the Franciscan Guest House (28 Beach Avenue, Kennebunkport, 207-967-4865, *www.franciscanguesthouse.com*), located adjacent to a sixty-acre monastic estate. A hearty breakfast is included; daily maid service is not.

In Old Orchard Beach

At White Lamb Cottages (3 Odessa Avenue, 207-934-2221 or 800-203-2034, *www.theedgewatermotorinn.com/lambhome.html*), stay privately nestled within one of ten cottages just 100 feet from the beach and have muffins, coffee, and the newspaper delivered to your door each morning. Royal Anchor Resort (203 East Grand Avenue, 207-934-4521 or 800-934-4521, *www.royalanchor.com*) provides beachfront family accommodations about a mile away from the hubbub of the Pier. Also at the quiet northern end of Old Orchard Beach, Ocean Walk Hotel (197 East Grand Avenue, 207-934-1013 or 800-992-3779, *www.oceanwalkhotel.com*) is a comfortable family property just steps from the sand; if it rains, you'll be glad to have access to their indoor pool and extensive library of children's videos for your in-room VCR.

Want to rent a beach home? Seashore Property Management (80 First Street, Old Orchard Beach, 207-934-3400, *www.seashore propertymanagement.com*) specializes in vacation rentals in Old Orchard Beach. If camping is your thing, head to Bayley's Camping Resort (275 Pine Point Road, Scarborough, 207-883-6043, *www .bayleys-camping.com*), where you can camp in your own tent, trailer, or RV, or rent one of their camping trailers. Bayley's offers three heated pools, bike and boat rentals, three playgrounds, an arcade, miniature golf, and a jam-packed schedule of daily activities, plus a complimentary shuttle to Old Orchard Beach, which is a half-mile away.

The Old Orchard Beach Chamber of Commerce provides information on the dozens of additional motels and cottages in the area at its Web site, *www.oldorchardbeachmaine.com*, or call them at 207-934-2500 or 800-365-9386 to request a free vacation planner.

Family Dining

Salty air definitely whets the appetite, but no worries. There are dining delights aplenty in Portland and southern Maine, whether you want to grab a fried bite on the Pier in Old Orchard Beach or relax at a charming, historic restaurant. You'll want to budget a bit more for family meals than you ordinarily do; it may be difficult to convince the kids to eat hot dogs when there's lobster on every menu.

Lobstermania

Many vacationers begin salivating over the thought of lobster the moment they make their Maine travel reservations. Warren's Lobster House (11 Water Street/Route 1, Kittery, 207-439-1630, *www.lobster house.com*) is one of the state's most southerly seafood spots. This waterside restaurant is also known for its expansive salad bar. Kids who are new to lobster can order the "Captains Claws"—two boiled lobster claws with fries.

≡FAST FACT

If you see something green and squishy when you break your lobster's tail away from its body, that's tomalley: the lobster's liver. While some consider this a delicacy, children shouldn't eat it, and adults should also steer clear. Maine's Division of Environmental Health warns that lobster tomalley may contain environmental contaminants, such as mercury.

Need a break from outlet shopping? Weathervane Seafood Restaurant (306 Route 1, Kittery, 207-439-0330, *www.weathervane-seafoods.com*) is located in the heart of "outlet row" and serves lobster and other sea treats in a boisterous, casual environment.

The ever-popular Maine Diner (2265 Post Road/Route 1, Wells, 207-646-4441, *www.mainediner.com*) is known for its lobster pie, but you may find it hard to resist the clam-o-rama combo: clam chowder, fried whole Maine clams, clam strips, and clam cake. If you're craving lobster for breakfast, this is also the place to go. Be prepared to wait in line.

Near Old Orchard Beach, no one goes hungry at Clambake Seafood Restaurant (Route 9, Scarborough, 207-883-4871, *www.clambake restaurant.com*), which specializes in lobster dinners and seats 700; the restaurant is renowned for its big portions. Surf 6 Oceanfront Grille & Bar (6 Cortland Street, Old Orchard Beach, 207-934-2058, *www.oldorchardbeachlodging.com/Surf6/Surf6home.htm*), where the bar was once a lobster boat, has lovely views of the Pier and Old Orchard Beach, plus a Lil' Mates menu for kids and fresh steamed lobsters for the grownups.

 TRAVEL TIP

If you want to take live lobsters home so you can enjoy one last taste of Maine while you're unpacking, stop by the Pine Point Fisherman's Co-op (96 King Street, Scarborough, 800-741-3146, *www.lobsterco-op.com*) for some of the freshest—and cheapest—lobsters to go.

For a true experience of eating lobster in the rough, dine outdoors at The Lobster Shack (225 Two Lights Road, Cape Elizabeth, 207-799-1677, *www.lobstershack-twolights.com*). A local tradition since the 1920s, this seasonal restaurant offers good food and incomparable views. Inside seating is available for rainy, chilly days.

In Freeport, just like L.L. Bean, which is a mere two blocks away, The Lobster Cooker (39 Main Street, 207-865-4349, *www.lobster cooker.net*) is open every day of the year, serving lobster, homemade chowders, and other seafood selections.

A Taste of History

Step back in time at the Jameson Tavern (115 Main Street, 207-865-4196, *www.jamesontavern.com*), the 1779 pub where Freeport folks first talked about asserting their freedom from Massachusetts. The Tavern has a number of dining rooms, including the casual taproom.

At The Goldenrod (Route 1A, York Beach, 207-363-2621, *www .thegoldenrod.com*), you can watch candy makers concoct world-famous Goldenrod Kisses, much as they have been since 1896 when this restaurant and saltwater-taffy shop opened. Breakfast is served all day, and lunch and dinner are available, too, from late May through Columbus Day. With 135 homemade ice-cream flavors and an antique soda fountain, you may want to stop in between meals, too.

For home-style Maine cooking, head inland to Cole Farms (Route 100, Gray, 207-657-4714, *www.colefarms.com*), which has been serving filling food to travelers and locals since 1952. Kids will like the picnic area and playground, not to mention the forty-item dessert menu.

Memorable Meals

Portland has a vibrant culinary scene, and there are a number of unique eating experiences to contemplate when you're in the city. For starters, you can float while you feast at DiMillo's Floating Restaurant (Commercial Street/Route 1A, 207-772-2216, *www.dimillos .com/restaurant/index.html*), a former car ferry turned into one of the largest floating restaurants in the country.

At Becky's Diner (390 Commercial Street, 207-773-7070, *www .beckysdiner.com*), breakfast is served from 4 A.M. until 4 P.M.; after that, you'll have to order from the "Breakfast in the Evening" menu. For food that's affordable and amusing, take your bunch to Silly's (40 Washington Avenue, 207-772-0360, *www.sillys.com*), known for its fried pickles, big burgers, and eclectic décor. If your brood has been good, let them wash down their kids' meals with S'mores Shakes.

The number of brewpubs in Portland has dwindled in recent years, but you'll still find bar food and local brews at Gritty McDuff's (396 Fore Street, 207-772-BREW, *www.grittys.com*) and Sebago Brewing Company (164 Middle Street, 207-879-ALES, *www.sebagobrewing .com*). The Great Lost Bear (540 Forest Avenue, 207-772-0300, *www .greatlostbear.com*) isn't a brewpub, but it does showcase more than a dozen Maine beers among the fifty-four on tap. You're bound to find just the right ale to wash down every item on the restaurant's eclectic menu. If you like your brew with a water view, then Federal Jack's Restaurant and Brewpub (8 Western Avenue, Kennebunk, 207-967-4322, *www.federaljacks.com*) is the place for you.

If you're able to escape for an evening without the munchkins, head to Fore Street (288 Fore Street, Portland, 207-775-2717, *www .forestreet.biz*). It might not look like much from the outside, but dining here is a coveted experience, so you'll need reservations. Specialties include turnspit-roasted chicken and pork loin and wood oven–roasted mussels. Further south, you'll find romantic fine dining at Clay Hill Farm (220 Clay Hill Road, Cape Neddick, 207-361-2272, *www.clayhillfarm.com*), the country's only restaurant that has been designated as a wildlife habitat and bird sanctuary by the National Wildlife Association. For an extraordinary, four-course, prix fixe dinner, the restaurant at the White Barn Inn (37 Beach Avenue, Kennebunkport, 207-967-2321, *www.whitebarninn.com*) is coastal Maine's most distinguished dining enclave. Reservations and jackets for men are required.

CHAPTER 14

Midcoast and Downeast Maine

AS YOU TRAVEL NORTH, Maine's coast becomes less populated and more rugged, less predictable and more strikingly beautiful. Here, high school students seriously consider careers as lobstermen; windjammer captains keep nineteenth-century sailing traditions alive; and wealthy philanthropists' foresight ensures that more than 47,000 acres of dramatic seacoast remain forever preserved for the public's enjoyment. If you're ready to stretch your legs, to be invigorated by fresh, salt-tinged air, and to sleep soundly under star-filled skies, Midcoast and Downeast Maine offer a true escape from your everyday routines.

An Introduction to Midcoast Maine

You can get a sense of the psyche of Midcoast Maine—the coastal region that runs from Brunswick to Searsport—simply by examining the calendar of annual events held here. Winter brings the Christmas by the Sea celebration and the National Toboggan Championships. Warmer weather sprouts events such as the Fishermen's Festival, where Miss Shrimp Princess is crowned, the annual Lobster Boat Races, and Windjammer Days. At the height of summer, Midcoast Maine is home to the Maine Blueberry Festival and the Maine Lobster Festival. And when the leaves begin to turn, an annual Fall Foliage Festival and a Festival of Scarecrows mark this season's splendor as well.

In essence, Midcoast Maine is all about everything that makes Maine delicious. From the vibrancy of the changing seasons to the majesty of rocky ledges standing starkly against the azure ocean, from the loveliness of tiny island towns to the palpable energy of fishing villages, this is a region that is at once exhilarating and soothing.

What to See and Do in Midcoast Maine

No matter what the season, the sea plays an integral part in the region's activities and attractions.

Boat Tours

Maine's windjammer fleet offers families the opportunity to embark on multiday sailing adventures. If you can't take the time for a full-blown windjammer cruise, there are several other boat excursions that will allow you to see Midcoast Maine from the water.

Balmy Day Cruises
Pier 8, Commercial Street, Boothbay Harbor
207-633-2284 or 800-298-2284
www.balmydayscruises.com

Board one of this cruise company's boats for a scenic harbor tour, a mackerel fishing trip, a sailing jaunt, or a journey to Monhegan Island, where you can spend a day hiking, picnicking, and visiting art galleries and a lighthouse.

Bugeye Schooner Jenny Norman
Harbor Park, Rockland
207-273-4731
www.sailmainebugeye.com

Join Captains Mike and Julie Rogers for a relaxing, two-hour scenic sail aboard the two-masted bugeye schooner *Jenny Norman*. All ages are welcome, and kids may even get a chance to take the wheel if they ask nicely. You'll enjoy hearing tales of finding and restoring this Maryland-built traditional wooden vessel. Ask about their schedule of special outings, such as Monday morning coffee-break sails, Sea Chanties at Sunset, and Moon-rise Dessert Cruises.

Captain Jack Lobster Boat Adventure
⌨Middle Pier, Rockland
☎207-542-6852 or ☎207-594-1048
✎*www.captainjacklobstertours.com*

Captain Steve Hale named his lobster boat after his grandson, who frequently accompanies groups on these 1¼-hour adventures that are fun even for preschoolers. Just be sure to visit a restroom before departing, as there are no facilities on board. For a real treat, purchase the lobsters you see hauled up in Captain Steve's traps; they don't get any fresher! Or make arrangements in advance to enjoy a complete lobster lunch or dinner on the boat as you tour Rockland Harbor.

 RAINY DAY FUN

At the Project Puffin Visitor Center (311 Main Street, Rockland, 207-596-5566 or 877-4-PUFFIN, *http://puffin.bird.audubon.org*), kids can crawl inside a recreated puffin burrow, control robotic cameras that broadcast images of puffins on remote Seal Island, print souvenir images of the scenes they capture, and learn about the National Audubon Society's efforts to restore these fascinating birds to their Maine island nesting sites.

Lively Lady Too
⌨Bay View Landing Wharf, Camden
☎207-236-6672
✎*www3.sympatico.ca/lively.lady*

The *Lively Lady Too* will take you on a lobster fishing and eco-tour. The boat's onboard camcorder and TV monitor system provide up-close views of underwater creatures, and seals, dolphins, and water birds are also frequently spotted on these two-hour trips.

Maine Windjammer Cruises
☎800-807-WIND

✎*www.sailmainecoast.com*

Ever dreamed of being part of the crew aboard a tall ship? The twelve schooners that are members of the Maine Windjammer Association make that dream a reality for hundreds of folks during the sailing season each year. Actually, you can do as much or as little as you like. These tall ships depart from Camden and Rockland in Midcoast Maine from late May to mid-October for three- to six-day excursions that include all meals. Because the ships sail in protected inlets for the most part, you're not likely to get seasick. Be forewarned, though, that there are no electrical outlets and only a few hot showers on board. Each ship has specific policies regarding children on board; some welcome children as young as five or six, while others only allow older children to sail.

Schooner Surprise
⌖Camden Public Landing, Camden

☎207-236-4687

✎*www.camdenmainesailing.com*

For a sampling of windjamming, this 1918 tall ship offers two-hour sightseeing sails. Passengers must be at least twelve years old.

Museums, Lights, and Historic Sites

The history of Midcoast Maine is kept alive, not only inside museum walls but through the preservation of picturesque coastal structures. Visit one or more of these historic attractions for insight into life along the seacoast and a chance to "meet" some remarkable Mainers.

Boothbay Railway Village
⌖586 Wiscasset Road / Route 27, Boothbay

☎207-633-4727

✎*www.railwayvillage.org*

Chug on over to Boothbay Railway Village, and ride a vintage train through a re-created, turn-of-the-century New England village featuring twenty-eight historic buildings. This attraction is open from Memorial Day weekend through late October.

Farnsworth Art Museum

⌨16 Museum Street, Rockland

☎207-596-6457

✎*www.farnsworthmuseum.org*

The Farnsworth Art Museum is one of Maine's premier art habitats. Home to six galleries, plus the Jamien Morehouse Wing, the Farnsworth Homestead, a great museum shop, and the Wyeth Center featuring the works of Maine's painting dynasty—N. C., Andrew, and Jamie Wyeth—you could easily spend a day here. The museum is open daily Memorial Day through Columbus Day and Tuesday through Sunday the remainder of the year. Admission to the Homestead, the Victorian-era residence of the Farnsworth family, is included between Memorial Day and Columbus Day.

Maine Lighthouse Museum

⌨One Park Drive, Rockland

☎207-594-3301

✎*www.mainelighthousemuseum.com*

Open year-round—daily in season and Thursdays through Saturdays in the winter and early spring—this repository for lighthouse and Coast Guard artifacts is an interesting place to learn about the mechanics of lighthouse lenses, as well as to discover the history of some of the state's most notable lights.

Maine Maritime Museum

⌨243 Washington Street, Bath

☎207-443-1316

✎*www.bathmaine.com*

Located on the site of a nineteenth-century shipyard, this museum is a good place to become acquainted with the state's seafaring history. It features paintings, models, artifacts, and exhibits related to maritime technology and life at sea. The museum is open daily year-round.

Pemaquid Point Light
⌨Pemaquid Point Road, Bristol

✆207-563-2739

✑*www.lighthousefoundation.org/alf_lights/pemaquidpoint/
pemaquid_info.htm*

Plan a scenic drive to the end of Route 130, where you'll find Pemaquid Point Light, originally constructed in 1827 and rebuilt in 1835. This photogenic beacon remains an active aid to navigation.

Penobscot Marine Museum
⌨Route 1 and Church Street, Searsport

✆207-548-2529

✑*www.penobscotmarinemuseum.org*

Explore eight historic fishing village buildings, which house collections of watercraft, marine art, and artifacts. The museum is open daily May through October. During the summer, the Peapod, a children's room in the museum's Education Center, features hands-on activities for young visitors.

Rockland Breakwater Light
⌨Samoset Road, Rockland

✑*www.rocklandlighthouse.com*

You'll need to watch your step, but you won't be able to beat the views as you stroll along the breakwater that leads to this lovely lighthouse. Completed in 1901, the breakwater required more than 750,000 tons of stone and cost more than $850,000 to build. Open houses are held at the lighthouse on weekends from late May through mid-October.

Outdoor Recreation
Whether you're looking for a place to swim at the peak of Maine's heat or a stretch of sand that's quiet and serene in the off-season, here are some places for outdoor recreation.

Popham Beach State Park
⌨10 Perkins Farm Lane, Phippsburg

☎207-389-1335 or ☎207-389-9125

✎*www.state.me.us/cgi-bin/doc/parks/find_one_name.pl?park_id=22*

Popham Beach is a good "day at the beach" destination, the surf is rather vigorous for young children. The park is open mid-April through October, and lifeguards are on duty during the summer months. Day-use fees are charged.

 **TRAVEL TIP**

> Little animal lovers will enjoy a visit to Winters Gone Farm (245 Alna Road, Wiscasset, 207-882-9191 or 800-645-0188, *www.win-tersgone.com*), which bills itself as "The Softest Farm in Maine." Picnic, walk the nature trails, and observe the farm's furry inhabitants—about twenty alpacas. The farm's store sells alpaca-fiber fashions, rugs, blankets, and teddy bears.

Reid State Park

⌨Seguinland Road, Georgetown

☎207-371-2303

✎*www.state.me.us/cgi-bin/doc/parks/find_one_name.pl?park_id=13*

Reid State Park has the distinction of being Maine's first state-owned saltwater beach, thanks to the generosity of land donor Walter E. Reid. You'll find three lovely beaches at this ocean-side destination, a favorite spot for birding, hiking, swimming, biking, saltwater fishing, cross-country skiing, and snowshoeing. There is an admission charge.

Shopping

Wiscasset and Boothbay Harbor are picturesque shopping villages where you can explore streets clustered with antique purveyors, galleries, and curiosity shops. If you'd like to support the work of Maine artisans and food producers, you'll also find many galleries and shops.

Art of the Sea Gallery
⌨Route 73, South Thomaston
✆207-594-9396
✐*www.artofthesea.com*
Housed within a former post office, this gallery displays diverse works of marine art including paintings, photographs, scrimshaw, nautical instruments, and ship models.

Cellardoor Winery & Vineyards
⌨367 Youngtown Road, Lincolnville
✆207-763-4478
✐*www.mainewine.com*
Maine's oldest vineyard offers tastings and wine sales from mid-May through mid-October.

Georgetown Pottery
⌨Route 127, Georgetown
✆207-371-2190 or 866-936-7687
✐*www.georgetownpottery.com*
This pottery maker's studio and showroom on the island of Georgetown showcases its distinctive line of functional and decorative pieces handcrafted and hand-painted in Maine.

Maine Gold
⌨Route 1, Rockport
✆800-752-5271
✐*www.mainegold.com*
Take home maple syrup and other maple products and specialty foods made in Maine from this company, which has been sugaring since 1976. They also have a retail outlet on Bayview Street in Camden.

Reny's
⌨33 and 48–54 Main Street, Damariscotta
✆207-563-5757
✐*www.renys.com*

This chain of Maine discounters was founded in 1949. Visit the original bargain store, with outlets on both sides of Main Street—one for clothing and one for everything else.

Sheepscot River Pottery
⌨34 Route 1, Edgecomb
☎207-882-9410
✎*www.sheepscot.com*

Visit the studio and headquarters of this creator of original, hand-painted pottery pieces featuring uniquely Maine designs. The retail store is open daily year-round.

An Introduction to Downeast Maine

How did a place that's so far up there in Maine ever earn a nickname like "Downeast"? The term originated with sailors en route to this region from Boston, who had to sail downwind and to the east to reach the harbors of Maine. Today, the label is applied to the entire northern coastal region of the state, stretching to the Canadian border.

This is a land chock-full of superlatives:

- The easternmost point in the United States—Lubec
- The easternmost U.S. city—Eastport
- The highest tides in the Continental United States—near Calais
- The highest point on the Atlantic coast north of Rio de Janeiro—Cadillac Mountain
- Maine's largest island—Mount Desert Island
- The oldest national park east of the Mississippi River and Maine's top tourist attraction—Acadia National Park

However you choose to encounter the natural wonders of Downeast Maine—on foot, on two wheels, behind the wheel of your automobile, from a boat off the coast, or even aboard a trolley or horse-drawn carriage—you'll gain a renewed appreciation for the formations and creations of nature that could never be replicated by human hands.

What to See and Do in Downeast Maine

While Acadia dwarfs other attractions in the region, there are a few you may want to visit while you're in Downeast Maine.

Acadia National Park

Each year, more than 2 million tourists descend on the 54-square-mile park, which encompasses 41 miles of coastline, mountains, forests, and lakes. Auto touring, biking, bird watching, boating, camping, climbing, cross-country skiing, fishing, hiking, horseback riding, skiing, snowshoeing, stargazing, swimming, walking, wildlife viewing—that's the laundry list of Acadia activities provided by the National Park Service. Acadia National Park (*www.nps.gov/acad*) on Mount Desert (pronounced "dessert") Island and Isle au Haut is the gem of Downeast Maine; its 47,633 acres of mountains, forest, lakes, ponds, and shore provide millions of visitors each year the opportunity to reconnect with the natural world.

 TRAVEL TIP

The town of Lubec is the easternmost point in the United States, and thus the spot where the first rays of sunlight touch the nation each morning. Rise early, and head down to the Lubec Municipal Marina on Lubec Harbor to watch the sun rise.

Acadia History

The Wabanaki Indians inhabited what is now Acadia National Park 6,000 years ago. European explorer Samuel Champlain landed on and named Mount Desert Island in 1604—sixteen years before the Pilgrims arrived. The English and French battled over the region for a century and a half, with Britain finally winning out in 1759. By the mid-1800s, Mount Desert Island was a popular haven for artists and America's elite: the Rockefellers, Morgans, Fords, Carnegies, Astors, Vanderbilts, and Pulitzers. George B. Dorr, a conservationist, and other members of this social set began their efforts to preserve the region's natural wonders in 1901. By 1916, they had secured National Monument status for 6,000 acres donated by Dorr. Another 40,000 acres were added to the park through private donations. At donors' request, the park was named Acadia in 1929.

Exploring the Park

There are many ways to see and experience Acadia National Park; a drive along the twenty-seven-mile Park Loop Road serves as a good introduction. Get oriented first at the Hulls Cove Visitor Center (Route 3, Bar Harbor, 207-288-3338), open mid-April through October. There, pick up trail and driving maps and other free literature describing the park's history and facilities, plus the schedule of ranger-led activities. In the winter, visitor operations move to the Park Headquarters (Route 233 near Eagle Lake, 207-288-3338).

From late June through early October, a one-week entrance permit for Acadia costs $20 per vehicle; the fee is $10 per vehicle from May 1 through late June and during the remainder of October. For those who enter the park on foot, bicycle, or motorcycle, the individual admission fee is $5. Although the park is open year-round, the Park Loop Road is closed in the winter.

Allow the better part of a day to drive the Park Loop Road, especially during the busy months of July and August. You'll want to stop frequently to visit scenic landmarks, such as Otter Cliffs and Thunder Hole; when wave conditions are optimal, water blasts as high as forty feet in the air when forced through this natural cavern. Stop for lunch or afternoon tea inside the park at the historic Jordan Pond House (207-276-3316, *www.jordanpond.com*); kids will enjoy slathering jam on the restaurant's famous popovers. Be sure to turn off the Park Loop Road for the seven-mile drive to the summit of Cadillac Mountain, the highest point on the eastern seaboard.

Within the park, you'll also find the Abbe Museum at Sieur de Monts Spring (off the Park Loop Road and off Route 3, 207-288-3519, *www.abbemuseum.org*), where you can learn about Maine's native peoples from late May through mid-October.

Boat Tours

Downeast boat tour companies will help you explore points off-shore, including puffin-inhabited islands.

Downeast Windjammer Cruises & Ferries
⊡Bar Harbor Inn Pier, Newport Drive, Bar Harbor
☎207-288-4585
✍*www.downeastwindjammer.com*
Head out to sea aboard New England's only four-masted schooner, *Margaret Todd*, on a morning, afternoon, or sunset cruise.

Hardy Boat Cruises
⊡Route 32, New Harbor
☎207-677-2026 or ☎800-278-3346
✍*www.hardyboat.com*
This boat tour company operates a ferry to Monhegan Island, a peaceful artists' haven, and also offers lighthouse cruises, seal watches, fall coastal cruises, and Puffin Watch trips to Eastern Egg Rock with an Audubon naturalist. Since 1973, the National Audubon Society's Project Puffin has worked to restore the Gulf of Maine habitats of the bird with such colorful nicknames as "clown of the ocean" and "sea parrot." Hardy Boat Cruises donates a portion of each Puffin Watch cruise fare to Project Puffin.

Norton of Jonesport
⊡Jonesport Marina, Sawyer's Square Road, Jonesport
☎207-497-2560 or ☎207-497-5933
✍*www.machiassealisland.com*
This tour company, founded in 1939, takes passengers on early-morning trips to see the 3,000-plus population of puffins on Machias Seal Island from early June through mid-August.

☔ RAINY DAY FUN

See baby lobsters at the Lobster Hatchery at the Mount Desert Oceanarium (Route 3, Bar Harbor, 207-288-5005, *www .theoceanarium.com*), which is also home to the Maine Lobster Museum. A second Oceanarium site (Clark Point Road, Southwest Harbor, 207-244-7330) features a Marine Aquarium, Touch Tank, and Fisherman's Museum. Both locations are open daily except Sunday from Memorial Day weekend until late October.

Museums, Lights, and Historic Sites

As remote as Downeast Maine may seem, it is home to a number of intriguing historic and modern attractions, plus museums devoted to everything from Native American culture to telephones.

Abbe Museum

🖂26 Mount Desert Street/Route 3, Bar Harbor

📞207-288-3519

✍*www.abbemuseum.org*

In addition to its small facility inside Acadia National Park, the Abbe Museum has a contemporary museum in downtown Bar Harbor that allows visitors to discover the history and culture of Maine's native Wabanaki people. Open from Memorial Day weekend through mid-November, the museum boasts a collection of 50,000 artifacts and also exhibits contemporary art and basketry by tribal members.

Fort Knox

🖂Route 174, Bucksport

📞207-469-6553

✍*http://fortknox.maineguide.com*

Fort Knox was built of Maine granite in the mid-nineteenth century for protection against the British, who had twice invaded the

Penobscot River. A third attack never came, but the fort served as a garrison during the Civil War and the Spanish-American War. The fort is open daily from May 1 through November 1. Purchase a combination ticket, and you'll also be able to ascend to the top of Maine's tallest occupied structure, the Penobscot Narrows Bridge Observatory, which opened in 2007. From the 420-foot obelisk—only the third bridge observatory in the world—visitors will have panoramic views of the fort, the Penobscot River, and the surrounding coastal region.

Roosevelt Campobello International Park
⊞459 Route 774, Welshpool, New Brunswick, Canada
✆506-752-2922
✐*www.fdr.net*

See the cottage and the grounds where President Franklin Delano Roosevelt often vacationed from the time he was a boy, and where he was stricken with polio at the age of thirty-nine. This 2,800-acre international historic site is located at the southern end of Campobello Island in New Brunswick, Canada, and accessible from Lubec, Maine, via the FDR International Bridge. The grounds are open year-round, and the cottage and visitor center are open daily from Memorial Day weekend through Columbus Day. Admission is free. New Brunswick is in the Atlantic Time Zone, so it is one hour ahead of Maine.

The Telephone Museum
⊞166 Winkumpaugh Road, Ellsworth
✆207-667-9491
✐*www.ellsworthme.org/ringring*

Learn about the history of telephones at this quirky museum, open Thursdays through Sundays July through September and in May, June, and October by appointment.

West Quoddy Head Light
⊞Quoddy Head State Park, South Lubec Road, Lubec
✆207-733-2180
✐*www.westquoddy.com*

With its red and white candy-cane stripes, West Quoddy Head Light is one of Maine's most recognizable lighthouses. This active light was first established in 1808, and the present, photogenic structure was completed in 1858. The lighthouse visitor center is open daily from Memorial Day weekend through mid-October.

Shopping

Bar Harbor's village center is popular with shoppers. Boutiques, galleries, and specialty stores are clustered in the area of West, Cottage, Mt. Desert, and Main Streets. Stores stay open late into the evening during the summer months to accommodate the tourist population. Elsewhere in the region are a number of shops worth perusing.

Betts Bookstore
584 Hammond Street, Bangor
207-947-7052
www.bettsbooks.com

Horror writer Stephen King calls Bangor home, and Betts Bookstore, a fixture since 1938, is the place to find signed limited editions and directions to area landmarks that appear in King's books.

Big Chicken Barn
Route 1, Ellsworth
207-667-7308
www.bigchickenbarn.com/books.html

How can you resist a place called Big Chicken Barn? The 21,600-square-foot antique store holds an ever-changing selection of books and collectibles.

Rackliffe Pottery
Route 172, Blue Hill
207-374-2297 or 888-631-3321
www.rackliffepottery.com

For something truly Maine-made, head to this third-generation pottery studio, where hand-crafted pieces are made from native Maine clay.

Raye's Mustard Mill

⌨83 Washington Street, Eastport

✆207-853-4451

✎*www.rayesmustard.com*

Mustard has been made the same way at Raye's since 1903; tours are available when the mill is in operation. Sample and shop for these zesty condiments year-round at the Pantry Store.

Where to Stay

You'll find few cookie-cutter lodging properties along Maine's northern shore, and that's actually a good thing. Unique accommodations can enhance your Midcoast or Downeast adventure, whether you choose a family resort on the water or a snug sea captain's home turned inn.

Midcoast Overnights

While you'll find some modern motor and chain hotels in the region, particularly in the Brunswick area, by far the most enchanting options are the seaside resorts and cozy inns that dot the lodgings landscape.

In Boothbay Harbor, you'll enjoy the soothing views from the oceanfront outdoor pool or your own private balcony at Smugglers Cove Inn (Route 96 East, 800-633-3008, *www.smugglerscovemotel.com*), where a simple buffet breakfast and WiFi are complimentary. At the forty-five-acre, wooded, waterside Ocean Gate Inn & Resort (Route 27 South, 207-633-3321 or 800-221-5924, *www.oceangateinn.com*), accommodations are modest, but the kids will love the on-site miniature golf course and heated pool. Other perks include a free buffet breakfast and complimentary use of kayaks and canoes. Families might also like Brown's Wharf Motel and Marina (121 Atlantic Avenue, 207-633-5440 or 800-334-8110, *www.brownswharfinn.com*), which offers balcony rooms with marina views and a seafood restaurant on-site.

For something more upscale, escape to the Spruce Point Inn Resort & Spa (Atlantic Avenue, Boothbay Harbor, 207-633-4152 or

800-553-0289, *www.sprucepointinn.com*), situated on its private, 100-acre peninsula. Enroll the kids in the inn's Lighthouse Camp in July or August, then relax in a hammock or enjoy the saltwater and heated freshwater pools, two whirlpools, clay tennis courts, full-service spa, and more.

For historic charm, consider the Captain Daniel Stone Inn (10 Water Street, Brunswick, 207-725-9898, *www.captaindanielstoneinn .com*), a palatial 1819 Federal-style home turned thirty-four-room inn with its own restaurant.

At the Grey Havens Inn (Seguinland Road, Georgetown Island, 207-371-2616 or 800-431-2316, *www.greyhavens.com*), four of the eighteen guest rooms are located in the circular turret, providing 180-degree ocean views. Crisp white rockers on the wraparound porch are another prime vantage point to watch the waves. The 1904 inn, which accommodates children ages twelve and up, is believed to be the last classic "shingle-style" hotel still operating on Maine's coast.

Children of all ages are welcome at EdgeWater Farm Bed & Breakfast (71 Small Point Road/Route 216, Phippsburg, 207-389-1322 or 877-389-1322, *www.ewfbb.com*), which has two suites especially for families. On select weeks and weekends, particularly in the off-season, rent the whole house and enjoy six rooms, an indoor pool and hot tub, nearby beaches, and acres of gardens and fruit trees.

 TRAVEL TIP

Parents and children can go to summer camp together at the all-inclusive Medomak Camp (178 Liberty Road, Washington, 207-845-6001 or 866-633-6625, *www.medomakcamp .com*), a retreat center that was founded in 1904 as a farming camp for city boys. You'll enjoy traditional camp activities, such as canoeing, arts and crafts, archery, fishing, and campfires, of course. Week-long stays include all meals—even a lobster dinner.

The Samoset Resort (220 Warrenton Street, Rockport, 207-594-2511 or 800-341-1650, *www.samosetresort.com*) has welcomed guests to Midcoast Maine since 1889. Located on 230 rugged oceanside acres overlooking the Rockland Breakwater and Rockland Lighthouse, it is known for one of New England's most scenic golf courses, with ocean vistas from fourteen of the eighteen holes. Sam-O-Camp, a children's program, is available in the summer months for an additional fee.

For an affordable vacation, the off-season rates are great at the pet-friendly Belfast Harbor Inn (Route 1, Belfast, 207-338-2740 or 800-545-8576, *www.belfastharborinn.com*), which overlooks Penobscot Bay.

Downeast Digs

From campgrounds and rustic log cabins to elegant inns, modern hotels, and spacious resorts, whatever your style, there's likely a perfect lodging complement for you in Downeast Maine.

Located near Acadia National Park, Bar Harbor is Downeast Maine's most popular destination, and the diversity and number of lodging establishments definitely reflects this distinction. At the top is the four-star Bar Harbor Hotel~Bluenose Inn (90 Eden Street, 207-288-3348 or 800-445-4077, *www.barharborhotel.com*), which offers expansive ocean views, heated indoor and outdoor pools, a fitness center, restaurant, and ninety-seven rooms and suites. The main entrance to Acadia National Park is just a couple of minutes from the hotel. Acadia Inn (98 Eden Street, 207-288-3500 or 800-638-3636, *www .acadiainn.com*) is also conveniently located with more down-to-earth rates and a free continental breakfast; the Island Explorer shuttle stops here, providing free transportation to Acadia and downtown Bar Harbor in season. For a dramatic ocean setting, it's difficult to top Bar Harbor Inn & Spa (Newport Drive, 207-288-3351 or 800-248-3351, *www.barharborinn.com*), once home to the Oasis Club, a social club whose members included the Vanderbilts, Morgans, and Pulitzers.

There are two campgrounds in Acadia National Park (*www .nps.gov/acad/planyourvisit/campgrounds.htm*). Make reservations for Blackwoods campground by calling 877-444-6777 up to six months in advance. Seawall campground operates on a first-come, first-served basis and fills up early for July through September.

For many more Bar Harbor lodging and camping ideas, request the free guidebook from the Bar Harbor Chamber of Commerce (207-288-5103, *www.barharborinfo.com*).

 JUST FOR PARENTS

One of the few summer mansions to survive the devastating 1947 fire in Bar Harbor is now the Ledgelawn Inn (66 Mt. Dessert Street, 207-288-4596 or 800-274-5334, *www.ledgelawninn .com*). This gracious yet casual B&B features twenty-one guest rooms including many with four-poster beds, working fireplaces, and whirlpool tubs. The inn's location—just a short walk from shops, restaurants, and the waterfront—is ideal. Additional accommodations are available in the inn's modern Carriage House.

There are some intriguing accommodations to consider elsewhere in the region. For your own log cabin hideaway, Castine Cottages (Route 166, Castine, 207-326-8003, *www.castinecottages.com*) has six two-bedroom waterside units available—all furnished with lobster cooking equipment. Seclusion is also on the menu at Goose Cove Lodge (Goose Cove Road, Deer Isle, 207-348-2508 or 800-728-1963, *www.goose covelodge.com*), a casual resort offering lodge and cottage accommodations, a private beach, nature trails, spa services, stargazing evenings, and proximity to the quaint fishing village of Stonington. Children two and up may participate in the Lodge's Kid Camp, a complimentary dinner and activity program offered nightly in July and August.

For something out of the ordinary, the Pleasant Bay Bed & Breakfast and Llama Keep (West Side Road, Addison, 207-483-4490, *www .pleasantbay.com*) has four family-friendly guest rooms and is situated within a 110-acre working llama farm. You can reserve llamas to be your hiking companions for a morning walk along the property's trails.

Family Dining

Your family may well be famished after activity-filled days along Maine's northern coast. Slow down and savor the fresh flavors of Maine at some of the region's notable dining establishments.

Midcoast Meals

Start your day off at Mae's Café (160 Centre Street, Bath, 207-442-8577, *www.maescafeandbakery.com*), where breakfast is served all day. You may want to stock up on take-out bakery items to enjoy throughout your stay.

Moody's Diner (Route 1, Waldoboro, 207-832-7785, *www .moodysdiner.com*) opened for business in 1934, and travelers and locals have been drawn to its traditional, down-home cooking and reasonable prices ever since. Whoopie pies for the kids are a must if they eat well.

If you're in Camden at lunchtime, head to the Camden Deli (37 Main Street, 207-236-8343, *www.camdendeli.com*) for what may be the best views from any deli in America. The restaurant is situated atop a waterfall and offers Camden harbor views, too. You can also enjoy breakfast or lunch inside an 1893 drugstore complete with an original soda fountain at Boynton-McKay Food Co. (30 Main Street, 207-236-2465, *www.boynton-mckay.com*).

What happens when you turn an early twentieth-century automobile repair shop into a waterfront restaurant? Find out at Le Garage (15 Water Street, Wiscasset, 207-882-5409, *www.legarageres-taurant.com*), where you can select from seafood, meat, and vegetarian entrées.

By now, you know that lobster is the mainstay of Maine coast menus. At Young's Lobster Pound and Seafood Restaurant (4 Mitchell Avenue, Belfast, 207-338-1160, *www.acadiavacations.com/d344/d344-05.htm*), select your own from a lobster aquarium that holds 30,000 of the crustaceans! Indoor and outdoor waterfront seating areas are available, and they'll pack seafood to go, too. You'll find ocean views from every table and a children's menu and touch tank at Kaler's Crab and Lobster House (48 Commercial Street, Boothbay Harbor,

207-633-5839, *www.kalers.com*). Lobster, local brews, and ocean views go together at the Whale's Tooth Pub and Restaurant (Route 1, Lincolnville, 207-789-5200, *www.whalestoothpub.com*). Watch the lobstermen hard at work bringing home your dinner at the Lobstermen's Co-op (97 Atlantic Avenue, Boothbay Harbor, 207-633-4900 or 800-996-1740), a casual restaurant where you can eat indoors or out.

JUST FOR PARENTS

For an exquisite meal, make reservations at the Robinhood Free Meetinghouse (210 Robinhood Road, Georgetown, 207-371-2188, *www.robinhood-meetinghouse.com*), a five-star gem housed in a restored 1855 meetinghouse. Although you'll be tempted to fill up on the restaurant's signature seventy-two-layer Cream Cheese Biscuits, save room for a slice of Obsession in Three Chocolates.

On Bailey Island, you'll find Cook's Lobster House (Route 24, 207-833-2818, *www.cookslobster.com*), a highly regarded, casual seafood spot that's been around since 1955. From the restaurant, you'll have views of the Bailey Island Bridge, a crib bridge that is a civil engineering marvel listed on the National Register of Historic Places.

Downeast Dining

For lobster in the rough, Downeast vacationers often make their way to Thurston's Lobster Pound (Steamboat Wharf Road, Bernard, 207-244-7600, *www.acadiainfo.com/thurstons.htm*), an enclosed restaurant overlooking the fishing boats at work in Bass Harbor. You may not think that your taste buds could ever tire of lobster, but just in case, it's good to know that lobster is prepared ten different ways at Poor Boy's Gourmet Restaurant (300 Main Street, Bar Harbor, 207-288-4148, *www.poor boys gourmet.com*), where you'll also find affordable early-bird specials and an all-you-can-eat "Bottomless Pasta Bowl" deal. "Lobster 10 Ways" is a claim of Jasper's Restaurant (High Street, Ellsworth, 207-667-5318, *www.jaspersmaine.com*), too, and there's a motel right there in case you want to stay over and try lobster another way tomorrow.

Save some room for lobster ice cream. Believe it or not, Ben and Bill's Chocolate Emporium (66 Main Street, Bar Harbor, 207-288-3281 or 800-806-3281, *www.benandbills.com*) dishes up this cold, creamy blend of vanilla and lobster chunks.

TRAVEL TIP

The whole family can enjoy dinner, water views, and a show at the Deck House Restaurant and Cabaret Theater (11 Apple Lane, Southwest Harbor, 207-244-5044, *www.thedeckhouse .com*), where the waiters become the Deck House Players when the houselights dim. Make reservations for an evening of food and tunes.

If you want to take something tasty home as a souvenir, head to Nervous Nellie's Jams and Jellies (598 Sunshine Road, Deer Isle, 207-348-6182 or 800-777-6845, *www.nervousnellies.com*), where you can watch the action in the jelly kitchen Monday through Thursday mornings or shop daily from May through Christmas and most days the rest of the year. If you want to sample before you buy, you can spread Wild Maine Blueberry Preserves, Strawberry Rhubarb Conserve, or one of Nellie's other fruit jams on homemade scones at the Mountainville Café.

Before you leave, have dessert at Helen's Restaurant (Route 1, Machias, 207-255-8423, *www.helenspies.com*), where home-baked pies have been a specialty since 1950. Helen's is best known for its award-winning wild Maine blueberry pie; you can order one (or two!) online if you can't get to Machias.

CHAPTER 15

Western Maine and the Northern Wilds

THE INLAND AND NORTHERN reaches of Maine don't offer the same amusements you'll find along the coast, but for some families that's just fine. Teens will relish the thrill of whitewater rafting; elementary-aged youngsters will get a kick out of learning how to cast a line or paddle a canoe; and everyone can share the delight of spotting Maine's state animal on a moose safari. As you spend your days at a rustic resort, a lakeside campground, or an uncrowded ski mountain, you'll have opportunities to truly connect with nature—and each other.

An Introduction to Western Maine's Lakes, Mountains, Rivers, and Valleys

Lobster and moose—the tasty crustacean and the gangly mammal symbolize Maine's duality, and when you leave the rocky coastline behind for inland reaches, you'll experience a different Maine entirely. The western part of the state is freshwater Maine—a land where mountain peaks reflect in shimmering lakes, rivers roar, and snow piles up on pine branches.

Outdoor adventures, particularly water sports, are what draw most travelers to this region. Make this your vacation destination if you are longing to canoe or kayak on limpid lakes, to bond with your loved ones on a camping trip, to brave Maine's most vigorous rivers on a whitewater rafting run, to snowmobile along miles of powdery trails, or to ski by day and hunker down in front of a tension-melting fire at night. Western Maine is also home to the state's capital, Augusta, a riverside city that began as a frontier trading post and now showcases the state's history and way of life.

What to See and Do in Western Maine

If you see SUVs with skis, mountain bikes, kayaks, or canoes strapped to the top as you drive along the Maine Turnpike, they're likely bound for this region. No matter what the season, outdoor recreation is western Maine's chief draw. There are also, however, a number of singular historic attractions and even some unique shops that you may want to explore.

═FAST FACT

Maine's largest agricultural fair is held in Fryeburg each fall. The Fryeburg Fair, a tradition since 1851, features livestock exhibitions, sheepdog trials, harness racing, a midway with rides and games, musical entertainment, Woodsmen's Day events, and more. On-site camping is available. For a schedule and information, visit *www.fryeburgfair.com* or call 207-935-3268.

Museums and Historic Sites

Western Maine's museums and historic sites are one-of-a-kind places to learn about the state's history and its people.

Maine State Museum
230 State Street, Augusta
207-287-2301
www.maine.gov/museum

Learn about Maine's evolution; four floors of exhibits showcase the state's land, history, products, and people.

Sabbathday Lake Shaker Village
⌨Shaker Road
☎207-926-4597
✎*www.shaker.lib.me.us*

Open to visitors daily except for Sunday from Memorial Day through Columbus Day, this working farm is home to the last practicing community of Shakers in America. Visit the museum, learn about the Shaker faith on a guided tour, purchase handcrafted items in the Shaker Store, or just appreciate the bucolic scene of apple orchards and grazing farm animals.

Stanley Museum
⌨40 School Street, Kingfield
☎207-265-2729
✎*www.stanleymuseum.org*

See the collection of antique Stanley Steamer automobiles at the Stanley Museum, open daily except for Mondays from June through October and Tuesday through Friday in May and November. The Stanley brothers were born in Kingfield.

 RAINY DAY FUN

Embark on a ride aboard the only steam train in Maine at the Belfast & Moosehead Lake Railroad Company (1 Depot Square, Unity, 207-948-5500 or 800-392-5500, *www.belfastrailroad.com*). As you enjoy your two-hour, narrated tour through Maine's countryside, you can visit the café car for a light lunch.

Washburn-Norlands Living History Center & Museum

290 Norlands Road, Livermore

207-897-4366

www.norlands.org

Step out of the twenty-first century at the former home of a prominent Maine family. As you participate in hands-on farm activities, you'll get a taste for rural life in the nineteenth century. If you're game for a totally immersive experience, make reservations for Washburn-Norlands' two-day live-in program, and your family can wake up in 1870. How authentic is this weekend in the past? There are no bathrooms: only chamber pots and privies.

Wilhelm Reich Museum

Dodge Pond Road, Rangeley

207-864-3443

www.wilhelmreichmuseum.org

Visit the Wilhelm Reich Museum and the Orgone Energy Observatory at Orgonon, open Wednesday through Sunday in July and August and Sundays only in September. A student of Sigmund Freud, Reich claimed to have discovered a previously unknown form of energy, orgone. He even developed the Orgone Energy Accumulator, later labeled a fraud by the U.S. Food and Drug Administration, to make the energy accessible to people who needed a boost.

Outdoor Recreation

Don't automatically rule out western Maine if you're not a family of rugged, outdoorsy types. There are natural wonders of incomparable beauty here that you can appreciate without ever leaving your car. And outfitters and guides are happy to help novices wet their feet, so don't be shy about trying a new outdoor pursuit.

Northern Outdoors

Route 201, the Forks

207-663-4466 or 800-765-7238

www.northernoutdoors.com

Book a whitewater rafting adventure with Northern Outdoors; Kennebec River outings are appropriate for children ages eight and up. Northern Outdoors also offers lake kayaking, rock climbing, fishing, and snowmobiling excursions.

Saco River Canoe & Kayak

⌨1009 Main Street, Fryeburg

✆207-935-2369 or ✆888-772-6573

✐*www.sacorivercanoe.com*

Rent a kayak or canoe, and explore one of New England's most perfect-for-paddling rivers.

Songo River Queen II

⌨Route 302, Naples

✆207-693-6861

✐*www.songoriverqueen.net*

Cruise Long Lake or the Songo River aboard the 92-foot *Songo River Queen II*, a Mississippi riverboat replica that operates from July through Labor Day.

Sun Valley Sports

⌨129 Sunday River Road, Bethel

✆207-824-7533 or ✆877-851-7533

✐*www.sunvalleysports.com*

In the winter, Sun Valley Sports is your headquarters for snowmobile rentals and guided tours; ask about their ride, dine, and fireworks packages. In the spring, summer, and fall, they'll rent you a canoe, kayak, or ATV, or teach you how to fly-fish in the Sunday, Androscoggin, or Magalloway Rivers.

Sugarloaf/USA

⌨5092 Access Road, Carrabassett Valley

✆207-237-2000 or ✆800-THE-LOAF

✐*www.sugarloaf.com*

This American Skiing Company—owned resort on Maine's

second tallest mountain offers skiing lessons for Mooseketeers as young as three and 133 trails and glades for more experienced skiers. From the 4,237-foot summit, accessible via the Timberline Quad, skiers can enjoy views of Vermont, New Hampshire, Canada, and Maine's Mount Katahdin on a clear day.

 ## RAINY DAY FUN

Who says being stuck indoors has to be boring? At the Carrabassett Valley Antigravity Recreation Complex (1001 Carriage Road, Carrabassett Valley, 207-237-5566, *www.carrabassettvalley .org/attractions/agc.asp*), developed as a training center for Olympians, kids six and up can learn trampoline tricks and scale the thirty-five-foot climbing wall. The skate park is open to Rollerbladers and skateboarders four and up. Call ahead for public hours.

Sunday River
⊞ Sunday River Road, Bethel
✆ 207-824-3000
✐ *www.sundayriver.com*

With eight peaks, 131 trails, and eighteen lifts, Sunday River is one of Maine's largest ski areas, with terrain for all levels, including beginners. Families will also love the tubing park, the lighted ice-skating rink, and the arcade.

Shopping

While western Maine can't hold a candle to the shopping splendors of Kittery and Freeport, there are some notable retail outposts.

Beech Hill Bison Ranch
⊞ 630 Valley Road, North Waterford

☎207-583-2515

✐www.beechhillbison.com

Buy bison meat and gifts at the Beech Hill Trading Post at this working ranch. Call ahead for a schedule of hayrides among the herd in the summer and early fall.

Cry of the Loon

✉Route 302, South Casco

☎207-655-5060

This gift shop can keep shopaholics occupied for hours with its multiple buildings filled to overflowing with Maine-made gifts and goodies in every nook and cranny.

Mount Mica Rarities

✉191 Main Street, Greenwood

☎207-875-3060

✐www.megalink.net/~mtmica

This colorful shop specializes in jewelry featuring tourmaline mined at Mt. Mica.

Pooh Corner Farm

✉436 Bog Road, Mason Township

☎207-836-FARM or ☎800-625-4708

✐www.poohfarm.com

Winnie the Pooh fans will adore this greenhouse and garden shop complex where the kids can chat with a live pig, donkey, rabbit, and wallaby named Piglet, Eeyore, Rabbit, and Roo, while you shop for garden gifts and Pooh collectibles.

An Introduction to Moosehead Lake and Maine's North Woods

If you want to see wild, untamed Maine, point your compass north and inland and drive, drive, drive. It's a long way from Maine's southern border to the vast, unspoiled region that features the state's largest lake, Moosehead Lake, and Maine's only mile-high mountain, glorious Mount Katahdin.

It's farther still to "The County," as Maine's northernmost county, Aroostook, is called. Just about 73,000 people live in this county, which is the size of Connecticut and Rhode Island combined. Aroostook is home to more than 2,000 rivers, lakes, and streams. Agriculture and forestry play a dominant role in the economy, and the county is renowned for its annual potato crop, celebrated each July at the Maine Potato Blossom Festival in Fort Fairfield.

What to See and Do Up North

If you're feeling a bit wild and untamed, you'll find some of the state's best whitewater rafting here and challenging kayaking and canoeing on the St. John, the Northeast's longest, free-flowing river. Landlubbers can hike and camp in Baxter State Park, set out on a planetary scavenger hunt, or, what the heck—you only live once—embark on a moose photo safari.

Museums and Historic Sites

A few sites of historic and cultural interest are worth a visit, too.

Acadian Village

Route 1, Van Buren

207-868-2691

www.connectmaine.com/acadianvillage

This collection of original and replica buildings displays artifacts related to the life of the French Acadians who populated the St. John Valley in the mid-eighteenth century. The village is open daily from mid-June to mid-September.

Fort Kent State Historic Site

Off Route 1, Fort Kent

207-941-4014

www.maine.gov/cgi-bin/doc/parks/find_one_name.pl?park_id=56

The Fort Kent Blockhouse is one of a handful of National Historic Landmarks in Maine. Constructed of cedar logs, it was built in 1839 during the Aroostook War, a border dispute that ended without bloodshed. Visitors can climb inside the blockhouse from Memorial Day through Labor Day.

Patten Lumbermen's Museum
⌨Shin Pond Road, Patten
✆207-528-2650
✎*www.lumbermensmuseum.org*

You'll find 4,000 artifacts from Maine's lumbering history displayed in nine buildings, open daily except for Mondays in July and August, Friday through Sunday from Memorial Day through June and September through mid-October.

RAINY DAY FUN

The University of Maine at Orono boasts the state's first planetarium. The Maynard F. Jordan Planetarium & Observatory (5781 Wingate Hall, 207-581-1341, *www.galaxymaine.com*) offers a regular schedule of public planetarium shows. Also at the university, visit the Hudson Museum (5746 Maine Center for the Arts, 207-581-1901, *www.umaine.edu/hudsonmuseum*), which has a permanent exhibit dedicated to the culture of Maine's Penobscot tribe. The museum is open free year-round.

Outdoor Recreation

From the soft adventure of a moose safari to the strenuous challenge of a hike along Mount Katahdin's sometimes treacherous Knife Edge trail, northern Maine offers recreational opportunities for all interests and ability levels. Before you embark on any outdoor trip, be sure you have the proper gear, maps, and supplies to ensure a safe outing. Guided trips are often the best choice for families.

Baxter State Park

⌨64 Balsam Drive, Millinocket

☎207-723-5140

✎*www.baxterstateparkauthority.com*

Baxter is the largest state park in Maine. Its 202,064 acres were gifted to the state by one of its governors, Percival P. Baxter. Within its boundaries, you'll discover legendary Mount Katahdin—its summit is known as Baxter Peak—just one of forty-six peaks and ridges within the park. There are also 175 miles of trails, ten campgrounds, canoe rentals, and plenty of wildlife to entrance and entertain bird watchers, photographers, and hikers. Most vehicles can handle the drive through Baxter along the Park Tote Road, so this is a good sightseeing option for families traveling with younger children or elderly relatives. The Appalachian Trail (304-535-6331, *www.appalachiantrail.org*) also ends within the park, so you may just have a chance to greet hikers who have completed the 2,167-mile trek from Springer Mountain in Georgia to Mount Katahdin in Maine. Stop at the park headquarters in Millinocket or at the Togue Pond Visitor Center for maps and information on all of the park's recreational possibilities.

TRAVEL TIP

Maine's vast network of more than 13,000 miles of mapped and maintained snowmobile trails makes the state a snowmobiler's heaven. The most popular snowmobiling areas are Baxter State Park, the Jackman/Moose River area, the Moosehead Lake and Rangeley Lakes regions, and Aroostook County. Sled ME (877-275-3363, *www.sledme.com*) is an organization of outfitters that can help you plan your Maine snowmobiling adventure.

Katahdin Lake Cruises
☎Moosehead Marine Museum, Route 15, Greenville
✆207-695-2716
✐*www.katahdincruises.com*

Moosehead Lake is forty miles long with 400 miles of shoreline, and it beckons to those who want to canoe or kayak on its waters, fish, search for moose from a pontoon boat, or watch seaplanes take off and land. Get to know the lake on a 1914 steamship, *The Katahdin*, from Moosehead Marine Museum. Cruises are available late June through early October; call ahead for a schedule and reservations.

Moose Safaris

Did you know that you can go on a safari in Maine . . . a moose safari? Grab your camera and call one of these tour providers that will lead you to where you're most likely to spot these gangly, homely, but nevertheless lovable creatures:

- Katahdin Air Service Inc., Millinocket, 207-723-8378 or 888-PICK-KAS, *www.katahdinair.com*. Spy on moose from above on a scenic flight aboard a small aircraft.
- Mainely Photos Moose and Photo Tour, Millinocket, 207-723-5465, *www.mainelyphotos.com*. Professional photographer Dale Stevens takes you to prime moose-viewing spots aboard an air-conditioned van.
- Northwoods Outfitters Moose/Wildlife Safaris, Greenville, 207-695-3288 or 866-223-1380, *www.maineoutfitter.com*. You'll have a good chance of seeing moose up close when you canoe or kayak with this outfitter.

New England Outdoor Center
☎Medway Road, Millinocket
✆207-723-5438 or ✆800-766-7238
✐*www.neoc.com*

The Penobscot River, which flows through Baxter State Park, provides some of New England's finest whitewater-rafting rapids. New

England Outdoor Center is one of northern Maine's largest outfitters, offering day and overnight rafting trips, some of which are appropriate for children as young as ten. They also offer fishing, kayaking, backpacking, geocaching, and snowmobiling adventures.

Shopping

Sure, there are a few cute shops in Greenville, but in northern Maine, shopping is mostly about acquiring necessities. Maine-made syrup is definitely a necessity.

Bob's Sugar House

252 East Main Street, Dover-Foxcroft

207-564-2145

www.mainemaplesyrup.com

For a sweet souvenir, visit this sugar house, which sells its own Maine maple syrup, maple sugar candy, and even maple popcorn.

Fraser's Trading Post

15 Main Street, Patten

207-746-3938 or 877-746-3938

www.fraserstradingpost.com

You'll look the part on your Maine adventures when you shop here for deerskin gloves, beaver fur earmuffs, and Daniel Boone hats. Fraser's Trading Post also sells Maine-made products, bearskin rugs, and mounted birds, fish, and animals.

Indian Hill Trading Post & Supermarket

Routes 15, Greenville

800-675-4487

www.indianhill.com

Need fishing supplies, camping supplies, hiking supplies, or a canoe of your own? This 35,000-square-foot store sells everything you need for your northern Maine adventures.

Where to Stay

In western and northern Maine, more vacationers sleep in lean-tos than in five-star hotels. That's not to say there aren't plenty of places where families will feel right at home. But you will need to adjust your expectations if you're accustomed to luxury lodgings and first-class amenities. Lodging properties described as "rustic" in other parts of New England may actually be "charming," but in Maine's interior regions, you can pretty much take "rustic" at face value.

In many parts of northern Maine, the critters outnumber the people, so it's not surprising that lodging choices are more limited here than in other regions of the state. Some accommodations are downright primitive, designed primarily for those who have come to fish, hunt, raft, snowmobile, and engage in other outdoor activities that aren't necessarily compatible with frilly bed canopies and antique appointments. That said, while you won't find huge luxury hotels, you will find comfortable lodgings that provide a cozy nest to tuck into at the end of an active day.

Family Campgrounds, Resorts, and Lodges

As you consider lodging properties, some of your best bets will be those that cater specifically to families. In the western part of the state, Point Sebago Resort (261 Point Sebago Road, Casco, 207-655-3821 or 800-530-1555, *www.pointsebago.com*) is a 775-acre family playground with an extensive menu of organized and supervised activities for toddlers to teens, and adults, too. Facilities include an eighteen-hole championship golf course, a driving range, a marina, tennis courts, and a beach. Camp in your RV or travel trailer, or stay in one of the resort's rental cottages, park homes, or vacation homes.

If your family seeks seclusion, Attean Lake Lodge (Attean Road, Jackman, 207-668-3792, *www.atteanlodge.com*) is situated on a wild island within the lake. All meals are included. Family reunions are welcomed.

For all of the amenities of a four-season resort, the 200-acre, 140-room Bethel Inn Resort (On the Common, Bethel, 207-824-2175 or 800-654-0125, *www.bethelinn.com*) offers an 18-hole golf course, cross-country and snowshoeing trails, tennis courts, a heated year-round outdoor pool, and both fine and casual family dining.

Moosehead Lake is surrounded by diverse accommodations choices. The Birches Resort (1 Birches Drive, Rockwood, 207-534-7305 or 800-825-9453, *www.birches.com*) is situated within an 11,000-acre wilderness preserve on the lake's shores. It is the home base for Wilderness Expeditions, a rafting and paddling outfitter, and also offers a variety of other adventures including ice fishing, cross-country skiing, snowmobiling, moose cruises, and mountain biking. Choose from cabins, lodge rooms, cabin tents, and even yurts—updated versions of the primitive, circular shelters that originated in Siberia.

 JUST FOR PARENTS

The Lodge at Moosehead Lake (Lily Bay Road, Greenville, 207-695-4400, *www.lodgeatmooseheadlake.com*) is an award-winning small inn that cleverly blends pampering and elegance with a rustic theme. Eight unique rooms and suites, such as the Bear Room, the Moose Room, and the Katahdin Suite come with Jacuzzis for two, fireplaces, and bedposts hand-carved to reflect the room's theme.

Budget-Friendly Hotels, Motels, and Inns

If you're looking for simple, value-priced lodging and don't mind the inconvenience of having to bring your own towels and soap, consider the three inns and cottages at the 800-acre Poland Spring Resort (543 Maine Street, Poland Spring, 207-998-4351, *www.polandspringinns.com*). Rates at this old-fashioned country inn are surprisingly affordable even before you factor in that all-you-can-eat, buffet-style meals are included.

Western Maine's resort ski areas are terrific places for families, even after the snow melts. To inquire about hotel and condominium lodging options, call Bethel's Sunday River at 800-543-2754 or Sugarloaf/USA in Carrabassett Valley at 800-THE-LOAF.

Up north, Gateway Inn (Route 157, Medway, 207-746-3193, *www .medwaygateway.com*) is a good landing spot for snowmobilers, as it's located near Maine's network of snowmobiling trails. It also welcomes pets and features an indoor pool, exercise room, and some rooms with Mount Katahdin views. Katahdin Inn (740 Central Street, Millinocket, 207-723-4555 or 877-902-4555, *www.katahdininn.com*) is convenient to northern Maine's prime outdoor sporting activities and features eighty-two rooms including some with Jacuzzis, an indoor pool and hot tub, a children's pool, exercise room, free continental breakfast, and a massage therapist on-site.

 TRAVEL TIP

Camping and Maine are a natural fit, and the sheer number of campsites in the state is proof positive of camping's popularity. The Maine Campground Owners Association (207-782-5874, *www.campmaine.com*) counts 228 RV parks and campgrounds among its ranks. Search their database online or call them to request a free camping guide.

In Aroostook County, Caribou Inn and Convention Center (19 Main Street, Caribou, 207-498-3733 or 800-235-0466, *www.caribouinn .com*) has seventy-three rooms and three suites and modern hotel amenities including a heated indoor pool and restaurant. Northern Lights Motel (72 Houlton Road, Presque Isle, 207-764-4441, *www .northernlightsmotel.com*) provides family-friendly accommodations and special touches such as in-room refrigerators and free wireless Internet access.

Family Dining

Food always seems to taste better after a day of fresh air and outdoor activity. If you're staying at a remote resort or sporting camp or participating in an organized rafting or other outing, your meals will likely be provided. If not, here are some eateries—from down-home to offbeat—to look for in western or northern Maine.

Western Maine Dining Finds

The Lakes Region's first brewpub, Bray's Brewpub & Eatery (Routes 302 and 35, Naples, 207-693-6806, *www.braysbrewpub.com*), opened in 1995 in a 120-year-old Victorian farmhouse. Lunch and dinner are available daily, and tours of the brewing operation are available Thursday afternoons. The children's menu features the likely suspects.

In Bethel, Maine-brewed beer is also on tap at Sunday River Brewing Co. (Route 2 and Sunday River Road, 207-824-4ALE). The Shipyard Brew Haus at Sunday River (White Heat Lane, Bethel, 207-824-5138, *www.shipyardbrewhaus.com*) is popular with the après-ski crowd. And although they don't brew their own ales, you'll find twenty-nine regional beers on draught at the family-friendly Suds Pub at the Sudbury Inn (151 Main Street, Bethel, 207-824-2174, *www.sudburyinn.com*).

When you're ready for a sweet treat, visit the farm animals and savor homemade ice cream at Gillmor Farms (615 Enfield Road, Lincoln, 207-794-6565).

Northern Noshing

You could literally step right into Moosehead Lake from your table on the deck at Kelly's Landing (Routes 6 and 15, Greenville Junction, 207-695-4438, *www.kellysatmoosehead.com*), where hungry vacationers love the all-you-can-eat breakfast buffet on Sundays. Lakeside dining is also available at The Black Frog (Pritham Avenue, Greenville, 207-695-1100, *www.theblackfrog.com*), where you watch the seaplanes take off and land as you munch on fried chicken or chish and fips—they have a sense of humor, here.

If whitewater rafting isn't your cup of tea, you can still dine at the New England Outdoor Center's River Drivers Restaurant (Medway Road, Millinocket, 207-723-5438 or 800-766-7238, *www.neoc.com*), where entrées range from fresh seafood preparations to rack of lamb. They promise: "Here, no one will frown at your kids."

Of course, if you're more worried about putting smiles on your little ones' faces, you may let them to talk you into simply grabbing a hot dog at Magic City (237 Penobscot Avenue, Millinocket, 207-723-4404, *http://mysite.verizon.net/magiccityminigolf*), a year-round indoor entertainment center featuring an arcade, kiddie rides, golf simulator, and miniature golf course.

≡FAST FACT

Your palate may not appreciate just any potatoes once you've tasted the Maine-grown variety. So, order organic potatoes grown in Aroostook County from Wood Prairie Farm online at *www.woodprairie.com* or by calling 800-829-9765. They even have a Maine Potato Sampler of the Month Club.

In Aroostook County, the Blue Moose (Route 1, Monticello, 207-538-0991, *www.connectmaine.com/bluemoose*) welcomes snowmobilers—the log cabin restaurant with a cozy wood stove and children's menu is just 400 feet from snowmobile trails. The Elm Tree Diner (146 Bangor Road, Houlton, 207-532-3181, *www.mallplexusa.com/elmtreediner*) has been serving home-cooked breakfasts, lunches, and dinners for more than sixty years. The Lakeview Restaurant (9 Lakeview Drive, St. Agatha, 207-543-6331), serves everything from prime rib to seafood in a family-friendly setting. Their all-you-can-eat Sunday brunch will fill your family up without costing a fortune.

New Hampshire

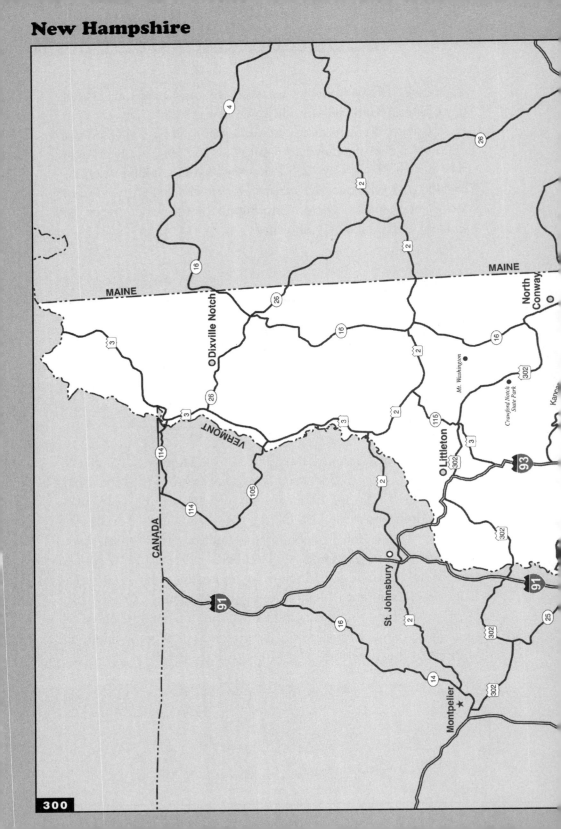

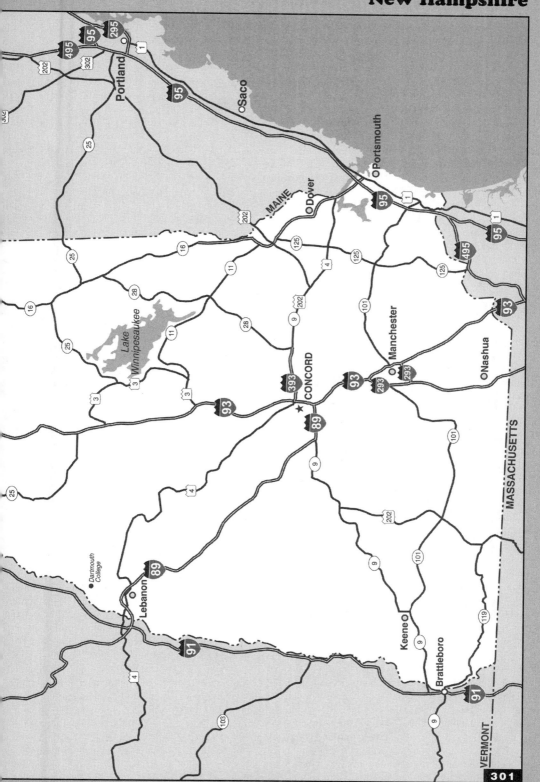

Portsmouth, New Hampshire

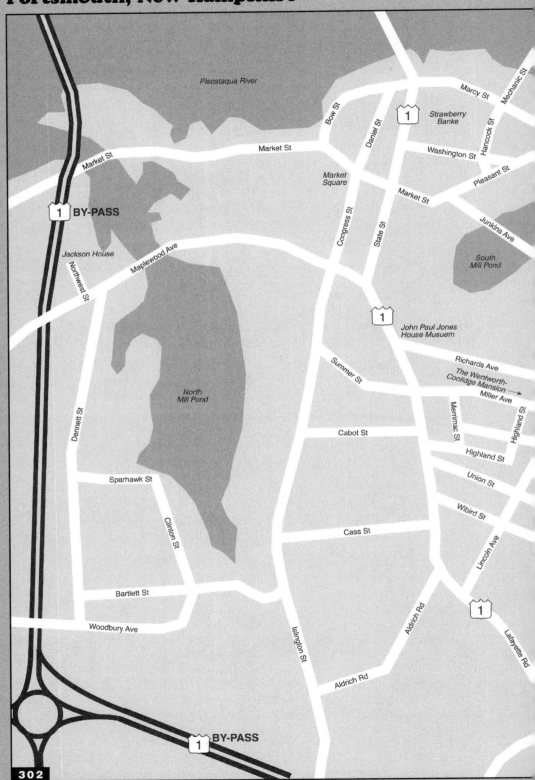

Piscataqua River

Market St

1 BY-PASS

Jackson House

Northwest St

Maplewood Ave

Dennett St

North
Mill Pond

Sparhawk St

Clinton St

Bartlett St

Woodbury Ave

Bow St

Market St

Daniel St

Market
Square

Congress St

State St

Summer St

Cabot St

Cass St

Islington St

Aldrich Rd

Aldrich Rd

1

Marcy St

Mechanic St

1 Strawberry
Banke

Hancock St

Washington St

Pleasant St

Market St

Junkins Ave

South
Mill Pond

1

John Paul Jones
House Musuem

Richards Ave

The Wentworth-
Coolidge Mansion →

Miller Ave

Merrimac St

Highland St

Highland St

Union St

Wibird St

Lincoln Ave

1

Lafayette Rd

1 BY-PASS

302

CHAPTER 16
New Hampshire

CHOOSING JUST ONE NEW England state to visit is an unenviable task, but if you must, New Hampshire is a solid bet. Not only will you find a smattering of all that is New England here, you'll also discover one-of-a-kind attractions, such as the Mt. Washington Cog Railway, that are completely unique to this realm. With "Live Free or Die" as its motto, you can almost guarantee that fiercely independent New Hampshire will dish up a few surprises all its own.

An Introduction to the Granite State

New Hampshire's official nickname is "The Granite State," but a more fitting moniker might just be "The Little Bit of This and a Little Dash of That State." Whether you picture majestic mountains, sparkling lakes, rushing rivers, bustling cities, sleepy villages, or seashore as the backdrop to your New England adventure, you can find the perfect setting within New Hampshire's borders.

The first European settlement in New Hampshire was a fishing colony established in 1623. New Hampshire has 1,300 lakes and ponds and 40,000 miles of rivers and streams—115,000 acres of water in all—that provide opportunities for fishing and recreation. Fittingly, in 1865, New Hampshire was the first New England state to establish a fish and game department and to promote active conservation. New Hampshire also has an ocean coast, and while it is just eighteen miles long, it provides not only fertile saltwater fishing and lobstering grounds, but vacation enticements for those who heed the call of the beach.

≡FAST FACT

The Old Man of the Mountain, which you may recognize from the New Hampshire state quarter, was a rock formation in the Franconia Mountains that looked distinctly like the profile of a weathered old man. Sadly, this natural wonder was discovered missing on the morning of May 3, 2003. Visitors can see what the Old Man looked like before he fell by gazing through high-tech viewers that have been installed at viewing areas along the Franconia Notch Parkway.

Mountains are another prominent feature of New Hampshire's landscape, and the state's peaks hold the promise of skiing in the winter, hiking in the spring and summer, and fabulous foliage sightseeing come autumn. Thanks to the dream of one man, Sylvester Marsh, the summit of Mt. Washington is accessible via the world's first mountain-climbing cog railway. Though members of the New Hampshire Legislature scoffed at Marsh and told him he "might as well build a railway to the Moon," this 1869 engineering feat continues to take visitors the 6,288 feet to the mountain's top.

When to Visit

New Hampshire has four distinct seasons—five if you count the "mud season," which occurs in late March and early April. Snow in the mountains makes for wonderful skiing vacations beginning in late November and lasting through April.

New Hampshire really comes to life in late spring and early summer, and you'll find festivals celebrating the state's floral bounty, including lilac festivals in Rochester and Lisbon and a lupine festival in the

Sugar Hill area. Summer is a perfect time to explore seacoast beaches and to take a whale-watch cruise. New Hampshire is at its most breathtaking in autumn, when the White Mountains are ablaze with color. You'll bring home vacation photos of crystal-smooth lakes and covered bridges against a background palette of dazzling autumn hues.

TRAVEL TIP

Outdoor adventurers will want to avoid New Hampshire's infamous, three-week "black fly season," which generally occurs in early May in the southern part of the state and may occur as late as mid-June in the far north. An insect repellent containing DEET may provide some defense against the painful bite of these pests, but young children may be sensitive to the chemical, so use it with caution.

Getting There and Getting Around

The growth of Manchester-Boston Regional Airport and the redevelopment of Pease Air Force Base as a civilian trade and aviation hub have broadened arrival options for New Hampshire visitors. Still, the state remains primarily a drive-to destination. And once you've arrived, having a car at your disposal will be crucial, not only for transportation to your vacation destination but for access to the spectacular scenes that await along some of New England's most scenic and exhilarating roadways.

Manchester-Boston Regional Airport (MHT)

Manchester-Boston Regional Airport (603-624-6556, *www .flymanchester.com*), is conveniently located off I-93 and is a growing transportation hub that serves northern New England. It is also an alternative for some travelers to Boston's busy Logan International Airport. Passenger traffic tripled at Manchester Airport between

1997 and 2000 and has continued to grow, setting new records in both 2004 and 2005.

To reach Manchester-Boston Regional Airport, follow signs from I-93 to I-293/Route 101 to exit 2 for Brown Avenue. Follow Brown Avenue for 1.4 miles to Airport Road.

MAJOR AIRLINES SERVING MANCHESTER-BOSTON REGIONAL AIRPORT

Airline	Phone Number	Web Site
Air Canada	☎888-247-2262	✎www.aircanada.ca
Continental	☎800-525-0280	✎www.continental.com
Delta	☎800-221-1212	✎www.delta.com
Northwest	☎800-225-2525	✎www.nwa.com
Southwest	☎800-435-9792	✎www.southwest.com
United	☎800-241-6522	✎www.ual.com
US Airways	☎800-428-4322	✎www.usair.com

≡FAST FACT

If New Hampshire's Seacoast region is your destination, you may want to check the schedule of flights into Portsmouth International Airport (603-433-6536, *www.peasedev.org*), located off I-95 within the Pease International Tradeport. Allegiant Air (*www.allegiantair.com*) and Pan Am Clipper Connection (*www.flypanam.com*) operate at this former military base, providing a limited schedule of arrivals and departures.

Airport shuttles are operated by Flight Line (603-893-8254 or 800-245-2525), Hampton Shuttle (603-659-9893 or 800-225-6426), Mermaid Transportation Company (207-885-5630 or 800-696-2463), and Thomas Transportation Services (603-352-5550 or 800-526-8143). Taxis and limousines are also readily available.

For ticketed passengers, the airport also offers the free Manchester Shuttle (603-624-6539, ext. 324, *www.flymanchester.com*), which provides transportation to and from the Anderson Regional Transportation Center in Woburn, Massachusetts, and the Sullivan Square subway station, located two stops from downtown Boston.

Trains and Buses

New Hampshire has just a handful of train stations serviced by Amtrak (800-872-7245, *www.amtrak.com*). Claremont, in the southwest corner of the state, is a stop on Amtrak's Vermonter route, and Exeter, Durham, and Dover are serviced by Amtrak's Downeaster, a coastal train that runs between Boston's North Station and Portland, Maine.

Concord Coach Lines (800-639-3317, *www.concordtrailways.com*) is the primary bus transportation company in the state. Its Dartmouth Coach connects Hanover, Lebanon, and New London, New Hampshire, with Boston's South Station and Logan Airport. Concord Trailways buses travel several routes including Concord-Manchester-Boston, Berlin-Conway-New Hampton, and Littleton-Plymouth-Tilton.

Greyhound (603-436-0163 or 800-231-2222, *www.greyhound.com*) also offers service to a number of New Hampshire bus stations via its affiliate, Vermont Transit Lines (800-552-8737, *www.vermonttransit.com*).

Getting Around

For flexibility and ease, you'll most likely want to rent a car if you haven't traveled to New Hampshire in your own vehicle. The free Visitors Guide, available from the state's Division of Travel and Tourism Development (800-386-4664, *www.visitnh.gov*), has a pull-out road map that will help you to navigate the state's highways and byways.

Winter driving can be treacherous; proceed slowly, and stick to main highways whenever possible following a major snowfall. During "mud season" in the spring, avoid unpaved roads. Stay alert—particularly as you travel in the White Mountains and the Great North Woods—for moose. A collision with one of these hulking creatures can cause serious injuries and vehicle damage.

Must-See Activities and Attractions

Healthful mountain air and elegant grand hotels lured New Hampshire's first vacationers in the mid-nineteenth century. Today, nostalgia reigns at the state's family-friendly attractions, many of which have entertained generations of visitors. Among these highlights, you'll find amusements where the focus is on spending time together—not spending a ton of money.

 **RAINY DAY FUN**

New Hampshire teacher Christa McAuliffe captured the world's imagination when she became the first civilian astronaut. Her untimely death in the 1986 explosion of the space shuttle Challenger devastated a nation that had followed her dream. The Christa McAuliffe Planetarium (2 Institute Drive, Concord, 603-271-7827, *www.starhop.com*) features hands-on exhibits and a changing menu of multimedia shows that take visitors on a virtual flight through space.

America's Stonehenge
⌨105 Haverhill Road, Salem
✆603-893-8300
✍*www.stonehengeusa.com*

You don't have to travel to England to see a prehistoric archaeological enigma. New England has its own Stonehenge in Salem, New Hampshire. Explore thirty acres of cave-like dwellings, astronomically aligned rock formations, and other mysterious structures left behind on "Mystery Hill" by an unknown people.

Canterbury Shaker Village

⌨288 Shaker Rd, Canterbury

✆603-783-9511 or ✆800-982-9511

✐*www.shakers.org*

Step back in time to the simple ways espoused by the Shaker religious community formed at Canterbury in 1792. This 694-acre National Historic Landmark has twenty-five original Shaker buildings to explore, plus nature trails, gardens, costumed guides, daily craft demonstrations, a gift shop featuring Shaker reproductions, and a restaurant, the Creamery, that serves traditional Shaker cuisine.

Cathedral of the Pines

⌨Cathedral Road, Rindge

✆603-899-3300 or ✆866-229-4520

✐*www.cathedralpines.com*

This outdoor memorial honors Americans who have died in service to their country. The Altar of the Nation is constructed of rock from every U.S. state and territory. Norman Rockwell designed the bronze tablets you'll see inside the Memorial Bell Tower, which also houses bells from around the world.

Clark's Trading Post

⌨Route 3, Lincoln

✆603-745-8913

✐*www.clarkstradingpost.com*

One of the White Mountains' most unusual attractions, Clark's Trading Post is best known for its trained black bears that perform daily. Clark's has been delighting families for more than seventy-five years with its interesting collection of entertainment, which includes a scenic train ride on the White Mountain Central Railroad, water bumper boats, the mysterious Tuttle House, Merlin's Mystical Mansion, and a museum of Americana.

Hampton Beach
⌨Ocean Boulevard, Hampton Beach
☏603-926-8717
✍*www.hamptonbeach.org*
This classic beach community offers all of the old-fashioned ingredients you need for the perfect summer vacation: a white sand beach open free to the public, gentle ocean surf, casual restaurants, colorful souvenir shops, deep-sea fishing charters, arcades, miniature golf courses, weekly fireworks, and nightly outdoor concerts.

The Isles of Shoals Steamship Company
⌨315 Market Street, Portsmouth
☏603-431-5500 or ☏800-441-4620
✍*www.islesofshoals.com*
Take a scenic cruise tour of historic Portsmouth Harbor and see lighthouses, forts, and coastal landmarks. Narrated trips feature tales of ghosts, pirates, fierce storms, and other legendary people and events. Also check their schedule of fall foliage outings and lobster clambake dinner cruises.

Santa's Village
⌨528 Presidential Highway, Jefferson
☏603-586-4445
✍*www.santasvillage.com*
You can't blame Santa for spending his summers in the picturesque White Mountains. This enchanting, Christmas-themed amusement park enthralls little ones and offers enough thrilling rides—including a log flume and a roller coaster—to excite older children, too.

Scenic Railways
Three railroad sightseeing options provide New Hampshire visitors with a nostalgic, leisurely means of viewing the state's natural beauty. Most famous is the Mount Washington Cog Railway in Bretton Woods (603-278-5404 or 800-922-8825, *www.thecog.com*). The coal-fired steam engine trains take passengers up one of the steep-

est tracks in the world—6,288 feet to the summit of Mount Washington. Conway Scenic Railroad (603-356-5251 or 800-232-5251, *www .conwayscenic.com*) offers excursions aboard the vintage Valley Train from Conway to Bartlett or the Notch Train through Crawford Notch, one of the state's most spectacular spots. Or, climb aboard the historic Winnipesaukee Scenic Railroad (603-279-5253, *www .hoborr.com/winni.html*) from departure points at Weirs Beach or Meredith for a fabulous tour of the lake's shore.

Story Land
⌨Route 16, Glen
✆603-383-4186
✍*www.storylandnh.com*

Kids' favorite fairy tales and nursery rhymes come to life at this enduring amusement park that opened its doors in the White Mountains in 1954. Pay one admission price for unlimited rides and shows. The park is geared primarily to preschoolers and young children, who will lead the charge to see all of the park's magical attractions the moment you step through the gates.

═FAST FACT

There is no sales tax on purchases anywhere in New Hampshire. That makes the state's outlet shopping centers an even better bargain. Many New Hampshire shops will gladly ship purchases for visitors.

Water Country
⌨Route 1, Portsmouth
✆603-427-1111
✍*www.watercountry.com*

Water Country is New England's largest water amusement park, with more than a dozen different water slides and rides ranging from big thrillers to tamer options appropriate for the tiniest of tots. Water Country also boasts New England's largest wave pool; it's 700,000 gallons! One admission price includes all water rides and attractions.

Family Fun Plans

When you're traveling with children, it's always best to have a plan. Make your reservations well in advance for summer weekends at New Hampshire's lake and ocean beaches and fall days in the incomparable White Mountains. These suggested itineraries are just a starting point; use them to inspire a travel plan that suits your family's needs.

A Jam-Packed, Three-Day New Hampshire Summer Sampler

You can cram plenty of activity into a long summer weekend when you choose southern New Hampshire as your destination. This itinerary takes you from the ocean all the way to outer space in just three days.

Day One: Arrive in Portsmouth and spend the afternoon at sea on a sightseeing cruise with the Isles of Shoals Steamship Co. (315 Market Street, 603-431-5500 or 800-441-4620, *www.islesofshoals.com*). In the evening, take a scenic drive along Route 1A, which follows New Hampshire's shoreline, and watch the shadows dance on wave crests as the day disappears. Treat yourself to a seafood feast at La Bec Rouge (73 Ocean Boulevard, Hampton Beach, 603-926-5050, *www. labecrouge.com*) before calling it a night.

Day Two: Enjoy the sun and fun at Hampton Beach (Ocean Boulevard, Hampton Beach, 603-926-8717, *www.hamptonbeach.org*). When you're waterlogged from swimming and boogie boarding, you'll find plenty of other enticements at the shops, arcades, restaurants, and entertainment venues across the street from the beach.

Day Three: On your last day in the Granite State, head inland and spend the morning at the historic Canterbury Shaker Village (288 Shaker Rd, Canterbury, 603-783-9511 or 800-982-9511, *www.shakers.org*). Be sure to have lunch at the village's Creamery restaurant, where you can sample authentic Shaker cuisine. In the afternoon, drive south to Concord and take a side trip to outer space at the Christa McAuliffe Planetarium (2 Institute Drive, C603-271-7827, *www.starhop.com*) before blasting off for home.

Five Fabulous Fall Days

New Hampshire is a leaf peeper's dream. It is impossible to predict exactly when leaves will be at their peak, so fill your fall itinerary with plenty to do, and consider colorful foliage a bonus.

Day One: Start in North Conway for sales tax–free outlet stores galore. When you've tired of the shopping frenzy, take a peaceful leaf-peeping trip aboard the Conway Scenic Railroad (Route 16, North Conway, 603-356-5251 or 800-232-5251, *www.conwayscenic.com*). In the evening, head north on Route 16 and pass through the covered bridge gateway to the town of Jackson, where you can sup on New England cuisine at Highfield's at the Eagle Mountain House (Carter Notch Road, Jackson, 603-383-9111 or 800-966-5779, *www.eaglemt.com*).

Day Two: Follow Route 302 through the White Mountain National Forest to Bretton Woods, where you have made reservations at the Mount Washington Hotel and Resort (Route 302, 603-278-1000 or 800-314-1752, *www.mtwashington.com*), a picturesque and historic grand hotel that welcomes families. Spend the remainder of the day enjoying the resort's many amenities.

Day Three: In the morning, enjoy the views from a horse-drawn carriage ride, offered to guests by the Stables at the Mount Washington Resort. Then, head south to Franconia Notch for an aerial view of the colorful landscape aboard the Cannon Aerial Tramway (Franconia Notch Parkway, Franconia Notch, 603-823-8800, *www.cannonmt.com*).

Day Four: Grab your camera and take the Mount Washington Cog Railway (Route 302, Bretton Woods, 603-278-5404 or 800-922-8825, *www.thecog.com*) 6,288 feet to the summit for breathtaking views. In the afternoon, head south on Route 3 and then west to

North Woodstock for a visit to Lost River Gorge (Route 112, North Woodstock, 603-745-8031, *www.findlostriver.com*), where you can see waterfalls and steep rock walls as you follow walkways through the gorge.

Day Five: Travel New Hampshire's most scenic road, the 34-mile Kancamagus Highway (Route 112), east to Conway. You'll be treated to spectacular mountain scenery as the road climbs to nearly 3,000 feet. Time permitting, make the trip an hour south to explore Castle in the Clouds (Route 171, Moultonborough, 603-476-5900 or 800-729-2468, *www.castleintheclouds.org*), a wonderful spot to savor your last images of autumn in New Hampshire.

Family Fun in the Lakes and Mountains

Summertime is family time, and if you head to New Hampshire for a holiday, your kids will go back to school with plenty of experiences to share in their "What I Did on My Summer Vacation" essays. This suggested itinerary takes you to the Lakes Region and the White Mountains, but if your budget is tight, plan a shorter escape to one destination and save the other for next summer.

Day One: Base yourself in North Conway for the first two days of your trip; it's an ideal central location to enjoy the White Mountains. If you arrive by late afternoon, you may have time to visit Story Land (Route 16, Glen, 603-383-4186, *www.storylandnh.com*) or to enjoy a train ride aboard the Conway Scenic Railroad (Route 16, North Conway, 603-356-5251 or 800-232-5251, *www.conwayscenic.com*).

Day Two: It's theme park day! Younger children will love Story Land or Santa's Village (528 Presidential Highway, Jefferson, 603-586-4445, *www.santasvillage.com*). The Old West–themed Six Gun City and Fort Splash Waterpark (1492 Presidential Highway, Jefferson, 603-586-4592, *www.sixguncity.com*) will appeal to older kids.

Day Three: Follow Route 112, the Kancamagus Highway, west from Conway to Lincoln, stopping often to enjoy the impressive mountain vistas. In Lincoln, explore Clark's Trading Post (Route 3, 603-745-8913, *www.clarkstradingpost.com*); there's something for everyone. If it's a steamy afternoon, cool off at Whale's Tale Water Park (Route 3, Lincoln, 603-745-8810, *www.whalestalewaterpark.net*) before driving south to the Lakes Region for the night.

Day Four: Enjoy a relaxing day at Weirs Beach (Weirs Boulevard, Weirs Beach, *www.weirsbeach.com*) on Lake Winnipesaukee, where you can swim, sunbathe, stroll the boardwalk, dine outdoors, take a scenic train ride or cruise, play arcade games, and more. In the evening, treat the kids to an old-fashioned entertainment experience at the Weirs Beach Drive-In Theater (Route 3, Weirs Beach, 603-366-5777).

 TRAVEL TIP

For the best Story Land value, purchase your admission tickets after 3 P.M. (2 P.M. when the park operates on a weekends-only schedule), enjoy all of the amusements until closing time, and receive a complimentary pass to return for another full day anytime during the same year.

Day Five: It won't be easy to say farewell to New Hampshire, so you may want to promise the kids one last stop as you leave the state. The ancient archaeological mystery that is America's Stonehenge (105 Haverhill Road, Salem, 603-893-8300, *www.stonehengeusa.com*) is located at exit 3 off I-93. Buy lucky rock amulets in the gift shop to wear on your journey home and to remind you of your stay in New Hampshire.

CHAPTER 17

New Hampshire's Seacoast and Lakes Regions

ALTHOUGH ITS OCEAN COAST is only eighteen miles long, New Hampshire offers families plenty of liquid refreshment. That's because much of the state's Atlantic shoreline is accessible to the public. Plus, just an hour northwest of the coastal city of Portsmouth, vacationers will discover the delights of the state's largest lake—Winnipesaukee—which sparkles at the center of a region graced with more than 200 freshwater pools. Whether you're drawn to the salty sea or the still, clear waters of glacier-carved lakes, New Hampshire provides waterside fun for everyone.

A Petite Seacoast

You're the first president of the United States, and you've just wrapped up the first session of the first Congress—where do you go to get away from it all? Well, in 1789, George Washington chose Portsmouth, the Seacoast region's largest city, as the final destination of his tour through New England. Since then, millions of other vacationers have followed suit, choosing the diminutive shoreline area with 350 years of history for its sandy beaches, ocean excursions, old-fashioned clambakes, boutiques and antiques, and family attractions.

Proximity also makes the region a popular choice. Portsmouth is just an hour north of Boston, and a stay in the Seacoast region puts you within a short drive of the outlets and other enticements of southern Maine and the beaches and seafood delights of the North Shore.

Even though you won't be greeted with quite the pomp and ceremony that accompanied George Washington's arrival in Portsmouth, you won't have to steal away on your fifth day of vacation to have some seaside fun without your military entourage cramping your style.

What to See and Do in the Seacoast Region

Beaches are the number-one reason to pull off I-95 in New Hampshire, but the Seacoast region also dishes up a full menu of family fun. Take time out to explore museums and historic sites that tell the story of New Hampshire's early history.

Seacoast Beaches

With its boardwalk, amusements, eateries, and entertainment, Hampton Beach is New Hampshire's premier destination for those who love the sun and sand. You won't be disappointed, however, if you prefer a quieter place to spread your blanket and build your sandcastles. The Seacoast region is home to several public beaches, each with its own unique character.

Hampton Beach State Park
Route 1A, Hampton
603-926-3784
http://www.nhstateparks.org/state-parks/alphabetical-order/ hampton-beach-state-park

On busy summer weekends, it can be difficult to see the beach beneath the colorful array of sun umbrellas and towels. Parking is at a premium, but admission to the beach is free. Affordable rates are available for overnight RV camping. The Seashell complex features not only an outdoor band shell but a bathhouse and first-aid station. There's plenty to do along the boardwalk when you tire of swimming.

Jenness State Beach
Route 1A, Rye
603-436-1552
www.nhstateparks.org/state-parks/state-beaches

Arrive early in the day at this family beach in order to score a metered parking spot. A bathhouse is available, and lifeguards are on duty in season.

═FAST FACT

You'll need to bring plenty of quarters to feed the meters at New Hampshire beaches, or purchase tokens, which are good for four hours of parking, at these locations: the parking lot south of the Hampton Seashell complex; the restrooms on Ross Avenue; or the restrooms at North Beach, Jenness Beach, and North Hampton State Beach. Parking meters operate from 8 A.M. until midnight every day from May 1 through October 1.

North Beach
Route 1A, Hampton
603-436-1552
www.nhstateparks.org/state-parks/state-beaches

Positioned north of Hampton Beach, this smaller stretch of sand is an ideal family spot. The bathhouse is open year-round, and lifeguards are stationed here during the summer season. Limited metered parking is available.

North Hampton State Beach
Route 1A, North Hampton
603-436-1552
www.nhstateparks.org/state-parks/state-beaches

Located about two miles north of North Beach, this beach is popular with surfers and families; lifeguards are on duty. A bathhouse is available. Metered parking is available along Route 1A.

 TRAVEL TIP

Although it does not have a swimming beach, Odiorne Point State Park (Route 1A, Rye, 603-436-7406, *www.nhstateparks.org/state-parks*) is a scenic place for a picnic. The oceanside park has an extensive system of trails to explore and is also home to the Seacoast Science Center (*www.seacoastsciencecenter.org*), where you can learn about the coastal region's human and natural history. An admission fee is charged in season, and additional entrance fees apply at the Science Center.

Seabrook Beach

⌖Ocean Drive (Route 1A), Seabrook

✆603-474-5746

Parking is limited at this quiet alternative to Hampton Beach, located just north of the Massachusetts border.

Wallis Sands State Beach

⌖Route 1A, Rye

✆603-436-9404

✑*www.nhstateparks.org/state-parks/state-beaches*

You'll enjoy views of the Isles of Shoals as you play in the sand and surf at this lifeguard-protected family beach. Ample parking is available, and families pay one price per car for admission to the park. Facilities include a bathhouse with showers and a store that sells food, beverages, and sundries.

Family Amusements

Many families opt to vacation for a week or more in the Seacoast region. Without venturing far from shore, you'll find amusements that can provide a nice break from the beach.

Fuller Gardens

⌨ 10 Willow Avenue, North Hampton

✆ 603-964-5414

✍ *www.fullergardens.org*

This seaside estate garden was planted in the early 1920s at the former summer home of Massachusetts Governor Alvan T. Fuller. Designed by landscape architect Arthur Shurtleff, it features 1,500 rosebushes of all types, brilliantly colored annuals, a Japanese garden, perennial borders, a hosta display garden, and a conservatory filled with tropical and desert plants. This historic and fragrant property is open to the public for a fee from mid-May through mid-October.

Hampton Beach Casino Ballroom

⌨ 169 Ocean Boulevard, Hampton Beach

✆ 603-929-4100

✍ *www.casinoballroom.com*

This century-old venue brings top musical acts and entertainers to the seashore each summer. Call ahead or visit their Web site to see who'll be in town while you're visiting.

 JUST FOR PARENTS

Seabrook Greyhound Park (Route 107 West, Seabrook, 603-474-3065, *www.seabrookgreyhoundpark.com*) hosts live greyhound racing seasonally and offers simulcast wagering and Texas Hold 'Em Poker year-round. Call for a schedule of day and evening sessions, and ask about special weekend getaway packages.

The Isles of Shoals Steamship Co.

315 Market Street, Portsmouth

603-431-5500 or 800-441-4620

www.islesofshoals.com

Don't miss the chance to head out to sea for a sightseeing excursion or to cruise inland along the Piscataqua River as you feast on chowder and lobster aboard a Victorian-style steamship, the *M/V Thomas Laighton*. This tour company offers a variety of departures from spring through fall.

Water Country

Route 1, Portsmouth

603-427-1111

www.watercountry.com

Let the kids brave the water slides while you float along on the Adventure River tube ride at New England's largest water amusement park.

Museums and Historic Sites

Portsmouth was founded in 1623 and has a long history as a commercial and military port city. Early colonists named their settlement Strawbery Banke because of the wild berries that thrived along the Piscataqua River, which empties into the Atlantic Ocean near Portsmouth. The area's historic sites whisk travelers back in time, offering insight into the region's development and significance.

John Paul Jones House Museum

43 Middle Street, Portsmouth

603-436-8420

www.portsmouthhistory.org/jpjhouse.html

Learn about the Father of the American Navy at this museum, where the Revolutionary War hero stayed on one of his visits to Portsmouth. Operated by the Portsmouth Historical Society, the 1758 boarding house is open to visitors daily from Memorial Day weekend through mid-October.

Strawbery Banke Museum

⌨Hancock Street, Portsmouth

✆603-433-1100

✑*www.strawberybanke.org*

Get a glimpse of New Hampshire's origins at this ten-acre, water-front, living-history complex on the site of one of the city's oldest neighborhoods. It is open daily from May through October for self-guided tours. Winter walking tours are also available on weekends from November through April.

RAINY DAY FUN

Kids can play Dino Detective, don raincoats and life vests before they climb aboard a fifteen-foot lobster boat with a working lobster trap, and orbit Earth inside a simulated space shuttle cockpit at The Children's Museum of Portsmouth (280 Marcy Street, Portsmouth, 603-436-3853, *www .childrens-museum.org*). Open year-round, the museum's interactive exhibits are designed to stimulate children's natural curiosity.

USS Albacore

⌨Albacore Park, 600 Market Street, Portsmouth

✆603-436-3680

✑*www.ussalbacore.org*

Designed and built at the Portsmouth Naval Shipyard, the USS *Albacore* was a prototype that influenced the course of submarine development. Commissioned in 1953, the underwater vessel set a record as the world's fastest submarine in 1966. In 1985, the decommissioned sub returned home to Portsmouth, where it is now open year-round for tours.

Wentworth-Coolidge Mansion Historic Site
🖳Little Harbor Road, Portsmouth
📞603-436-6607
✎*www.nhstateparks.org/ParksPages/WentworthCoolidge/
WentCoolHom.html*

The forty-room Wentworth-Coolidge Mansion is an interesting structure that reflects five architectural periods. It was home from 1741 to 1767 to New Hampshire's first royal governor. Tours, available seasonally on weekends only, offer insight into colonial life in New Hampshire.

Shopping

The Kittery, Maine, outlets are just minutes away, but don't overlook some shopping finds tucked away in this area.

Antique Alley
🖳Route 4 in Northwood, Lee, Epsom, and Chichester
✎*www.nhantiquealley.com*

The thirty-mile stretch of Route 4 between Portsmouth and Concord is called "Antique Alley"; you'll find dozens of antiques shops to poke around in.

Maine-ly New Hampshire
🖳33 Deer Street, Suite 5A, Portsmouth
📞603-422-9500
✎*www.mainelynewhampshire.com*

Souvenir hunters will love this store, which specializes in New Hampshire–made products including herbal soaps and fragrant soy candles made at nearby Sweet Grass Farm.

Market Square
🖳Market Square, Portsmouth

Located in the center of the historic city, this popular, walkable shopping district has dozens of galleries, gift shops, cafés, and boutiques.

🧳 TRAVEL TIP

The nonprofit Seacoast Growers' Association (603-658-0280, *www.seacoastgrowers.org*) operates six farmers' markets in the region, where shoppers can buy fresh fruits and vegetables, plus New Hampshire–made crafts and food products. Visit their Web site for a schedule of dates and locations.

Salmon Falls Stoneware
🖼 The Engine House, Oak Street, Dover
📞 603-749-1467
✍ *www.salmonfalls.com*

For traditional New England salt-glaze pottery made by New Hampshire artisans, visit this studio and shop housed inside a 1920s-era building where train engines were once serviced.

Where to Stay in the Seacoast Region

The Seacoast region is compact, so wherever you choose to stay, the area's attractions are just minutes away. The Sheraton Harborside Portsmouth (250 Market Street, 603-431-2300, www.sheratonportsmouth.com) is one of the larger options with more than 200 rooms, an indoor heated pool, and its own restaurant and Riverwatch Lounge. Another location convenient to the shops and sights of Portsmouth is the Inn at Strawbery Banke (314 Court Street, 603-436-7242 or 800-428-3933, *www.innatstrawberybanke.com*), an early-1800s home turned B&B that welcomes children ages ten and older.

The bustling Hampton Beach area is your best bet for waterfront lodging. The landmark Ashworth by the Sea (295 Ocean Boulevard, 603-926-6762 or 800-345-6736, *www.ashworthhotel.com*) has offered lodgings overlooking the Atlantic for more than ninety-five years. Book a two-and-a-half-room suite with its own ocean-view porch at Sea Spiral Suites (449 Ocean Boulevard, 603-926-2222 or

800-303-9933, *www.seaspiralsuites.com*), where they'll even stock your galley kitchen on request. The Hampton Beach Area Chamber of Commerce will gladly send you a free accommodations guide with dozens of additional choices. Call them at 603-926-8718, or request your guide online at *www.hamptonchamber.com*.

 JUST FOR PARENTS

Couples will find luxury and a quiet haven at D.W.'s Oceanside Inn (365 Ocean Boulevard, Hampton Beach, 603-926-3542 or 866-623-2674, *www.oceansideinn.com*), an adults-only inn with nine individually furnished guest rooms. Amenities include private, gated parking one block from the inn; a self-service bar on the deck; and inn-wide WiFi. D.W.'s welcomes guests from Memorial Day weekend through Columbus Day weekend.

If you're seeking historic charm, Three Chimneys Inn (17 Newmarket Road, Durham, 603-868-7800 or 888-399-9777, *www .threechimneysinn.com*) provides accommodations for adults and well-mannered children within a restored 1649 mansion and carriage house. While you're there, dine beside the 1649 cooking hearth at the ffrost Sawyer Tavern. Or consider Rock Ledge Manor (1413 Ocean Boulevard, Rye, 603-431-1413, *www.rockledgemanor.com*), a classic gingerbread Victorian that was once part of a resort colony; it's now a B&B with sea views from all guest rooms. Children ages ten and older are welcome.

For a truly extraordinary stay, immerse yourselves in the grandeur of the grand hotel era at Wentworth by the Sea, A Marriott Hotel & Spa (Wentworth Road, New Castle, 603-422-7322 or 866-240-6313, *www.wentworth.com*). This beautifully restored 1874 hotel has indoor and outdoor pools, tennis courts, two restaurants, and a full-service spa.

Family Dining in the Seacoast Region

The Seacoast region is known for two things: seafood and beer. You'll be able to indulge in both, and to treat your family to some very memorable dining experiences, while you vacation at the New Hampshire shore.

Seafood Delights

Don't miss the affordable Lobster Clambake dinners piled high on paper plates at the casual and fun Little Jack's Seafood Restaurant (539 Ocean Boulevard, Hampton Beach, 603-926-8053). Go for the Triple Lobster Dinner if you're really hungry, or save room for some of the other sea specialties including clam fritters, scallop rolls, fisherman's chowder, seafood stew, crab legs, and fresh fried salmon. Prefer your seafood au naturel? The Sea Ketch Restaurant & Lounge (127 Ocean Boulevard, Hampton Beach, 603-926-0324, *www.seaketch .com*), a waterfront restaurant that serves breakfast, lunch, and dinner, is home to the Ketch 22 Raw Bar. Families also flock to La Bec Rouge (73 Ocean Boulevard, Hampton Beach, 603-926-5050, *www .labecrouge.com*) for everything from traditional clambake dinners and baked lobster pie to cider-glazed pork chops. Kids will find satisfying choices on the "Small Fries" menu.

For upscale seafood dining, consider The Oar House (55 Ceres Street, Portsmouth, 603-436-4025, *www.portsmouthnh.com/ oarhouse*), located in the city's historic Merchant's Row building overlooking the old harbor. In season, you can choose to dine on the restaurant's outdoor deck.

Casual Food and Brews

Portsmouth is home to the East Coast operations of Redhook Ale Brewery (35 Corporate Drive, 603-430-8600, *www.redhook.com*). Explore the beer-making process on a guided tour—they're offered daily and end with a sampling session for adults—then stop into the family-friendly Cataqua Public House for tasty, pub-style eats and more crafted–in–New Hampshire beers.

Portsmouth Brewery (56 Market Street, Portsmouth, 603-431-1115, *www.portsmouthbrewery.com*) is the region's original brewpub. In addition to beers brewed on the premises, you'll also find selections brewed at the brewpub's sister company, Smuttynose Brewing Company, plus pub-style food and kid-pleasing Squamscot sodas, bottled in Newfields, New Hampshire, since 1863.

Memorable Meals

Want ice cream for breakfast? The University of New Hampshire Dairy Bar housed in the old Durham train station (Depot Road, Durham, 603-862-1006, *www.unh.edu/dairy-bar*) is open year-round, except during school breaks, as a training facility for restaurant management students—and yes, ice cream is served during all hours of operation.

At lunchtime, kids will get a kick out of selecting from the menu of more than 125 star-inspired selections at Celebrity Sandwich (171 Islington Street, Portsmouth, 603-433-7009, *www.celebritysandwich.com*), where almost every sandwich can be ordered kid-size for those tykes who are ready to order something more adventurous than the Barney (peanut butter and jelly) or the Kermit the Frog (bologna and mustard).

Isles of Shoals Steamship Co. (315 Market Street, Portsmouth, 603-431-5500 or 800-441-4620, *www.islesofshoals.com*) and Foster's Downeast Clambake of Maine have teamed up to offer cruise passengers a true New England dining experience. Reservations are required for their lobster clambake dinner cruises; children's dinner tickets include barbecued chicken instead of lobster.

Land of Lakes

How many lakes and ponds does it take to make a Lakes Region? In New Hampshire, the answer is 273. If you love lakes and the quiet, calming influence a day on or beside the water can have, you may actually find yourself emitting a squeal of delight when you catch your first glimpses of these sparkling blue gems as you drive the region's rolling, winding roads.

The crown jewel is Lake Winnipesaukee, the state's largest lake. It's 182 miles around, covers 72 square miles, and contains 238 confirmed islands—some estimates put the number over 300. The lake's unusual shape and jagged coastline provide for sheltered coves, bays, and inlets that create a sort of optical illusion, making Winnipesaukee appear much less enormous from many perspectives. Situated around the lake you'll find storybook New England towns, private residential areas, resorts, and even a carnival-esque boardwalk area at Weirs Beach.

 TRAVEL TIP

Each year in mid-June, an estimated 350,000 motorcycle enthusiasts converge on the Lakes Region for Laconia Motorcycle Week (*www.laconiamcweek.com*), one of the largest rallies of its kind in America and the oldest continuously held event of the sort. Weirs Beach is the central hub of activities during the nine-day event. Nonbikers usually avoid the overrun area entirely during this annual powwow.

While your natural tendency may be to gravitate toward the big blue diamond that is Winnipesaukee, don't overlook some of the region's smaller, less crowded, and less hurried lakes, including Squam Lake, Winnisquam Lake, and Newfound Lake.

What to See and Do in the Lakes Region

Winnipesaukee is a Native American term that means "smile of the Great Spirit." Spend a few days near the shores of this natural attraction, and you'll soon understand its heavenly appeal. There are myriad ways to occupy your days, and yet, you'll also experience a sense of calm and restfulness that is likely missing from your everyday life.

Family Amusements

Weirs Beach on Lake Winnipesaukee is a summertime family favorite, and the kids will hardly know in which direction to pull you first. While the region's family amusements are concentrated in this area, don't miss some of the other nearby attractions, including New Hampshire's own NASCAR track.

New Hampshire International Speedway

⌨Route 106, Loudon

✆603-783-4931

✍*www.nhis.com*

If motor sports get your heart pumping, the speedway has your ticket to a day of exhilarating racing action. Each year, more than 500,000 fans descend on New England's largest sports facility, which hosts not only NASCAR NEXTEL Cup races but also a variety of professional and amateur motor sports competitions, motorcycle racing, and driving and racing schools from late spring through early fall. Call for a schedule of racing events or to order reserved seats. Tickets may also be purchased online.

Surf Coaster USA

⌨1085 White Oaks Road, Weirs Beach

✆603-366-5600

✍*www.surfcoasterusa.com*

Pay one admission price for day-long or afternoon access to all of the wet and wild slides and rides at this waterpark.

Weirs Beach

⌨Weirs Boulevard/Route 3, Weirs Beach

✆603-524-5046

✍*www.weirsbeach.com*

Weirs Beach on Lake Winnipesaukee is the epicenter of family fun in the Lakes Region. Although the beach is rather small, there are a variety of nearby amusements to enjoy after a refreshing swim. Along the wooden boardwalk, you'll find arcades, bumper cars, mechanical fortunetellers, shops, restaurants, miniature golf, bowling, and bingo. You can always simply lie on the beach, or, if you're feeling more adventurous, rent a boat or Jet Ski. Lifeguards are on duty in season, and facilities at the beach include a bathhouse with restrooms and a playground.

Weirs Beach Drive-In Theater

▣ Route 3, Weirs Beach

✆ 603-366-5777

At night, a blast from the past awaits at the Weirs Beach Drive-In Theater, New Hampshire's oldest drive-in with four screens and room for 800 cars.

Drive-in movie theaters are a rarity these days, so kids will get a kick out of enjoying a feature film under the stars. Movies begin at dusk; arrive early and play free video games in the snack bar before the show.

Winnipesaukee Scenic Railroad

✆ 603-279-5253

✍ *www.hoborr.com/winni.html*

Clamber aboard the Winnipesaukee Scenic Railroad, which departs from stations in Weirs Beach and Meredith, for scenic shoreline rides. The train operates weekends from late May through late June and during fall foliage season, and daily from late June through Labor Day.

Museums and Historic Sites

You won't have to disrupt your "play time" to slot in a visit to a museum or historic site. The Lakes Region's educational attractions offer memorable experiences in truly remarkable settings.

Castle in the Clouds

▣ Route 171, Moultonborough

✆ 603-476-5900 or ✆ 800-729-2468

✍ *www.castleintheclouds.org*

Castle in the Clouds is by far the most enthralling place you can tour while in the Lakes Region. The architecturally extravagant and eccentric home of industrialist Thomas Plant is situated on a 5,500-acre estate high in the Ossipee Mountains. After paying your admission at the entrance gate, you'll be in for scenic treats including views of Lake Winnipesaukee as you follow the winding road up the mountain. Take the time to hike the 200 yards from the first parking area to Falls of Song, a 50-foot natural waterfall. Guided tours of the castle are available, and forty-five miles of hiking trails allow visitors to further explore the property.

 TRAVEL TIP

What's that haunting cry you hear in the night? It's the call of the common loon, a water bird common to the lakes of New Hampshire. The Chippewas believed the loon's cry was an omen of death. Other Native tribes believed loons held magical powers. New Hampshire's Loon Preservation Committee operates the Loon Center (Lee's Mills Road, Moultonborough, 603-476-5666, *www.loon.org*), which is open free year-round. Here you can learn more about these birds and walk two nature trails.

Squam Lakes Natural Science Center
⌨23 Science Center Road, Holderness
☏603-968-7194
✎*www.nhnature.org*

Exhibits and trails at this multifaceted science center give visitors of all ages an appreciation for New Hampshire's ecology and wildlife. Children will especially enjoy observing the live animals that are on display from May through October.

Wright Museum
⌨77 Center Street, Wolfeboro
✆603-569-1212
✐*www.wrightmuseum.org*

Exhibits and special events at this museum transport visitors to World War II era on the American home front. The museum is open daily from May through October.

Outdoor Recreation
There are many ways to enjoy the outdoors in the Lakes Region, whether you want to get out on the water or climb high above it.

Rattlesnake Mountain
⌨Route 113, Holderness

Challenge older children by planning a hike up Rattlesnake Mountain for breathtaking views of New Hampshire's lakes. From the trailhead on Route 113, it's just under a mile to the summit.

Mount Washington Cruises
✆603-366-5531 or 888-843-6686
✐*www.cruisenh.com*

Sit back and relax aboard the 230-foot *M/S Mount Washington*, which departs for scenic lake cruises daily from mid-May through late October from docks in Weirs Beach, Wolfeboro, Center Harbor, Meredith, and Alton Bay. Ask about Family Party Night and Jazz Champagne Brunch cruises, too.

Opechee Park
⌨North Main Street/Route 106, Laconia
✐603-524-5046

If you're looking for a quiet family beach with free admission, head to this city park on Opechee Lake. Lifeguards are stationed here in season, and facilities include two playgrounds, two changing rooms with restrooms, and a concession stand.

Shopping

If you appreciate handcrafted things, you'll be tickled pink by the selection of shops in the Lakes Region. Deal seekers will find an outlet center to explore, too.

Annalee Outlet Store & Doll Museum

50 Reservoir Road, Meredith

603-279-6542 or 800-433-6557

www.annalee.com

If you collect Annalee dolls, you'll definitely want to see where these whimsical creations came to life and shop for hard-to-find items on your wish list. The Annalee Outlet Store and Doll Museum are located in the town where Annalee Thorndike transformed her hobby into a tremendously successful venture.

Country Braid House

462 Main Street, Tilton

603-286-4511

www.countrybraidhouse.com

Shop for traditional New England braided wool rugs made on the premises, or buy a kit and teach yourself this Old-World craft.

Hampshire Pewter

43 Mill Street, Wolfeboro

603-569-4944 or 800-639-7704

www.hampshirepewter.com

At Hampshire Pewter, free tours are offered weekdays in the summer and fall, giving you the opportunity to watch craftsmen transform pewter into beautiful objects. Shop for pewter items Monday through Saturday in the summer and fall at the workshop gift shop.

Keepsake Quilting

⌨Route 25B, Center Harbor

✆603-253-4026

✍*www.keepsakequilting.com*

Whether you're a beginning quilter or an expert, you'll lose yourself inside this enormous quilt shop—one of the largest in the country. Even if you have no interest in picking up a needle and thread, browse the selection of hundreds of American-made quilts for sale.

Pepi Herrmann Crystal

⌨3 Waterford Place, Gilford

✆603-528-1020

✍*www.handcut.com*

Watch artisans craft bowls, glasses, jewelry, vases, and other sparkling pieces on a free tour of Pepi Herrmann Crystal, where the art of crystal cutting is kept alive.

Tanger Outlet Center

⌨120 Laconia Road, Tilton

✆603-286-7880

✍*www.tangeroutlet.com*

Savvy shoppers won't want to miss the Tanger Outlet Center, home to more than fifty outlets including J. Crew, Eddie Bauer, Carter's, OshKosh, and Tommy Hilfiger.

 **RAINY DAY FUN**

For a yesteryear shopping experience, visit the Old Country Store and Museum (1011 Whittier Highway, Moultonborough, 603-476-5750, *www.nhcountrystore.com*), which has been peddling wares since 1781. Its nooks and crannies are packed with unique items for sale, and its upstairs "museum" is crowded with eclectic antiques that will give kids an appreciation for modern living.

Where to Stay in the Lakes Region

From lakefront cottages to family-oriented motels and sprawling resorts, you'll have your choice of intimate accommodations or grand lodgings.

Christmas Island Family Resort (630 Weirs Boulevard, Laconia, 603-366-4378 or 800-832-0631, *www.christmasresort.com*) offers a variety of Winnipesaukee lakefront accommodations including motel rooms, efficiency apartments, and housekeeping cottages. Whichever you choose, your family will have access to two private beaches, a boat dock, and an indoor pool. Anchorage at the Lake (725 Laconia Road, Tilton, 603-524-3248, *www.anchorageatthelake.com*) on Lake Winnisquam has thirty rustic cottages with screened front porches and thirty private acres for peaceful recreation.

Looking for a larger hotel or resort? The Inns at Mill Falls (312 Daniel Webster Highway, Meredith, 800-622-6455, *www.millfalls.com*) is a complex that actually includes four country inns, a covered bridge, a spa, and a marketplace with adorable shops, galleries, and seven restaurants—all overlooking Lake Winnipesaukee. The selection of getaway packages is unparalleled, so be sure to ask about deals that include meals, skiing, spa treatments, or sightseeing excursions. The Margate on Winnipesaukee (76 Lake Street, Laconia, 603-524-5210, *www.the-margate.com*) is a family-friendly, full-service hotel that boasts its own private white-sand beach, indoor and outdoor pools, a fitness center, and a gazebo beach bar. The charming Wolfeboro Inn (90 North Main Street, Wolfeboro, 603-569-3016, *www.wolfeboroinn.com*) was built in 1812 as a private residence and has expanded to feature forty-four guest rooms and a casual New England pub. Shalimar Resort (660 Laconia Road/Route 3, Winnisquam, 603-524-1984 or 800-742-5462, *www.shalimar-resort.com*) offers guests an indoor pool and a private beach, plus free use of paddleboats, rowboats, and canoes.

Renting a vacation home for a week or more is also a popular option in the Lakes Region. Preferred Vacation Rentals (Route 25, Center Harbor, 603-253-7811, *www.preferredrentals.com*) provides an extensive online directory of hundreds of available rental properties, or call for a free brochure.

Contact the Lakes Region Association (603-744-8664 or 800-605-2537, *www.lakesregion.org*) for additional lodgings assistance.

 TRAVEL TIP

> The New Hampshire Campground Owners' Association has 140 members, so campers have plenty of choices in all the state's diverse regions. The association's online campground directory, *www.ucampnh.com*, is a great place to start your search. New Hampshire also boasts more than a dozen state parks that offer everything from tent sites to full RV hookups. For complete information and state park camping reservations, call 603-271-3628. ·

Family Dining in the Lakes Region

The region's restaurants cater to vacationers' hearty appetites. When you're ready to refuel, consider one of these notable establishments.

Family Feasts

It's Thanksgiving every day at Hart's Turkey Farm (Routes 3 and 104, Meredith, 603-279-6212, *www.hartsturkeyfarm.com*), where, on a busy day, they serve 1 ton of turkey, 40 gallons of gravy, 1,000 pounds of potatoes, 4,000 rolls, and 100 pies. There are turkey nuggets for the kids and plenty of other choices, three meals a day.

Dine inside a rustic, homey, nineteenth-century farmhouse and barn at The Woodshed (128 Lee Road, Moultonborough, 603-476-2311, *www.thewoodshedrestaurant.com*). Kids eat well here, with everything from king crab to a kids' filet on the pricey "Young Folks" menu.

It's not easy to find Southern-style barbecue in New England, but Yankee Smokehouse (Routes 16 and 25, West Ossipee, 603-539-RIBS, *www.yankeesmokehouse.com*) claims the largest open pit north of the Mason-Dixon line. They're known not only for their smoky ribs but for creamy corn chowder and strawberry shortcake. The Smoke-house Feast is a good value for families with hungry teens.

If your kids have been good all day, treat them to the ice-cream-sundae buffet at Kellerhaus (259 Endicott Street North, Weirs Beach, 603-366-4466, *www.kellerhaus.com*), a Lakes Region tradition for thirty years.

Memorable Meals

You'll remember the food and the views at Walter's Basin (Route 3, Holderness, 603-968-4412, *www.waltersbasin.com*), a good choice for lunch, dinner, or Sunday brunch. Squam Lake is so close you can almost dip your toes in. Dine outdoors at the fry shack in the summer.

Italian food and music go perfectly together, and at Giuseppe's Show Time Pizzeria (Routes 3 and 25, Meredith, 603-279-3313, *www .giuseppesnh.com*), there's live entertainment on the menu every night.

Flash back to the 1950s at the Tilt'n Diner (61 Laconia Road, Til-ton, 603-286-2204, *www.thecman.com/html/restaurants_Tiltn.html*), a stainless-steel diner car where the food is affordable, and breakfast is served all day.

Popcorn is passé at Smitty's Cinema (630 West Main Street, Tilton, 603-286-4444, *www.smittyscinema.com*), where you can enjoy a full pub-style menu of appetizers, burgers, main dishes, kids' selections, beer, wine, and desserts along with your choice of six movies.

Don't leave the Lakes Region without going to Camp (300 Dan-iel Webster Highway/Route 3, Meredith, 603-279-3003, *www.thecman .com/html/restaurants_camp.html*). This rustic restaurant is styled to resemble an Adirondack Great Camp and serves family-style salad, steaks, S'mores, and more.

CHAPTER 18

The White Mountains and the Great North Woods

THE WHITE MOUNTAINS ARE to New Hampshire what Orlando is to Florida—a mecca of family entertainment where children are thoroughly enchanted. Of course, New Hampshire's amusement parks can't match Disney for technological feats of wonder. But the sputtering motor powering Cinderella's pumpkin coach doesn't faze Story Land's small visitors and parents love the manageable lines, affordable prices, and lack of commercialism at New Hampshire's parks. Plus, there's no charge at all to enjoy the dramatic mountain backdrop, which proves Mother Nature is as talented as any Imagineer.

An Introduction to Northern New Hampshire

There are a few places on Earth that seem to have been tailor-made for vacationers. The White Mountains certainly make that list. This hospitable region opens its arms to visitors, providing just the right mix of grand, romantic inns and affordable motels; out-of-the-ordinary family attractions and natural wonders; novelty shopping and serious outlet bargains. With thousands of acres of public park land including the 780,000-acre White Mountain National Forest, twenty-six covered bridges, more than 100 waterfalls, thousands of miles of walking and hiking trails, two National Scenic Byways—the Kancamagus Highway and the White Mountains Trail, the

Northeast's tallest mountain peak, ten downhill ski areas, and a posse of performing bears at Clark's Trading Post, you may just be able to tick off everything on your New England checklist, all in one spot.

The White Mountains didn't always seem so inviting to visitors, though. The rugged terrain served as a deterrent to travelers until about 200 years ago, when tourists first began to discover the region's scenic riches. Businesses catering to the needs of travelers followed quickly on their heels, and today, vacationers will find that everything they need is at hand. However, scenic vistas and backcountry treasures have been left mostly undisturbed.

If the White Mountains aren't quite remote enough for you, continue north to New Hampshire's largely undeveloped, pristine Great North Woods, a favorite among hunters, snowmobilers, fishing enthusiasts, and those who truly are looking to get away from it all.

What to See and Do

In northern New Hampshire, your biggest question will be, "What should you do first?" Year-round, this region offers gorgeous sights, outdoor adventures, and one-of-a-kind attractions. While families tend to gravitate to the area in the summer and winter, this is also one of New England's most awe-inspiring autumn destinations, and even spring—with its mud and early blossoms—holds a certain appeal, especially for those who want to see the numerous waterfalls at their most spectacular time.

Family Amusements

Generations of families have created lasting memories in the White Mountains. Enduring theme parks and roadside attractions still charm youngsters, while offering parents an opportunity to recall their own childhood vacation joys.

Clark's Trading Post
⌨Route 3, Lincoln
✆603-745-8913
✐*www.clarkstradingpost.com*

If you've never seen North American black bears playing bear-sketball and eating ice cream, then you haven't been to Clark's Trading Post, where trained bruins have been drawing crowds since 1949. The bear show is just one of many reasons to include this eclectic attraction on your vacation itinerary. Kids will also enjoy scaling the Old Man climbing tower, riding the White Mountain Central Railroad, exploring Merlin's Mystical Mansion, and more. Clark's is open daily from mid-June through Labor Day and weekends only from Memorial Day through mid-June and from Labor Day through mid-October.

Santa's Village
528 Presidential Highway, Jefferson
603-586-4445
www.santasvillage.com

You'll have a merry day at this Christmas-themed amusement park, which operates daily from mid-June through August and on weekends starting Memorial Day and from Labor Day through early October. Santa's Village also reopens after Thanksgiving for exhilarating weekends filled with holiday cheer leading up to Christmas Eve. In between rides, children will enjoy feeding Santa's reindeer and playing the Elfabet game.

Six Gun City and Fort Splash Waterpark
1492 Presidential Highway, Jefferson
603-586-4592
www.sixguncity.com

Since 1957, this amusement park has transported visitors back to the Old West with its horse shows, carriage museum, trading post, and themed rides. Recent enhancements, including the Gold Rush Express Runaway Train Roller Coaster and an adjacent campground, make this an even more exciting destination for you and your little buckaroos.

Story Land
Route 16, Glen
603-383-4186
www.storylandnh.com

For the under-six set, there's no better attraction in the region than Story Land, where the pages of their favorite books spring to life. With dozens of old-fashioned rides, including swan boats, antique cars, and the dizzying Cuckoo Clockenspiel, plus the thrilling Polar Coaster and wet-and-wild raft ride, there is plenty to keep kids amused. Pause to take in a show, visit Cinderella at her castle, or cool off at the Oceans of Fun Sprayground. Story Land is open daily from mid-June through Labor Day and operates on weekends only from Memorial Day weekend through mid-June and in September and early October.

RAINY DAY FUN

The Mount Washington Valley Children's Museum (2936 White Mountain Highway, North Conway, 603-356-2992, *www.mwvchildrensmuseum.org*) debuted in 2006 with a variety of exhibits designed to educate and entertain young children ages eight and under. There's even a safe area where infants and toddlers can develop sensory awareness and motor skills as they play and explore.

Whale's Tale Water Park
⌨ Route 3, Lincoln
📞 603-745-8810
✎ *www.whalestalewaterpark.net*

With its giant wave pool, lazy river, curvaceous slides, warm water swimming pool, hot tubs, and Beluga Boggin for the little ones, Whale's Tale is the place to be on a hot summer day. Save money by purchasing your admission tickets online.

Natural Attractions
From caverns to cascades, natural wonders abound in the region. Here are a few of nature's gifts that you might want to make a point of visiting.

TRAVEL TIP

New Hampshire is home to New England's only commercial caves, and they're cool places to visit during the hot summer months. Take an hour-long, self-guided tour of Lost River Gorge and Boulder Caves (Route 112, North Woodstock, 603-745-8031, *www.findlostriver.com*). Or, head to Polar Caves Park (705 Old Route 25, Plymouth, 603-536-1888, *www.polarcaves. com*) for an intriguing look at caves and passageways formed about 50,000 years ago.

Arethusa Falls
Crawford Notch State Park, Route 302, Harts Location
603-374-2272
www.nhstateparks.org

Of all of New Hampshire's waterfalls, Arethusa Falls has the longest drop. The access road to the start of the 1.4-mile Arethusa Falls Trail, a fairly rocky and moderately steep hike, is off Route 302 just south of Dry River Campground. Return via the same route, or complete the three-mile loop past Frankenstein Cliff, which also brings you back to the starting point.

Flume Gorge
Franconia Notch State Park, I-93 exit 34A, Franconia
603-745-8391
www.flumegorge.com

Open from early May through late October, Flume Gorge is an impressive, river-carved chasm that you can see up-close as you navigate wooden stairs and walkways along the gorge's 700-foot rock walls. This geologic wonder was discovered accidentally in 1808 by a 93-year-old woman, Aunt Jess Guernsey. Her stories soon attracted tourists who traveled by stagecoach to marvel at the flume.

Scenic Touring

Whether you choose to explore on foot, in the car, on a train, or aboard a skyride, your most indelible vacation memories are likely to be of the dramatic scenery. The scenic touring possibilities are endless. Here are a few highlights.

Cannon Mountain Aerial Tramway

⌨Franconia Notch State Park, I-93 exit 34B, Franconia

☎603-823-8800

✍*www.cannonmt.com/summer/SummerPages/tram.html*

See the scenery from aloft aboard the eighty-passenger aerial tramway that takes you 4,180 feet up to the summit of Cannon Mountain for views of New Hampshire, Vermont, Maine, and Canada.

Conway Scenic Railroad

⌨Route 16, North Conway

☎603-356-5251 or ☎800-232-5251

✍*www.conwayscenic.com*

Both railroad aficionados and sightseers alike won't want to miss this stop. You can embark on your choice of three scenic excursions through the Mount Washington Valley aboard a restored antique train.

The Frost Place

⌨Ridge Road, Franconia

☎603-823-5510

✍*www.frostplace.org*

Robert Frost lived here from 1900 to 1909. On a limited schedule from late May until early October, you can tour the famous poet's home and wander the grounds that inspired his works, including a nature trail where excerpts from his poems are posted.

Moose Alley

⌨Route 3, Pittsburg

If you're hoping to see a moose while you're visiting New England, one of your best bets is the stretch of Route 3 that runs north from Pittsburg, New Hampshire, to the Canadian border. Nicknamed "Moose Alley," this highway undulates past the lakes that form the headwaters of New England's longest river, the Connecticut, so you'll enjoy picturesque views, even if you don't see any moose.

≡FAST FACT

At the summit of Mount Washington sits the Mount Washington Observatory (603-356-2137, *www.mountwashington .org*), where you can visit the Weather Discovery Center, an interactive atmospheric science museum. Mount Washington is located in the path of three major storm tracks, and its reputation for extremely cold temperatures, high winds, and icing conditions has earned it the nickname "Home of the World's Worst Weather."

Mount Washington Auto Road
⌨Route 16, Gorham
✆603-466-3988
✍*www.mountwashingtonautoroad.com*

You really should get to the top of Mount Washington, the Northeast's tallest peak, while you're in the neighborhood. The good news is that even though folks have been climbing the mountain since explorer Darby Field first did it in 1642, you don't have to. The 7.6-mile Mount Washington Auto Road was opened to travelers in 1861. Once the snow is cleared away sometime in May, the toll road is open daily through mid-October. Be forewarned that the narrow, cliff-hugging road makes for a rather stressful drive, so you may want to opt for a guided tour aboard an Auto Road van.

Mount Washington Cog Railway
⌨ Off Route 302, Bretton Woods
☎ 603-278-5404 or ☎ 800-922-8825
✍ www.thecog.com

Another way to see Mount Washington is aboard the world's first mountain-climbing cog railway. The Mount Washington Cog Railway makes the steep, three-mile climb up the mountain in about an hour and a half, May through late November. It's a good idea to call ahead for schedule information and to purchase your ticket in advance, particularly during leaf-peeping season. Snowflake Express winter trains take passengers as far as Upper Waumbek weekends only from late November through April.

Northern Extremes
⌨ Routes 16 and 302, North Conway
☎ 603-356-4718 or ☎ 877-722-6748
✍ www.northernextremessnowmobiling.com

Explore New Hampshire's snowy beauty. In addition to snowmobile rentals, Northern Extremes also offers guided one-, two-, or three-hour snowmobile tours for novices. Children five and under ride free with an adult; teenagers sixteen to eighteen can operate their own snowmobiles if accompanied on the tour by a parent or legal guardian.

White Mountains Trail/Kancamagus Highway
☎ 603-528-8721
✍ www.byways.org

This 100-mile loop is the most scenic drive in New Hampshire and perhaps all of New England. Begin at the White Mountains Visitor Center at the intersection of Route 112 and I-93 in North Woodstock, and proceed north on I-93. Travel east on Route 3 to Twin Mountain; then follow Route 302 southeast to North Conway. Travel north on Route 16 to Conway, where you will pick up the Kancamagus Highway/Route 112. Drive west on "the Kanc" to complete the loop. Along this route, you'll see waterfalls, covered bridges, and some of the region's most popular natural and human-made attractions. There are also abundant opportunities to park and hike.

Skiing

New Hampshire has more than twenty alpine ski areas that lure downhill skiers every winter, and many of the most exhilarating peaks are in the northern part of the state. Call one toll-free number, 800 88-SKI-NH, for information on ski areas and conditions statewide. Here's a quick look at the region's largest ski resorts.

- **Attitash** (Route 302, Bartlett, 603-374-2368 or 800-223-7669, *www.attitash.com*) is a complete winter sports complex. In addition to 70 downhill trails on two peaks, twelve lifts, a terrain park, and 97 percent snowmaking coverage, the resort also offers cross-country skiing, snowshoeing, and dog sledding. Instruction is available for children ages three and up.
- **Bretton Woods Mountain Resort** (Route 302, Bretton Woods, 603-278-3300, *www.brettonwoods.com*) boasts 434 acres of skiable terrain with 101 trails and glades, nine lifts, 92 percent snowmaking coverage, and a Family Learning Center designed to introduce children gently to the sport. There are even Apres Ski parties for kids ages four to twelve.
- **Cannon Mountain** (Franconia Notch State Park, I-93 exit 34C, Franconia, 603-823-8800, *www.cannonmt.com*) is an easily accessible ski area with 55 trails, nine lifts, and a day camp program featuring skiing instruction for kids four and up.
- **Loon Mountain** (Route 112, Lincoln, 603-745-8111 or 800-229-LOON, *www.loonmtn.com*) offers an unconditional satisfaction guarantee and has 45 trails, ten lifts, and 96 percent snowmaking coverage. Lessons are available for children three and up. If you're not a downhill skier, try snow tubing. There's also plenty of winter fun at the Adventure Center, where you can head out on cross-country skis, snowshoes, or ice skates, or stay inside and scale the indoor climbing wall.
- **Waterville Valley Resort** (1 Ski Area Road, Waterville Valley, 603-236-8311 or 800-GO-VALLEY, *www.waterville.com*) is widely known for its family appeal. You'll find fifty-two trails, twelve lifts, and an impressive 100 percent snowmaking capacity here.

Snowboarders will dig the ski area's five parks and pipes. Kids Kamps make learning to ski fun for ages three and up.

- **Wildcat Ski Area** (Route 16, Pinkham Notch, 603-466-3326 or 888-SKI-WILD, *www.skiwildcat.com*) will take your breath away before you even begin your descent with its fabulous views of Mount Washington's Tuckerman Ravine. Wildcat provides forty-seven trails, four lifts, and snowmaking coverage of 90 percent. It is located entirely within the White Mountain National Forest. Introduction to skiing programs are offered for children ages three and up.

═══FAST FACT

In the summer, Attitash is transformed into a family playground. A one-day, two-day, or afternoon ticket entitles guests to unlimited use of the alpine slides, lift-serviced mountain biking trails, skate park, water slides, Buddy Bear's Playpool, the EuroBungy Trampoline and the climbing wall. Additional fees apply for guided horseback tours, scenic sky rides, and use of the golf driving range.

Shopping

Looking for an old-fashioned Main Street shopping district? You'll find craft shops, gift boutiques, antiques stores, gourmet food purveyors, and other retail treasures along Main Streets in Lincoln, North Woodstock, and Littleton. Here are some additional retail highlights you won't want to miss.

Garnet Hill Firsts and Seconds Store

279 Main Street, Franconia

603-823-5545

www.garnethill.com

Grant and Pegge Dowse began selling flannel sheets from their tiny Franconia sugarhouse turned home in 1976; when they placed a one-inch ad in *Yankee* magazine and a two-inch ad in *Country Journal*, the orders came rolling in. More than thirty years later, the company they founded is still headquartered in Franconia, and Garnet Hill offers a variety of household linens, plus women's and kids' apparel, made from fine natural fibers.

The Handcrafters Barn

⌨Main Street / Route 16, North Conway

✆603-356-8996

✐*www.handcraftersbarn.com*

For one-stop shopping for American-made crafts, visit this eighteenth-century barn filled with the works of more than 300 artisans.

Harman's Cheese and Country Store

⌨1400 Route 17, Sugar Hill

✆603-823-8000

✐*www.harmanscheese.com*

Don't let this quintessential New England country store fool you with its petite size and quaint atmosphere. It's just a "front" for a family-run business that sells more than ten tons of really-aged cheddar cheese each year to mail-order customers across the nation. You'll enjoy exploring the store's eclectic selection of unique food and gift items.

Outlet Shopping in North Conway

⌨Route 16, North Conway

North Conway is the outlet-shopping capital of New Hampshire. In fact, the outlets along Route 16 are some vacationers' primary reason for visiting the region! Remember, the savings are multiplied here because New Hampshire has no state sales tax. The largest outlet center along Route 16 is Settlers' Green Outlet Village (888-667-9636, *www.settlersgreen.com*), with more than sixty stores including Brookstone, KB Toy, Harry & David, Rockport, and Banana Republic. The White Mountain Outlets (508-362-0360), include an L.L. Bean Factory Store, plus designer outlets Nautica, Liz Claiborne, and Polo Ralph Lauren.

The Wooden Soldier Catalog Outlet

24 Kearsarge Road, North Conway

800-375-6002

www.woodensoldierltd.com

This outlet store is tucked away on a North Conway side street, but you won't want to miss it if you have little children you just adore outfitting in gorgeous dress-up clothes. While this retailer's catalogs feature hefty prices, the outlet shop has some reasonable buys on fanciful, heirloom-quality special–occasion clothing.

Zeb's General Store

Main Street, North Conway

800-676-9294

www.zebs.com

All of the more than 5,000 products stocked at Zeb's were made in New England, including an incredible variety of specialty foods. If you're looking for gifts for the folks back home, this is the place to shop.

Where to Stay

Lodgings in the White Mountains quite literally come in every size, shape, and variety. Availability is the only potential problem during the peak fall foliage season and busy summer weekends, when you should definitely make reservations well in advance. In the Great North Woods, lodgings are sparser, and hunting lodges and cabins are predominant.

Grand Hotels

Relive the days of the Great North Woods and White Mountains grand hotels at one of the turn-of-the-century landmarks that remain. You will find these historic, amenity-laden properties surprisingly family-friendly.

The Balsams Grand Resort Hotel

Route 26, Dixville Notch

603-255-3400 or 800-255-0600

www.thebalsams.com

This four-season paradise is a destination all by itself. The 15,000-acre resort dates to 1866 and has skiing, ice skating, golf, tennis, and a private lake within its confines. The Balsams is known for its fine dining, and breakfast and dinner are included with most vacation packages. A day-long children's program for ages five through ten is available seven days a week in the summertime.

Eagle Mountain House
Carter Notch Road, Jackson
603-383-9111 or 800-966-5779
www.eaglemt.com

Built in 1879, this ninety-three-room grand hotel is one of the best choices for family vacationers seeking a yesteryear atmosphere. Children will get a kick out of operating the manual doors on the hotel's 1920s-era elevator, and they'll enjoy the array of recreational facilities including an outdoor pool, game room, nine-hole golf course and cross-country ski trails. Children under eighteen stay free when they share a room or suite with adults.

The Mount Washington Resort at Bretton Woods
Route 302, Bretton Woods
603-278-1000 or 800-314-1752
www.mtwashington.com

The incredibly picturesque Mount Washington Hotel still treats guests to the same lavish hospitality afforded visitors who arrived in 1902. Winston Churchill, Thomas Edison, Babe Ruth, and three U.S. presidents have stayed here. You may never want to check out once you discover the resort's indoor and outdoor pools, adventure center, eighteen- and nine-hole golf courses, clay tennis courts, horseback riding trails, downhill and cross-country ski trails, and children's programs. In addition to the grand hotel, the resort also offers more casual and affordable lodging options, including the nearby Lodge at Bretton Woods, which has its own indoor pool and pizzeria. Stay at any of the resort's properties, and you'll have full access to all resort amenities.

Family Resorts

Amusement parks, outdoor sports, and natural wonders aren't the only things that lure vacationers to northern New Hampshire. The region's resorts know how to make families feel at home, and they offer plenty to keep all ages entertained right on-site. That makes them particularly good choices for extended stays.

Adventure Suites

⌂3440 White Mountain Highway, North Conway

✆603-356-9744 or ✆888-NCONWAY

✐*www.adventuresuites.com*

Your kids might not care if you ever leave the room when you book one of the sixteen themed suites at this unique lodging property. Which will you choose? The Cave, with its tunnel, cavern, dino bones, waterfall shower, fireplace, and video game console? Show Time, with its own movie theater and commercial popcorn machine? The two-story authentic Tree House, with a climbing wall, a two-person Jacuzzi, a remote-controlled moon, and tents for the kids? Or leave the little ones with a sitter and book the Love Shack.

Highland Center at Crawford Notch

⌂Route 302, Bretton Woods

✆603-278-HIKE

✐*www.outdoors.org/lodging/lodges/highland/index.cfm*

The Appalachian Mountain Club's Highland Center offers year-round hostel and lodge accommodations for families who want to immerse themselves in outdoor adventure. Guests have access to daily activities such as guided hikes, naturalist talks, bird-watching outings, and educational programs, and they enjoy complimentary use of L.L. Bean gear. A buffet breakfast and family-style dinner are included with lodge accommodations.

Indian Head Resort
⌨664 U.S. Route 3, Lincoln
✆800-343-8000
✐*www.indianheadresort.com*

The prices are modest at this 180-acre resort where kids twelve and under stay and eat breakfast and dinner free when adults choose the Modified American Plan (MAP) dining package. Lodging options range from lakeside or lake-view motel rooms to cottages and bungalows, and resort amenities include indoor and outdoor pools; a game room; cross-country skiing and snowmobiling trails; a private lake for fishing, skating, and paddleboating; and supervised children's activities nightly throughout the summer and weekends during ski season.

Red Jacket Mountain View
⌨Route 16, North Conway
✆603-356-5411 or ✆800-RJACKET
✐*www.redjacketresorts.com*

With its central location, variety of accommodations, lovely views, and superb on-site facilities, this forty-acre resort is an ideal choice for families. While children splash in the outdoor pool, parents can sip frozen drinks at the poolside bar; and while the kids participate in the supervised summer children's program, Mom and Dad can sneak off to the full-service spa or one of the resort's two restaurants for some quiet time. You'll all enjoy the indoor pool, family barbecue nights, and horse-drawn sleigh or wagon rides.

Waterville Valley
⌨1 Ski Area Road, Waterville Valley
✆800-GO-VALLEY
✐*www.waterville.com*

Don't just think of Waterville Valley for your winter ski vacation. In the summer, this multifaceted resort village becomes a recreational paradise for active families. You'll be able to choose from a variety of accommodations—condos, hotels, lodges—and enjoy all of the resort's facilities, shops, restaurants, and special events.

TRAVEL TIP

For an array of accommodations options in the Mount Washington Valley, call Luxury Mountain Getaways (603-383-9101 or 877-LMG-STAY, *http://lmgnh.com*), which operates a string of resort complexes featuring everything from townhouses and penthouses to two-bedroom villas to inn rooms at the Victorian Nestlenook Farm on the River. The Mill at Loon Mountain (Route 112, Lincoln, 603-745-6261, *www.mainstream. com/millatloon*) is another resort village with three hotels, plus restaurants and shops, all on the site of an old lumber mill.

The White Mountain Hotel and Resort
2660 West Side Road, North Conway
800-533-6301
www.whitemountainhotel.com

This charming and warm resort hotel has many amenities that appeal to families including a year-round outdoor heated pool and Jacuzzi, a fitness center, a nine-hole golf course, outdoor tennis courts, a game room, hiking trails, and two restaurants.

Budget-Friendly Hotels and Motels

From chain hotels to small, family-run motels, there are dozens of lodging properties that make a White Mountains vacation afford-able for families. Because of its central and easily accessible location, North Conway is one of the best places to base your stay. The town has many budget-friendly accommodations choices. The Colonial Motel (2431 White Mountain Highway/Route 16, 603-356-5178, *www.the colonial motel.com*) has an outdoor pool and marshmallow-roasting by the outdoor fire on Saturday evenings in season. Comfort Inn & Suites (2001 White Mountain Highway/Route 16, 603-356-8811 or 866-647-8483, *www.northconwaycomfortinn.com*) offers free wireless high-speed Internet access, complimentary continental breakfast, and an indoor pool.

The Green Granite Inn & Conference Center (Route 16, 603-356-6901 or 800-468-3666, *www.greengranite.com*) has indoor and outdoor pools, a playground, and free family movie nights on Fridays and Saturdays.

There are also many affordable places to stay near Santa's Village. At the Lantern Resort Motel & Campground (Route 2, Jefferson, 603-586-7151, *www.thelanternresort.com*), the outdoor pool has underwater music and the schedule of family events includes hayrides and old-fashioned bonfires and sing-alongs. The Town & Country Motor Inn (Route 2, Shelburne, 603-466-3315, *www.townandcountry inn.com*) features an indoor pool, complimentary wireless Internet access, an arcade, and live bands on Friday and Saturday nights. Staying at the Coos Motor Inn (209 Main Street, Lancaster, 603-788-3079, *www.coosmotorinn.com*) includes continental breakfast and two kids fifteen and under can stay free in a room with adults.

Outdoor enthusiasts will feel at home at Tall Timber Lodge (609 Beach Road, Pittsburg, 800-83-LODGE, *www.talltimber.com*), which offers lodge rooms, rustic log cabins, and luxury cottages with Jacuzzis, plus access to fishing, snowmobiling, moose watching, and other outdoor pursuits in the Great North Woods.

Family Dining

You'll probably wind up eating lunches at amusement park concessions or fast-food restaurants, so be sure to start or end your day with an out-of-the-ordinary, uniquely New Hampshire dining experience.

Meals on the Move

The views will change throughout your meal when you decide to dine aboard the Café Lafayette Dinner Train (Route 112, North Woodstock, 603-745-3500 or 800-699-3501, *www.nhdinnertrain.com*). During the two-hour trip, you'll be seated at a table for four in an antique Pullman car and served five gourmet courses.

Conway Scenic Railroad invites passengers aboard the Dining Car Chocorua (Route 16, North Conway, 603-356-9009, *www.conwayscenic .com*) for a leisurely and scenic lunch or dinner. Lunch trains accommodate tiny diners, but dinner is available only for those ages four and up.

Memorable Meals

For a divine breakfast, eat at Polly's Pancake Parlor (672 Route 117, Sugar Hill, 603-823-5575, *www.pollyspancakeparlor.com*), a local institution since 1938. Adults and teenagers with hearty appetites will be tempted by the all-you-can-eat pancake or waffle options, and everyone will enjoy designing their own perfect pancakes from the choice of batters, add-ins, and maple toppings.

Red Fox Bar and Grille (Route 16, Jackson, 603-383-4949, *www.redfoxpub.com*) is known for its amazingly affordable, all-you-can-eat Jazz Breakfast Buffet on Sunday mornings. Parents will find this a good choice for dinner or a weekend lunch, as well. The restaurant has its own toy-filled toddler playroom, where you can pass the time if there's a wait for a table, and there's a children's movie room in the center of the restaurant, so the two of you can linger over your meal long after your offspring get fidgety.

You've never had pizza quite like the wood-fired pies made at the Flatbread Company (2760 White Mountain Highway/Route 16, North Conway, 603-356-4470, *www.flatbreadcompany.com*), where organic toppings include many items from local farms.

The rustic, always popular Muddy Moose Restaurant & Pub (2344 White Mountain Highway/Route 16, North Conway, 603-356-7696, *www.muddymoose.com*) has a menu just for "Little Hikers." Most kids' selections come with moose fries.

Seafood lovers won't want to miss the Friday night seafood buffets at the Ledges Dining Room at the White Mountain Hotel and Resort (2660 West Side Road, North Conway, 800-533-6301, *www.whitemountainhotel.com*). For one price, you'll enjoy a raw bar, salads, clam and seafood chowders, fresh fish selections, and a pasta and shellfish station. A children's menu is available for those under twelve.

Vermont

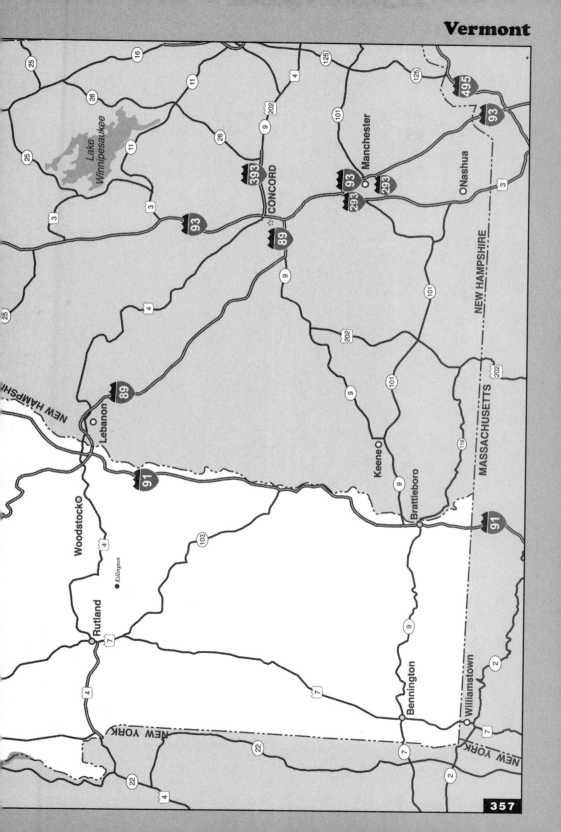

Vermont

357

Skiing and Hiking Trails of Vermont

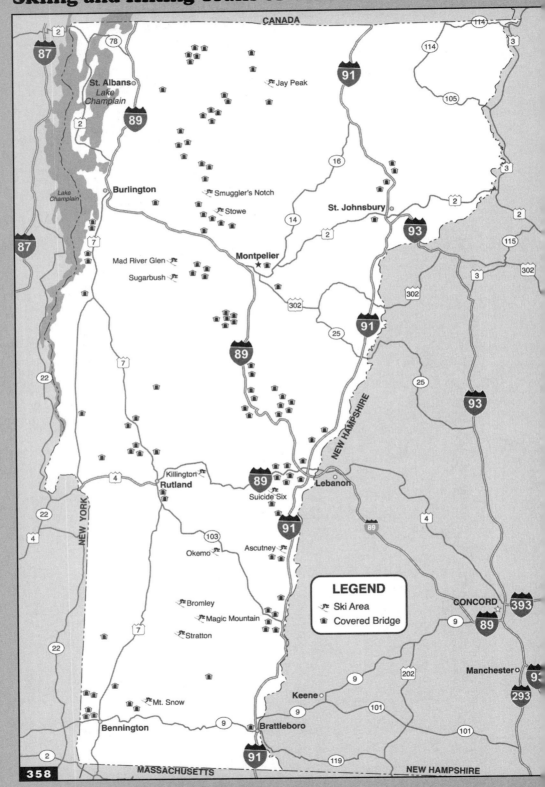

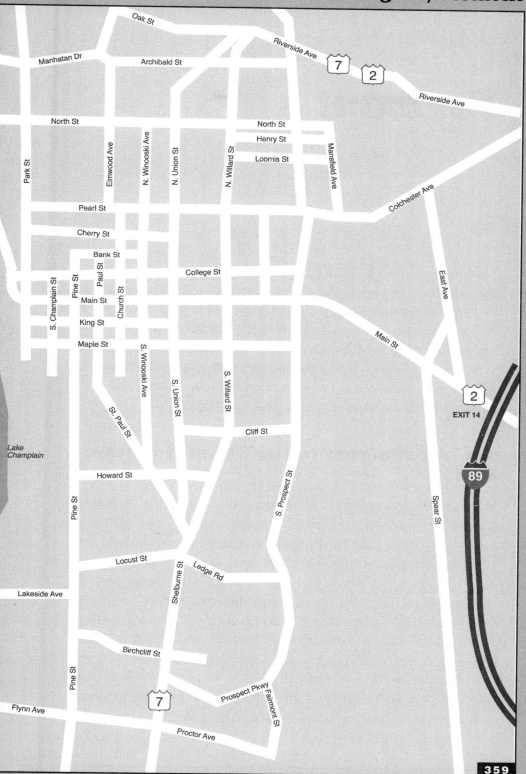

CHAPTER 19

Vermont

EVEN IF YOU'VE NEVER set foot in Vermont, you've probably had a taste of New England's most agrarian state, whether it was Vermont-made maple syrup, cheddar cheese, apple cider, or Ben & Jerry's ice cream. Vermont was the last New England state to be settled. For the brief period from 1777 to 1791, before it became the fourteenth state in the Union, Vermont was its own country—an independent republic with its own postal service, currency, and laws. Today, there is still a different drummer leading Vermont's march through time.

An Introduction to the Green Mountain State

Vermont's unspoiled forests, mountains, and countryside beckon to travelers to come and play—and they holler even louder when they're coated in sparkling, cold white stuff. Vermont is New England's undisputed winter sports capital—from skiing to snowmobiling to snowshoeing to sledding. Don't overlook Vermont's other three seasons, though. Spring brings the annual magic of maple sap simmering to become glorious, amber syrup. Summer is chock-full of outdoor recreational possibilities including hiking, biking, boating, fishing, and golfing—in fact, Vermont has one of the highest numbers of golf courses per capita in the United States. And fall is, in a word, spectacular. Vermont's covered bridges and white church spires are photographed incessantly when autumn provides its vivid backdrop.

═FAST FACT

You can hike Vermont end-to-end by following the Long Trail, a 270-mile, backcountry route that runs from the Canadian border to the Massachusetts state line. Built between 1910 and 1930 by the Green Mountain Club (802-244-7037, *www.greenmountainclub.org*), America's first extensive hiking path remains a unique, scenic, and challenging way to see the Green Mountains and Vermont's rugged landscape. About seventy primitive shelters are located along the trail at intervals of about a day's hiking distance.

In Vermont, the cities are more like small towns, and even though there are no longer more cows than people, the total population still barely tops 600,000. You'll feel right at home among the natives and the thousands of "transplants" who have discovered that a taste of Vermont is simply not enough.

When to Visit

With more than twenty downhill ski areas and nearly fifty cross-country skiing centers, winter is a popular time to be in mountainous, snowy Vermont. And as winter turns to spring, Vermont's ski resorts remain open longer than those in neighboring states, and visitors have the additional treat of being able to observe the annual "sugaring off" as sap is transformed into world-renowned Vermont maple syrup. In the summer, Vermont's glorious outdoor expanses provide opportunities for warm-weather recreation including hiking, bird watching, horseback riding, sailing, and swimming. And the color show put on each fall by Vermont's forests is one of the best in all of New England.

Getting There and Getting Around

Scenic country lanes and bucolic back roads are Vermont's calling card. If your vacation time is scarce, however, and leisurely driving is out of the question, two interstate highways, an easy-to-navigate inter-national airport, and rail and bus services offer convenient access to many of the most appealing destinations. You can also arrive via the water—even though Vermont is the only New England state without an ocean coast.

Burlington International Airport (BTV)

Burlington International Airport (802-863-2874, *www.burlington intlairport.com*), is located four miles east of Burlington off Route 2. Welcoming nearly 700,000 passengers annually, the airport serves as a point of arrival not only for visitors to the state's largest city but for mountain-bound skiers and other vacationers.

MAJOR AIRLINES SERVING BURLINGTON INTERNATIONAL AIRPORT

Airline	Phone Number	Web Site
Continental	800-525-0280	*www.continental.com*
Delta	800-221-1212	*www.delta.com*
JetBlue Airways	800-538-2583	*www.jetblue.com*
Northwest	800-225-2525	*www.nwa.com*
United	800-241-6522	*www.ual.com*
US Airways	800-428-4322	*www.usair.com*

Trains, Buses, and Ferries

Amtrak (800-872-7245, *www.amtrak.com*) provides regularly scheduled rail service to Vermont. The Ethan Allen Express travels from New York City's Penn Station to Rutland in five-and-a-half hours. Amtrak's Vermonter train visits nine Vermont stations on its daily run, which begins in Washington, D.C., and terminates near the Canadian border in St. Albans.

Vermont Transit Lines (800-552-8737, *www.vermonttransit.com*), an affiliate of Greyhound Lines (617-526-1800 or 800-231-2222, *www .greyhound.com*), provides inbound bus service to several Vermont destinations. During the ski season, Adventure Northeast Transportation Service (917-861-1800, *www.adventurenortheast.com*) runs buses between Manhattan and four Vermont ski areas.

If you're headed to Vermont from New York's Adirondacks region, Lake Champlain Ferries (802-864-9804, *www.ferries.com*) offers relaxing and scenic transportation connecting Plattsburgh, New York, and Grand Isle, Vermont; Port Kent, New York, and Burlington, Vermont (seasonal); and Essex, New York, and Charlotte, Vermont. All three ferries can accommodate both passengers and vehicles; if you're planning to take your car aboard the Burlington-bound ferry, an advance reservation is a good idea.

Getting Around

Inside Vermont, public transportation opportunities are not plentiful, but there are some ways to explore the state if you don't have a car at your disposal. Amtrak is one option, although the schedule of train connections between points in Vermont is rather limited. Likewise, Vermont Transit/Greyhound offers a compact schedule of trips within the state. The Green Mountain Transit Agency (802-223-7287 or 866-864-0211, *www.gmtaride.org*) serves central Vermont with public buses that operate in the capital region, the Mad River Valley, and the Lamoille Valley, including the weekday LINK Express connection between Burlington and Montpelier.

Must-See Activities and Attractions

There's something about Vermont that brings out the kid in everyone. These prime attractions combine educational elements with a healthy dose of fun.

Ben & Jerry's Factory

⌨Route 100, Waterbury
✆866-BJ-TOURS
✐*www.benjerry.com*

From its humble 1978 origins in a renovated gas station in Burlington, Ben & Jerry's has grown to become an enormous Vermont success story. The makers of such original ice-cream flavors as Cherry Garcia and Chunky Monkey invite you to take a tour and to taste their sweet frozen concoctions daily year-round.

Bennington Battle Monument

⌨Monument Avenue, Bennington

☎802-447-0550

✍*www.historicvermont.org/bennington*

More than a monument to the pivotal Revolutionary War Battle of Bennington, this 306-foot obelisk made of blue-gray magnesian limestone is Vermont's tallest structure. Take the elevator to the top, and you'll enjoy panoramic views of Massachusetts, New York, and Vermont.

Cabot Creamery

⌨Route 215, Cabot Village

☎800-837-4261

✍*www.cabotcheese.com*

View the cheese-making process, and then nibble on Cabot's award-winning cheeses on a tour of Cabot Creamery, the farmer-owned company that has been a Vermont institution since 1919.

Lake Champlain

Vermont's largest lake is the place to go for scenic cruises, waterfront dining, fishing, and monster watching. You'll find relaxing recreational opportunities here—that is, unless you do spot "Champ," the fabled prehistoric sea serpent that reputedly lives in the lake, in which case your coronary unit may get more of a workout than you bargained for.

Maple Sugaring

In the late winter and early spring, Vermont turns into a hotbed of boiling sap. Dozens of sugarhouses welcome the public to watch the syrup-making process in action. Even if you don't visit during the annual sugaring season, you'll at least want to be sure to order pancakes with pure Vermont maple syrup for breakfast.

Outlet Shopping in Manchester

Manchester rivals Kittery, Maine, when it comes to outlet shopping. If you're looking for designer duds, housewares, shoes, and other retail items at factory store prices, you'll definitely want to include a visit to Manchester on your itinerary.

Shelburne Museum

⌨ Route 7, Shelburne

✆ 802-985-3346

✍ *www.shelburnemuseum.org*

If you want to see a lot of Vermont in a short time, visit the Shelburne Museum, where you can explore exhibition buildings and twenty-five historic structures including a lighthouse that once stood beside Lake Champlain, a covered bridge, and a one-room schoolhouse. You'll also get a peek at the museum's 150,000-item collection of art and Americana, including tools, quilts, carriages, circus memorabilia, American paintings, and impressionist works.

Stephen Huneck's Dog Chapel

⌨ 143 Parks Road, Saint Johnsbury

✆ 800-449-2580

✍ *www.dogmt.com*

If you've ever had a four-legged family member, then you will want to include a visit to artist Stephen Huneck's remarkable Dog Chapel on your Vermont itinerary. Your canine companions are welcome to visit, too. Huneck created this life-size work of art following a near-death experience. The marvelously detailed chapel is set atop picturesque Dog Mountain, where you can celebrate the companionship of your family pet and explore nature trails that wind through the wooded, 400-acre property.

 JUST FOR PARENTS

Cliff House Restaurant (Stowe Mountain Resort, Stowe, 802-253-3500, *www.stowe.com*) sits atop Vermont's tallest mountain, Mt. Mansfield, at the Stowe Mountain Resort, and you'll need to hop a chair lift to enjoy its amazing views. While the prix-fixe dinner menu isn't cheap, the good news is, the ten-minute gondola ride is free when you have a dinner reservation.

Vermont Teddy Bear Factory

⌕Route 7, Shelburne

✆802-985-3001 or ✆800-829-BEAR

✑*www.vtbear.com*

There's a Vermont Teddy Bear for practically every occasion, and you can see where these adorable keepsakes come to life on a tour of the company's factory in Shelburne. While you're there, you can also select, stuff, and stitch up a bear all your own.

Windsor-Cornish Covered Bridge

⌕Route 5, Windsor Village

America's longest wooden covered bridge connects Windsor, Vermont, with Cornish, New Hampshire.

Skiing in Vermont

Vermont is home to more than twenty alpine (aka downhill) ski resorts and nearly fifty cross-country ski areas, making it a winter paradise for skiers and snowboarders. From small, family-oriented hills to challenging peaks, skiing enthusiasts will find diverse terrain statewide.

 TRAVEL TIP

You can check on snow conditions at ski resorts throughout Vermont by visiting *www.skivermont.com*. The Vermont Ski Areas Association Web site also features photos, videos, podcasts, and information on learning to ski or ride at the state's ski areas. A free e-mail newsletter delivers the latest updates to your inbox.

Southern Skiing

Ski resorts in southern Vermont are plentiful and very accessible.

- **Bromley Mountain Resort** (3984 Route 11, Peru, 802-824-5522, *www.bromley.com*) is known for affordable family skiing. It offers forty-four trails, ten lifts, and snowmaking on 80 percent of its skiable terrain. Not skiers? Bromley offers a variety of other family activities including ice skating, sleigh rides, snowshoeing, and snowmobiling.
- **Magic Mountain** (495 Magic Mountain Access Road, Londonderry, 802-824-5645, *www.magicmtn.com*) is home to the Ala Kazaam Tube Park and challenging slopes for skiers and snowboarders. Magic Mountain has forty-eight trails, three lifts, and snowmaking on 87 percent of its terrain. Lessons are available for ages five and up.
- **Mount Snow Resort** (12 Pisgah Road, West Dover, 802-464-3333 or 800-245-SNOW, *www.mountsnow.com*) is the big mountain closest to major cities in the Northeast. It boasts four mountain areas including North Face, 106 trails, nineteen lifts, four terrain parks, a superpipe, and a tubing park. Skiing and snowboarding lessons are available for children as young as three years old.
- **Stratton Mountain Resort** (Stratton Mountain Road, Stratton Mountain, 802-297-4000 or 800-STRATTON, *www.stratton .com*) was the first major ski area to allow snowboarding— back in 1983. Today, you'll find the resort is home to four terrain parks for beginner to expert snowboarders, ninety downhill trails, and fourteen lifts. Ski and snowboard instruction are offered for "Little Cubs" as young as age four.

Central Peaks

The central region is home to some of Vermont's best skiing.

- **Ascutney Mountain Resort** (485 Hotel Road, Brownsville, 802-484-7711 or 800-243-0011, *www.ascutney.com*) is an especially good choice for families with teens. You'll find fifty-seven trails, six lifts, cross-country and snowshoe trails, and a tubing slope here. Lessons for children ages three and up provide a solid initiation to the sport.

- **Killington** (4763 Killington Road, Killington, 802-422-6200, *www.killington.com*) is the East's largest ski and snowboard resort, and it's among New England's first ski areas to open and last to close each year. Killington consists of a ring of seven mountains with 150 trails, thirty-three lifts, and 752 acres of snowmaking. There are plenty of activities for nonskiing family members, from snowmobile tours and dogsled outings to arcade games and inflatable bounce houses inside the Kids Zone.

- **Mad River Glen** (Route 17, Waitsfield, 802-496-3551, *www.madriverglen.com*) has a unique story—it is the only cooperatively owned ski area in America. In 1995, loyal skiers were invited to become shareholders when the resort was put up for sale. Today, you'll find Mad River Glen, which gets about 250 inches of natural snowfall annually, home to forty-five trails, five lifts including the last surviving single-chair lift in the nation, and a ski school that offers small-group instruction for kids ages four and up.

- **Middlebury College Snow Bowl** (Middlebury College campus, Middlebury, 802-388-4356, *www.middlebury.edu/campuslife/facilities/snowbowl*) offers an affordable, uncrowded skiing option. The Snow Bowl has fifteen trails, three lifts, and a snow school for ages six and up.

- **Okemo Mountain Resort** (77 Okemo Ridge Road, Ludlow, 802-228-4041 or 800-78-OKEMO, *www.okemo.com*) is a family-owned ski mountain with extensive snowmaking capabilities. Okemo has 117 trails, eighteen lifts, and a learning program for children as young as age two.

- **Pico Mountain** (4763 Killington Road, Killington, 802-422-3333 or 866-667-7426, *www.picomountain.com*) is a classic Vermont ski area with exciting terrain. Six lifts and fifty trails keep serious downhillers busy, and the Ministars program provides safe, fun instruction for the youngest skiers starting at age four.

- **Sugarbush** (1840 Sugarbush Access Road, Warren, 802-583-SNOW or 800-53-SUGAR, *www.sugarbush.com*) offers varied terrain on six interconnected mountain peaks and a relaxed, away-from-it-all atmosphere. Sugarbush features 111 trails, sixteen lifts, and 68 percent snowmaking coverage. The Ski & Ride School offers on-snow learning programs for kids three and up.
- **Suicide Six** (Fourteen the Green, Woodstock, 802-457-6661 or 800-448-7900, *www.woodstockinn.com/vermont-ski-resort.php*) is the intimate ski area at the Woodstock Inn & Resort. It features twenty-three trails, three lifts, and a ski school.

Skiing in Northern Vermont

You'll find resorts specializing in family fun when you head north to Vermont's highest peaks.

- **Bolton Valley** (4302 Bolton Valley Access Road, Bolton Valley, 802-434-3444 or 877-9-BOLTON, *www.boltonvalley.com*) is a winter wonderland where you can ski downhill, snowshoe, or cross-country ski. You will find sixty-four trails, six lifts, special programs for women, and group lessons for children starting at age four.
- **Burke Mountain** (223 Sherburne Lodge Road, East Burke, 802-626-7300, *www.skiburke.com*) is located in Vermont's Northeast Kingdom and provides an alternative to some of the more crowded and commercial ski centers. Burke has forty-five trails, four lifts, and a Snowsports Learning Center with programs for ages four and up.
- **Jay Peak** (4850 Route 242, Jay, 802-988-2611 or 800-451-4449, *www.jaypeakresort.com*) has the highest average annual snowfall of any ski area in the East, so if you're looking for natural snow, this is the place. Jay provides seventy-six trails, eight lifts including Vermont's only aerial tramway, and ski lessons for children as young as three.
- **Smugglers' Notch** (4323 Route 108 South, Smugglers' Notch, 802-644-8851 or 800-419-4615) is a three-mountain family

ski area with a renowned Snow Sport University. You'll find plenty of alpine action with seventy-eight trails and eight lifts, plus an incredible lineup of other winter adventures including cross-country skiing, snowshoe and snowmobile tours, dogsledding, tube sliding, ice skating, airboarding, and guided nature walks.

- **Stowe** (5781 Mountain Road, Stowe, 802-253-3000 or 800-253-4754, *www.stowe.com*) can brag of Vermont's highest peak and longest average trail length. It also offers an entire mountain—Spruce Peak—devoted to beginners. Stowe has forty-eight trails, thirteen lifts, and one of America's oldest ski schools, where children three and up can learn to ski in a no-pressure environment.

Family Fun Plans

The activities your family can enjoy in Vermont vary with the seasons. This means, of course, that you'll have to plan more than one vacation in the Green Mountain State. These suggested travel plans will help you sample the state's highlights in winter, summer, and luminous fall.

A Five-Day Winter Sports Sampler Keeping Near Route 100

Having a hard time choosing just one mountain resort for your winter escape? Vermont's Route 100 is "ski alley" in the snow season, and a multiday trip along this corridor can be filled with cold weather pleasures.

Day One: Start at Stratton Mountain Resort (Stratton Mountain Road, Stratton Mountain, 802-297-4000 or 800-STRATTON, *www .stratton.com*) where four high-speed, six-passenger lifts mean you'll get in more runs before the day is done. Stratton prides itself on its professional ski instructors who can help beginners master the sport and guide experienced skiers and snowboarders seeking to become experts.

Day Two: Drive north to the Viking Nordic Center (615 Little Pond Road, Londonderry, 802-824-3933, *www.vikingnordic.com*). You may want to consider spending the night at the Viking Guest House, as that entitles you to free access to the center's 35 kilometers of cross-country trails.

Day Three: Your day of rest. Continue north along Route 100 at a leisurely pace, exploring the many shops in Weston, particularly the Vermont Country Store (802-824-3184, *www.vermontcountrystore .com*). Later in the afternoon, visit the Green Mountain Sugarhouse (820 Route 100 North, Ludlow, 800-643-9338, *www.gmsh.com*) for a taste of Vermont-made maple syrup and other goodies. Get to your inn, B&B, or condo near Killington early and rest up for another big day on the slopes!

Day Four: Conquer Killington (4763 Killington Road, Killington, 802-422-6200, *www.killington.com*), where good snow is guaranteed. That's right—if you're unhappy with the conditions after at least one run within your first hour of arrival, you can exchange your lift ticket for a voucher to return on another day.

Day Five: Venture off Route 100 just a bit and arrive early at the Woodstock Inn & Resort (Fourteen the Green, Woodstock, 802-457-1100 or 800-448-7900, *www.woodstockinn.com*). Spend the afternoon nestled inside the inn's old–New England ambience, or venture out on snowshoes at the inn's Ski Touring Center. Before you check out, be sure to visit the off-site Fitness Center for a swim in the indoor pool, a soak in the whirlpool, or a relaxing spa treatment.

A Three-Day Summer Getaway

Have time for just a brief summer retreat? Head to the shores of Lake Champlain, and use Burlington as your central hub of exploration.

Day One: Get to know Vermont's largest city including the shops and restaurants concentrated in the Church Street Marketplace (*www.churchstmarketplace.com*). If the weather is hot, head to North Beach (Institute Road, *www.enjoyburlington.com/NorthBeach.cfm*) for a swim in Champlain. Dine in the evening at one of the area's many waterfront restaurants.

Day Two: Drive north and stop briefly at Snow Farm Vineyard (190 West Shore Road, South Hero, 802-372-9463), where you can sample a variety of reds and whites produced by the state's oldest winery. Continue north to North Hero Island to visit the Herrmann's Royal Lipizzan Stallions (Knights Point State Park, 44 Knight Point Road, North Hero, 802-372-8400) and see a horse show on select summer dates. Return to Burlington later in the afternoon, and get a different view of Lake Champlain from aboard the Spirit of Ethan Allen II (802-862-8300, *www.soea.com*), which departs from the Burlington Boathouse on College Street.

Day Three: It's time for the ultimate summer activity—eating ice cream. Drive southwest to Waterbury for a tour of Ben & Jerry's (Route 100, 866-BJ-TOURS, *www.benjerry.com*), which concludes sweetly with the opportunity to sample several of the company's one-of-a-kind flavors. If you haven't ruined your appetite, have lunch at one of the three New England Culinary Institute restaurants (877-223-6324, *www.necidining.com*) in nearby Montpelier before heading for home.

A Week of Autumn Hues and Views

Fall is a glorious time to visit Vermont, but keep in mind that it's also the season when lodging rates are highest and reservations are nearly impossible to come by unless you've planned well in advance.

Day One: Start your fall foliage journey in Bennington, where you can ascend to the top of the Bennington Battle Monument (Monument Avenue, 802-447-0550, *www.historicvermont.org/bennington*) for views of three states. Bennington also boasts five covered bridges within close proximity, so spend time discovering these charming landmarks.

Day Two: Follow Route 7A toward Manchester and visit Hildene (802-362-1788 or 800-578-1788, *www.hildene.org*), the summer home of Robert Todd Lincoln. Stroll through lush formal gardens and take in spectacular views of the autumn-painted Green Mountains. Spend the afternoon shopping for bargains at the Manchester outlets, which are concentrated in the area of Routes 7A and 11/30 in Manchester Center.

Day Three: Pack a picnic, pay the toll, and make the drive along the 5-mile Mount Equinox Skyline Drive (802-362-1114, *www.equinoxmoun tain.com/skylinedrive*). When you're ready to tear yourselves away from the amazing views, leave southern Vermont behind and drive along scenic Route 7. Rutland is a good stopping place for the night.

Day Four: Wake up early and venture off Route 7, following Route 4 East to Killington (4763 Killington Road, Killington, 802-422-6200, *www.killington.com*), which boasts the highest Vermont peak serviced by a chair lift. The K-1 Gondola ride provides views of five states and Canada. Return to Route 7 and continue north, stopping whenever the colors warrant reaching for the camera. Spend the night in Middlebury.

Day Five: Continue north on Route 7 to Shelburne. You'll want to photograph the covered bridge at the Shelburne Museum (Route 7, 802-985-3346, *www.shelburnemuseum.org*), against the backdrop of autumn leaves. In the afternoon, tour the Vermont Teddy Bear factory (Route 7, Shelburne, 802-985-3001 or 800-829-BEAR, *www .vtbear.com*), and make your own bear dressed for Halloween.

Day Six: Again, continue north on Route 7 to Burlington. At the King Street Dock, choose between the scenic lake cruises offered by Northern Lights Lake Champlain Cruises (802-864-9669, *www .lakechamplaincruises.com*) or a Lake Champlain Ferries (802-864-9804, *www.ferries.com*) trip across the lake to view the colors in New York State.

Day Seven: Make sure your camera battery is charged for your final day of scenic Vermont driving. From Burlington, follow Route 15 East through quaint towns along the way to Jeffersonville, where you'll pick up Route 108 South, which will take you through the mountainous Smugglers' Notch area and eventually to Stowe, home to Vermont's tallest mountain peak. Spend the rest of your day exploring Stowe, or continue south on Route 100 for a visit to the Ben & Jerry's Factory (Route 100, Waterbury, 866-BJ-TOURS, *www.benjerry.com*) before heading for home.

CHAPTER 20

Southern Vermont

THE VAST MAJORITY OF Vermont's visitors enter from the south, traveling Interstate 91 or Routes 7, 8, or 112 through Massachusetts en route to northern retreats. While their ultimate destination may still lie as much as three hours away, they are treated to distinctly Vermont scenes the moment they cross the state line. History, art, apples, sport, and syrup are all reasons to make southern Vermont, including Bennington, Brattleboro, and Manchester, more than a drive-by destination.

An Introduction to Vermont's Southern Gateway

Vermont's southern gateway allows you to sample a smattering of all of the enticements the state serves up for visitors—pretty little villages, mountains dotted with ski resorts, historic landmarks, quintessential New England inns, made-in-Vermont foods and handicrafts, working farms, and family attractions. The region has characteristics all its own, too, including top-notch outlet shopping and battlefields and monuments that spotlight the state's heroic history.

This is the land, after all, of the Green Mountain Boys—the valiant bunch under Ethan Allen's command who successfully fought attempts by New Yorkers to encroach upon Vermont's independence. They also played a vital role in the American Revolution, capturing

Fort Ticonderoga in 1775 and defeating the British in 1777 at the Battle of Bennington.

Your clan just might call you a hero, too, when you choose southern Vermont as the destination for your next family furlough.

What to See and Do

If your family members have divergent interests, southern Vermont can minimize your squabbling. There are ample opportunities for togetherness, but also reasons to go your separate ways. Some members can learn to fly-fish; others (and you know who you are) can browse outlet stores. While the little ones nap after an exciting morning at Santa's Land USA, older children can whiz down an alpine slide. There's one thing you'll all agree on: your vacation in this stimulating and scenic region will be over too soon.

Farms and Family Amusements

Wonderful family activities abound in southern Vermont.

Adams Farm

⊞ 15 Higley Hill, Wilmington

✆ 802-464-3762

✑ *www.adamsfamilyfarm.com*

Memorable agricultural experiences await at this sixth-generation family farm, where kids can enjoy fun activities year-round, from milking goats to gathering eggs to pony or hay or sleigh rides. Check the farm's Web site for a calendar of special events, from the annual Easter Egg Hunt to fall Bonfire Parties and winter Fudge Fondue Nights.

The Apple Barn

⊞ Route 7 South, Bennington

✆ 802-447-7780 or ✆ 888-8APPLES

✑ *www.theapplebarn.com*

The Apple Barn is one of southern Vermont's best "agritainment" attractions, with a seasonally changing lineup of activities for children, along with a farm store and country bake shop. Fall is an especially good time to visit, with opportunities to pick apples and pumpkins, weekend special events, and a chance to get lost inside Vermont's oldest cornfield maze.

≡FAST FACT

For a complete list of working Vermont farms that are open to the public, visit *www.vtfarms.org*. The Web site of the Vermont Farms! Association allows you to search for farms by region and by type. From alpaca farms to Christmas tree farms to pick-your-own orchards, you'll find dozens of opportunities to experience farm life—even farms that welcome overnight guests.

Bromley Mountain Thrill Zone
3984 Route 11, Peru
802-824-5522
www.bromley.com

At Bromley, the fun continues long after the snow melts. Each summer, the Bromley Mountain Thrill Zone gives kids and teens reasons to scream with its Alpine Slide, Condor Coaster, Space Bikes, climbing wall, and Trampoline Thing. For littler kids, there's a Bounce House, miniature golf, and bumper boats.

Harlow's Sugar House
563 Bellows Falls Road / Route 5, Putney
802-387-5852
www.vermontsugar.com

From March through mid-April, head to Harlow's Sugar House, where you can watch the syrup-making process in action on weekends. The fourth-generation farm also offers pick-your-own strawberries, blueberries, and raspberries in the summer and apples in the fall.

Santa's Land USA

⌨Route 5, Putney

✆802-387-5550 or ✆800-SANTA-99

✎*www.santasland.com*

Visit Santa, meet his furry friends, ride the alpine train, and embrace the Christmas spirit at this antique amusement park for small children, open Memorial Day weekend through Christmas Eve.

 TRAVEL TIP

Riding the rails is a wonderful way to see Vermont's scenery, particularly in the fall. Green Mountain Railroad (54 Depot Street, Bellows Falls, 802-463-3069 or 800-707-3530, *www.rails-vt.com*) operates three historic sightseeing trains. The Green Mountain Flyer travels the southernmost route, providing fabulous views of covered bridges, a waterfall, and farmlands along the ride from Bellows Falls to Chester Depot.

Monuments and Museums

You may hear a groan or two when you inform the kids that you're spending a day visiting monuments and museums. So instead, tell them you'll be zooming in an elevator to the top of Vermont's tallest structure, visiting Grandma, traipsing through a cemetery, looking at famous people's fishing poles, and learning about "kissing bridges." Or, maybe scratch that last one.

The American Museum of Fly Fishing

⌨Route 7A and Seminary Avenue, Manchester

✆802-362-3300

✎*www.amff.com*

Fishing enthusiasts will want to make a stop at this museum, where you can see tackle that belonged to such notable fishermen as Dwight D. Eisenhower, Ernest Hemingway, Andrew Carnegie,

Ted Williams, and Bing Crosby. It is the world's largest repository of angling-related art and artifacts.

Bennington Battle Monument
⌨Monument Avenue, Bennington
✆802-447-0550
✐*www.historicvermont.org/bennington*

This monument to a battle that actually occurred across the border in New York looms over the town of Bennington. At 306 feet, 4½ inches, it is Vermont's tallest structure, and an elevator trip to the top provides views of three states, which are particularly spectacular in the fall.

Bennington Museum
⌨75 Main Street, Bennington
✆802-447-1571
✐*www.benningtonmuseum.com*

One of the oldest and largest decorative and fine-arts museums in New England, the Bennington Museum dates to 1875 and has been at its present location since 1928. The museum houses the largest public collection of works by Anna Mary Robertson Moses, better known as Grandma Moses, who began painting when she was in her seventies, as well as the Grandma Moses Schoolhouse, the 1834 one-room building where the legendary painter attended school in nearby Eagle Bridge, New York.

Hildene
⌨Route 7A, Manchester
✆802-362-1788
✐*www.hildene.org*

Visit the former summer home of Robert Todd Lincoln, Abraham Lincoln's son. The twenty-four-room Georgian manor house on the 412-acre estate is open for tours year-round. Children will enjoy the property's farm animals, formal gardens, and hiking trails. In the winter, cross-country skiing and snowshoeing are permitted on the property.

Robert Frost Gravesite

⌨Old First Church, Route 9 and Monument Avenue, Old Bennington

✐*www.oldfirstchurchbenn.org/visiting.html*

Next door to the Bennington Museum, wander around the cemetery at Old First Church, where you'll find the grave of beloved New England poet Robert Frost (1874–1963), which is inscribed, "I had a lover's quarrel with the world."

Vermont Covered Bridge Museum

⌨Bennington Center for the Natural and Cultural Arts, West Road at Gypsy Lane, Bennington

✆802-442-7158

✐*www.benningtoncenterforthearts.org/VtCBM*

The world's only covered-bridge museum opened in 2003. Exhibits explore the evolution of these unique structures, the tools used to construct them, the variety of designs, and the people and stories associated with Vermont's "kissing bridges."

≡FAST FACT

In the days of horse and buggy courtships, covered bridges were nicknamed "kissing bridges" because they provided young lovers with a measure of privacy. There are five historic covered bridges still standing in Vermont's Bennington County, and the Bennington Area Chamber of Commerce (800-229-0252, *www.bennington.com*) has information online and in print to help you find them all.

Outdoor Recreation

Whether you prefer the exhilaration of whitewater rafting or the tranquility of fly-fishing, recreational opportunities in southern Vermont are diverse and rewarding. You can even raise your pulse rate by taking a drive toward the sky.

Mount Equinox Skyline Drive

☎ 802-362-1114

🖱 *www.equinoxmountain.com/skylinedrive*

Don't miss the chance to drive the winding five-mile Equinox Skyline Drive, which rises from 600 to 3,835 feet at the top of Mt. Equinox. There are parking and picnic areas along the drive and at the summit.

TRAVEL TIP

Vermont Bicycle Tours (800-BIKE-TOUR, *www.vbt.com*) will lead you on an invigorating inn-to-inn cycling excursion through colorful Vermont towns and exquisite scenery. Call to request their free catalog of bike trips worldwide. Children ages thirteen and up may accompany adults on North American trips.

Orvis Fly Fishing School

▣ Manchester

☎ 800-235-9763

🖱 *www.flyfishing.orvis.com*

Charles F. Orvis opened a fly-fishing shop on Main Street in Manchester, in 1856. Today, the world-renowned fishing and outdoor-gear retailer still calls Vermont home, and its fly-fishing school—the oldest in the country—continues to introduce adults and older children to the fine art of the sport. The Battenkill River, which runs through Manchester, remains one of New England's finest fly-fishing streams.

Zoar Outdoor

☎ 800-532-7483

🖱 *www.zoaroutdoor.com*

Zoar Outdoor offers whitewater rafting adventures on southern Vermont's West River near Stratton Mountain. The intermediate-level trip is appropriate for adults and children ages twelve and up and concludes with a hearty chicken barbecue.

Shopping

Shopping is reason alone to visit southern Vermont, whether you're hunting for bargains or eager to buy products handcrafted in the Green Mountain State. As an added incentive, clothing items priced at $110 or less are exempt from the state's usual 6 percent sales tax.

Basketville

Main Street, Putney

802-387-5509

www.basketville.com

For a unique shopping experience, visit the headquarters of Basketville. Learn about traditional basket-making techniques at this family-owned business founded in Vermont in 1842 and peruse the myriad of baskets, wicker furniture, foodstuffs, and kitchen gear for sale.

Candle Mill Village

Old Mill Road, Arlington

802-375-6068

Combine shopping with a history lesson at this old mill built by one of Ethan Allen's Green Mountain Boys back in 1764. It now houses a collection of antique shops.

Green Mountain Spinnery

Depot Road, Putney

802-387-4528 or 800-321-9665

www.spinnery.com

This petite shop sells patterns, as well as yarn and knit items made from locally harvested wool. Mill ends are available at reduced prices.

The Outlet Center
📧 580 Canal Street, Brattleboro
📞 802-254-4594 or 800-459-4594
✍ *www.vermontoutlets.com*

This outlet shopping center is home to a small collection of outlet stores such as Dress Barn, Bass, Carters Childrenswear, and more.

Outlet Shopping in Manchester

Manchester is one of New England's premier outlet shopping towns. Routes 7A and 11/30 in Manchester Center are literally littered with outlet stores. Manchester Designer Outlets (800-955-SHOP, *www.manchesterdesigneroutlets.com*) is an association of nearly forty outlet shops including J. Crew, Brooks Brothers, Coach, Polo/Ralph Lauren, and Timberland. Battenkill & Highridge Outlet Centers (*www.outletfind.com*) are home to factory stores from Gap, Bose, Anne Klein, Liz Claiborne, Tommy Hilfiger, Nine West, and more.

Where to Stay

From cozy motor hotels and country inns to resort and condominium accommodations at the region's ski areas, lodging choices in southern Vermont are quite diverse.

Bennington Lodging

Bennington's motels and chain hotels offer value-priced accommodations for family travelers. The Bennington Motor Inn (143 West Main Street, 802-442-5479 or 800-359-9900, *www.coolcruisers.net/bennington motorinn.htm*) offers sixteen guest rooms and a central location from which to walk to attractions in town. The Best Western New Englander (220 Northside Drive, 802-442-6311, *www.bestwestern.com*), about a mile from the center of town, offers an outdoor pool and complimentary continental breakfast. With its indoor pool, complimentary hot breakfasts, and hotel-wide high-speed wireless Internet, the Hampton Inn Bennington (51 Hannaford Square, 802-440-9862, *www.hamptoninnbennington .com*), which opened in 2005, is a good choice for longer stays.

Manchester Lodging

In Manchester, lodging tends to be more expensive, and accommodations exude a bit more Vermont charm. The Equinox Resort & Spa (Route 7A, 802-362-4700 or 800-362-4747, *www.equinox .rockresorts.com*) is a famed, exceedingly family-friendly hotel that dates to 1769 and has hosted such distinguished guests as Mary Todd Lincoln, Ulysses S. Grant, and Theodore Roosevelt. In addition to luxurious accommodations, you'll find unique activities, such as an Off-Road Driving School, indoor tennis courts, an archery school, and the British School of Falconry, not to mention the 18-hole Gleneagles golf course and the Avanyu Spa, with its indoor pool and treatments that include the Mountain Man Facial and a maple sugar scrub.

The Inn at Willow Pond (Route 7A, 802-362-4733 or 800-533-3533, *www.innatwillowpond.com*) features colonial touches in its spacious guest suites; some have fireplaces. Manchester View (Route 7A, 802) 362-2739, *www.manchesterview.com*) has individually decorated rooms, including several spacious suites that can accommodate family groups.

You'll find more reasonable rates and free continental breakfast and in-room wireless Internet at North Shire Motel (Route 7A, 802-362-2336, *www.northshiremotel.com*), where you can borrow from an extensive library of games and movies to play in your room.

Places to Stay Near Stratton and Mount Snow

Stratton Mountain provides several of its own lodging options including more than 150 one- to four-bedroom condominiums; the seventy-five-room, chalet-style Lift Line Lodge; and the 119-room Inn at Stratton Mountain. Call 800-787-2886 for reservations at mountain lodging properties.

The 200-room Grand Summit Resort Hotel (Route 100, West Dover, 800-498-0479, *www.mountsnow.com/grandsummit.html*) is located at the base of Mount Snow. The ski resort also has a variety of condominium and other lodging facilities available. Call 800-498-0479 for information and reservations.

Want to stay at a B&B while you ski? The Inn at Mount Snow

(Route 100, West Dover, 802-464-8388 or 866-587-SNOW, *www .innatmountsnow.com*) serves a home-cooked country breakfast each morning and offers fourteen rooms and suites.

Southwestern Vermont Accommodations

Brattleboro is your best bet if you're looking for family accommodations in the southwestern corner of the state. Here, you'll find affordable rooms at chain hotels like the Hampton Inn Brattleboro (1378 Putney Road, 802-254-5700, *www.hamptoninn.com*) with its indoor pool, high-speed wireless Internet access, and free hot breakfast; or the Econo Lodge of Brattleboro (515 Canal Street, 802-254-2360, *www.econolodgebrattleboro.com*), which offers an outdoor pool and complimentary continental breakfast; kids eighteen and under stay free in a room with their parents.

 JUST FOR PARENTS

The Four Columns Inn (230 West Street, Newfane, 802-365-7713 or 800-787-6633, *www.fourcolumnsinn.com*) is a romantic Greek Revival mansion built more than 160 years ago by local craftsmen who used hand-hewn beams and timbers harvested from local forests. Even if you don't spend the night, try to sneak away for dinner at the inn's much acclaimed restaurant.

If you're looking for more distinctive accommodations, Brattleboro has the Latchis Hotel (50 Main Street, 802-254-6300 or 800-798-6301, *www.latchis.com*), a thirty-room, 1938 Art Deco landmark that shares a building with a brew pub, two shops, and a theater that screens art and commercial films. Or consider The Putney Inn (57 Putney Landing Road, 802-387-5517 or 800-653-5517, *www.putneyinn .com*), a small country inn that welcomes all family members—pets included—and serves a hearty Vermont farmer's breakfast each morning.

Family Dining

In Vermont, it's easy to turn eating into an adventure—three meals a day! From pancakes doused in locally produced maple syrup to wiener schnitzel with a view, here are a few dining establishments that will fill your belly and capture your imagination.

≡ FAST FACT

The Vermont Fresh Network (802-229-4706 or 800-658-8787, *www.vermontfresh.net*) is a statewide collaboration of farmers and chefs who share the goal of bringing fresh products grown and made in Vermont to the table. This means you'll have bountiful opportunities to feast on tasty, locally inspired cuisine. Visit the organization's Web site for links to dozens of member restaurants.

Breakfast

Breakfast is one of the best meals of the day in Vermont. At Jensen's Family Restaurant (Route 7, Bennington, 802-442-3333, *www.jensensrestaurant.com*), Vermont breakfast favorites are super affordable, and two children ages five and under eat free with each adult. Or go where the locals go—Alldays & Onions (519 Main Street, Bennington, 802-447-0043, *www.alldaysandonions.com*)—for the omelet of the day and a cider slushie.

At Backside Café (24 High Street, Brattleboro, 802-257-5056), breakfast is served all day. Even if you're not a morning person, get to Up For Breakfast (710 Main Street, Manchester Center, 802-362-4204) for a bistro omelet with Granny Smith apples, brie, and maple-cured bacon or one of this breakfast-only restaurant's other signature selections.

Lunch

After you've worked up an appetite from outlet shopping, have lunch at Zoey's Deli & Bakery (Route 11/30, Manchester, 802-362-0005, *www.zoeys.com*), where sandwiches are served on freshly baked bread with warm, homemade potato chips.

If you're vacationing on the other side of the state, pick up the makings of a picnic at the Brattleboro Food Co-op (2 Main Street, 802-257-0236, *www.brattleborofoodcoop.com*), a natural foods market and deli that has an extensive selection of local cheeses and Vermont-brewed beers.

Dinner

For outdoor dining with a spectacular view, Dalem's Chalet (78 South Street, West Brattleboro, 802-254-4323 or 800-462-5009, *www.dalemschalet.com*) offers balcony seating and a menu featuring German, Swiss, and Austrian dishes.

Johnny Seesaw's (Route 11, Peru, 802-824-5533 or 800-424-CSAW, *www.jseesaw.com*) is a storied inn at the base of Bromley Mountain. Enjoy heaping plates of Yankee cooking inside this 1920s-era log lodge.

Dine in a vintage Vermont barn at The Barn Restaurant and Tavern (Route 30, Pawlet, 802-325-3088, *www.barnrestaurant.com*). This rustic yet lovely eatery boasts of the "perfect children's menu" and serves tots Kool Kocktails, too. Or round up your posse and mosey on over to the Sirloin Saloon (135 Depot Street, Manchester Center, 802-362-2600, *www.sirloinsaloon.com*) for a buckle-busting supper featuring steakhouse selections and an all-you-can-eat salad bar.

CHAPTER 21

Central and Northern Vermont

THE CENTRAL AND NORTHERN regions of Vermont are home to the state's best known family vacation destinations: Killington, Ludlow, Woodstock, the Mad River Valley, Burlington, Smugglers' Notch, and Stowe. Montpelier, the country's tiniest capital city, is also here. As you journey into Vermont, you'll also find small towns seemingly unaltered by time, pristine wilderness areas, crystal clear lakes, and family farms. If your getaway goals are to slow down, appreciate simple pleasures, and reconnect with the people you cherish, you'd be hard-pressed to find a more suitable setting.

An Introduction to Central Vermont

Need a reason to set your sights on central Vermont? If the Northeast's largest ski area, the world's largest granite quarry, or Vermont's "Little Grand Canyon" don't pique your interest, then perhaps free samples of some of the world's finest cheeses and some of Earth's quirkiest ice-cream flavors will do the trick.

The state's central core dishes up more of everything: scenic wonders, downhill exhilaration, distinctive inns, fishable lakes and streams, points of historic interest, and unlimited recreational possibilities.

What to See and Do in Central Vermont

Central Vermont is naturally gifted. Its significant attractions are mostly linked to the land—its bounty and its beauty. Even the most intriguing shops are purveyors of products for which Mother Nature deserves most of the credit.

Farms and Food Producers

Agriculture is alive and well in central Vermont, and dairy operations owe their strength to companies that transform milk into food products coveted on the national and even global stage.

Ben & Jerry's Factory

Route 100, Waterbury

866-BJ-TOURS

www.benjerry.com

Ben & Jerry's offers ice-cream factory tours daily. Learn how childhood friends Ben Cohen and Jerry Greenfield turned a $5 correspondence course on ice-cream making into one of Vermont's best known and most socially and environmentally progressive businesses. Then, sample a selection of their original frozen flavors at the conclusion of your tour.

Billings Farm & Museum

Route 12 and River Road, Woodstock

802-457-2355

www.billingsfarm.org

This working farm, established in 1871, provides a firsthand look at Vermont dairying past and present through exhibits, films, and hands-on activities for kids.

Cabot Creamery

Route 215, Cabot Village

800-837-4261

www.cabotcheese.com

Head to award-winning cheese maker Cabot for a factory tour and free tastings, including their highly acclaimed cheddars. The Cabot Creamery Cooperative was founded by local dairy farmers in 1919.

Museums and Historic Sites

From syrup history to presidential homes, Vermont has a wide array of sites for history and museum buffs.

New England Maple Museum

⌨ Route 7, Pittsford

☎ 802-483-9414

✎ *www.maplemuseum.com*

At the world's largest maple museum, you can watch demonstrations of the syrup-making process, try maple foods in the tasting room, and shop for Vermont foods and crafts daily from mid-March through late December.

RAINY DAY FUN

Vermont's gold-domed, granite-columned State House (115 State Street, Montpelier, 802-828-2228, *www.vtstatehouse.org*) is open to the public for free tours Monday through Saturday from July through October when the state legislature is not in session. The beautifully restored Greek Revival building, Vermont's third state house, was designed in 1857.

Norman Rockwell Museum of Vermont

⌨ 654 Route 4 East, Rutland

☎ 877-773-6095

✎ *www.normanrockwellvt.com*

Beloved New England illustrator Norman Rockwell's Vermont years are commemorated here with more than 2,500 magazine covers, advertisements, calendars, and other works on exhibit.

President Calvin Coolidge State Historic Site

3780 Route 100A, Plymouth

802-672-3773

www.historicvermont.org/coolidge

Vermont native Calvin Coolidge is the only U.S. president born on the Fourth of July. The thirtieth president was actually sworn in by his father here at his boyhood home following the death of Warren Harding. The homestead remains exactly as it was that night, and tours are offered from Memorial Day weekend through mid-October. While you're in Plymouth, stop into the Plymouth Cheese Factory to sample curd cheese and witness the cheese-making process.

Wilson Castle

Hollow Road, Proctor

802-773-3284

www.wilsoncastle.com

From Memorial Day weekend through October, take a guided tour of this thirty-two-room, European-inspired architectural fascination. The 115-acre estate also has stables, a carriage house, and cattle barns.

Natural Attractions

Central Vermont's natural attractions are no ordinary holes in the ground.

Quechee Gorge

Route 4, Quechee

802-295-2990 or 800-299-3071

Visit Quechee State Park for a picnic and a peek at glacier-carved Quechee Gorge. The Ottauquechee River courses through this rocky chasm, dubbed Vermont's "Little Grand Canyon." The scene is a favorite subject for photographers.

Rock of Ages

773 Graniteville Road, Barre

802-476-3119

www.rockofages.com

Rock of Ages is home to the world's largest deep-hole dimension granite quarry, and it's still an active industrial site. From the Visitors Center, open daily from May through October, narrated shuttle tours depart for the quarry, where massive blocks of granite are harvested. Self-guided factory tours allow you to watch artisans at work, and kids can sandblast their own souvenirs at the Cut-In-Stone Activity Center, open Monday through Saturday in the summer months.

Vermont Marble Museum

52 Main Street, Proctor

802-459-2300 or 800-427-1396

www.vermont-marble.com

Vermont is famous for marble, and the world's largest marble display is at this multifaceted museum. Learn about the history of marble, view the works of marble sculptors, visit the Hall of Presidents, shop for unique gifts, and follow a quarter-mile walkway to the original Proctor quarry.

Shopping

Central Vermont is home to legendary shopping possibilities.

The Bowl Mill

45 Mill Road, Granville

800-828-1005

www.bowlmill.com

The Bowl Mill has been producing turned hardwood bowls and other woodenware from Vermont timber since 1857. The store is open daily, but you can tour the factory on a weekday. A barn filled with factory rejects is popular with bargain seekers.

Cold Hollow Cider Mill

3600 Waterbury-Stowe Road / Route 100, Waterbury Center

802-244-8771 or 800-3-APPLES

www.coldhollow.com

Watch cider being pressed the old-fashioned way, munch on cider donuts, and shop for made-in-Vermont specialties at this mill store that is open year-round.

═ FAST FACT

The Mad River Green Farmers' Market (Route 100, Waitsfield, 802-496-5856), held Saturdays from May through October, is worth the drive from anywhere in central Vermont. Of course, it's just one of more than fifty farmers' markets that operate statewide each summer. The Vermont Agency of Agriculture, Food & Markets provides a comprehensive list at *www.vermontagriculture.com/farmmkt.htm*.

Green Mountain Sugarhouse
820 Route 100 North, Ludlow
800-643-9338
www.gmsh.com
You'll find sweet deals at this authentic sugarhouse and Vermont country gift shop.

Morse Farm Sugarworks
1168 County Road, Montpelier
802-223-2740 or 800-242-2740
www.morsefarm.com
This maple products maker is open daily year-round for tours, tastings, and shopping for gifts from the farm. In March, at the height of sugaring season, line up for an old-fashioned taste of sugar on snow.

The Vermont Country Store
Route 100, Weston
802-824-3184
Route 103, Rockingham

✆802-463-2224

✍*www.vermontcountrystore.com*

The Vermont Country Store is known nationwide for its mail-order catalog crammed with items you probably thought no longer existed. The original store in Weston was founded in 1946; the Rockingham store opened in 1967. Both are open daily, and travelers are welcome to explore their unique product array including Vermont foodstuffs and hard-to-find goods.

An Introduction to Northern Vermont

The top of Vermont is a land of juxtapositions. You'll find Vermont's largest city here—Burlington. Its tallest peak is here, too—Mount Mansfield, home to the Stowe ski resort. And while we're talking about superlatives, not just Vermont's but New England's largest lake is here—Lake Champlain. However, this is also the location of the Northeast Kingdom, a wild, insular, three-county area where winters are long and hard, forests are dense, and those who have lived here for generations cling fast to traditions. With the international border close at hand, you'll also find bilingual signs and other welcoming touches for tourists visiting from Canada.

With all of this diversity, a getaway in northern Vermont is one that can satisfy all of your dualities. Join the crowds on the slopes one day, and the next surge through an uninhabited forest aboard a snowmobile. Visit a family-run farm market one summer morning, then tour a multimillion-dollar teddy bear factory later that same day. Delve into history at the Ethan Allen Homestead, or kick back on a scenic cruise aboard the *Spirit of Ethan Allen II*. You may just depart from northern Vermont with the uncanny feeling you've enjoyed two vacations for the price of one.

What to See and Do in Northern Vermont

If you like being cooped up inside, northern Vermont probably isn't for you. Then again, if you only plan to ski or hike or fish or bike, you'll miss some of the quirky attractions that make this region unique. Be sure to interrupt your outdoor pursuits to visit a few of these local highlights.

Family Amusements

Animals enchant children, and in northern Vermont, roadside bovines aren't the only critters that will tickle their fancy.

ECHO at the Leahy Center for Lake Champlain
1 College Street, Burlington
802-864-1848
www.echovermont.org

Open year-round, this waterfront lake aquarium and science center is home to more than sixty fish, amphibian, and reptile species. Watch as 800 million years of history zip by in six minutes inside the Awesome Forces Theater; then immerse yourselves in the ecology, history, culture, and opportunity of the Lake Champlain Basin through interactive exhibits. Children can meet some of ECHO's inhabitants up close during three daily feeding and demo sessions.

Vermont Teddy Bear Factory
Route 7, Shelburne
802-985-3001 or 800-829-BEAR
www.vtbear.com

Tours of the Vermont Teddy Bear Factory, offered daily year-round, offer a behind-the-scenes glimpse at the creation of one of Vermont's best-loved products. After you see where bears are born, head to the Make a Friend for Life area, where you can actually create your very own bear. Just don't overstuff him!

Museums and Historic Sites

Museums and historic places celebrate this region's riches and the individuality of Vermonters.

Ethan Allen Homestead
1 Ethan Allen Homestead, Burlington

☎802-863-5744

✍www.ethanallenhomestead.org

Get to know Vermont's founder and flamboyant Revolutionary War hero at his final home, situated just outside Burlington on scenic grounds overlooking the Winooski River. Tours are available daily May through October.

Fairbanks Museum & Planetarium

⌨1302 Main Street, St. Johnsbury

☎802-748-2372

✍www.fairbanksmuseum.org

This Victorian building contains more than 160,000 objects including an expansive collection of mounted New England mammals and birds. Founded in 1889 by local industrialist and naturalist Franklin Fairbanks, the museum also has permanent exhibits devoted to art and history, plus Vermont's only public planetarium.

Lake Champlain Maritime Museum

⌨4472 Basin Harbor Road, Vergennes

☎802-475-2022

✍www.lcmm.org

Hands-on exhibits help to tell Lake Champlain's storied history at this museum, where you can even climb aboard a replica of the Revolutionary War gunboat *Philadelphia II*. Young children will enjoy the playground while older youngsters can converse with boatbuilders and blacksmiths. The museum is open late May through mid-October.

Shelburne Museum

⌨Route 7, Shelburne

☎802-985-3346

✍www.shelburnemuseum.org

This forty-five-acre complex is home to a compendium of folk art, Americana, and traditional New England structures including a lighthouse. Late May is the most colorful—and fragrant—time for a visit, when more than 400 lilac bushes bloom.

Outdoor Recreation

You'll be surrounded by opportunities to explore the great outdoors when you spend time in northern Vermont. Here are a few outdoor experiences you may want to enjoy.

Burke Mountain Toll Road
⌷Off Mountain Road, East Burke
☏802-626-7300

From May through late October, follow the winding and scenic toll road to the summit of Burke Mountain, and then climb the steel tower for sweeping views.

≡FAST FACT

The Northeast Kingdom's Lake Willoughby, framed by Mounts Pisgah and Hor, is one of the Northeast's top ice-climbing destinations. On frozen winter days, you can often observe adventurous climbers scaling these sheer walls of ice. If you're interested in giving this extreme sport a try, Vermont Adventure Tours (802-773-3343, *www.vermontadventuretours. com*) offers private and group instruction and guide service.

North Beach
⌷Institute Road
✎*www.enjoyburlington.com/NorthBeach.cfm*

Burlington's North Beach is one of the nicest beaches on Lake Champlain. There is a parking fee, and facilities include a snack bar, picnic area, playground, and restrooms. Lifeguards monitor the beach in season.

Spirit of Ethan Allen III
⌷Burlington Boathouse, College Street, Burlington
☏802-862-8300
✎*www.soea.com*

CENTRAL AND NORTHERN VERMONT

Aboard this 400-passenger cruise ship, which departs from the waterfront in downtown Burlington, you can dine, drink in the views, and even keep your eyes peeled for Champ, the Lake Champlain monster.

Shopping

If you're ready to invest in some warm woolies or a set of moose antlers, then you've come to the right place. Even window-shopping can be an adventure in northern Vermont.

Church Street Marketplace

⌨ Church Street, Burlington

✆ 802-863-1648

✍ *www.churchstmarketplace.com*

If shopping is in your genes, you will adore the Church Street Marketplace, which runs along four blocks in downtown Burlington and features more than 100 retail stores. To encourage visitors, two hours of free parking is provided at the following downtown garages: Marketplace Garage, South Winooski between Bank and Cherry; College Street Garage at the Wyndham Hotel, 60 Battery Street; Burlington Town Center, Cherry Street; and Lakeview Parking Garage, Cherry Street.

Johnson Woolen Mills

⌨ Main Street, Johnson

✆ 877-635-WOOL

✍ www.*johnsonwoolenmills.com*

You'll find discounts on woolen wear and blankets at the Johnson Woolen Mills, an authentic factory store that has been a fixture in Vermont since 1842.

Moose River Lake & Lodge Store

⌨ 370 Railroad Street, St. Johnsbury

✆ 802-748-2423

✍ www.*allroutes.to/mrl*

You're bound to find something of interest at this store, featuring taxidermy and antlery, hickory furniture and other lodge decor, Vermont-made products, and a wine vault.

Stowe Craft Gallery

⌨55 Mountain Road, Stowe

☎877-456-8388

✎*www.stowecraft.com*

This Stowe shop showcases fine jewelry, pottery, blown glass, home furnishings, and kaleidoscopes made by American craftspeople.

Where to Stay

Whether you choose a slope-side condo or a lakeside cabin, a family resort or a pop-up tent, you will feel at home in central and northern Vermont. Whatever your budget and desired level of comfort, options abound. In addition to these suggestions, many other lodgings are listed at the official Web site of the Vermont Department of Tourism and Marketing (*www.vermontvacation.com*), where you can search for suitable accommodations by type, location, and amenities.

 ## JUST FOR PARENTS

Jimmy LeSage's New Life Hiking Spa (The Inn of the Six Mountains, Killington Road, Killington, 800-228-4676, *www .newlifehikingspa.com*) combines Green Mountains hikes, healthy cuisine, and activities for relaxation and stress reduction. Stay for two days or longer from mid-May through September, and leave rejuvenated.

Family Resorts and Inns

The upper regions of Vermont are known for resorts and inns that cater specifically to families. These lodging properties provide a full range of activities for little ones, which means that parents can enjoy a real vacation, too.

Smugglers' Notch

4323 Route 108 South, Smugglers' Notch

800-419-4615

www.smuggs.com

This 3,000-acre, four-season fun zone is one of the top family resorts not only in New England but in the nation. With programming and child care for children as young as six weeks, two teen centers, and plenty of adult activities, it's a destination the whole family can agree on. Stay in one- to five-bedroom mountain condominiums and choose from a variety of activities. A free shuttle provides easy access to all the resort's facilities, which include four water playgrounds, eight pools, four water slides, six playgrounds, two trout ponds, a driving range, three ski mountains, a snowboard terrain park, and a Nordic Center.

Trapp Family Lodge

42 Trapp Hill Road, Stowe

802-253-8511 or 800-826-7000

www.trappfamily.com

Perhaps the most storied inn in all New England, this resort was built by the Von Trapp family, the inspiration for the musical and movie *The Sound of Music*. Stowe reminded them of their home in the Austrian Alps, from which they'd fled during World War II. Maria and her husband are buried in the cemetery near the lodge, and Johannes von Trapp, the youngest of the singing children, is president of the inn today. Families will enjoy a variety of activities from sing-alongs and outdoor concerts to guided snowshoe treks.

Tyler Place Family Resort

Route 7, Highgate Springs

802-868-4000

www.tylerplace.com

This all-inclusive family resort on the shores of Lake Champlain has been nurturing babies, kids, and parents, too, for more than seventy years. Rates include all activities, meals, and accommodations in a family suite or cottage with a separate bedroom for children. The resort operates from late May through early September, and a week's stay is required at most times.

The Wildflower Inn
⌨2059 Darling Hill Road, Lyndonville
📞802-626-8310 or 📞800-627-8310
✎*www.wildflowerinn.com*

If you thought you couldn't bring your children to a charming Vermont country inn, this Northeast Kingdom hideaway will prove you wrong. The Wildflower Inn enchants little ones with its farm animals, teddy bear–shaped pancakes, and full range of outdoor activities. In the summer, children ages four to eleven can participate in a supervised morning session, as well as a themed evening meal and entertainment programs. Special getaways tailored to parents of infants and preschoolers are available in June and September.

Staying on the Slopes

In the wintertime, you can't beat the convenience of staying on-property at Vermont's premier ski areas, which offer a variety of lodging options ranging from hotel rooms to condominiums to chalet rentals. These same accommodations become a convenient and often affordable choice in the spring, summer, and fall. Because many ski area lodging units are equipped with full kitchens and multiple bedrooms, they're perfect for longer stays and for families. Call one of these toll-free central reservations numbers to inquire about options and availability.

SKI AREA ACCOMMODATIONS IN CENTRAL AND NORTHERN VERMONT

Ski Area	Location	Central Reservations	Web Site
Ascutney	Brownsville	📞800-243-0011	✎*www.ascutney.com*
Bolton Valley	Bolton Valley	📞877-9BOLTON	✎*www.boltonvalley.com*
Jay Peak	Jay	📞800-451-4449	✎*www.jaypeakresort.com*
Killington	Killington	📞800-621-MTNS	✎*www.killington.com*
Okemo	Ludlow	📞800-78OKEMO	✎*www.okemo.com*
Pico Mountain	Killington	📞877-232-PICO	✎*www.picomountain.com*
Stowe	Stowe	📞800-253-4754	✎*www.stowe.com*
Sugarbush	Warren	📞800-53SUGAR	✎*www.sugarbush.com*

🧳 TRAVEL TIP

If you're interested in locating off-mountain accommodations in the Stowe area, the Stowe Area Association (*www.gostowe .com*) can help. Call their toll-free central reservations line, 877-GOSTOWE, and a representative will help you find available lodging to suit your preferences and budget at local B&Bs, inns, hotels, and resorts. This reservations service is free.

Burlington Overnights

Burlington is Vermont's largest city and an eclectic college town where you'll find a number of business-class hotels and smaller motels that appeal to families, including the centrally located, 257-room Wyndham Burlington (60 Battery Street, 802-658-6500, *www .wyndhamburlington.com*), the modern and convenient Courtyard by Marriott Burlington Harbor (25 Cherry Street, 802-864-4700, *www .marriott.com*), the 309-room Sheraton Burlington Hotel & Conference Center (870 Williston Road, South Burlington, 802-865-6600, *www .sheratonburlington.com*), and the no-frills Ho Hum Motel (1660 Williston Road, South Burlington, 802-863-4551, *www.hohummotel.com*).

Nearby, the Hampton Inn Burlington/Colchester (42 Lower Mountain View Drive, Colchester, 802-655-6177, *www.hamptoninnburlington .com*) offers family-friendly amenities like an indoor pool and free breakfast buffet. For something a bit different, The Inn at Essex (70 Essex Way, Essex, 802-878-1100, *www.vtculinaryresort.com*) offers 120 individually decorated rooms including some with fireplaces, gas stoves, rocking chairs, kitchenettes, and whirlpool tubs. The New England Culinary Institute operates the inn's restaurants.

Family Dining

Cozy pubs and casual restaurants that appeal to both the after-ski crowd and to families dominate the dining landscape in central and northern Vermont. The Stowe area, alone, is home to more than forty eateries. It's always a good idea to ask locals for recommendations.

Central Vermont Dining Ideas

There are a number of unique restaurants to tempt you in central Vermont's scenic towns. A great place to start your day is The Farmers Diner (Quechee Gorge Village, 5573 Woodstock Road/Route 4, Quechee, 802-295-4600, *www.farmersdiner.com*), where hearty breakfasts are made with ingredients fresh from Vermont farms. Can't get there early? Breakfast is served all day, along with lunch and dinner selections.

For a memorable fine-dining experience, Simon Pearce Restaurant (The Mill at Quechee, 1760 Main Street, Quechee, 802-295-1470, *www.simonpearce.com*) offers gourmet delights served on tablewear by the famed pottery and glass designer. Watch potters and glass-blowers at work inside the historic mill before or after your meal.

The New England Culinary Institute operates three restaurants (877-223-6324, *www.necidining.com*) in Vermont's capital city, Montpelier, where you can sample the culinary creations of up-and-coming chefs-in-training.

Want to dine in a historic environment? Countryman's Pleasure (Townline Road, Mendon, 802-773-7141, *www.countrymanspleasure.com*) near Pico Mountain and Killington serves German- and Austrian-inspired cuisine by firelight within a red-shuttered 1824 farmhouse. Windsor Station Restaurant (Depot Avenue, Windsor, 802-674-2052, *www.windsorstation.com*) serves family-friendly fare in a converted 1900 train station. The Common Man Restaurant (3209 German Flats Road, Warren, 802-583-2800, *www.commonmanrestaurant.com*) near Sugarbush is set in a 150-year-old barn with hand-hewn beams and an open fireplace, dressed up with crystal chandeliers and art. Contemporary American cuisine will please your palates, and a children's menu with favorites like thick-crust pizza is also available.

Northern Vermont Dining Ideas

Burlington is the place to eat if you're craving variety. Ice House (171 Battery Street, 802-864-1800) is an old icehouse turned steak-and-seafood restaurant with views of Lake Champlain. Rí~Rá (123 Church Street, 802-860-9401, *www.rira.com*) is an authentic pub built in Ireland and moved to Vermont. On summer days, dine outdoors at Isabel's on the Waterfront

(112 Lake Street, 802-865-2522), housed inside a restored mill building with brick walls and large windows that provide panoramic views of Lake Champlain. Perry's Fish House (1080 Shelburne Road, South Burlington, 802-862-1300) specializes in fresh seafood dishes; kids will like the nautical decor. Watch Burlington go by as you dine at Sweetwaters (120 Church Street, 802-864-9800, *www.sweetwatersvt.com*), a European-inspired, outdoor café; they offer an affordable kids' menu.

In Stowe, start your day at the Dutch Pancake Café at Grey Fox Inn (990 Mountain Road, 802-253-8921, *www.greyfoxinn.com*), where you'll find more than eighty varieties of Dutch pancakes on the menu. The Shed Restaurant & Brewery (1859 Mountain Road, 802-253-4364) is a favorite family place at lunch and dinnertime.

In the Northeast Kingdom, The Wildflower Inn (2059 Darling Hill Road, Lyndonville, 802-626-8310 or 800-627-8310, *www.wildflowerinn .com*) welcomes non-guests to dine at its Juniper's Restaurant, where dishes are prepared with all-natural ingredients and highchairs and sippy cups ensure that families feel right at home. If your crew is really hungry, head to Anthony's Diner (50 Railroad Street, St. Johnsbury, 802-748-3613) for Woodsman Burgers. Got the late-night munchies? The P&H Truck Stop (Route 302, Wells River, 802-429-2141), known for its all-day breakfast and fresh-baked breads, is the Kingdom's only twenty-four-hour restaurant.

Resources for Visitor Information

Connecticut

Connecticut Commission on Culture & Tourism
755 Main Street
Hartford 06103
860-256-2800 or 888-CT-VISIT
www.ctvisit.com

Central Regional Tourism District
31 Pratt Street, 4th Floor
Hartford 06103
860-244-8181 or 800-793-4480
www.visitctriver.com

Coastal Fairfield County Convention & Visitors Bureau
297 West Avenue
Norwalk 06850
203-853-7770 or 800-866-7925
www.visitfairfieldcountyct.com

Greater Hartford Convention & Visitors Bureau
31 Pratt Street, 4th Floor
Hartford 06103
860-728-6789 or 800-446-7811
www.enjoyhartford.com

Greater New Haven Convention and Visitors Bureau
169 Orange Street
New Haven 06510
203-777-8550 or 800-332-STAY
www.visitnewhaven.com

Mystic Coast & Country Travel

Industry Association, Inc.
101 Water Street, Suite 102
Norwich 06360
860-204-0310 or 877-286-9784
www.mysticcountry.com

Northwest Connecticut Convention & Visitors Bureau
P.O. Box 968
Litchfield 06759-0968
860-567-4506
www.litchfieldhills.com

Maine

Maine Office of Tourism
#59 State House Station
Augusta 04333-0059
888-624-6345
www.visitmaine.com

Bar Harbor Chamber of Commerce
93 Cottage Street
Bar Harbor 04609
207-288-5103
www.barharbormaine.com

Bethel Area Chamber of Commerce
P.O. Box 1247
8 Station Place
Bethel 04217
207-824-2282 or 800-442-5826
www.bethelmaine.com

Convention & Visitors Bureau of Greater Portland
245 Commercial Street

Portland 04101
207-772-5800
www.visitportland.com

Freeport Merchants Association
P.O. Box 452
23 Depot Street
Freeport 04032
207-865-1212 or 800-865-1994
www.freeportusa.com

Greater Bangor Convention & Visitors Bureau
40 Harlow Street
Bangor 04401
207-947-5205 or 800-916-6673
www.bangorcvb.org

Kennebec & Moose River Valley Tourism Council
79 Main Street
Waterville 04901
800-393-8629
www.kennebecvalley.org

The Maine Beaches Association
P.O. Box 388
York 03909
www.southernmainecoast.net

Maine's Downeast & Acadia Region
P.O. Box 4
87 Milbridge Road
Cherryfield 04622
207-546-3600 or 888-665-3278
www.downeastregion.com

Moosehead Lake Region Chamber of Commerce
P.O. Box 581
Greenville 04441-0581
207-695-2702 or 888-876-2778
http://mooseheadlake.org

Massachusetts

Massachusetts Office of Travel & Tourism
10 Park Plaza, Suite 4510
Boston 02116
617-973-8500 or 800-227-MASS
www.mass-vacation.com

Berkshire Hills Visitors Bureau
3 Hoosac Street
Adams 01220
413-743-4500 or 800-237-5747
www.berkshires.org

Cape Cod Chamber of Commerce
Junction of Route 6
and Route 132
Hyannis 02601
508-362-3225 or
888-33-CAPECOD
www.capecodchamber.org

Central Massachusetts Convention and Visitors Bureau
30 Elm Street, 2nd Floor
Worcester 01609
508-755-7400 or 800-231-7557
www.worcester.org

Greater Boston Convention & Visitors Bureau
Two Copley Place, Suite 105

Boston 02116-6501
888-SEE BOSTON
www.bostonusa.com

Greater Merrimack Valley Convention & Visitors Bureau
9 Central Street, Suite 201
Lowell 01852
978-459-6150
www.lowell.org

Greater Springfield Convention and Visitors Bureau
1441 Main Street
Springfield 01103
413-787-1548 or 800-723-1548
www.valleyvisitor.com

Martha's Vineyard Chamber of Commerce
P.O. Box 1698
Vineyard Haven 02568
508-693-0085 or 800-505-4815
www.mvy.com

Mohawk Trail Association
P.O. Box 1044
North Adams 01247
413-743-8127
www.mohawktrail.com

Nantucket Island Chamber of Commerce
48 Main Street
Nantucket 02554
508-228-1700
www.nantucketchamber.org

North of Boston Convention and Visitors Bureau
17 Peabody Square
Peabody 01960
978-977-7760 or 800-742-5306;
www.northofboston.org

Plymouth County Development Council, Convention & Visitor's Bureau
170 Water Street, Suite 24
Plymouth 02360
508-747-0100 or 800-231-1620
www.seeplymouth.com

Southeastern Massachusetts Convention and Visitors Bureau
P.O. Box 976
70 North Second Street
New Bedford 02741
508-997-1250 or 800-288-6263
www.bristol-county.org

New Hampshire
New Hampshire Division of Travel and Tourism Development
P.O. Box 1856
172 Pembroke Road
Concord 03302-1856
603-271-2665 or 800-FUN-IN-NH
www.visitnh.gov

Greater Portsmouth Chamber of Commerce
P.O. Box 239, 500 Market Street
Portsmouth 03802-0239
603-436-3988
www.portcity.org

Monadnock Travel Council
P.O. Box 358, Keene 03431
800-HEARTNH
www.monadnocktravel.com

Mt. Washington Valley Chamber of Commerce
P.O. Box 2300
2617 White Mountain Highway
North Conway 03860
603-356-5701 or 877-948-6867
www.mtwashingtonvalley.org

Androscoggin Valley Chamber of Commerce
164 Main Street
Berlin 03570
603-752-6060 or 800-992-7480
www.northernwhitemtnchamber.org

Ski New Hampshire, Inc.
P.O. Box 528
North Woodstock 03262
603-745-9396 or 800-88 SKI NH
www.skinh.com

Waterville Valley Region Chamber & Information Center
12 Vintinner Road
Campton 03223

603-726-3804 or 800-237-2307
www.watervillevalleyregion.com

White Mountain Attractions
P.O. Box 10
North Woodstock 03262
603-745-8720 or 800-FIND-MTS
www.visitwhitemountains.com

Rhode Island

Rhode Island Tourism Division
315 Iron Horse Way, Suite 101
Providence 02908
800-556-2484
www.visitrhodeisland.com

Blackstone Valley Visitor Center
175 Main Street
Pawtucket 02860
401-724-2200 or 800-454-2882
www.tourblackstone.com

Block Island Tourism Council
P.O. Box 356
Water Street
Block Island 02807
401-466-5200 or 800-383-BIRI
www.blockislandinfo.com

Newport County Convention & Visitor's Bureau
23 America's Cup Avenue
Newport 02840
401-849-8048 or 800-976-5122
www.gonewport.com

Providence Warwick Convention & Visitors Bureau
One West Exchange Street
Providence 02903
📞401-456-0200 or 📞800-233-1636
✎*www.pwcvb.com*

South County Tourism Council
4808 Tower Hill Road
Wakefield 02879
📞401-789-4422 or 📞800-548-4662
✎*www.southcountyri.com*

Vermont

Vermont Chamber of Commerce
P.O. Box 37
Montpelier 05601
📞802-223-3443
✎*www.vtchamber.com*

Vermont Department of Tourism and Marketing
National Life Bldg., 6th
Floor, Drawer 20
Montpelier 05620-0501
📞802-828-3237 or 📞800-VERMONT
✎*www.1-800-vermont.com*

Lake Champlain Regional Chamber of Commerce
60 Main Street, Suite 100
Burlington 05401
📞802-863-3489 or 📞877-686-5253
✎*www.vermont.org*

Mad River Valley Chamber of Commerce
P.O. Box 173
General Wait House, Route 100
Waitsfield 05673
📞802-496-3409 or 📞800-82-VISIT
✎*www.madrivervalley.com*

Manchester and the Mountains Chamber of Commerce
5046 Main Street, Suite 1
Manchester Center 05255-3451
📞802-362-2100 or 📞800-362-4144
✎*www.manchestervermont.net*

Northeast Kingdom Travel & Tourism Association
P.O. Box 212
East Burke 05832
📞802-626-8511 or 📞800-884-8001
✎*www.travelthekingdom.com*

Stowe Area Association
P.O. Box 1320
51 Main Street
Stowe 05672
📞802-253-7321 or 📞877-GO STOWE
✎*www.gostowe.com*

Woodstock Area Chamber of Commerce
P.O. Box 486
Woodstock 05091
📞802-457-3555 or 📞888-496-6378
✎*www.woodstockvt.com*

Portland 04101
☎207-772-5800
✍*www.visitportland.com*

Freeport Merchants Association
✉P.O. Box 452
23 Depot Street
Freeport 04032
☎207-865-1212 or ☎800-865-1994
✍*www.freeportusa.com*

Greater Bangor Convention & Visitors Bureau
✉40 Harlow Street
Bangor 04401
☎207-947-5205 or ☎800-916-6673
✍*www.bangorcvb.org*

Kennebec & Moose River Valley Tourism Council
✉79 Main Street
Waterville 04901
☎800-393-8629
✍*www.kennebecvalley.org*

The Maine Beaches Association
✉P.O. Box 388
York 03909
✍*www.southernmainecoast.net*

Maine's Downeast & Acadia Region
✉P.O. Box 4
87 Milbridge Road
Cherryfield 04622
☎207-546-3600 or ☎888-665-3278
✍*www.downeastregion.com*

Moosehead Lake Region Chamber of Commerce
✉P.O. Box 581
Greenville 04441-0581
☎207-695-2702 or ☎888-876-2778
✍*http://mooseheadlake.org*

Massachusetts
Massachusetts Office of Travel & Tourism
✉10 Park Plaza, Suite 4510
Boston 02116
☎617-973-8500 or ☎800-227-MASS
✍*www.mass-vacation.com*

Berkshire Hills Visitors Bureau
✉3 Hoosac Street
Adams 01220
☎413-743-4500 or ☎800-237-5747
✍*www.berkshires.org*

Cape Cod Chamber of Commerce
✉Junction of Route 6
and Route 132
Hyannis 02601
☎508-362-3225 or
☎888-33-CAPECOD
✍*www.capecodchamber.org*

Central Massachusetts Convention and Visitors Bureau
✉30 Elm Street, 2nd Floor
Worcester 01609
☎508-755-7400 or ☎800-231-7557
✍*www.worcester.org*

Greater Boston Convention & Visitors Bureau
✉Two Copley Place, Suite 105

Boston 02116-6501
☎888-SEE BOSTON
✑www.bostonusa.com

Greater Merrimack Valley Convention & Visitors Bureau
✉9 Central Street, Suite 201
Lowell 01852
☎978-459-6150
✑www.lowell.org

Greater Springfield Convention and Visitors Bureau
✉1441 Main Street
Springfield 01103
☎413-787-1548 or ☎800-723-1548
✑www.valleyvisitor.com

Martha's Vineyard Chamber of Commerce
✉P.O. Box 1698
Vineyard Haven 02568
☎508-693-0085 or ☎800-505-4815
✑www.mvy.com

Mohawk Trail Association
✉P.O. Box 1044
North Adams 01247
☎413-743-8127
✑www.mohawktrail.com

Nantucket Island Chamber of Commerce
✉48 Main Street
Nantucket 02554
☎508-228-1700
✑www.nantucketchamber.org

North of Boston Convention and Visitors Bureau
✉17 Peabody Square
Peabody 01960
☎978-977-7760 or ☎800-742-5306;
✑www.northofboston.org

Plymouth County Development Council, Convention & Visitor's Bureau
✉170 Water Street, Suite 24
Plymouth 02360
☎508-747-0100 or ☎800-231-1620
✑www.seeplymouth.com

Southeastern Massachusetts Convention and Visitors Bureau
✉P.O. Box 976
70 North Second Street
New Bedford 02741
☎508-997-1250 or ☎800-288-6263
✑www.bristol-county.org

New Hampshire
New Hampshire Division of Travel and Tourism Development
✉P.O. Box 1856
172 Pembroke Road
Concord 03302-1856
☎603-271-2665 or ☎800-FUN-IN-NH
✑www.visitnh.gov

The Best New England Web Sites

For General Information

About.com New England Travel
✍ *www.gonewengland.about.com*

Yankee **magazine**
✍ *www.yankeemagazine.com*

The Boston Globe's **boston.com**
✍ *www.boston.com*

Citysearch Boston
✍ *www.boston.citysearch.com*

TimeOut Boston
✍ *www.timeout.com/travel/boston*

For Places to Stay

Bed & Breakfast Inns ONLINE
✍ *www.bbonline.com*

BedandBreakfast.com
✍ *www.bedandbreakfast.com*

CyberRentals Vacation Properties
✍ *www.cyberrentals.com*

Historic Hotels of America
✍ *www.historichotels.org*

New England Inns & Resorts Association
✍ *www.newenglandinns.com*

10kVacation Rentals Inc.
✍ *www.10kvacationrentals.com*

Vacation Rentals by Owner
✍ *www.vrbo.com*

For Places to Eat

Gayot.com, The Guide to the Good Life
✍ *www.gayot.com*

OpenTable
✍ *www.opentable.com*

Phantom Gourmet
✍ *www.phantomgourmet.com*

The Vermont Fresh Network
✍ *www.vermontfresh.net*

Major New England Newspapers

Connecticut

Connecticut Post
✍ *www.connpost.com*

Hartford Courant
✍ *www.courant.com*

New Haven Register
✍ *www.nhregister.com*

New London The Day
✐www.theday.com

Stamford The Advocate
✐www.stamfordadvocate.com

Maine

Bangor Daily News
✐www.bangornews.com

Kennebec Journal
✐www.kennebecjournal.mainetoday.com

Portland Press Herald
✐ www.pressherald.mainetoday.com

Massachusetts

The Boston Globe
✐www.boston.com/news/globe

The Boston Herald
✐www.bostonherald.com

The Boston Phoenix
✐http://thephoenix.com

Cape Cod Times
✐www.capecodtimes.com

The Patriot Ledger
✐www.southofboston.com

The Republican
✐www.masslive.com

Worcester Telegram & Gazette
✐www.telegram.com

New Hampshire

Concord Monitor
✐www.concordmonitor.com

Nashua Telegraph
✐www.nashuatelegraph.com

Portsmouth Herald
✐www.seacoastonline.com

The Union Leader
✐www.theunionleader.com

Rhode Island

Bristol Phoenix
✐www.bristolri.com

The Newport Daily News
✐www.newportdailynews.com

The Pawtucket Times
✐www.pawtuckettimes.com

The Providence Journal
✐www.projo.com

Vermont

The Barre Montpelier Times Argus
✐www.timesargus.com

The Burlington Free Press
✐www.burlingtonfreepress.com

The Rutland Herald
✐www.rutlandherald.com